The Arab Oil Weapon

The Arab Oil Weapon

by
JORDAN J. PAUST
ALBERT P. BLAUSTEIN

With
ADELE HIGGINS

1977 OCEANA PUBLICATIONS, INC./DOBBS FERRY, NEW YORK
A.W. SIJTHOFF/LEYDEN

PERMISSIONS

Jordan J. Paust and Albert P. Blaustein, "The Arab Oil Weapon — A Threat to International Peace", reprinted with the permission of the authors and publisher from *American Journal of Internatinal Law,* Vol. 68, 1974, pp. 410-439.

Ibrahim F.I. Shihata, "Destination Embargo of Arab Oil: Its Legality Under International Law", reprinted with the permission of the author and publisher from *American Journal of International Law,* Vol. 68, 1974, pp. 591-627.

Jordan J. Paust and Albert P. Blaustein, "The Arab Oil Weapon: A Reply and Reaffirmation of Illegality", reprinted with the permission of the authors and publisher from *Columbia Journal of Transnational Law,* Vol. 15, 1976, pp. 57-73.

Richard B. Lillich, "Economic Coercion and the International Legal Order", reprinted with the permission of the author and publisher from *Internatinal Affairs,* Vol. 51, 1975, pp. 358-371.

Timothy Stanley, "Some Politico-Legal Aspects of Resource Scarcity", reprinted with permission of the author and publisher from *American University Law Review,* Vol. 24, 1975, pp. 1106-1121.

Jahangir Amuzegar, "OPEC in the Context of the Global Power Equation", reprinted with the permission of the author and publisher from the *Denver Journal of International Law and Policy,* Vol. 4, 1974, pp. 221-228.

Robert W. Tucker, "Oil: The Issue of American Intervention", reprinted from *Commentary,* January 1975, by permission; copyright (c) 1975 by the American Jewish Committee.

Andrew Tobias, "War — The Ultimate Antitrust Weapon", copyright (c) 1974 by the NYM Corp. Reprinted from the issue of October 14, 1974, with the permission of *New York* Magazine.

John H. Jackson, "The Need for Negotiated Reforms", reprinted with the permission of the author and publisher from *American University Law Review,* Vol. 24, 1975, pp. 1154-1163.

Library of Congress Cataloging in Publication Data

Main entry under title:

The Arab oil weapon.

1. Petroleum industry and trade — Arab countries — History — Sources. 2. Organization of Petroleum Exporting Countries. 3. Embargo. I. Paust, Jordan J., 1943- II. Blaustein, Albert P., 1921- III. Higgins, Adele.
HD9578.A55A77 338.2'7'2820956 77-2937

ISBN 0-379-00797-5 (Oceana)
ISBN 90 286 0507 X (Sijthoff)

Manufactured in the United States of America

THE ARAB OIL WEAPON

PART I
THE EMBARGO

Documents

Commentary

PART II
THE RESPONSE

Documents

Commentary

PART III
LEGAL FRAMEWORK
(REFERENCES)

United Nations

Treaties

CONTRIBUTORS

JORDAN J. PAUST; Associate Professor of Law, University of Houston.

ALBERT P. BLAUSTEIN; Professor of Law, Rutgers University School of Law-Camden.

IBRAHIM F.I. SHIHATA; Legal Advisor, Kuwait Fund for Arab Economic Development.

RICHARD B. LILLICH; Professor of Law, University of Virginia School of Law.

TIMOTHY STANLEY; President, International Economic Policy Association.

JAHANGIR AMUZEGAR; Ambassador-at-Large and Chief of the Iranian Economic Mission, Washington, D.C.

ROBERT W. TUCKER; Professor, Department of Political Science, The Johns Hopkins University.

ANDREW TOBIAS; Contributing Editor, *New York* Magazine.

JOHN H. JACKSON; Professor of Law, University of Michigan.

PART I

THE EMBARGO

HISTORICAL CHRONOLOGIES

Chronology of the Arab Oil Embargo

Throughout the late spring and summer of 1973, the Arab nations brandished the "oil weapon" with increasing frequency. The "weapon" was alternately described as an embargo directed at consuming states "unfriendly" to the Arab cause or as a production cutback of a more general nature. Whatever the means, there was little doubt that the ends were from the outset intensely political—designed to produce a "satisfactory" outcome to the long-standing Arab-Israeli conflict. At no time prior to the embargo was the curtailment of production as a means of raising prices publicly discussed. When the embargo came, it was in response to political and military concerns; nevertheless, its impact on the price of oil was immediate and dramatic.

The first rattles were from Saudi Arabia (where in April Sheikh Yamani warned the United States that the SAG would not acquiesce to Aramco's ambitious expansion program unless the United States would alter its "pro-Israeli" stance). On May 3, 1973, King Faisal delivered a similar lecture to Aramco President Jungers threatening a curtailment of the rate of production expansion. At the end of May, the same message was sounded by Dr. Pachachi, former Secretary General of OPEC, who proposed a crude production "freeze" to force withdrawal of Israeli forces from the 1967 cease-fire lines.

In Libya, production cutbacks accompanied demands for participation in oil company operations. Qadafi embargoed Bunker Hunt liftings of Sarir crude at the end of May, prior to "nationalization" of the company on June 11. The Libyan leader justified the action by asserting the U.S. deserved a "good hard slap on its insolent face." On July 19, Iraq threatened the use of embargoes and nationalizations as a "political" weapon. In anticipation of the Arab foreign ministers meeting in Kuwait, scheduled for September 4, the "oil weapon" became a popular subject for speculation throughout the Arab world, while the thrust of developments within OPEC continued to concentrate on pricing. At its 35th meeting on September 15, OPEC demanded renegotiation of the Teheran Agreement, scheduling the first round for October 8 in Vienna.

Although the Vienna talks began on October 8, they were rapidly overtaken by events in the Middle East following the fighting which erupted on October 7, 1973. Initially, the impact on the petroleum market was curiously muted. There were, however, some significant developments. Iraq nationalized U.S. (Exxon and Mobil) interests in

Basrah Petroleum Company on October 7. Military action curtailed up to two-thirds of the 2 million barrels per day exports from major Eastern Mediterranean pipeline terminals. In Europe, Italy and Spain imposed product export controls while France tightened existing product export controls.

On October 9, Kuwaiti Minister Atiqi responded to pressure from his National Assembly and called for an emergency meeting of Arab oil ministers. While pressure for the use of the oil weapon mounted, Aramco was directed to supply crude oil and products to fuel the Arab war effort. Even though the oil and the products had been contracted for and were destined for other customers, the Saudi Office of Aramco informed the shareholders that the request was a "matter of state priority" and that Aramco had "no alternative but to comply." In his first cable on this problem, Jungers told the shareholders that "we can probably expect more of this as time goes on." The first request was for crude oil for Egypt, the second was for crude oil and products for Iraq.

On October 15, Jungers cabled from Saudi Arabia that the Saudis were upset over what they believed to be a major American role in the war on the side of the Israelis. He said that Yamani was unhappy about the remarks of a number of United States Government officials, including then Vice President Ford, and that unless there was a major change in the tone of remarks coming from the highest level of the United States Government the companies could expect the imposition of a boycott. Yamani said that the pressure for curtailment came mainly from the Libyans and the Iraqis but that the effort was also being pushed hard by the Kuwaitis and would, therefore, be very difficult to turn around.

Yamani was designated by his government as the principal Saudi official discussing the Saudi role in imposing an oil embargo and as the Saudi Government representative at the oil ministers meeting in Kuwait.

On October 16, the "Gulf" committee of OPEC met in Kuwait. They decided to raise prices by 70 percent unilaterally. The following day, the OPEC Ministers convened in the same city and agreed on an immediate 5 percent production cutback from September production. The communique further warned:

> The same percentage will be applied in each month compared with the previous one, until the Israeli withdrawal is completed from the whole Arab territories occupied in June 1967 and the legal rights of the Palestinian people restored. The conferees are aware that this reduction should not harm any friendly state which assisted or will assist the Arabs actively and materially. Such countries would receive their shares as before the reduction.

In the week following this decision, the Arab states individually imposed a rapidly escalating series of restrictions on the supply of crude oil, briefly summarized in the following chronology:

Date	Country	Production cutback (percent)	Embargoes: United States	Netherlands	Other
Oct 18	Saudi Arabia	10			
	Qatar	10			
	Libya	5			
	Abu Dhabi		×		
	Algeria		×[1]		
Oct 19	Libya		×		
Oct 20	Bahrain	5	×		Cancellation 1971 U.S. Navy base agreement.
	Saudi Arabia		×		
	Algeria	10			
Oct 21	Kuwait	10	×		
	Dubai		×		
	Qatar		×		
	Bahrain		×		
	Algeria			×	
Oct 22	Iraq				Nationalized Royal Dutch Shell interest in BPC.
Oct 23	Kuwait			×	
	Abu Dhabi			×	
Oct 24	Qatar			×	
Oct 25	Oman		×	×	
Oct 30	Libya			×	
	Bahrain			×	
Nov 2	Saudi Arabia			×	

[1] Originallly imposed Oct. 6.

By early November, the embargoes and cutbacks were firmly in place. The net impact on crude production was approaching a 20 percent reduction due to the fact that both Saudi Arabia and Kuwait first shut in liftings for the embargoed nations and then applied the cutback percentage. Moreover, the rules of the game laid down by the Arabs (with most following the Saudi level) had been refined. The complete embargo applied to all exports to the United States, but also to Canada, the Bahamas, Trinidad, Netherlands Antilles, Puerto Rico, Guam, and the Netherlands. In a separate action, shipments to South Africa and South Yemen were cut off by the SAG.

As the embargo continued, transshipments to other European destinations via Holland and limited deliveries to Canada for domestic consumption were permitted.

In addition to the "embargoed" nations, the Arabs maintained an "exempt" or "most favored" list of "friendly" nations, including: France, Spain, United Kingdom, Jordan, Lebanon, Malaysia, Pakistan, Tunisia, and Egypt. These countries were to receive 100 percent of their September 1973 supplies, notwithstanding the production cutbacks. Accordingly the remaining "neutral" states were effectively cut back well over the announced percentages.

On November 4, OAPEC Ministers reassembled in Kuwait to coordinate the embargo/cutback. They immediately raised the cutback to 25 percent, but agreed to include the shut-in volumes for embargoed states in this percentage. This move was designed to raise the smaller producers to the Saudi Arab level and to establish a uniform calculating procedure.

In addition, the embargo of the U.S. was expanded by all Arab States to include all indirect shipments as well as direct deliveries to the American market, including deliveries to refiners supplying U.S. forces in Bahrain, Italy and Greece. The "most favored" list was expanded to include India, and all African states which had broken diplomatic relations with Israel. The cutback of 25 percent from the September 1973 levels equated to a 32 percent slash of Aramco's projected November production. Conformity was not complete, however. Iraq participated in the U.S. and Dutch embargo, but refused to subscribe to the production cutbacks. Both Libya and Algeria publicly announced cutback formulas different from that announced in Kuwait. Saudi Arabia subsequently added Brazil to the "most favored" list while announcing an embargo against Portugal.

In mid-November, Saudi Arabia and Kuwait announced goals of well beyond the 51 percent participation level. In Vienna, OPEC made no progress on pricing issues, delaying the decision until December 22. Ecuador was admitted to OPEC and Gabon was offered associate status. The Arab Ministers also agreed to exempt on a one-time basis all the EEC nations (except Holland) from the scheduled 5 percent December cutback. The spotlight then shifted to the Arab summit meeting held on November 26–28 in Algiers.

At their summit, the ministers made a number of changes in the use of the oil weapon. Specifically, they decided:

(1) That notwithstanding the embargoes and cutbacks, no producing state would be expected to tolerate reductions of more than 25 percent in petroleum export earnings;

(2) To establish a special Ministerial Committee to "classify" consuming nations as friendly, neutral or hostile;

(3) To exempt Japan and the Philippines from the December cutbacks only;

(4) To impose an all-Arab embargo on South Africa, Portugal and Rhodesia;

(5) To establish an Arab Development Bank for Africa;

(6) To draw up a schedule for production increases to correspond to the various stages of an Israeli withdrawal; and

(7) To compensate non-embargoed European nations for the loss of supplies normally transshipped via Holland.

Following the summit, the Saudi Arab and Algerian oil ministers made a trip to major European capitals to emphasize Arab demands for Israeli withdrawals, but offering to restore production progressively in response to a staged Israeli pullback. On December 8, the Arab oil ministers again assembled in Kuwait to reaffirm the embargo, but Saudi Arabia postponed its scheduled 5 percent December cutback until January. The SAG also announced it would not consider restoring production above the September 1973 level, even if the Israelis withdrew immediately.

As December drew to a close, a series of momentous decisions were undertaken by the oil producing nations. On December 21, Libya banned sales to Caribbean refineries (where production is virtually all for U.S. consumption), thus plugging the major "leak" in the Arab embargo of the U.S. The 37th OPEC Meeting in Teheran opened the following day. Concern for the quantity of supply was rapidly transformed into concern for the cost of supply as OPEC raised posted prices by 130%. Leading the drive for a major price hike were the Iranians, flushed with the unprecedented $17/bbl prices received at an NIOC auction the week before. During the week of this announcement, OPEC established a simplified pricing system utilizing Arabian Light (34°) as the "marker crude" with standard adjustments for specific gravity, sulfur content and transportation differentials. Also, the Arabs agreed to relax their production cutbacks from 25 percent to 15 percent effective January 1, 1974.

The embargo on exports to the U.S. and Holland was maintained while Japan, the Philippines and Belgium were granted preferential status. In the case of Belgium, this gesture was retroactive until December 1, 1973. In addition, certain "friendly" countries were granted additional preferences, permitting them to receive more than their September 1973 imports. This special list included the U.K. (then being crippled by a coal strike) and several Islamic and African nations.

With this action, the Arabs effectively established four categories of consuming nations:

(1) "*Most favored*"—exports to meet current demand;

(2) "*Preferential*"—receiving September 1973 levels or average of January–September 1973 levels;

(3) "*Neutral*"—receiving remaining production, prorationed on January–September 1973 averages;

(4) "*Embargoed*"—receiving no crude oil or refined products.

The internal politics of the December OPEC meeting were instructive. The Saudi representative, Sheikh Yamani, attempted to hold the line on the price rise, under strict instructions from the King, who was anxious to maintain the "political" tone of the embargo. The Shah, on the other hand, was committed to a spectacular price hike—to $17/barrel or more. A compromise emerged.

In January and February 1974, rumors of an impending end to the Arab boycott of the United States proliferated. Speculation was extremely high prior to an Arab oil ministers meeting scheduled for Tripoli (13–14 February 1974) which was cancelled at the last moment. The intensive shuttle diplomacy of U.S. Secretary of State Kissinger finally bore fruit in mid-March. The embargo against the United States was lifted by most Arab states on March 18, 1974 but continued against Holland. In addition, Iraq and Libya continued an embargo against the U.S. The curtailment of U.S. petroleum supplies had lasted exactly five months.

A Chronology of Events in the Middle East, October 6 to November 26, 1973 [1]

October 6—Heavy fighting erupted between Israeli and Arab forces along the Suez Canal and Golan heights ceasefire lines.

Official announcements by Israel and Egypt agreed that Egyptian forces had cross the Suez Canal and established footholds in the Israeli-occupied Sinai Peninsula.

On instructions from President Nixon, Mr. Kissinger urged restraint to avoid the undermining and violation of the ceasefire in effect since August, 1970.

October 7—Israel said her jets struck deep inside Egypt and Syria and crippled Syrian air defenses and severed 9 of 11 Egyptian bridges across the Suez Canal. This action isolated 400 Egyptian tanks and other forces on the eastern bank. Both Egypt and Syria said that their forces had repelled the Israeli counterattacks. Each side blamed the other for starting the fighting, although the United Nations observers on the scene agreed with Israeli assertions that the Arabs had simultaneously attacked on two fronts first.

October 8—Preceded by large-scale Israeli air strikes against Arab military airfields, Israeli units launched major counterattacks on two broad fronts. Although Israeli forces had apparently succeeded in turning back Arab advances, the Israeli counterattack was encountering heavier resistance than expected.

The Soviet Union indicated that it shared the American desire to limit the fighting in the Middle East.

The United States asked the United Nations Security Council to bring an end to the fighting in the Middle East and restore the 1967 ceasefire lines.

October 9—Administration officials in Washington said that although the Soviet Union had avoided direct involvement in the Middle East conflict, Moscow had encouraged other Arab Governments to support Egypt and Syria in their fight with Israel.

Pentagon officials have concluded that Israeli forces will evenutally prevail in the Middle East conflict, but only after several more days of costly fighting.

October 10—Administration officials said there were indications that the Soviet Union was air lifting military equipment to resupply Egyptian and Syrian forces in their fight against Israel.

October 11—Mounting Israeli losses of jet warplanes and tanks make it likely that additional F-4 Phantom fighter-bombers and A-4 Skyhawk attack will be sent to Israel. Israeli tanks and infantry started a major thrust toward Damascus.

October 12—Some Syrian Army units appeared to be in full retreat as Israeli forces advanced to within 18 miles of Damascus.

Egypt continued to pour men and heavy equipment across the Suez Canal to make the area secure against Israeli recapture.

Secretary of State Kissinger said that while the Middle East war had the potentialities for getting out of hand both the United States and the Soviet Union had acted so far to keep it from widening into a world conflict.

October 13—The Jordanian command announced that it had begun moving a detachment of its best military formations to Syria to help in the defense of that land.

The United States prepared to ship jet fighter planes to Israel to replace some of those lost in the first week of the Middle East war.

---

[1] Compiled by the Congressional Research Service from newspaper accounts, mainly New York Times.

FEA Office of International Energy Affairs, 94th Cong., 1st Sess., Report on U.S. Oil Companies and the Arab Oil Embargo: The International Allocation of Constricted Supplies (Senate Foreign Relations Comm. Print 1975)

October 14—American officials have concluded after eight days of efforts that a diplomatic solution to the Middle East conflict will have to wait until the fighting stops. So far none of the combatants have shown any wish for a ceasefire and the Soviet Union has refused to endorse a truce as long as the Egyptians feel they can gain more by fighting.

October 15—The State Department announced that the United States had begun to supply Israel with aircraft and equipment to replace her losses.

Saudi Arabia's Oil Minister was reported to have told Western oil executives that his country would cut crude oil production by 10 percent now and by 5 percent a month in future if the United States overtly undertook to resupply Israel.

Egypt has said that she will accept a ceasefire only if she is given guarantees that Israel will withdraw to the pre-1967 lines.

October 16—President Anwar el-Sadat of Egypt called for a ceasefire coupled with Israeli withdrawal from Egyptian territory seized in 1967. Sadat also proposed that the truce be followed by a peace conference at the United Nations.

Golda Meir said that the Middle East war would end when Israel had succeeded in beating the enemy.

Melvin R. Laird accused the Soviet Union of blocking efforts to achieve a Middle East ceasefire.

October 17—The Soviet Union has begun high-level efforts to persuade Egypt and Syria to move toward a diplomatic settlement of the Middle East conflict.

The Arab oil states said they had imposed a 5 percent cut each month in the flow of oil to the United States and other countries supporting Israel in the Middle East conflict.

Four Arab Foreign Ministers, who said they represented 18 Arab nations, submitted a general peace proposal to President Nixon and asked the United States to help mediate the Middle East conflict.

The Pentagon plans to ask Congress for an extra $2 billion to replace American arms shipments being rushed to Israel.

October 18—Israeli and Egyptian forces reported locked in a huge tank battle on the Egyptian side of the Suez Canal.

Egypt announced that Soviet Premier Kosygin had held three long meetings in Cairo with Sadat.

Saudi Arabia announced a 10 percent oil production cutback to put pressure on the United States into reducing its support for the Israeli cause.

Jets piloted by North Koreans clashed with Israeli planes.

October 19—Libya ordered a halt to all shipments of crude oil and petroleum products to the United States and raised prices to almost twice the former level.

President Nixon asked Congress for $2.2 billion in emergency security assistance for Israel and $200 million for Cambodia.

October 20—Secretary of State Kissinger arrived in Moscow and entered into talks with Brezhnev on the two week old Middle East war.

Saudia Arabia has decided to stop all oil exports to the United States.

October 21—The Security Council unanimously adopted a joint Soviet-U.S. resolution which called for a cease-fire in place in the Middle East within twelve hours—about 1 p.m. (October 22, 1973) EDT—and immediate negotiations for a just and durable peace.

October 22—A cease-fire between Egypt and Israel went into effect about 12 hours after the UN Security Council called for an end to hostilities. Syria, where fighting continued, was said to be "considering" the UN resolution, while Iraq rejected the proposal. Jordan, while accepting the proposal, said its troops were under command of Syria.

October 23—Full-scale war continued between Israeli and Egyptian forces on the southern part of the Suez Canal, with each side blaming the other for violating the technical cease-fire. The UN Security Council adopted a resolution again calling for cease-fire and Syria informed the Secretary General that it would abide by the cease-fire.

October 24—As a new cease-fire went into effect on the Syrian and Suez fronts, Egyptian President Anwar el-Sadat issued an urgent appeal for the United States and the Soviet to send troops to supervise the agreement they had originated. The United States rejected his request and expressed optimism about the truce.

October 25—The United States ordered its military forces on a worldwide "precautionary alert" because of concern that the Soviet Union might be planning to send troops to the Middle East.

Secretary of State Kissinger said that the United States does not want a confrontation with the USSR.

The UN Security Council unanimously voted to establish a UN emergency force made up of troops from smaller nations to supervise a cease-fire.

October 26—President Nixon said that the U.S. and the USSR had agreed to put more pressure on the Israelis and Arabs to reach a permanent settlement. Soviet party leader Brezhnev accused the U.S. of artificially increasing tensions in the Middle East with rumors of alleged Soviet plans to intervene. The United Nations moved swiftly to get a 7,000-man force into the Middle East.

October 27—Egypt and Israel agreed to negotiate face-to-face on implementation of the cease-fire along the Suez Canal as a result of the "good offices" provided by Secretary of State Kissinger, according to the State Department.

October 29—Israel said that continuation of the cease-fire was contingent on the early identification and release of more than 400 Israeli soldiers believed captured by Egypt and Syria.

The first truckloads of medicine and food were ferried across the Suez Canal to the Egyptian III Corps trapped on the east bank, under supervision of UN officials.

Ismail Fahmy, Egyptian Acting Foreign Minister, arrived in Washington and met with Secretary of State Kissinger.

October 30—President Nixon conferred with the Acting Foreign Minister of Egypt, Ismail Fahmy.

Egypt offered the release of Israeli prisoners of war on condition that Israeli troops withdraw to the cease-fire line of October 22.

November 1—Israel Premier Golda Meir met for more than an hour with President Nixon and said that she was "reassured" of continued U.S. support for Israel's security. She denied that Israel was under any pressure from the U.S. to make one-sided concessions or that the U.S. was trying to end Israeli encirclement of the Egyptian III Corps troops.

November 2—Syrian Deputy Foreign Minister Muhammed Ismail met with Secretary of State Kissinger, making Syria's first significant diplomatic contact with the United States in a year.

November 3—Secretary of State Kissinger continued to attempt to create dialogue between the contending sides as he held talks with Egyptian Foreign Minister Ismail Fahmy and Premier Golda Meir of Israel. The UN Emergency Forces reported some successes in easing tensions between Egyptian and Israeli troops, particularly in the areas west of the Suez Canal.

November 5—Secretary of State Kissinger arrived in Morocco on the first leg of an extensive trip.

November 6—Israel announced that 1,854 Israeli soldiers were killed during the latest war.

Secretary of State Kissinger arrived in Cairo for talks with President Sadat.

The European Common Market, under threat of an Arab oil boycott of all none member-countries unless they remain neutral in the Middle East war, called on Israel and Egypt to return to the lines they held October 22, before Israeli forces sourrounded the Egyptian III Corps.

November 7—After a meeting between Secretary of State Kissinger and President Sadat, the United States and Egypt announced that they would resume diplomatic relations and exchange ambassadors within two weeks. Senior members of the Kissinger delegation then departed for Israel to convey "ideas" developed at the meeting.

November 8—Officials traveling with Secretary of State Kissinger said that Egypt and Israel agreed on new arrangements under the cease-fire that would take effect within a few days and lead to full-scale peace negotiations by the end of the year. The plan, worked out by Kissinger and Sadat and accepted by the Israeli Cabinet, called for a supply corridor to the Egyptain III Corps, a prompt exchange of prisoners, negotiations to adjust the cease-fire line, and later negotiations on a broader basis.

November 9—The Israeli Government announced that it had accepted "in principle" the American-sponsored cease-fire agreement with Egypt, but said it would seek further clarification of the details from the United States.

November 9—Secretary of State Kissinger was unable to obtain a relaxation of Saudi Arabia's oil embargo against the United States. Mr. Kissinger was told that production cuts imposed since October 17 would not be relaxed until there was physical withdrawal of Israeli forces from Arab territory occupied during the 1967 war.

November 10—Egypt and Israel agreed to sign a six-point American sponsored cease-fire agreement on the Cairo-Suez road. The signing, originally scheduled for yesterday, was postponed to give Israel time to ask the United States for "clarifications" on some of the six points.

November 11—Egypt and Israel signed the case-fire agreement sponsored by the United States and immediately began direct discussions on carrying it out. The discussions marked the first time since the 1949 armistice that higher officers of the two nations met in negotiations over issues larger than the establishment and maintenance of local cease-fire arrangements.

November 11—The United States has proposed that an Israeli-Arab peace conference be convened in Geneva in early December under American and Soviet auspices, Israeli sources in Jerusalem reported.

November 12—Secretary of State Kissinger said that the United States was considering a mutual security treaty with Israel as one of the possible ways of guaranteeing Israel's boundries once a formal peace agreement has been achieved in the Middle East.

November 12—Israeli sources said that unless the question on control of the strategic Cairo-Suez road was resolved and war prisoners promptly returned, Israel would have to reconsider the entire cease-fire agreement with Egypt, including her pledge to permit provisions to continue to go to the Egyptian III Corps.

November 12—Finnish troops of the United Nations Emergency Force established two checkpoints on the Cairo-to-Suez road and held them in spite of a threat of attack by Israeli force, highly placed sources reported. They said fistfights broke out between Finns and Israelis.

November 13—Israeli forces demonstrated that they retained full control of the road leading to the city of Suez despite the two United Nations checkpoints that were set up November 12. Israeli soldiers held back about 120 newsmen and cameramen who had come from Cairo to the point on the Cairo-Suez road called Kilometer 101.

November 13—Premier Golda Meir told the Israeli Parliament that she believed Israel and Egypt would be able to overcome their differences and carry out the American-sponsored cease-fire agreement along the Suez Canal.

November 14—Israeli and Egyptian negotiators ended a three-day impasse by agreeing on an immediate exchange of prisoners. The agreement appeared to clear the way for a full-scale Arab-Israeli peace conference that is expected to open in Geneva next month. Under the terms of the exchange agreement, prisoners will be returned on direct flights between Cairo and Tel Aviv by Red Cross planes.

November 15—Twenty-six wounded Israeli prisoners of war arrived in Tel Aviv aboard a Red Cross plane that later returned to Cairo with 44 wounded Egyptian prisoners, as Israel and Egypt began their prisoner exchange which is expected to last a week. Afterward, another plane took 250 wounded Egyptian prisoners to Cairo.

November 15—The United Nations began exercising its right to supervise the daily flow of food, water and medical supplies to Suez city under the cease-fire arrangement, but in other respects Israeli forces remained in control of all access roads.

November 16—President Nixon expressed hope that what he called the "real progress" in the Middle East might lead to a lifting of the Arab embargo on oil shipments to the United States.

November 17—Egypt has asked the United States to put diplomatic pressure on Israel to carry out the six-point cease-fire agreement more rapidly, according to well-informed Cairo sources. The requests were addressed to Herman F. Eilts, the newly appointed American Ambassador, by Foreign Minister Ismail Fahmy and other high officials.

November 18—Arab oil exporters made a conciliatory gesture to Western Europe with the announcement that petroleum supplies will not be cut back further to most European Common Market countries. An embargo will continue to apply to the Netherlands and the United States in punishment for what the Arabs believe to be Dutch and American policies favoring Israel.

November 18—It was reported that large quantities of new Soviet weapons have been put into service by the Syrian Armed Forces, which are offering Western suppliers cash in advance for quick delivery of radar and other air-defense equipment.

November 19—Syria, after long hestiation, has reportedly declared itself willing to attend a peace conference under United Nations auspices aimed at establishing a durable Middle Eastern peace, it was disclosed in Cairo. Officials said, the Syrian Foreign Minister, Abdel Halim Khaddam conveyed Syria's position to President Anwar el-Sadat.

November 19—The Administration's bill proposing $2.2 billion in military aid to Israel would give President Nixon the power to determine how much would be a loan and how much a gift, and this is being interpreted in different ways in Washington. No previous aid bill has ever provided a President with this authority, according to Senate and Pentagon sources.

November 20—The Soviet note that, along with intelligence data on certain Soviet sea and air activities, led to a precautionary alert of United States forces around the world on the night of October 24 carried an implied threat rather than an actual threat of the dispatch of Soviet troops to the Suez war zone. "We strongly urge that we both send forces to enforce the cease-fire and, if you do not, we may be obliged to consider acting alone," the Soviet note said, according to two officials who have read it.

November 21—Secretary of State Kissinger said the United States would not change its Middle East policies because of the Arab oil embargo and warned that "countermeasures" would have to be considered if the embargo continued "unreasonably and indefinitely." During the news conference on the Middle East Mr. Kissinger also repeated his objections to the United States' proposing a detailed peace plan.

November 21—Defense officials said that the United States had intelligence information suggesting that the Soviet Union might have moved nuclear warheads into Egypt at the height of the Arab-Israeli war. Despite reported disagreements over how conclusive the evidence is, the information is said to have raised Administration suspicions that some Soviet-controlled weapons may now be in Egypt.

November 22—Egyptian and Israeli generals met on the Cairo-Suez road as the two sides held their first formal session in eight days to discuss the details of disengaging their troops under the cease-fire agreement. While no agreement was reached, the session was relaxed, and the discussion progressed to detailed debates of each side's proposals.

November 22—Saudi Arabia's Oil Minister threatened to cut oil production by 80 per cent the United States, Europe or Japan tried to counter current Arab embargoes and reductions. The minister, Sheik Ahmed Zaki al-Yamani, also threatened to blow up some oil fields if the United States should take any military action.

November 23—Col. Muammar el-Qaddafi of Lybia arrived in Paris and was expected to demand that the French deliver more and better arms, possibly including atomic weapons, and lift restrictions on transfer of French arms to Egypt and Syria.

November 23—Israel's Defense Minister, Moshe Dayan, said that he did not share the optimism generated by the talks between Egyptian and Israeli generals on carrying out the six-point cease-fire agreement. The talks at Kilometer 101 on the Cairo-Suez road, at which the disengagement of forces was discussed, continued to show some progress.

November 23—The editor of Egypt's semiofficial newspaper Al Aharam stressed that the Arab world needed to build, buy or borrow nuclear weapons as a deterrent to any use of such weapons by Israel. The editor, Mohammed Hassanein Heykal wrote that he had become convinced that Israel had nuclear weapons and might attempt to use them as psychological "blackmail" against the Arabs.

November 24.—Israeli officials said that a major gap was still separating Israel and Egypt on the question of disengaging their forces along the Suez Canal. They said that "no meaningful progress" had been made at an 80-minute meeting between Israeli and Egyptian negotiators on the Cairo-Suez highway.

November 24.—Anti-Israeli militancy was the keynote as ministers and other high officials representing 16 Arab nations and Palestinian refugees gathered at the Arab foreign ministers conference in Staoueli, Algeria, in the first large-scale Arab meeting since the October war against Israel.

***November 25.*—Israel's Cabinet decided to accept an American proposal that Israel attend peace talks with Egypt, Syria and Jordan on December 18. Arab hijackers seized a Dutch jet with 288 passengers and crew members in a flight over the Middle East, and sent a message to Archbishop Makarios, President of Cyprus, demanding release of seven Arabs who had bombed the home of the Israeli ambassador to Cyprus.**

***November 26.*—Arab hijackers agreed to release passengers of a Dutch jet in Malta, and conference of Arab heads of state opened in Staoueli, Algeria with spokesmen speaking of the Arab "oil weapon" and its impact on the outside world, but adding notes of caution about its use.**

THE UNITED STATES OIL SHORTAGE AND THE ARAB-ISRAELI CONFLICT

The burgeoning U.S. energy crisis has dealt our Nation the most serious threat to its national security since World War II. Although world petroleum shortages have been increasing in recent years, the latest Arab-Israeli war has dangerously impeded our country's ability to obtain the amount of oil necessary for its security and well-being.

In addition to aggravating the worldwide petroleum squeeze, the October Arab-Israeli war imposed unspeakable human losses on both sides, destroyed materiel and infrastructure to the extent that the economies of the warring parties were dealt serious setbacks, and precipitated a potentially deadly United States-Soviet confrontation reminiscent of the Berlin wall and Cuban missile crisis.

THE OIL PROBLEM

The United States has only recently become aware of the scope of its dependence on oil produced in the Arab nations of the Middle East. As late as the second week of the October Arab-Israeli war, certain White House spokesmen, as well as some Members of the House and the Senate, were asserting that the United States was only 5 to 6 percent dependent on petroleum from Arab oil-producing countries. The American public was in for a "crude" shock—for the inaccuracy of such estimates has not only slowed the response of our Government to the oil embargo, but it has also done a great disservice to the American consumers who were led to believe that the embargo would not affect them severely.

The study mission's research and inquiries into the dimensions of our Nation's dependence on Arab oil revealed four factors which must be taken into consideration when the full amount of Arab oil finding its way to the United States is measured. These factors are: (1) crude oil imported directly from Arab countries; (2) Arab crude oil exports transshipped through other countries to the United States; (3) refined petroleum products from Arab refineries and from refineries of other countries such as the Netherlands which process Arab crude oil for U.S. markets; and (4) imports which represent trades of oil with countries like Canada, which finds it profitable to engage in such a transaction due to its own Arab oil imports. Taking all four factors into consideration, one finds that the United States is currently dependent on Arab oil for 14 to 18 percent of its total petroleum requirements, the significance of which the executive branch has recognized belatedly.

Putting U.S. dependence on Arab oil into the perspective of our total energy requirement, one finds that it was necessary for Americans to import one-third of its daily consumption of oil (averaging 17.3 million barrels in 1973) with at least one-third of those imports

Staff of House Comm. on Foreign Affairs, 93d Cong., 1st Sess, The United States Oil Shortage and the Arab-Israeli Conflict (Comm. Print 1973)

related to Arab production. The significance of U.S. imports of Arab oil looms even larger when one considers that oil furnishes at least 50 percent of the total U.S. energy requirement, and, had the embargo not been imposed, U.S. imports of Arab oil were scheduled to increase greatly in coming months.

While it is too early to forecast the medium- to long-term effects of the Arab embargo on the United States, it is clear that if the embargo is prolonged, the economic consequences will be serious, notwithstanding efforts to conserve available energy and to develop new and alternative sources. Already, some executive branch estimates put the unemployment rate at 8 to 9 percent by 1975 (8 million people) if the embargo continues. Moreover, to borrow an economic term, a continuing critical shortfall of oil could have an adverse "multiplier" effect on the economy. Industries, businesses, and offices will be forced to cut back operations, resulting in a retardation of our economic growth and a new round of inflation.

In addition to causing long-term economic dislocations, the Arab oil embargo will have an immediate effect on two areas of the Nation—New England and the upper Midwest. For example, one-fourth of the residual oil (used to produce electricity) and 80 percent of the distillate fuel (heating oil) imported by the east coast States is refined from Arab oil.

Even more critically affected by the Arab embargo and production cuts are the countries of Western Europe which depend on Arab countries for 87 percent of their petroleum requirements and Japan with a 40 percent dependence. Thus, the Arab actions have produced a worldwide oil squeeze which will sharply increase competition for the limited supplies of other producing countries, such as Venezuela, Nigeria, and Iran.

The Arab oil states have been able to inflict a serious oil shortage on the industrialized nations of the non-Communist world due to their ability to present a united front to a disorganized group of oil-consuming nations. That united front derives its power and cohesiveness from two organizations—the Organization of Petroleum Exporting Countries (OPEC), which includes the world's principal oil exporting countries and its sister group, the Organization of Arab Petroleum Exporting Countries (OAPEC).

In 1971 the OPEC countries first showed their muscle when they concluded an agreement in Teheran with the major oil companies which gained them a major price increase and participation in oil company assets and profits. It was this agreement which saw the balance of power tip in favor of the producers.

In the first week of October 1973, coinciding with the opening guns of the October Arab-Israeli war, OPEC again presented the major oil companies with a set of price increase demands in Vienna. When the Vienna meeting failed to produce a compromise, the six Persian Gulf State members of OPEC met in Kuwait on October 16 and unilaterally announced a 17-percent increase in the base market price of a barrel of oil ($3.65). This action enabled producing countries to greatly increase the amount of money made on each barrel of crude oil and paved the way for the Arab producers' subsequent embargo and production cuts.

Meeting again in Kuwait, the oil ministers of OAPEC imposed a total embargo on the United States and the Netherlands for their support of Israel. South Africa, Rhodesia, and Portugal were added later. In addition, the Arab oil states also announced a cut in production totaling 25 percent of their September 1973 output.

To enforce the embargo, the OAPEC countries instituted a sophisticated plan which has enabled them to keep detailed information on every barrel of oil leaving their borders. In addition, the Arab oil producers have been receiving the cooperation of recipient countries who, for fear of being included in the embargo, have discontinued both transshipments of crude oil and refined products to the United States.

Thus far, the only cracks in OAPEC's solidarity on the embargo appear to be Libya and Iraq, who reportedly are exporting crude oil in amounts exceeding the OAPEC 25 percent reduction level. In the case of Libya, it is believed that some of its crude oil exports are still going to Caribbean refineries for final shipments to U.S. markets, but not in enough amounts to have a beneficial effect on the shortfall caused by the embargo.

The role of Saudi Arabia has been crucial to the effectiveness of OAPEC's actions. The study mission found that Saudi Arabia originally supported the production cut policy but opposed embargoing the United States and the Netherlands. However, when the President's $2.2 billion military assistance request for Israel was made public, Saudi Arabia changed its position and the embargo went into effect.

What allows Saudia Arabia its position as the most influential and powerful member of OAPEC? First, it's soil contains the largest known oil reserves in the world—150 billion barrels. Second, it is the world's largest exporter of crude oil. Third, it's revenue from oil sales far exceeds its expenditure requirements. The latter attribute has led Saudi Arabia to embrace a policy which has already had a profound effect on the oil market. Recognizing that even their enormous reserves are finite, they have opted to reduce production, maximize income through increased prices, and let as much oil as possible "appreciate" in the ground. With few exceptions, major oil producers around the world have followed suit in this policy as a hedge against the future.

In summary of the oil problem, the following observations can be made. With some exceptions (Libya and Iraq), the embargo and production cuts are being faithfully applied by the Arab oil states. The embargo is being enforced. Coupled with the production cuts, the embargo is causing serious shortfalls in the oil supplies in the United States, Western Europe, and Japan. As a result, most of the nations of Western Europe and Japan have altered their Middle East policies, which was the purpose of the Arab oil states actions.

Given the impact of the embargo on the United States what can be done to deal with it? For the long term, it is imperative that the United States become less dependent on foreign sources of energy, especially such politically unstable sources as the Middle East. To do so will require a crash research and development program similar to the Manhattan and Apollo projects in which America achieved seemingly impossible goals in relatively short-time frames. In the short run, it will be necessary to stringently conserve existing energy supplies while doing what can be done within reason to convince the Arab producers to lift the embargo.

Findings and Conclusions

Current dependence on Arab oil

The United States is currently dependent on Arab sources of oil for between 14 and 18 percent of its total petroleum use.

Future dependence

Barring an indefinite application of the Arab embargo and the rapid development of alternative sources of energy, U.S. importation of Arab oil, both direct and indirect, will increase dramatically by 1980. The National Petroleum Council estimates that, without effective conservation measures or other restraints on demand, U.S. consumption by 1980 could reach 24 million barrels per day. At least one-fourth of that total would have to be imported from Arab sources.

The embargo

Saudi Arabia only agreed to participate in the embargo after the President's $2.2 billion military aid request for Israel was made public. The study mission learned that the U.S. Embassy in Saudi Arabia was not consulted on the timing or possible effect of the request. Failure to consult adequately with appropriate Department of State personnel may have contributed to our present crisis.

As long as the embargo is in effect, the United States will not be able to import essential refined products from the Netherlands, Italy, or Spain, all three of which are normally sellers to U.S. markets.

The embargo has forced U.S. naval fleets normally reliant on Arab oil to dip into domestic supplies.

Importance of Saudi Arabia

Experts believe that Saudi Arabia's estimate of its oil reserves (150 billion barrels) is low. Therefore, it is believed that Saudi Arabia could easily increase its production. If the embargo were lifted, availability of Saudi Arabian oil would not solve the U.S. energy crisis but it could fill much of the current gap between supply and demand for oil.

Because of Saudi Arabia's leadership among the Arab oil states and its strong financial position, it is in the interest of the United States to maintain good relations there. Last year alone, American firms and contractors in Saudi Arabia repatriated over $1 billion in profits to the United States.

Alternative sources of oil

According to the Department of State's Office of Fuels and Energy, the possibility for compensating for the Arab embargo by increasing imports from non-Arab producers is virtually nil.

Production of U.S. oils can be raised but only to a small extent. Any significant jump could permanently damage the wells.

Increased off-shore drilling within the Continental Shelf would not be of any significant relief in the petroleum shortage in the immediate future nor in the long range.

Counterembargo

To be effective, a counterembargo against the Arab oil states would have to be a multilateral effort involving a majority of the industrialized nations. The lack of cooperation among the countries of Western Europe in face of the embargo and production cuts makes such a response unlikely in the immediate future.

Nevertheless, in spite of the present disunity among the nations dependent on Arab oil, the industrialized countries must recognize that international cooperation is imperative if they are to effectively confront such energy cartels as OPEC and OAPEC. Therefore, the study mission believes that the United States should promote the formation of an "International Organization of Energy Importing Nations" under the auspices of the 24-member Organization for Economic Cooperation and Development (OECD).

Recommendations

To increase domestic production

Congress should approve the executive branch's request to open up the Elk Hills Naval Petroleum Reserve. This reserve can produce, almost immediately, 160,000 barrels per day, and after a year and some improvements, 300,000 barrels per day.

To conserve available fuel

In order to deal with the immediate crisis, we must conserve our available fuel supplies. The best conservation measure is to allow fuel prices to rise to a level sufficient to induce consumers to limit their nonessential use of energy.

In addition to the voluntary and mandatory gasoline conservation measures already being applied, the study mission recommends that consideration be given to an indefinite exemption from emission control devices for four-cylinder automobiles. Such a measure would encourage both the manufacturer and the buyer to turn to more economical private automobiles.

The United States should, as a general policy, encourage people to live nearer their jobs. We should also make better utilization of our high-rise office buildings. The present 40-hour-per-week use of these buildings is one of the most inefficient uses of energy.

Long term measures

The United States should encourage the acceleration of the development of energy resources in the deep seabed.

One of the reasons which forces the United States to rely on so much imported refined oil, is the shortage of domestic refineries. A major cause of the reluctance to build new refineries is the feared environmental danger inherent in such projects. Therefore, we must seek to develop a technology which will minimize the environmental effect of much needed new oil refineries.

Consideration should be given to those actions that would immediately stimulate a maximum feasible effort by the oil companies in exploring new oil and gas wells. Such incentives could include, but not be limited to: Allowing the price of gas at the wellhead to rise to a level that would induce increased production and increased exploratory efforts; and providing tax incentives which would permit an accelerated depreciation of capitalization on a short-term basis.

Regulatory procedures should be revised to discourage the switch from coal to oil by electric utilities.

One of the most abundant resources of energy available to this country are our domestic reserves of anthracite coal. This is a hard, clean-burning coal. The initial capital investment necessary to extract this coal, however, precludes profitable extraction of this resource. Therefore, consideration should be given to providing financial incentives to the extractive industry that would encourage the immediate opening of mines. These incentives could be in the form of either preferential tax incentives or a direct subsidy of the initial capitalization.

We must undertake a massive program of research and development aimed at freeing ourselves from excessive dependence on oil. This should include, in addition to undersea exploration, research into solar, thermal and hydrogen fusion energy. However, it should be well understood that such an effort will not bear fruit soon enough to deal with the immediate effects of the embargo.

THE OCTOBER WAR AND PEACE PROPOSALS

Hopefully, the fourth Arab-Israeli war will serve as a watershed in the history of the Middle East conflict.

For both sides, the results of the latest war changed nothing in the basic dispute. The principal Arab combatants, Egypt and Syria, ostensibly began the war to regain lands lost in the June 1967 war. Yet when the cease-fire took hold, Israeli forces had forged even deeper into Egyptian and Syrian territories. While in a narrow sense, it can be said that Israel won a military victory, it was a pyrrhic victory in other respects. Their casualties (the U.S. equivalent would be 155,000 dead and 500,000 wounded) were the worst since the 1948 war of independence. The initial successes of the Arab forces shattered Israel's image of invincibility and shed doubt in the minds of many Israelis on the effectiveness of the occupied territories as buffer zones in defense of Israel's real borders.

Although the Arabs failed in their military objectives, they made considerable diplomatic advances and achieved greater solidarity among Arab countries than ever before. Israel emerged from the war diplomatically isolated except for the United States, the Netherlands, South Africa, Rhodesia, and Portugal, all of whom have been embargoed by the Arab oil states.

On the positive side, the study mission was given a strong impression that the principal parties involved in the Middle East conflict now are willing to make a serious effort to resolve the territorial disputes and to attempt to find a solution to the Palestinian issue. Finally, the study mission received indications that the thorniest issue, Jerusalem, can be separated from other issues more amenable to compromise.

Findings and Conclusions

Israel's ability to turn back the Arab forces on two fronts shows that the Israeli Defense Force remains the single most effective military establishment in the Middle East.

However, Arab forces have improved to the extent that they are capable of inflicting serious-to-unacceptable losses on Israel.

The Golan Heights region is Israel's most vulnerable point. The study mission learned that, at one point, Syria could have invaded the Jordan Valley of northern Israel but did not due to logistical problems.

The war has shaken Israel's economy but has not severely dislocated it. However, if negotiations do not allow for an Israeli pullback on the two contested fronts and demobilization in the near future, severe economic dislocations may begin to develop.

President Sadat of Egypt and King Faisal of Saudi Arabia have emerged from the war as coleaders of the Arab world. Sadat's leadership is based on his political ability to forge an unprecedented state of unity among traditionally factional Arab nations. King Faisal's ascendancy has resulted from his leadership in the oil embargo, his economic support for the Arab combatants, and his insistence on the return of the Old City of Jerusalem to Arab control.

King Hussein represents a moderating influence in the Middle East. His adroitness kept Jordan in a minor role during the October war and his willingness to permit a plebiscite in the West Bank may offer the best opportunity to resolve the Palestinian issue.

Recommendations

In the opinion of the study mission, a negotiated settlement of the disposition of the Golan Heights and the Sinai is the most urgent requirement of the forthcoming peace conference. There are strong indications that such a settlement would convince the Arab oil states to ease the oil embargo. It is clear that Israel will agree to a return of large areas of the Sinai and the Golan Heights only if it can be assured of defensible borders and a credible external guarantee of security. Therefore, in order to encourage Israel to negotiate a territorial settlement, the United States should consider supporting the following provisions:

(1) In the event of an agreement involving a phased Israeli pullback in the Sinai and the Golan region, a buffer zone should be maintained by U.N. observers with the possible Israeli and Arab participation. Such a provision is essential in the Golan Heights where Israel is particularly vulnerable.

(2) In order to encourage a permanent boundary settlement, the Sinai and Golan areas should be demilitarized under the auspices of the United Nations.

(3) The United States should consider entering into a formal bilateral agreement to guarantee Israel's territorial integrity. Such a guarantee should meet the following criteria: (a) It should seek to give Israel reliable assurance of physical security in territory defined by borders accepted by all sides of the conflict; (b) it should be entered into only parallel to a general territorial settlement; (c) it should seek to avoid any further polarization of United States and Soviet roles in the Middle East.

However, in the absence of a territorial settlement, a military balance between Israel and its adversaries must be maintained. Anything less could severely endanger Israel's security and chances for successful peace negotiations.

In order to facilitate negotiations on the Palestinian issue, the study mission believes the following steps should be taken: (1) Coinciding with peace negotiations, the United States should encourage U.N. members to increase the funding of UNRWA to alleviate the plight of the refugees; (2) because a major repatriation of the refugees inside Israel proper is not a viable alternative, an indemnity program for those who lost property, jobs, and businesses should be considered. Such a program could be

formulated and administered by the U.N. or any other multilateral organization acceptable to the parties involved; (3) the offer of King Hussein for a plebiscite on the West Bank should be explored as well as a similar solution for the Gaza area.

In order to ease tensions in the Middle East, the United States should press for an understanding with the Soviet Union to control arms flows to that area. One method of curbing the arms flow to the area would be to link our granting of "most favored nation" trading status to the Soviet Union to a Middle East arms limitation agreement.

OIL NEGOTIATIONS, OPEC, AND THE STABILITY OF SUPPLY

HEARINGS

BEFORE THE

SUBCOMMITTEE ON FOREIGN ECONOMIC POLICY

AND THE

SUBCOMMITTEE ON THE NEAR EAST AND SOUTH ASIA

OF THE

COMMITTEE ON FOREIGN AFFAIRS HOUSE OF REPRESENTATIVES

NINETY-THIRD CONGRESS

FIRST SESSION

APRIL 10; MAY 14, 16; JULY 11; SEPTEMBER 6 AND 18, 1973

OPEC

Since its inception in 1960, the OPEC has achieved significant gains in negotiations with international oil companies. Supply disruptions since 1967, such as the Suez Canal closure, the Tapline rupture and curtailments in Libyan production, as well as the vigorous negotiating stance of OPEC, have brought increases in posted oil prices, new formulas for calculating royalty payments and taxes, and, most recently, agreements on participation in ownership. OPEC has also forced changes in the price of crude oil to reflect devaluation of the dollar. These actions by OPEC's members will bring considerable increases in revenue as well as control of the local assets of oil companies. Conversely, these same events have brought problems to the oil companies and concern to the consuming nations.

The Tehran and Tripoli agreements set forth a four-step increase in posted prices through 1975. This increase varies by type and source of crude and will raise oil company payments to the Persian Gulf nations by $1.50 per barrel or 80 percent over 1969 levels. To place these payments in historic perspective, let me point out that there was virtually no increase in per barrel payments in the 1950's and only a 12-percent-per-barrel increase in the 1960's.

RESULTS OF OIL NEGOTIATIONS

I might add that there has been a rise in the posted price and, hence, the tax paid per barrel as a result of the devaluation of the dollar. The resulting increase in the cost to the U.S. consumer is governed by a formula agreed to by the Western oil companies and the producer nations at Geneva in January 1972. It provides that posted prices will be adjusted every time the U.S. exchange rate differs from an index of nine major currencies by more than 2 percent. Posted prices rose by 8.55 percent in February 1972 and are expected to rise by another 5.8 percent this month. Negotiations on the 5.8 percent rise are scheduled for April 12 between OPEC and the representatives of the oil companies.

OPEC's most recent demands have concerned the extent to which host countries would participate in oil production. Some agreements call for the transfer of a majority share to host governments, while others, such as that with Iran, call for total ownership by the producing country and future cancellation of concessions. In most cases, the oil companies have agreed to buy back a country's share at prices lower than could be realized from third-party purchasers. Compensatory payments to the companies are to be made in crude oil.

Oil producing countries can be expected to press for further increases. Their spokesmen claim that they have not been adequately compensated for their oil given the prices the oil companies realize in the marketplace.

OIL REVENUES OF EXPORTING COUNTRIES

In the case of most oil-producing countries, income from oil is likely to lead to an equivalent expansion of imports. However, a few of the oil producing states, particularly those located on the Persian Gulf, have small populations and only limited development potential, making it highly unlikely that they could increase expenditures in consumption and investment as fast as their oil revenues. These countries will spend part of their revenues on aid to other countries. They may invest part in Europe and the United States. And, what has given some cause for concern, they may hold much of their earnings as international reserves.

The major oil producers on the Arabian Peninsula—Saudi Arabia, Kuwait, Abu Dhabi, and Qatar—had an estimated income of about $5 billion in 1972. This is likely to increase to $10 billion by 1975, and up to $20 to $30 billion by 1980. These countries could absorb about $10 billion in imports annually by 1980, leaving $10 to $20 billion to be allocated to foreign aid, foreign investments, and foreign exchange reserves. If annual excess earnings were added to reserves, the holdings of these countries would rise to $40 to $70 billion by 1980. This is a very substantial pool of dollars that obviously could play a most important role in the international monetary system.

RECOGNIZING MONETARY POWER OF OPEC COUNTRIES

Fortunately the oil producing countries have been participating fully in discussions on international monetary reform. It is to be expected that, in determining the use of their oil income, they will primarily be motivated by the normal investment opportunities that pay the highest return. In accordance with that desire the United States should serve as an excellent investment area.

Some producing countries have already expressed their willingness to invest in the U.S. oil industry. This, in turn, would benefit their own economies. Other possibilities might include their participating in large investment projects elswhere, such as the exploitation of the Siberian oil and gas fields. Since the ability of most Middle Eastern governments to develop and provide adequate supervision for large-scale investment projects is limited, assistance by the United States and other governments may be necessary in getting the oil producers to commit their funds to these projects.

The Middle East has been the predominant supplier of oil to Europe and Japan for some time and is rapidly becoming a major source of U.S. petroleum requirements. The security of these supplies is of paramount concern to the importing nations.

IMPORTANCE OF PERSIAN GULF

The bulk of the world's oil reserves are in the Middle East. At present, this area has 67 percent of the world's known reserves.

Three countries—Saudi Arabia, Iraq, and Iran—possess oil reserves sufficient to allow substantial increases in production above current levels. But Iran has indicated that the output of crude oil will not expand much beyond a maximum of 8 to 9 million barrels per day.

Saudi Arabia holds the largest reserves of oil, about 140 billion barrels or 24 percent of the world's proven reserves. Saudi reserves are equivalent to four times U.S. reserves, including the North Slope's estimated 10 billion barrels. Thus, Saudi Arabia will play a key role in the balance between world oil supply and demand.

The Middle East must greatly expand its production from its reserves to meet the anticipated growth in demand for oil in the United States, Western Europe, and Japan. While the exporting nations may choose different strategies in exploiting their remaining reserves so as to maximize their flow of revenues, it is reasonable to expect that oil production in the Middle East and North Africa will increase from 22 million barrels per day in 1970 to about 40 to 50 million barrels in 1980. Saudi Arabia will supply about 75 percent of the expected growth in Middle Eastern oil production through 1980 and Iran another 20 percent. On a global basis, the Middle East will be producing 50 percent of the world's oil and Saudi Arabia and Iran will, together, supply half of this oil by 1980. In other words, the world's oil economy has changed drastically from when the oil import program was first initiated.

Oil imports from the Middle East will be supplemented by imports of natural gas shipped to the United States either as liquefied natural gas (LNG) or methanol. Although an LNG contract was, after long delay, consummated last week with Algeria for delivery in 1977, it is unlikely that arrangements could be made with Persian Gulf governments to deliver gas to the United States before 1980.

SECURITY PROBLEM FOR UNITED STATES

Greater reliance on Middle East oil could represent a security problem for the United States for several reasons.

First, despite their ties to the United States, all producing countries have shown an increasing tendency to demand more for their oil. Some have actually threatened withholding supplies to assure that their demands are met.

Second, the Middle East is not trouble-free. War has broken out several times during the past three decades, and supplies from this area have suffered frequent interruptions.

Third, some governments might be tempted to threaten longstanding agreements with the oil companies and use their oil resources as a political weapon.

The relationships between oil-producing nations and the international oil companies operating within their borders are changing rapidly. Most OPEC members are seeking participation in oil production within their borders. Agreements have been signed which provide that host governments will obtain a 25-percent ownership in international oil companies, beginning last January, and eventually reaching 51 percent of 1982.

INCREASED POWER FOR OPEC STATES

Participation in exploration and development will give producing countries their own oil which they may use as they wish. Revenues from this oil, together with the taxes from nonparticipation oil, will yield extremely high foreign exchange earnings for several producing nations. In 1980 alone this oil-derived revenue to the Middle East could well total as high as $60 billion per year. Hopefully, these sums will find a use within the Middle East or will be invested abroad, perhaps in the United States. If not, we face the prospect that some producers will find other, less desirable uses for their revenues or may decide that it is in their best interests to keep their oil in the ground.

Under these circumstances, how best can our security interests in the Middle East be served? The new strength of the oil producing nations is well known and it has been used to advantage in recent months. It will be difficult to coordinate the energy policies of a large group of consuming nations and to secure a joint approach to common supply problems. We are convinced, however, that the consuming countries should begin to explore this approach seriously.

What actions can the United States take at home to protect against a cutoff of the supply of crude oil? In the last few years we have investigated various ways of responding to interruption in foreign supplies. We have, for example, begun to consider storage and shut-in production of oil and coal reserves. We also have some dual capability in our powerplants. We can switch some of these plants back to coal if, in the meantime, we have not put our coal industry out of business. If disruption of imports should be serious enough to threaten U.S. security, the Government can evoke the power to set priorities and allocate supplies under title I of the Defense Production Act of 1950. But let us resolve that it shall not come to this.

RECOMMENDATIONS

First, we must produce more oil here at home. We cannot be content with declining levels of production. We must provide the incentives to increase U.S. production.

Second, the Mandatory Oil Import program, as presently constituted has become obsolete. We must end the stop-and-go operations of the program that have created uncertainty in the industry and deterred needed investment in drilling and new refinery construction. Our mission, as previously stated, is to have a vigorous domestic petroleum industry. We must encourage exploration and production as well as new refinery construction and expansion.

In the end, industry, consumers and the national interest should all benefit.

OIL NEGOTIATIONS, OPEC, AND STABILITY OF SUPPLY

MONDAY, MAY 14, 1973

HOUSE OF REPRESENTATIVES,
COMMITTEE ON FOREIGN AFFAIRS,
SUBCOMMITTEES ON FOREIGN ECONOMIC POLICY
AND ON THE NEAR EAST AND SOUTH ASIA,
Washington, D.C.

The subcommittees met at 10:06 a.m., pursuant to call, in room 2255, Rayburn House Office Building, Hon. John C. Culver and Lee H. Hamilton (chairmen of the subcommitees) presiding.

Mr. HAMILTON. The subcommittees will come to order.

Today, the Subcommittee on the Near East and South Asia and the Subcommittee on Foreign Economic Policy resume their joint hearings on "Oil Negotiations, OPEC and the Stability of Supply."

We are fortunate to have with us today Mr. W. F. Penniman who is a petroleum consultant currently based in Beirut, Lebanon, and who has developed over the years important contacts and relationships with the major figures in the oil industry in the Middle East and with the leaders of the oil exporting countries.

The major issues that we wish to discuss with Mr. Penniman are:

First, what has occurred in the oil negotiations that have taken place and are still taking place and what are the implications of their likely outcome on the ability of the United States to be able to maintain access to Persian Gulf oil?

Second, what is and what should be the role of the U.S. Government in these negotiations?

Third, what degree and kind of consuming country cooperation and coordination do you consider advisable and profitable?

Fourth, how can the United States best assure a stable relationship with the oil exporting countries for the future? What policies will promote continued access to oil?

And finally, what do you think the members of OPEC and the specific leaders of oil producing states want in these negotiations. What are their concerns? What are their priorities? And what is likely to be the future role of OPEC?

Mr. Penniman, we appreciate your coming here today. You have a prepared statement and you may proceed as you wish, by reading or summarizing the statement.

STATEMENT OF WILLIAM F. PENNIMAN, JR., PETROLEUM CONSULTANT, CURRENTLY BASED IN BEIRUT, LEBANON

Mr. PENNIMAN. Thank you, Mr. Chairman.

That is quite a list of questions that you have given me.

I am going to summarize in part, although I will follow the prepared statement fairly closely.

OPEC'S SUCCESS

I am here to discuss OPEC and the Middle East in light of my experience in the area.

1. I will attempt to show that, historically, OPEC sets objectives and realizes them; that it is the moderate voice in the Middle East; that OPEC members have, in the past, felt a moral obligation to supply the oil-consuming nations and, so far, have used oil as a weapon to a very limited degree.

2. I will consider the four main options of OPEC in relation to the oil companies and try to indicate that there should be no crude supply problem provided man-made difficulties do not arise.

3. I will show that the predicted outcome of direct government participation and consumer confrontation would be to provoke an instant reaction and inject into an already complex equation a myraid of new but irrelevant variables.

4. I will suggest that the U.S. Government should provide a favorable climate within which the companies may operate efiiciently.

I would like first to point out that I do not profess to be an oil statistician, nor am I directly concerned with the domestic energy problems of the United States. I would also like to state that, at the request of the committee, I do not intend to concentrate on the Arab-Israeli problem.

The OPEC of 1960, reaffirmed in 1968, can be summarized as:

1. Unification of the petroleum policies of the member countries;
2. Stabilization of prices in international markets, and
3. Efficient, economic regular supply to consuming nations, and a fair return on their capital to those investing in the petroleum industry.

PARTICIPATION GOAL

The current objective of the participation was first implied, though the exact term was not used, 11 years ago in OPEC's 1962 Resolutions.

First, then, OPEC tends to do as it says. Second, the OPEC resolutions represent the moderate view in the Arab world today. A workable formula followed the Djakarta Agreement of 1965 to the effect that the OPEC position should be the moderate one and individual members would be permitted to depart from the position if they so desired. Leapfrogging by individual member countries stemmed from that agreement and is not regarded as a breach of OPEC unity.

OPEC members are not ogres; neither are they paper tigers. They are a group of disparate countries that see themselves in a powerful economic position after years of drought.

It is interesting to note that since OPEC's XXV Conference in September 1971 only four members have implemented participation: Saudi Arabia, Kuwait, Abu Dhabi and Qatar in October and December 1972. Of the other members Iraq has nationalized, Iran has reached a separate alternative with the producing companies, and Libya has in the last few days delivered new and stringent conditions to at least one group of companies operating there.

OPEC resolved to negotiate participation "individually or in groups" largely because they realized in advance that gradual equity acquisition is not the only effective formula to gain control of a wasting national asset.

Estimates of world production capacity in 1980, exclusive of the Communist bloc countries, average about 76 million barrels a day, only 28 million of which will be low-sulfur crude oil. Demand for this sweet crude, however, will be upwards of 40 million barrels a day. Furthermore, this oil still has to be developed and capital expenditures as well as the leadtime involved will be considerable. Any delay in the development of this crude could upset all forecasts and necessary steps to insure continued, uninterrupted development should be taken as soon as possible.

Still, barring man-made interventions, the availability of crude will be governed by demand and not by supply. Certainly OPEC is not going to produce more than is actually required.

OIL AS A POLITICAL WEAPON

There is a long history of threats arising out of the Arab countries, however, to use oil as a weapon against those whose policies are considered anti-Arab. The first to advocate the denial of oil were the Egyptians. They were not, however, prepared to apply it themselves and they did not try to persuade other oil-producing states to follow through, especially those upon whom they were dependent for large subsidies. Iraq and Kuwait also made noises in this direction but, characteristically, they too did not intend to apply their recommendations.

In the past 22 years Arab oil has been used as a political weapon only three times but the picture now has become more serious. In the past there was little danger of any real application of these threats by the Arab countries, individually or unilaterally. However, now that Saudi Arabia's Zaki Yamani, speaking on behalf of King Faisal, has appealed to the United States to reconsider its pro-Israeli policy, a serious study of the motivating forces must be made.

Saudi Arabia represents the traditional conservative friends of the West in the Middle East. They are the United States-trained, anti-Communist power in the area. Sheikh Yamani himself is OPEC's spokesman for moderation. The Saudi Government recognizes furthermore, a moral obligation to provide the United States and the world with crude oil, for which so far there has been little reciprocal consideration. They consider that beyond a certain level of production it becomes an economic sacrifice of the nation's wasting asset.

PRESSURE ON SAUDI ARABIA

The Saudis are under great pressure, from within and without. Arab voices have long been raised against the United States for its continued moral, economic and military support of Israel. The billions of dollars in aid, as well as continued arms shipments, add to a growing sense of frustration and bitterness which has been capitalized upon by numerous groups throughout the Middle East and in the gulf.

For the future, the political leverage of oil cannot be overlooked, as the Saudi announcement demonstrates. In this case it is not an embargo; it is not political blackmail; it is a withholding of further increases in output beyond a certain level, which means that the principal victim will be the United States.

The producing countries have only a few options: (1) To increase production and generate unneeded surplus funds, (2) restrict production—and leave their wealth in the ground, ignoring the requirements of consuming countries and particularly of the United States or (3) increase production in exchange for technical assistance, an improved political climate and the opportunity of investing abroad.

I must emphasize, at this point, that any outbreak of hostilities will result in immediate and extreme anti-American reactions, the total withholding of supplies to the United States and the immediate imposition of production controls.

A QUID PRO QUO

What is needed is a quid pro quo. The United States is asking the producing countries to produce. It should not seem unreasonble that these same countries should in turn ask the United States for something, and paper money is not going to be enough. In addition to the political aspect, at least two avenues for reciprocity lay open to us: downstream investments and industrialization.

In effect, industrialization can be seen as the next step after participation. The producing countries with their vast sums of inflowing capital are anxious to develop a solid industrial base within each of their countries. As of now the Arabs have only oil. So, while these countries still have a unique advantage, they will provide sufficient quantities of oil to satisfy world demand and, I repeat, only in return for something besides money. Economically, this means outside investment in all different sectors of the national economies, especially by joint venture, to build up other resources, industry, and agriculture, using outside expertise and know-how. At the same time, foreign markets in anticipation of this industrialization will have to be secured.

At the present time the Arab countries are not interested in downstream investment in the United States. They feel that too much still has to be done at home before outside investments are sought. Furthermore, there is a fear amongst the producing countries of establishing themselves in outside markets and becoming the hostages of those markets. There is no doubt that such investments will be forthcoming once excess funds become available but they will not consider investing heavily in consuming countries while the consumers' policies are so unsettled and while they continue to hear consumers threatening to undermine OPEC.

POSSIBLE CONSUMER COOPERATION

On the subject of consumer coordination at an international level, I feel strongly that such cooperation is important and necessary, but it should not be used to intensify confrontation.

Any change of the status quo to support the consumers' interest at the expense of the producers must be carefully constructed not to draw adverse reaction. This is not a threat but a predictable outcome. OPEC wants cooperation but will not accept being told who they can sell to and at what price. Anyway, without total solidarity among oil-consuming countries and the individual buyers and consumers within those countries, any effective leverage will be undermined.

Furthermore, there is a strong reluctance on the part of Europe and Japan to join any union organized for these purposes. France is riding high in Arab public opinion and has no desire to jeopardize this position. Japan believes our energy policy is too closely allied with our Middle East foreign policy and prefers to compete on its own. For example, they have recently formed an economic committee with Saudi Arabia for the joint promotion of industrial and major economic projects in exchange for crude contracts. This cooperation is being extended to other countries in the gulf. Japan is strongly in favor of cooperative relationships but only between the producing nation or nations and Japan. Japanese delegations have been attempting to negotiate long-term crude purchase contracts throughout the Middle East and North Africa.

I am in full agreement that the consumers should organize to promote international research and development of alternate sources of energy, draft conservation programs, propose modifications of ecological restraints, establish an international mechanism for dealing with energy questions in times of critical shortages, study the establishment of stockpiling facilities, furnish supply-and-demand statistics, and so forth. However, any attempt to form a buyers cartel is ill advised and foredoomed to failure.

ROLE OF U.S. GOVERNMENT

A number of recommendations have been made urging the U.S. Government to take a more active position and intervene directly in negotiations with the oil-exporting countries. Some critics claim that our energy position today would have been much stronger if the U.S. Government had stepped in to support the oil companies when they needed it most.

Before this initiative is considered, I would caution you to analyze the predictable outcome. For a government to come in as a prospective buyer of crude is one thing. For a government to intervene on behalf of one or more companies on critical issues and impose pressure on the producing countries, or to negotiate price or availability is quite another thing.

Bearing in mind the dual function that must be served, that is an economic interest to obtain oil at the best price and harmonious relationship between buyer and supplier to insure availability for the future—I would suggest that the U.S. Government should realize it cannot hope to fill both roles at the same time, at least not as well as the oil companies themselves have done in the past.

If the U.S. Government takes over, it creates a whole new set of rules. It is still inconceivable for Saudi Arabia to tell Aramco that its oil liftings will be curtailed unless it changes its foreign policy. Yet, once the U.S. Government assumes an active role it automatically opens a dialog with the producing countries on a political rather than economic or technical basis. If the U.S. Government wishes to assume this role, let us first do all we can to establish peace in the area, for under the present conditions it would be impossible for the Government to sit at the negotiating table.

POLITICAL PRESSURE WILL NOT WORK

Predictably, if the U.S. Government or any other attempts to employ political pressure as a means to achieve economic ends, such pressure would prompt a very harsh reaction among the producing countries' governments and peoples and persuade the producing countries on their part to use oil as an economic and/or political weapon. Once one tries to interfere and to regulate prices and availability, the rules of supply and demand become drastically altered. By cutting back on production and withholding deliveries the producing countries could create a supply situation which would break almost any agreement.

Obviously, there is a great potential for cooperation between governments, but having more to do with the development of Saudi Arabia, itself than with the oil industry alone.

And ultimately I think it most important that, somehow, the Arab states be brought into the industrial and financial world of today.

At the beginning of my statement I mentioned that I did not intend to belabor the details of the Arab/Israeli question but it is impossible to talk about Middle East oil for over 5 minutes without touching on this subject. The role of the U.S. Government in Middle East oil should be to eliminate the hostile, belligerent climate in which the oil companies have been forced to operate over the past decades. I am sure there is no one in Washington who does not know what should be done, but no one has been able to tell me how it can be done.

CONCLUSIONS

In closing, I would like to point out a few of the changes which have taken place since the 1967 war. It is no longer sufficient to say that our Middle East policy can be solved by support of the U.N. resolution of November 1967 alone. Other developments which must affect U.S. thinking and policy in the area are the weakening Russian influence, military aid to Israel and Iran, and the official absence of recognition of the Palestine problems.

Thank you for hearing out my views on this issue which is of overriding importance to U.S. foreign policy. The question of oil supply has been described as the jugular vein of America's greatness.

I see the danger as one that can still be avoided through the development of mutuality between producing and consuming countries and the promotion of a just and lasting solution to the Arab/Israeli conflict. An evenhanded policy is a step in the right direction but no longer sufficient in itself. It is peace in the Middle East which is absolutely vital to our national interest.

STATEMENT OF WILLIAM F. PENNIMAN, JR.

Thank you, Mr. Chairman:

I am here to discuss OPEC and the Middle East in light of my experience in the area.

1. I will attempt to show that, historically, OPEC sets objectives and realizes them; that it is the moderate voice in the Middle East; that OPEC members have, in the past, felt a moral obligation to supply the oil-consuming nations and, so far, have used oil as a weapon to a very limited degree.

2. I will consider the four main options of OPEC in relation to the oil companies and try to indicate that there should be no crude supply problem provided man-made difficulties do not arise.

3. I will show that the predicted outcome of direct government participation and consumer confrontation would be to provoke an instant reaction and inject into an already complex equation a myriad of new but irrelevant variables.

4. I will suggest that the U.S. Government should provide a favorable climate within which the companies may operate efficiently.

I would like first to point out that I do not profess to be an oil statistician, nor am I directly concerned with the domestic energy problems of the United States. I would also like to state that, at the request of the Committee, I do not intend to concentrate on the Arab/Israeli problem.

ORGANIZATION OF PETROLEUM EXPORTING COUNTRIES (OPEC)

The OPEC Statutes of 1960, reaffirmed in 1968, can be summarized as:

1. Unification of the petroleum policies of member countries,
2. Stabilization of prices in international markets, and
3. Efficient, economic, regular supply to consuming nations and a fair return on their capital to those investing in the petroleum industry.

Chiefly, the OPEC issues have concentrated on (1) price stabilization, (2) increased royalty expensing, (3) conservation, (4) compensation for monetary fluctuations, (5) development of national petroleum industry, and (6) equity sharing and control. Of the last three, parity talks are currently underway, participation has been achieved by some, and the vigorous formation and development of indigenous petroleum and other industries lies directly ahead of us.

First, then, OPEC tends to do as it says. Secondly, the OPEC Resolutions represent the moderate view in the Arab World today. A workable formula followed the Djakarta Agreement of 1965 to the effect that the OPEC position should be the moderate one and individual members would be permitted to depart from that position if they so desired. Leapfrogging by individual member countries stemmed from that agreement and is not regarded as a breach of OPEC unity.

OPEC's view of its situation is much as Venezuela's Sr. Hugo Saliva stated it. "This situation of crisis is not of our making. It gives us, however, at this moment, considerable power. Let us use it to secure economic justice for our peoples."

The producing countries are demanding that changes be made so as to get the most out of their oil. Some are less patient than others but for the most part the OPEC members, individually and/or together, are achieving these changes through negotiation.

Very briefly, these oil negotiations gained their momentum in October 1970 with the Tripoli Settlement, when Libya began to realize its distinct economic advantage arising out of the closure of the Suez Canal, the high freight rates, and the rare quality of its low sulphur fuel oil. By negotiation and enforcement of their new conservation regulations the Libyans gained 30 cents increase in tax reference prices in settlement of retroactive dues.

The Gulf producing countries subsequently made a five year settlement on prices in February 1971, gaining 35 cents per barrel plus additional increases in posted prices.

Algeria decided at this time to partially nationalize France's CFP by a 51% immediate takeover, negotiating matters of compensation afterwards.

With the Tripoli Agreement two months later the Libyans managed to get back on par with the new OPEC standard 55% tax rate and adopted the Teheran escalations of 5 cents a year to reflect market prices plus 2½% a year to reflect inflation, claiming the 1970 Settlement was for retroactive dues only. In addition Libya gained a required minimum level of reinvestment as well as tax and royalty payments calculated on a monthly basis. The Tripoli Agreement established that Libya would not be pegged to Gulf prices.

The six Gulf producers rectified the 1971 dollar devaluation with an 8.49% increase at the Geneva Agreement in January 1972. It specifically allowed for readjustment of posted prices on the Mediterranean should Libya obtain a higher percentage increase. In May the Libyan postings were also increased by 8.49%.

By June the Iraq-IPC negotiations had come to a head and nationalization was declared.

By December 1972 participation had been successfully negotiated by Saudi Arabia and Abu Dhabi, followed by Kuwait and Qatar. It provided 1) 25% government participation rising to 51% by 1982, 2) a detailed system allowing producers and consumers to have access to the crude needed to meet the requirements of each—involving bridging crude, phase-in crude and buy-back prices be renegotiable after 1975.

Libya refused OPEC's participation scheme and beginning January 1973 presented their own formula for equity control demanding, 1) 50% equity immediately, 2) compensation at net book value only, 3) buy-back optional and at higher prices, and 4) retroactive to January 1st, 1973.

At the same time Iran presented its own alternative to participation which was formalized in the February 1973 St. Moritz Agreement. In dollars and cents it is very close to participation, but provides that NIOC takeover 100% as operator with the Consortium purchasing their crude on a privileged long-term basis.

The two big issues still to be negotiated in the near future are 1) the current parity talks over the second dollar devaluation and 2) Libya's current demands which have now reached 100% control of oil operations.

OPEC members are not ogres; neither are they paper tigers. They are a group of disparate countries that see themselves in a powerful economic position after years of drought.

CURRENT DIRECTIONS

The 1968 Vienna Conference marks a turning point in the petroleum industry, bringing an end to the traditional concession agreements. There are several methods which the different oil producing countries have exercised to gain equity share and/or control in the existing producing concessions: partial nationalization (Algeria), nationalization (Algeria and Iraq), full control in return for long-term sales (Iran) and finally participation, which is the official OPEC option.

It is interesting to note that since OPEC's XXVth Conference in September 1971 only four members have implemented participation: Saudi Arabia, Kuwait, Abu Dhabi and Qatar in October and December 1972. Of the other members Iraq has nationalized, Iran has reached a separate alternative with the producing companies, and Libya has in the last ten days delivered new and stringent conditions to at least one group of companies. The remaining four, Algeria, Indonesia, Venezuela and Nigeria had established their own formulas for equity sharing beforehand.

OPEC resolved to negotiate participation individually or in groups largely because they realized in advance that gradual equity acquisition is not the only effective formula to gain control of a wasting national asset. The exploration and production of new areas, on the other hand, has been developed largely along the lines of an active partnership in the form of 51–49 joint ventures such as in Iran, embracing upstream and downstream operations.

I believe that fortunately the current headlong rush to buy crude is going to simmer down by year's end. The panic will be deflated by the realization that oil is there to be produced and sold.

Estimates of world production capacity in 1980, exclusive of the communist bloc countries, average about 76 million barrels a day, only 28 million of which will be low-sulphur crude oil. Demand for this sweet crude, however, will be upwards of 40 million barrels a day. Furthermore, a large part of this oil still has to be developed and capital expenditures as well the lead time involved will be considerable. Any delay in the development of this additional crude could upset all forecasts and necessary steps to insure continued, uninterrupted development should be taken as soon as possible.

Still, barring man-made interventions, the availability of crude will be governed by demand and not by supply. Certainly OPEC is not going to produce more than is actually required. There is a clear realization today that oil is a wasting asset, that world energy will not be dependent on oil forever, and that, for most of the producing countries, oil is their single valuable asset.

There is a long history of threats arising out of the Arab countries, however, to use oil as a weapon against those whose policies are considered anti-Arab. The first to advocate the denial of oil were the Egyptians. They were not, however, prepared to apply it themselves and they did not try to persuade other oil-producing states to follow through, especially those upon whom they were dependent for large subsidies. Iraq and Kuwait also made noises in this direction but, characteristically, they too did not intend to apply their recommendations.

In the past 22 years Arab oil has been used as a political weapon only three times.

First when Iraq cut off supplies to the Haifa refinery in April 1948.

Second following the Anglo-French-Israeli attack on Egypt in 1956.

Third when several countries imposed an embargo on oil supplies to the U.S., Britain and West Germany following the 1967 Arab-Israeli war.

But the picture has now become more serious. In the past there was little danger of any real application of these threats by the Arab countries, individually or unilaterally. However, now that Saudi Arabia's Zaki Yamani, speaking on behalf of King Faisal, has appealed to the United States to reconsider its pro-Israeli policy, a serious study of the motivating forces must be made.

Saudi Arabia represents the traditional conservative friends of the West in the Middle East. They are the U.S.-trained, anti-Communist power in the area. Sheikh Yamani himself is OPEC's spokesman for moderation. The Saudi government recognizes, furthermore, a moral obligation to provide the U.S. and the world with crude oil, for which so far there has been little reciprocal consideration. They consider that beyond a certain level of production it becomes an economic sacrifice of the nation's wasting asset.

The Saudis are under great pressure, from within and without. Arab voices have long been raised against the U.S. for its continued moral, economic and military support of Israel. The billions of dollars in aid, as well as continued arms shipments add to a growing sense of frustration and bitterness which has been capitalized upon by numerous groups throughout the Middle East and in the Gulf.

For the future, the political leverage of oil cannot be overlooked, as the Saudi announcement demonstrates. In this case it is not an embargo; it is not political blackmail; it is a withholding of further increases in output beyond a certain level, which means that the principal victim will be the United States.

The producing countries have only a few options: (1) to increase production and generate unneeded surplus funds, (2) restrict production—and leave their wealth in the ground, ignoring the requirements of consuming countries and particularly of the U.S. or (3) increase production in exchange for technical assistance, an improved political climate and the opportunity of investing abroad.

I must emphasize, at this point, that any outbreak of Arab/Israeli hostilities will result in immediate and extreme anti-American reactions, the total withholding of supplies to the United States and the immediate imposition of production controls.

INDUSTRIALIZATION

What is needed is a quid pro quo. The United States is asking the producing countries to produce. It should not seem unreasonable that these same countries should in turn ask the United States for something, and paper money is not going to be enough. In addition to the political aspect, at least two avenues for reciprocity lay open to us: downstream investments and industrialization.

In effect, industrialization can be seen as the next step after participation. The producing countries with their vast sums of inflowing capital are anxious to develop a solid industrial base within each of their countries. The OPEC members feel, and rightfully so, that the U.S. is a very rich country—rich in natural resources, technical expertise, capital and manpower. As of now the Arabs have only oil. So, while these countries still have a unique advantage, they will provide sufficient quantities of oil to satisfy world demand but, I repeat, only in return for something besides money. Economically, this means outside investment in all different sectors of the national economies, especially by joint-venture, to build up other resources, industry and agriculture, using outside expertise and know-how. At the same time, foreign markets in anticipation of this industrialization will have to be secured.

At the present time the Arab countries are not interested in downstream investment in the U.S. They feel that too much still has to be done at home before outside investments are sought. Furthermore, there is a fear amongst the producing countries of establishing themselves in outside markets and becoming the hostages of those markets. The energy policy in the U.S., the prevailing hysteria of buyers to secure crude supplies, as well as the political considerations of the producing countries have convinced OPEC that this avenue can be held in abeyance a while longer. There is no doubt that such investments will be forthcoming once excess funds become available but they will not consider investing heavily in consuming countries while the consumers' policies are so unsettled and while they continue to hear consumers threatening to undermine OPEC.

CONSUMER COORDINATION

On the subject of consumer coordination at an international level I feel strongly that such cooperation is important and necessary but it should not be used to intensify confrontation.

Any change of the status quo to support the consumers' interest at the expense of the producers must be carefully constructed not to draw adverse reaction. This is not a threat but a predictable outcome. OPEC wants cooperation but will not accept being told who they can sell to and at what price. Anyway without total solidarity among oil-consuming countries and the individual buyers and consumers within those countries, leverage will be undermined.

Furthermore, there is a strong reluctance on the part of Europe and Japan to join any union organized for these purposes. France is riding high in Arab public opinion and has no desire to jeopardize this position. Japan believes our energy policy is too closely allied with our Middle East foreign policy and prefers to compete on its own. For example, they have recently formed an economic committee with Saudi Arabia for the joint promotion of industrial and major economic projects in exchange for crude contracts. This cooperation is being extended to other countries in the Gulf. Japan is strongly in favor of cooperative relationships but only between the producing nation or nations and Japan. Japanese delegations have been attempting to negotiate long-term crude purchase contracts throughout the Middle East and North Africa. Even when Ecuador called for sealed bids four out of 24 bids received were from Japanese buyers.

I am in full agreement that the consumers should organize to promote international research and development of alternate sources of energy, draft conservation programs, propose modifications of ecological restraints, establish "an international mechanism for dealing with energy questions *in times of critical shortages*," study the establishment of stockpiling facilities, furnish supply and demand statistics, etc. However, any attempt to form a "buyers cartel" is ill-advised and foredoomed to failure.

In retrospect the oil companies have weathered the OPEC storm very well. Negotiations have been laborious but a workable formula for the future has been developed and mutual development is the key.

For the immediate future the oil companies will be gearing themselves to the requirements inherent in the program of participation and gradually adjusting to the producing countries' needs for wider industrialization. The role they must increasingly assume has been identified by Saudi Arabia's Minister Ahmed Zaki Yamani. When asked whether the intermediary role of the companies would now come to an end he said, "I do not want this role to be eliminated. In fact I believe that the international oil companies are wise enough to cooperate with our national oil companies. Then it will be possible for our national oil companies to team up with the international companies to fulfill jointly the same intermediary role between producer and consumer. Thus cooperation will grow, making the atmosphere between all the parties concerned a more healthy one." (3rd Nov. 1972). Spokesmen for other OPEC nations have expressed the same view.

ROLE OF THE U.S. GOVERNMENT

A number of recommendations have been made urging the U.S. Government to take a more active position and intervene directly in negotiations with the oil-exporting countries. Some critics claim that our energy position today would have been much stronger if the U.S. Government had stepped in to support the oil companies when they needed it most.

Before this initiative is considered I would caution you to analyze the predictable outcome. For a government to come in as a prospective buyer of crude is one thing. For a government to intervene on behalf of one or more companies on critical issues and to impose pressure on the producing countries, or to regulate prices or availability is quite another thing.

Bearing in mind the dual function that must be served, that is, an economic interest to obtain oil at the best price and harmonious relationship between buyer and supplier to insure availability for the future, I would suggest that the U.S. Government should realize it cannot hope to fill both roles at the same time, at least, not as well as the oil companies themselves have done in the past.

If the U.S. Government takes over it creates a whole new set of rules. It is inconceivable for Saudi Arabia to tell Aramco that its oil liftings will be curtailed unless it changes its foreign policy. Yet, once the U.S. Government assumes an active role it automatically opens a diologue with the producing countries on a political rather than economic basis. In this case, direct negotiation would not, I think, be in our favor. If the United States Government wishes to assume this role, let us first do all we can to establish peace in the area, for under the present conditions it would be impossible for the Government to sit at the negotiating table.

Predictably, if the U.S. Government or any other attempts to employ political pressure as a means to achieve economic ends, such pressure would prompt a very harsh reaction among the producing countries' governments and persuade these countries on their part to use oil as an economic and/or political weapon. Once one tries to interfere and to regulate prices and availability, the rules of supply and demand become drastically altered. By cutting back on production and withholding deliveries the producing countries could create a supply situation which would break almost any agreement.

Rather than intervene and use political pressure to reach its goals, where the underdeveloped nations are concerned, it would be much more effective if the United States could lend its assistance in developing relations with the producing countries by coordinating the various projects and joint-ventures which U.S.-based companies will be developing in the Middle East in the future.

It could be of great value, for example, were the American and Saudi Arabian governments to meet—as the world's largest petroleum consumer and the world's largest petroleum producer respectively—and work together in earnest on problems such as economic and political cooperation, upstream, and downstream investment, technical assistance, training and a number of other interests. Obviously there is a great potential for cooperation between governments, but having more to do with the industrial development of these countries than with the oil industry alone.

And ultimately I think it most important that, somehow, the Arab states be brought into the industrial and financial world of today.

At the beginning of my statement I mentioned that I did not intend to belabor the details of the Arab/Israeli question but it is impossible to talk about Middle East oil for over five minutes without touching on this subject. The role of the United States Government in Middle East oil should be to eliminate the hostile, belligerent climate in which the oil companes have been forced to operate over the past decades. I am sure there is no one in Washington who does not know what should be done, but no one has been able to tell me how it can be done.

In closing I would like to point out a few of the changes which have taken place since the 1967 war. It is no longer sufficient to say that our Middle East policy can be solved by support of the U.N. Resolution of November 1967 alone. Other developments which must affect U.S. thinking and policy in the area are the weakening Russian influence, military aid to Israel and Iran, and the official absence of recognition of the Palestine problems and the resulting increase of fedayeen activity.

Thank you for hearing out my views on this issue which is of overriding importance to U.S. foreign policy. The question of oil supply has been described as the jugular vein of America's greatness.

I see the danger as one that can still be avoided through the development of mutuality between producing and consuming countries and the promotion of a just and lasting solution to the Arab/Israeli conflict. An "even-handed" policy is a step in the right direction but no longer sufficient in itself. *Peace* in the Middle East is absolutely vital to our national interests.

OPEC RESOLUTIONS AND OTHER DOCUMENTS (1973)

COMMUNIQUE

CONFERENCE OF ARAB OIL MINISTERS

KUWAIT, OCTOBER 17, 1973

The Arab oil exporting countries contribute to the prosperity of the world and to the growth of its economy through their exports of this wasting natural resource. In spite of the fact that the production of many of these countries has exceeded the levels required by their domestic economies and the energy and revenue needs of their future generations, they have continued to increase their production, sacrificing their own interests in the service of international cooperation and the interests of the consumers.

It is known that huge parts of the territories of three Arab states were forcibly occupied by Israel in the June 1967 war. Israel has continued to occupy them in defiance of UN resolutions and various calls for peace from the Arab countries and peace-loving nations.

Although the international community is under an obligation to implement UN resolutions and to prevent the aggressor from reaping the fruits of his aggression and occupation of the territories of others by force, most of the major industrialized countries which are consumers of Arab oil have failed to take masures or to act in such a way as might indicate their awareness of this public international obligation. Indeed, the actions of some countries have tended to support and reinforce the occupation.

Before and during the present war, the United States has been active in supplying Israel with all the means of power which have served to exacerbate its arrogance and enable it to challenge the legitimate rights of others and the unequivocal principles of public international law.

In 1967, Israel was instrumental in closing the Suez Canal and burdening the European economy with the consequences of this action. In the current war, it hit East Mediterranean Oil export terminals, causing Europe another shortfall in supplies. This is the third such occurrence resulting from Israel's disregard of our legitimate rights with US backing and support. The Arabs have therefore been induced to take a decision to discontinue their economic sacrifices in producing quantities of their wasting oil assets in excess of what would be justified by domestic economic considerations, unless the international community hastens to rectify matters by compelling Israel to withdraw from our occupied territory, as well as letting the US know the heavy price which the big industrial countries are having to pay as a result of America's blind and unlimited support for Israel.

Therefore, the Arab Oil Ministers meeting in Kuwait today have decided to reduce their oil production forthwith by not less than 5 per cent of the September (1973) level of output in each Arab oil exporting country, with a similar reduction to be applied each successive month, computed on the basis of the previous month's production, until such time as total evacuation of Israeli forces from all Arab territory occupied during the June 1967 war is completed, and the legitimate rights of the Palestinian people are restored.

The conferees took care to ensure that reductions in output should not affect any friendly state which has extended or may in the future extend effective concrete assistance to the Arabs. Oil supplies to any such state will be maintained in the same quantities as it was receiving before the reduction. The same exceptional treatment will be extended to any state which takes a significant measure against Israel with a view to obliging it to end its occupation of usurped Arab territories.

The Arab Ministers appeal to all the peoples of the world, and particularly to the American people, to support the Arab nation in its struggle against imperialism and Israeli occupation. They reaffirm to them the sincere desire of the Arab nation to cooperate fully with all the peoples of the world and their readiness to supply the world with its oil needs as soon as the world shows its sympathy with us and denounces the aggression against us.

RESOLUTION

CONFERENCE OF ARAB OIL MINISTERS

KUWAIT, OCTOBER 17, 1973

The Oil Ministers of the member States of the Organization of Arab Petroleum Exporting Countries (OAPEC) held a meeting in the city of Kuwait on the 21st of Ramadan 1393 A.H., corresponding to the 17th of October 1973 A.D., to consider employing oil in the battle currently raging between the Arabs and Israel. Following a thorough discussion of this question the Oil Ministers,

Considering that the direct goal of the current battle is the liberation of the Arab territories occupied in the June 1967 war and the recovery of the legitimate rights of the Palestinian people in accordance with the United Nations resolutions;

Considering that the United States is the principal and foremost source of the Israeli power which has resulted in the present Israeli arrogance and enabled the Israelis to continue to occupy our territories;

Recalling that the big industrial nations help, in one way or another, to perpetuate the status quo, though they bear a common responsibility for implementing the United Nations resolutions;

Considering that the economic situation of many Arab oil producing countries does not justify raising oil production, though they are ready to make such an increase in production to meet the requirements of major consumer industrial nations that commit themselves to cooperation with us for the purpose of liberating our territories;

Decided that each Arab oil exporting country immediately cuts its oil production by a recurrent monthly rate of no less than 5 per cent to be initially counted on the virtual production of

September, and thenceforth on the last production figure until such a time as the international community compels Israel to relinquish our occupied territories or until the production of every individual country reaches the point where its economy does not permit of any further reduction without detriment to its national and Arab obligations.

Nevertheless, the countries that support the Arabs actively and effectively or that take important measures against Israel to compel its withdrawal shall not be prejudiced by this production cut and shall continue to receive the same oil supplies that they used to receive prior to the reduction. Though the cut rate will be uniform in respect of every individual oil exporting country, the decrease in the supplies provided to the various consuming countries may well be aggravated proportionately with their support to and cooperation with the Israeli enemy.

The participants also recommend the countries party to this resolution that the United States be subjected to the most severe cut proportionally with the quantities of crude oil, oil derivatives and hydrocarbons that it imports from every exporting country.

The participants also recommend that this progressive reduction lead to the total halt of oil supplies to the United States from every individual country party to the resolution.

COMMUNIQUE

CONFERENCE OF ARAB OIL MINISTERS

KUWAIT, NOVEMBER 4-5, 1973

The Arab oil ministers met again in Kuwait on November 4, 1973, to discuss the question further and decided that initial production cut be 25% of the September level, and a further 5% from the production of each of the following months. The 25% cut should also include the complete halt of all oil shipments to both the United States and the Netherlands.

The Arab Oil Halt to the United States and Holland

The Arab oil producing countries have decided to halt their oil supplies to the United States and Holland and to any other country supporting Israel.

This decision is by no means directed against the peoples of the United States or Holland. It is in fact directed against their governments' hostile policies towards the Arab people.

The Arab people fully realize the interests of other people and want to develop closer ti with the people of the United States and Holland, who must also realize where their interests lie.

The Arab Oil Exporting Countries would like the American and Dutch people to know that the halt in oil supplies to their countries will continue until such a time as Israeli forces are fully withdrawn from all occupied Arab territories and the Arab people of Palestine regain their lawful rights.

The Arab Oil Ministers would like to draw the attention of the American people to the fact that the United States' Government itself adopted similar policies of banning shipments of arms, strategic material, such as oil and even food stuff to countries considered hostile to the United States.

LETTER TO THE AMERICAN PEOPLE

published as an advertisement in
<u>The Washington Post</u>, November 14, 1973

Over the last few decades the Arab petroleum exporting countries have largely contributed to the world economy and the well-being and prosperity of mankind through the export of their natural resources.

In spite of the fact that production of many of these countries has surpassed the level necessary for their social and economic development and the need of their future generation for energy, they have nevertheless continued to increase their production, thus sacrificing their own interests in order to serve the interests of the consumers and promote international cooperation in general.

Since the June war of 1967, territories from three Arab countries have been occupied by the Israelis, and they still are, in defiance of U.N. Resolutions and the various peace efforts made by the Arab states and other peace loving countries. The international community is committed to the implementation of the U.N. resolutions which reaffirm the principle of the non-acquisition of territory by force, as stipulated in the United Nations Charter.

However, most of the major industrial countries which import Arab oil have taken no positive action to reflect their international obligation in this respect. Some of them even went as far as to support and consolidate the Israeli occupation. By insisting on supplying Israel with the most sophisticated weapons before and after the recent war, the United States has only encouraged the Israeli intransigence and arrogance in total disregard of international law.

This unbearable situation has forced the Arab oil exporting states to make certain decisions to expedite action on the part of the international community towards meeting their responsibilities in forcing the Israeli withdrawal from occupied Arab territories and restoring the legitimate rights of the Palestinian people.

In their meeting in Kuwait on October 17, 1973, the Arab ministers of petroleum decided that each Arab exporting country should cut its production by no less than 5% of the September production. In their subsequent meeting on November 4, 1973, they increased the rate of reduction to 25% of the September level, to be followed by subsequent 5% reduction each month.

In view of the unilateral action on the part of the U.S. to resupply Israel with weapons while the Arabs were struggling to liberate their occupied lands, the Arab countries have decided to halt all supplies of crude oil and its refined products to the U.S. and the Netherlands and to any other country which backs the Israeli aggression.

To understand these decisions, one has to bear the following in mind:

1. The reduction would not affect any friendly country which has or will take any positive action in resolving this unjust situation in the Middle East. Such countries will continue to receive the same amount of oil supply as before.

2. The decision to halt supplies to the U.S. was by no means directed against the peoples of the U.S. It was rather prompted by their government's total military support to the Israeli enemy during the recent war.

3. This course of action on the part of the Arab countries will hold until such a time when the Israeli forces are totally withdrawn from all occupied Arab territories and the legitimate rights of the Palestinian people are restored.

4. It is to be recalled that the U.S. herself adopted similar measures for political objectives when she banned arms, strategic products and even food stuff from certain countries.

The Arab nation, therefore, appeals to the peoples of the world, and particularly the people of the United States of America, to support their legitimate struggle in resisting Israeli expansionist policies and rectifying the injustices done to the Palestinian people.

ARAB OIL POLICY IN THE MIDDLE EAST CONFLICT

The following is the text of an advertisement under the title "Arab Oil Policy in the Middle East Conflict" which was placed by the Organization of the Arab Oil Exporting Countries (OAPEC) in *The Guardian*, November 15, 1973.

It is an irrefutable fact that the Arab Petroleum Exporting Countries have made over the past decades, and are continuing to make, a liberal and vital contribution to the enhancement of the World economy, and consequently to the well-being and prosperity of all nations, through exporting their gradually depleted, and irreplaceable, natural resource: OIL. Equally irrefutable is the fact that in many Arab countries production has long surpassed the limit required by their own local economy and the needs of future generations for continued sources of income and energy. Nevertheless, they willingly decided to give first consideration to the mounting world-wide demand for their oil necessitated by the increasing requirements of energy as a key factor in maintaining the growth of production in all spheres. Thus, demonstrating their unequivocal desire to play their role in promoting international cooperation and the well-being of mankind, they continued to increase their oil production and exports while being fully aware of the fact that by doing so they were indeed sacrificing their own interests.

On the other hand, for six years, the Arab Oil Exporting countries, saw vast areas of the territories of three Arab countries being perpetually occupied and ravished by the Israeli aggressors who acquired these Arab lands by force during the June War in 1967. During all these years, in spite of the innumerable peace offers and endeavours on the part of the Arab States and the peace-loving nations, and indeed by the United Nations Security Council and General Assembly, Israel remained intransigent and lent a deaf ear to all the efforts that have been made to induce her to respect and implement the U.N. resolution calling upon her to withdraw from the Arab occupied territories on the basis of the U.N. Charter's provision, asserted in its resolution, concerning the inadmissibility of the acquisition of lands by force.

It is, needless to say, that the responsibility for the implementation of the U.N. resolutions, representing the consensus of the world community's will, lies squarely on the shoulders of all member-states of the World Organisation, and particularly on the permanent members of the Security Council. However, most of the major industrial powers failed to show any intention of taking meaningful and effective action indicating their willingness to discharge their responsibility as they should. On the contrary, some powers acted in such a manner as to encourage the Israeli aggressors to maintain their intransigence, and even consolidate their occupation of the Arab lands by the creation of the so-called "new facts," blatantly defying the World Organization and breaking the principles of International law, as well as making mockery of the legitimate rights of the Arab people.

The 1967 Israeli aggression caused the closure of the Suez Canal, thus disrupting world trade and inflicting immeasurable damage to the interests of the world community. During the present war, Israel did not hesitate in raiding, bombarding and destroying the oil export terminals in the East Mediterranean, thus aggravating the shortage of oil supplies to Europe. Now, seeing for the third time that Israel, encouraged and abetted by the United States, is persisting in its aggressive policy and defying Arab rights, the Arab Petroleum Exporting Countries have found themselves constrained to end their self-imposed economic sacrifices; namely producing quantities of their depleting oil resources far exceeding the requirements of their own economic needs. They will continue to pursue this course of action until such time as the international community decides to act and take decisive and effective measures to remedy the situation and induce Israel to withdraw from Arab lands and impress upon the United States how costly the latter's policy of unlimited and unequivocal support for Israel has proved to be to the major industrial countries.

Consequently, the Arab Petroleum Ministers, meeting in Kuwait on the 17th October, 1973, have resolved that all Arab Oil Exporting Countries shall forthwith cut their production respectively by no less than 5% of the September production, and maintain the same rate of reduction each month thereafter until the Israeli forces are fully withdrawn from all Arab territories occupied during the June 1967 War, and the legitimate rights of the Palestinian people are restored.

However, the Arab countries represented in this conference wish to assure friendly countries, especially those who helped or are helping the Arabs in their just cause effectively, that they shall not be made to suffer from the Arab oil cut. Such countries will continue to receive the same quantities supplied to them from the Arab countries before the cut. On the other hand, countries which demonstrate moral and material support to the Israeli enemy will be subjected to severe and progressive reduction in Arab oil supplies, leading to a complete halt.

The U.S.A. & Holland

Acting upon the above resolutions (the official text of which is published in full), the Arab Oil Exporting Countries found it necessary to impose a total embargo on oil exports to the U.S.A. and Holland in view of the active support given to the Israelis during this war, in terms of massive arms supplies and facilities to help transporting the U.S. supply of deadly and sophisticated war material to Israel by air and sea.

The Arabs wish to make it plainly and explicitly known, however, that this embargo is not intended in any way to castigate the peoples of the countries concerned, with whom the Arabs wish to maintain the closest and warmest friendly relations; but this embargo is indeed directed against the Governments, or those responsible in the Governments, for the anti-Arab policy which the Arabs could only reply to in kind.

Evidently, the Arabs' embargo on the export of strategic products to hostile and unfriendly countries -- especially in time of war -- is entirely in line with similar policies pursued by other countries at war, and even by the U.S.A. which went so far with this policy as to place an embargo on wheat and food supplies <u>to countries which have no special relations nor share common interests with the United States</u>.

It is with deep regret that the Arab countries found it necessary to take this decision which is bound to bring suffering to the peoples of the countries concerned: but until such time as the Governments of the U.S.A. and Holland or any other country that takes a stand of active support to the Israeli aggressors reverse their positions and add their weight behind the World Community's concensus to end the Israeli occupation of Arab Lands and bring about the full restoration of the Legitimate rights of the Palestinian people, the Arab Oil Exporting Countries will not rescind their decision to impose a total embargo on oil exports to such countries.

ARAB SUMMIT DECISIONS

ALGIERS, NOVEMBER 26-28, 1973

TEXT OF THE SUMMIT COMMUNIQUE

[The official communique issued after the Sixth Arab Summit Meeting, which was held in Algiers from 26 to 28 November 1973, consisted of five statements. These were as follows: 1) Policy Statement; 2) Statement Western Europe; 3) Statement to the Socialist Countries; 4) Statement to Africa; and 5) Statement to the Non-Aligned Countries.]

1) Policy Statement

The Kings and Presidents of the States of the League of Arab States, at their meeting in the Palais des Nations in Algiers at the invitation of President Muhammad Anwar al-Sadat of the Arab Republic of Egypt and President Hafiz al-Asad of the Syrian Arab Republic, studied the Arab and international situation in the light of statements submitted by the Kings and Presidents, of the report of the Secretary General, and of the recommendations of the Foreign Ministers, and took the political defense and economic decisions which the situation requires.

The Arab world is passing through a decisive period in its history, and the battle against Zionist aggression is a long-term historic responsibility which demands further efforts and sacrifice. If the war of October 1973 demonstrated the determination of the Arab nation to liberate its occupied territories whatever the cost, then the ceasefire on the ground in no way means that the struggle is over or that a solution can be imposed on the Arab states which does not realize their just aims.

So long as the causes of the aggressive and expansionist wars which have brought the world to the brink of global conflict are not eliminated, no lasting peace or true security can be established in the Middle East. It is impossible to reconcile aggression, occupation, expansionism and hegemony with the principles of national independence, development, progress and a just peace.

The war of October 1973 is, like its predecessors, the inevitable result of the policy of aggression and fait accompli practiced by Israel in violation of international principles and resolutions and the rights of peoples. Since usurping the rights of the Palestinian people and expelling them from their country, Israel has not ceased its efforts to expand, relying on the collusion of the imperialist states and their economic, technological and military support, particularly from the United States of America. This collusion has recently come to light in the form of mobilizing unprecedented financial and material support, supplying specialist mercenaries, and organizing a political offensive which groups together all the enemies of the liberation of the Third World.

In addition to its policy of war and expansion, Israel also seeks as part of its imperialist strategy to rule out the possibility of development for the peoples of the area. Zionism thus appears, in an era which is witnessing the upsurge of national liberation movements and the eradication of imperialism, as a dangerous resurgence of the imperialist and racist system and of its methods of domination and economic exploitation.

Despite Israel's ties with world imperialism, which places various means and capabilities in the service of its aggressive aims, the Arab nation has never abandoned its national goals nor shrunk from the demands of the struggle. Setbacks and hardship have been unable to weaken its national will, but have rather strengthened its resolution and determination.

In October 1973 the armed forces of Egypt, Syria and the Palestinian resistance, accompanied by other Arab forces, were able to inflict very heavy losses on the Israeli aggressors, and during this battle there developed a growing awareness on the part of the Arab nation and governments of their responsibilities and their human and material potential. This awareness is manifested in a practical solidarity whose effectiveness has been proved and which has given a new impetus to the Arab liberation movement.

The Conference salutes our brave soldiers on the battlefronts, who have written the most glorious and bravest pages of our national history and whose determination to fight until victory is ever growing. The Conference also calls blessings upon our valiant and upright martyrs who have immortalized their memories and raised the stature of their nation.

Israel now appears in its true light and the expansionist nature of its policy is clear for all to see. Its bogus friendship towards the African peoples stands exposed and it no longer receives the slightest support in Africa except from the imperialist and racist regimes in South Africa, Rhodesia and Portugal.

Moreover, Israel is facing a general rejection of its policy in the Islamic countries, the non-aligned countries, the liberation organizations of the Third World, the socialist countries and in enlightened and unbiased world public opinion. As a result, Israel's diplomatic isolation has today become a palpable reality. A particular indication is that some European governments traditionally known for their support of Israeli positions have begun to question the validity of Israel's adventurist policy, which involves great danger to international peace and cooperation.

These factors, which represent important gains for the Arab cause, must be developed and reinforced in order to arrive at a solution which will guarantee Arab national rights.

The cease-fire of over one month ago continues to meet with maneuvering and sabotage from the Israeli side. Israel's official attitudes and its actions on the international level also confirm that Israel has in no way abandoned its old policy or renounced its imperialist and expansionist ambitions.

The cease-fire is not peace. Peace requires the fulfillment of a number of conditions, foremost among them two firm and fundamental ones:

(1) Israeli withdrawal from all the occupied Arab territories, with particular regard to Jerusalem.

(2) The recovery by the Palestinian people of their established national rights.

Unless these two conditions are met, it is useless to expect anything in the Middle East other than the aggravation of the explosive situation and the outbreak of new confrontations.

The Arab Kings and Presidents, aware of their historic responsibilities, confirm their readiness to participate in reaching a just peace on the basis of these two principles. It is up to those who talk of peace go give concrete proof of their desire to end a situation which grows daily more dangerous and explosive.

The Arab countries will not under any circumstances accept to mortgage their future against illusory promises and empty bargaining. Not the slightest doubt must be left in world public opinion, which has for so long been deceived by Zionist propaganda, about the Arab nation's intention and determination to recover its usurped rights and to liberate its occupied territories.

Peace can only be achieved through complete frankness and by avoiding maneuverings and deception, and on the basis of the principles set out in this statement. Therefore the Arab Kings and Presidents announce that any serious and constructive consultations must take place within this framework. If the conditions for a just peace are not forthcoming and if Arab efforts for peace meet rejection from Israel and its allies, the Arab countries will find themselves compelled to draw the natural conclusion and to continue their battle for liberation, however long it may take, by all means possible and in all fields.

The Arab nation is determined to do its duty and is prepared for further struggle, expenditure and sacrifice. It is up to the whole world to bear the responsibility for resisting aggression and to support the Arabs' just struggle.

2) Statement to Western Europe

The world, which is following with interest developments in the Middle East problem, has a right to know the definition of what we are seeking and to share ou hopes and views as to the future in our region and in the world as a whole.

We affirm to the world that we are endeavoring within the framework of international law to achieve a just and lasting peace on the basis of the restoration of our occupied territories and the recovery of the national rights of the Palestinian people. Within this framework we are endeavoring to establish a zone of peace in the Middle East which will ensure our interests and the interests of all the countries of the world, and we desire to remove international tension from the area, believing as we do in the UN Charter and the principles of non-alignment.

While expressing our deep appreciation of the positive and constructive participation undertaken by our brothers and comrades-in-arms in Africa, Asia, the non-aligned countries and the socialist countries, we are also watching with greater attention and interest the signs of an understanding of our position which have begun to appear in the states of Western Europe. We also announce our sincere readiness to cooperate in the efforts being undertaken within the framework of the United Nations to establish a just peace in the area.

Western Europe is linked across the Mediterranean to the Arab peoples by strong ties of civilization and vital interdependent interests which can only flourish in a framework of cooperation characterized by mutual interests and trust. It is therefore appropriate for it to adopt a clear and impartial stand in respect of our just cause, thereby proving the independence of its will and playing its full role in international affairs. It should accomplish this by committing itself to work by all possible means to bring about Israel's withdrawal from all the occupied Arab territories, with particular regard to Jerusalem, and the recovery by the Palestinian people of their national rights.

The Arabs desire the friendship of all peoples and wish for an exchange of benefits with them without discrimination on the basis of guaranteeing their legitimate rights and safeguarding their vital interests. They similarly desire to share in providing for the well-being of the world, as long as the world participates with them in providing security and justice in their region.

3) Statement to the Socialist Countries

At their meeting in Algiers from 26 November to 28 November 1973, the Arab Kings and Presidents studied the Arab and international situation. They express their appreciation of the socialist countries which cut their diplomatic relations with Israel following the Israeli aggression against the Arab countries in 1967. They note with pride the full political support of the Soviet Union and the other socialist countries, their military support and economic cooperation with the Arab countries, and their standing at the side of the just Arab struggle to liberate the occupied Arab territories and recover the rights of the Palestinian people. They also note with appreciation the continued support of the People's Republic of China for the struggle of the Arab nation.

They look forward to a reinforcement of this cooperation and a development of these ties by all possible means, in the service of mutual interests, of the fulfillment of common objectives and of the strengthening of Arab friendship with the socialist countries. They are confident that the socialist countries' solidarity with the just struggle will render ever increasing service to freedom and justice and ever increasing support for world peace.

4) Statement to Africa

The Arab Kings and Presidents who met in Algiers from 26 November to 28 November 1973 discussed the new situation in the Middle East resulting from Israeli aggression and its effects on international security. They took into consideration the growing movement towards solidarity which the fraternal African states have expressed in favor of the just Arab cause and the struggle to liberate the occupied Arab territories and to recover the national rights of the Palestinian people. This struggle is part of the battle which the forces of liberation are waging against the forces of imperialism, racism and Zionism.

Since they consider that Arab-African solidarity must manifest itself in a tangible form in all spheres, including the sphere of economic and political cooperation, with the aim of strengthening the bases of national independence and achieving development, they resolve:

(1) To send messages of appreciation to fraternal African states for the decisions they have taken to break their relations with Israel, thereby increasing its isolation from the world.

(2) To express their appreciation for the confirmation of this solidarity with the struggling Arab countries at the extraordinary meeting of the Ministerial Council of the Organization of African Unity.

(3) To extend full support to the African countries in their struggle for national liberation and economic progress and in their struggle against imperialism and racial discrimination.

(4) To welcome the decision of the Ministerial Council of the OAU at its recent emergency meeting to form a committee composed of seven countries to organize African-Arab cooperation. They resolve to take the following measures to strengthen Arab-African solidarity and embody it in practical form:

(a) Support for Arab-African cooperation in the political sphere and strengthening Arab diplomatic representation in Africa.

(b) Breaking off all diplomatic, consular, economic, cultural and other relations with South Africa, Portugal and Rhodesia by those Arab states which have not yet done so.

(c) The application of a total embargo on Arab oil exports to these three countries.

(d) The adoption of special measures to continue normal supplies of Arab oil to the fraternal countries of Africa.

(e) Strengthening and expansion of economic, financial and cultural cooperation with fraternal African states, at a bilateral level and at the level of Arab and African regional organizations.

(f) In order to speed up the application of these decisions and the establishment of continuous cooperation between the Arab and African countries, they charge the Secretariat General of the Arab League with taking steps to implement them and with contacting the Secretariat of the OAU and the committee of seven countries attached to it to organize regular consultations between the Arab and African countries at all levels, including the highest.

5) Statement to the Non-Aligned Countries

The Arab Kings and Presidents who met in Algiers from 26 November to 28 November 1973 consider that Israeli aggression has proved the soundness of the analysis made by the heads of state and governments of the non-aligned countries during their fourth conference in Algiers. This analysis establishes with precision that the prevailing situation in the Middle East is the result of Israeli obduracy and Israel's persistence in the policy of occupying the territories of three non-aligned countries, and that this aggression represents a threat to world peace and security.

The Kings and Presidents note the imperialist character of Israel as a factor causing tension and confrontation in a vital region of the Third World. They note with satisfaction the full solidarity the non-aligned countries have shown towards Egypt, Syria, Jordan and the Palestinian people in the struggle for the liberation of their territories, the integrity of their soil, and their national rights.

This solidarity has manifested itself particularly in the political and diplomatic activity which has played its part in the disapproval of the international community and its condemnation of Israel's aggressive, expansionist and annexationist plans.

Since the Kings and Presidents are sending messages of appreciation to the non-aligned countries in Africa for the effective solidarity they have shown towards the struggle of the Arab peoples, they urge all the non-aligned countries to redouble their individual and collective efforts to find a solution in the Middle East which accords with the principles and resolutions of the non-aligned countries and seeks to establish peace and security in the world.

Since the Kings and Presidents condemn the close collusion existing between Israel, imperialist and racist organizations, and American imperialism, they call upon the community of non-aligned nations, which represent the peoples of the Third World and a majority of the world's population, to shoulder their international responsibility to support right and justice not only in the Middle East but throughout the world. They will thus participate more fully, in accordance with the resolutions of the fourth summit conference, in the establishment of an international system based on democracy and in conformity with the peoples' aspirations towards progress, security and peace.

RESOLUTION ON OIL

SIXTH ARAB SUMMIT CONFERENCE

ALGIERS, NOVEMBER 28, 1973*

The Conference resolves to continue using oil as an economic weapon in the battle until such time as the withdrawal from the occupied Arab territories is completed and the national rights of the Palestinian people are restored, in accordance with the following bases:

-- Maintenance of the embargo on countries supporting Israel.

-- Maintenance of the progressive cuts in oil production to the extent that the reduction in income accruing to any of the producing countries should not exceed one-quarter on the basis of the 1972 income level.

-- Formation of a committee composed of the Ministers of Foreign Affairs and Oil of the Arab oil producing states with the following functions:

(1) To draw up a list classifying states in accordance with the following categories: friendly countries; neutral countries; and countries supporting the enemy.

(2) To follow up the implementation of the decision on the use of oil.

(3) To review the list of countries with a view to reclassifying a country from one category to another in the light of its commitment to implement the political line decided upon by the Arab Summit or if it adopts a political, economic or military stand in harmony with such political line.

---

* The Conference was attended by the Heads of State of sixteen Arab countries, not including Iraq and Libya; Jordan sent a lower level delegation.

(4) To give any neutral country which is reclassified into the friendly category the same quantities of oil as it used to import in 1972 on condition that it undertakes not to re-export such oil, either in the form of crude or refined products.

(5) The re-export of oil from any country to a hostile state is not permissible.

The above-mentioned committee will meet to draw up the classification of countries into the three categories, notification of which will be passed on to the Arab oil producing states and the states from which the oil is exported with a view to implementation.

RESOLUTION

ARAB OIL MINISTERS

ON LIFTING OIL EMBARGO AGAINST THE U.S.

KUWAIT, DECEMBER 8, 1973

The Arab Ministers of Oil and their representatives signatory to this resolution met in Kuwait on 8 December 1973, after reviewing their resolution issued on 18 November 1973 relating to the suspension of the five percent reduction for the European Common Market countries with the exception of Holland decided upon for December, subject to the proviso that the reduction of five percent of December production levels will continue thereafter for all non-exempted countries in January, have adopted the following resolution:

> Firstly: If agreement is reached on withdrawal from all the territories occupied since 1967, foremost amongst them Jerusalem, in accordance with a timetable which Israel agrees to and whose implementation is guaranteed by the United States, the embargo on exports to the United States will be lifted as soon as the withdrawal program begins, and at that point the general reduction applicable to it will be determined on the basis that it should not exceed or be less than the prevailing percentage applicable to the oil consuming countries at the time the embargo is lifted. The percentage reduction will then be applied to the United States in the same way as to Europe and the rest of the world.
>
> Secondly: When agreement on a timetable for a withdrawal is reached the Arab Oil Ministers implementing this resolution will meet to draw up a timetable for the gradual restoration of

production to the level of September 1973 in a manner corresponding to the stages of the withdrawal.

Thirdly: The friendly African and Islamic countries will be given the full quantities contracted for in concluded contracts, even if this necessitates an increase in production by a percentage which will guarantee that their domestic requirements are met, provided it is ascertained that there is no possibility to re-export to countries to which oil exports are embargoed.

The Representatives of
Abu Dhabi, Bahrain,
Algeria, Saudi Arabia,
Syria, Qatar, Kuwait,
Libya, Egypt

COMMENTARY

THE ARAB OIL WEAPON—A THREAT TO INTERNATIONAL PEACE

*By Jordan J. Paust * and Albert P. Blaustein ***

THE ARAB COERCION: BACKGROUND

The month of October, 1973, brought with it Arab coercion in two forms: the first was the military attack against Israeli forces begun on October 6;[1] the second was the use of economic coercion against countries that, in Arab eyes, either supported Israel or did not support the Arabs in their present quests (which include the return of claimed "Arab" lands, favorable settlement of the Palestinian peoples' claim for self-determination, and other political and military objectives).

On October 18, just twelve days after the joint Arab initiation of war against Israel, Saudi Arabia, the world's largest oil-exporting state, announced immediate cuts in oil production in an attempt to pressure the United States to reduce support for the state of Israel and also threatened to cut off all oil trade with the United States, if Arab demands were not met. By January, 1974, that trade had dried up completely.[2] On that same day in October, the Persian gulf state of Abu Dhabi announced that it was stopping all oil exports to the United States and would act similarly against any other country that supported Israel.

* J.S.D. Candidate, Yale University.

** Professor of Law, Rutgers University, Camden.

The authors are grateful for the comments and criticism offered by Myres S. McDougal, W. Michael Reisman, Eugene V. Rostow, Julius Stone, and Sidney Liskofsky. Of course, the views expressed and errors or imperfections are our own.

[1] We offer no detailed inquiry here into whether the joint Arab attack on Israeli forces violated UN S.C. Res. 242 and Article 2(4) of the UN Charter as amplified by UN G.A. Res. 2625, Declaration on Principles of International Law Concerning Friendly Relations and Co-operation Among States in Accordance with the Charter of the United Nations, 25 UN GAOR, SUPP. 18, at 122–24, UN Doc. A/8028 (1970), *reprinted at* 65 AJIL 243 (1971). Readers are referred to E. V. Rostow, THE MIDDLE EAST CONFLICT IN PERSPECTIVE (1973); and J. Stone, letter, Washington Post, Dec. 8, 1973. *See also* UN CHARTER, preamble and Arts. 1 and 2; W. M. REISMAN, NULLITY AND REVISION 842–43 (1971); and E. V. Rostow, *Legal Aspects of the Search for Peace in the Middle East,* PROC. AMER. SOC. INT. LAW, 64 AJIL 64 (No. 4, 1970) and remarks at 78–87.

[2] *See* N.Y. Times, Oct. 19, 1973, at 1, col. 6. On January 12, 1974, the Saudi Minister of Petroleum Affairs stated that his country was by then not supplying "a drop of oil" to the United States or to "any refinery that supplies petroleum products to the United States," *see* N.Y. Times, Jan. 13, 1974, at 14, col. 4. It has been alleged that President Nixon's October 17 request of $2.2-billion in military aid to Israel directly contributed to King Faisal's decision to use the oil weapon. *See* E. Sheehan, N.Y. Times, Magazine, Mar. 24, 1974, at 13, 54, col. 1. *Cf.* I. Sus, *Western Europe and the October War,* 3 J. OF PALESTINE STUDIES 65, 75 (1974).

Some six weeks later, the use and impact of this form of economic coercion had broadened and intensified. Amid an aura of proclaimed unity, Arab leaders adopted a joint resolution calling for the continued "use of oil as an economic weapon." [3] Already, the Netherlands had been boycotted and all other European Common Market countries and Japan had been placed under a 25 percent oil cut.[4] As part of this mounting coercion, a new "Arab solidarity," and the joint military attack against the state of Israel, this November resolution called for: (1) a continuation of an oil embargo against countries "supporting Israel"; (2) the continued reduction of oil production in any event; and (3) the creation of a joint Arab committee to categorize states as "friendly," "neutral," and "supporting Israel" so that implementation of the Arab objectives could be carried out.[5] In addition, periodic cuts in the oil trade were threatened with targeted countries that did not change their policies or engage in certain pro-Arab conduct—a sort of periodic intensification of the coercion. Interrelated with these threats were additional Saudi Arabian claims "to cut oil production by 80 percent if the United States, Europe or Japan took measures to counter current Arab oil boycotts and reductions" in production.[6] It was made quite clear that the Arabs would decide who was to get what amount of oil, when, and for what reasons. It was also made clear that general production was going to be cut in any event; [7] and, further, if any joint or unilateral resistance were made to this approach to energy production and trade, those who resisted would be made to suffer the consequences.

Despite the conclusion of a cease-fire agreement and a "six-point" disengagement agreement between Israel and Egypt by January 18, 1974, the attempts to initiate a more comprehensive Geneva conference for settlement of Middle East problems, and the partial withdrawal of Israeli forces from post-1967 positions under UN force supervision, no reduction

[3] *See* "Arabs Halt Oil Shipments to 3 Countries," N.Y. Times, Nov. 29, 1973, at 16, col. 6. The use of an oil boycott had first occurred in the 1967 war and was directed against the United States for about one month with little effect. *See* J. E. Akins, *The Oil Crisis: This Time the Wolf Is Here,* 51 FOREIGN AFFAIRS 462, 468 (1973).

[4] *See* N.Y. Times, Nov. 23, 1973, at 1, col. 6, quoting the Saudi Arabian Oil Minister, Ahmed Zaki al-Yamani. [5] *See supra* note 3.

[6] *See supra* note 4.

[7] Here, much broader questions are raised, such as the permissibility of increases in oil prices by oil producers; they are related to the whole process of coercion but will not be discussed here in great detail. Professor Rostow had insightfully suggested that an issue is raised as to whether Article 2(4) of the UN Charter is "the Sherman Act in disguise" in connection with the community regulation of a coercive and monopolistic manipulation of resources. The price increases can also be analyzed in terms of breach of contract or as a form of wealth deprivation and control in a global arena. *See* B. H. Weston, *International Law and the Deprivation of Foreign Wealth: A Framework for Future Inquiry,* 2 THE FUTURE OF THE INTERNATIONAL LEGAL ORDER: WEALTH AND RESOURCES 36, 38 n. 10, 79, *passim* (Falk and Black *eds.* 1970).

had occurred in the then total embargo of oil to the United States.[8] This situation continued for some five months after the initiation of the first cut in oil exports and states like France, Italy, Japan, the Philippines, and the United Kingdom lined up to trade guns and technology for oil under the pressure of economic coercion and new Arab strength.[9] A 25 percent cut in overall oil production in Arab states continued into mid March. Oil prices soared to record highs, while Europe continued under a 10–15 percent ban and many countries in the Third World experienced a loss of 25–35 percent of normal oil flow.

On March 18, five months after the initiation of the embargo by Saudi Arabia and Abu Dhabi, most of the Arab states announced in Vienna their decision to end the oil embargo against the United States and certain other countries. However, Iraq had refused to attend the meeting, and Libya and Syria refused to give their "assent" to the lifting of the embargo or to any increase in overall production. Moreover, Algeria stated that it was only lifting the embargo provisionally until June 1. The "ending" of the use of the oil weapon against the United States by participating Arab states [10] had occurred with a lingering threat to re-employ it. Additionally, there was no ending of the oil embargo against the Netherlands, Denmark, South Africa, Rhodesia, and Portugal.

This Arab strategy constitutes the deliberate employment of an economic instrument of coercion (the oil "weapon") against other states and peoples in order to place intense pressure upon their freedom of choice. Although this strategy is primarily dependent upon the use of an economic instrument of coercion, the full dimension of the coercive process has involved the interrelated use of diplomatic and ideological instruments as well as the coordinate use of military forces against the state of Israel. As such, the Arab oil embargo is in violation of international law, as formulated in the United Nations Charter and key supporting documents.

An Approach to Decision

At times we will merely refer to this overall process of coercion as the oil "weapon" or as the Arab economic coercion or oil embargo, but the full range of Arab effort should be kept in mind. We do not find it useful to classify the entire coercive process in terms of rigid, past categories—such as embargo, boycott, reprisal, or act of "blackmail." Nor do we find it useful to consider the coercive process merely in terms of "economic warfare" or "economic aggression." Not only are these terms generally too confining for a proper focus, but some are merely conclu-

[8] *See, e.g.,* "Kissinger Says a Continuation of the Arab Oil Embargo Would Be 'Blackmail'," N.Y. Times, Feb. 7, 1974, at 1, col. 4.

[9] Europe remained under an "officially" disclosed cut of 15% in oil imports from the Middle East through March 10, 1974, despite notable changes in positions and significant agreements to supply arms and technology to Arab states. *See* N.Y. Times, Mar. 9, 1974, at 5, col. 1.

[10] *See* N.Y. Times, Mar. 19, 1974, at 1, col. 1, and at 20, cols. 3–8.

sions that may be attached to a particular coercive process after fact and law have been fully considered.

Indeed, it is too simplistic to categorize events as acts of "war" or "peace," since coercion between states and peoples is continuous through time and space in differing types and levels of intensity. Far more is proscribed under international law than coercive acts which amount to acts of "war." Moreover, a great deal of coercion is "normal" or permissible in day to day relations.[11] International law takes cognizance, however, of the greater need for the regulation of varied types and intensities of coercion in this increasingly interdependent world.[12] The main concern is for a rational, policy-serving distinction between forms of permissible and impermissible coercion.

Does the conduct conform to legal policies (goal-values)[13] that the accepted prescriptions against the use of coercion seek to serve? Where a set of prescriptions discloses a complimentarity of purpose, as is often the case, and the conduct in question seems to serve certain community policies while impairing others, how is rational and policy-serving decision best promoted?[14] It is clear that rigid categories such as "embargo" or economic "war" are insufficient in reference to the full range of legal policy that is relevant or to the myriad of contextual factors that may usefully be considered in making a rational, realistic choice concerning the legality of the Arab coercive process. Similarly, it is clear that a mere reference to one set of the complementary goal-values (*e.g.*, norms of self-defense) without reference to the other (*e.g.*, proscriptions against certain forms of coercion) is insufficient.

Depending upon degrees of intent, intensities of impact, and a number of other factors, the use of the Arab coercive strategy may be found to constitute such a substantial impairment of the goals articulated in the United Nations Charter that decisionmakers can authoritatively characterize the use of the oil "weapon" as a violation of that instrument. The United Nations, for example, could declare that there has been a violation of those provisions dealing with the use of coercion, the promotion of friendly relations, the promotion of self-determination, the promotion of equal rights of nations large and small, the promotion of social progress and better standards of life in larger freedom, the peaceful settlement of

[11] For a useful example of this sort of recognition by a non-McDougalian and a related intellectual groping for distinctions, *see* D. Bowett, *Economic Coercion and Reprisals By States,* 13 VA. J. INT. L. 1, 2–5 (1972).

[12] *See* M. MCDOUGAL and F. FELICIANO, LAW AND MINIMUM WORLD PUBLIC ORDER 11–39 and 97 ff. (1961); and M. McDougal, *Peace and War: Factual Continuum with Multiple Legal Consequences,* 49 AJIL 63 (1955).

[13] Throughout this article we refer to the policies behind legal rules (or those documented in constitutive instruments and elsewhere) as legal policies, goal-values, or community goals.

[14] On the problem of complimentarity and the need for responsive decisionmaking which is rational and policy-serving *see* MCDOUGAL and FELICIANO, *supra* note 12, at 57.

disputes, and the maintenance of international peace and security.[15] In certain situations, the use of any economic coercion could constitute a form of "economic aggression."[16] And where the impact of economic coercion upon the target group results in intense fear or anxiety (not at all demonstrable in this case), the use of economic coercion could constitute a form of impermissible terroristic strategy.[17]

Here we cannot provide the ultimate, detailed analysis of the use of this economic instrument of coercion which is a necessary prerequisite to a comprehensive consideration of the full range of relevant legal policies, in this case or in any future inquiry into the legality of economic coercion. Our purpose here lies more in the disclosure of probable violations of international law and the danger to those legal policies that the international community seeks to effectuate than in a final characterization of certain Arab states as violators of the law. For the latter purpose, it is hoped that a comprehensive analysis by appropriate community decision-makers will be initiated and will involve a detailed inquiry into all aspects of the situation—participants in the coercive process (initiators, instrumental targets, primary targets, spillover victims), the objectives of the Arabs (and all other perspectives), actual arenas of interaction (Middle East and global), resources available to all participants, elements of the strategy, actual outcomes, and probable long-term effects.[18] Instead, we focus on the types of general community policy (goal-values) at stake, and briefly explore some of the features of context in order to demonstrate our concern and to outline factors that seem important both to facilitate the identification and clarification of policy and for the comprehensive assessment of the necessity and proportionality of the use of this particular strategy of coercion in actual context.

In any future inquiry, the important factors would include: (a) the objectives of the Arab initiators of the coercive strategy; (b) the number of

[15] *See* UN Charter, preamble and Arts. 1, 2, and 56. *See also* McDougal and Feliciano, *supra* note 12, at 177–206, *passim*, and references cited.

[16] *See, e.g.*, L. Chen, *The Legal Regulation of Minor International Coercion* 131–210 (1964), unpublished dissertation, Yale Law School. *See also* McDougal and Feliciano, *supra* note 12, at 30–32, 194–202, 325–29, and references cited; B. Ferencz, *Defining Aggression: Where It Stands and Where It's Going*, 66 AJIL 491 (1972); R. Falk, *Quincy Wright: On Legal Tests of Aggressive War, id.*, 560; and R. Tucker, *Reprisals and Self-Defense: The Customary Law, id.*, 586. On the related matter of justifiable "self-defense" responses to "economic aggression," *see infra* notes 24–27.

[17] On the legal regulation of international terroristic strategy *see, e.g.*, J. Paust, *Some Terroristic Claims Arising from the Arab-Israeli Context*, Symposium, International Terrorism: Mid East, 7 Akron L. Rev. (1974); and *Terrorism and the International Law of War*, 64 Mil. L. Rev. 1 (1974), *reprinted in* 13 Revue de Droit Penal Militaire et de Droit de la Guerre (1974). Also, *compare* T. M. Franck, B. B. Lockwood, *Preliminary Thoughts towards an International Convention on Terrorism*, 68 AJIL 69 (1974) *with* J. Paust *supra* and references cited; and J. Paust, Letter, 68 AJIL 502–03 (1974).

[18] *See generally*, McDougal and Feliciano, *supra* note 12.

participants affected; (c) the number and types of Charter goals affected; and (d) the extent to which Charter goals are affected.[19]

Traditional Rules and the Policies at Stake

The UN Charter.

Almost all states and peoples have pledged to each other and to all mankind their continued effort to practice tolerance; to develop friendly relations among nations based on respect for equal rights and self-determination; to cooperate in an effort to solve international economic and other problems; to live together in peace; and to settle disputes by peaceful means in such a manner that international peace, security, and justice are not endangered.[20] Article 2(4) of the Charter, containing the important pledge of all members to refrain from certain forms of impermissible coercion, provides:

> All Members shall refrain in their international relations from the threat or use of force against the territorial integrity or political independence of any state, or in any other manner inconsistent with the Purposes of the United Nations.

Thus, if the threat or use of force is against the "territorial integrity" or "political independence" of another state, Article 2(4) of the Charter has been violated. Additionally, the goal-values of Article 2(4) are impaired if the threat or use of force is "in any other manner inconsistent with the Purposes of the United Nations," many of which, as outlined above, are expressed in Article 1 and the preamble of the Charter. Thus, the substantial impairment of goals of the international community as articulated in the Charter through the deliberate use of coercion against other states, not counterbalanced by complementary policies relating to legitimate self-defense or the sanctioning of UN decisions, constitutes a violation of Article 2(4) as well as of other provisions of the Charter.[21]

What is the meaning of the word "force" in Article 2(4)? Does the Charter prohibit economic forms of coercion? It has been stated in the past that the type of "force" contemplated in Article 2(4) was "armed force." Some writers have even read into Article 2(4) the restrictive word "armed," which does not appear in the text and was not contemplated as a restriction in pre-Charter norms or in the drafting of the Charter it-

[19] *See* L. Chen, *supra* note 16, at 136–38, 159, *passim*; and McDougal and Feliciano, *supra* note 12, at 14–19, 30–32, *passim*.

[20] *See supra* note 15. It is significant that the preamble of the Charter begins with: "We the peoples of the United Nations . . ."

[21] *See, e.g.*, McDougal and Feliciano, *supra* note 12, at 178–79; J. Paust and A. Blaustein, Jurisdiction and Due Process: The Case of Bangladesh (1974); J. Paust, *A Survey of Possible Legal Responses to International Terrorism: Prevention, Punishment and Cooperative Action*, forthcoming; I. Brownlie, International Law and the Use of Force by States 266–68 (1963); and 2 Oppenheim's International Law 154 (H. Lauterpacht, *ed.*, 7th ed., 1952). *See also* UN G.A. Res. 2625, *supra* note 1.

self. They merely assume that, since the preamble of the Charter is more specific in stating that "armed force shall not be used save in the common interest," other forms of coercion (economic, diplomatic, ideological) were to go unregulated, despite the articulation of other Charter objectives concerning world public order and human dignity and the concomitant pledge of members in Article 56.[22] Moreover, they never fully explain, in terms of the fulfillment of Charter goals, the desirability of allowing "economic aggression" to remain unregulated, especially when such a mode of coercion can be of such significant intensity and impact that it is comparable to an armed attack upon another state.

Those writers who favor this myopic and restrictive approach to the regulation of coercion often maintain that to prohibit other forms of coercion would allow a state to exercise the right of self-defense in response to "economic aggression," "diplomatic aggression," impermissible propaganda, and so forth. Actually, such a conclusion would depend upon one's interpretation of the phrase "armed attack" in Article 51 of the Charter[23] and upon a contextual analysis that would disclose whether the actual "economic aggression," diplomatic coercion, and so forth were of such an intensity, efficacy, and magnitude as to threaten the security of another state significantly and, thus, properly justify the exercise of the right of "self-defense."[24] Here, we merely note that although Articles 2(4) and 51 are usually "complementary opposites" in terms of the basic policies at stake,[25] they do not exhaust the complementarity of norms that are relevant today.[26] Once it is realized that Article 2(4) proscribes much more than a use of force against the territorial integrity, political independence, or security interests of another state, it should also be realized that all violations of Article 2(4) do not automatically threaten the security interests of another state in a significant way or reach such an intensity

[22] *See* 2 Oppenheim, *supra* note 21, at 153; Goodrich, Hambro, Charter of the United Nations 104 (2d ed. 1949); Brierly, The Law of Nations 415 (6th ed. 1963). *Cf.* Brownlie, *supra* note 21, at 361–62 and 365–66; and Bowett, Self-Defense in International Law 54 and 119 (1958). *Contra* McDougal and Feliciano, *supra* note 12, at 177–202 and 240–41; Kelsen, The Law of the United Nations 915 (1951); and Paust and Blaustein, *supra* note 26.

[23] *Compare* the cogent analysis in McDougal and Feliciano, *supra* note 12, at 233–41 *with* the far less comprehensive approach and forecast offered in S. M. Schwebel, "A Takeover of Kuwait?," Washington Post, June 26, 1973, nearly four months before the actual use of the oil "weapon." *See also* Reisman, *supra* note 1, at 839 n. 6 and 849–50.

[24] *See* McDougal and Feliciano, *supra* note 12, at 179 n. 142, 200, 231–32, 235 and 240–41 and Reisman, *supra* note 1, at 839 n. 6. For those who think that claims to use responsive coercion in "self-defense" are not relevant to the case of the oil weapon, *see* remarks of Secretary of Defense Schlesinger as reported in N.Y. Times, Jan. 12, 1974, at 3, col. 1.

[25] *See* McDougal and Feliciano, *supra* note 12, at 57, 123, 126–27. *Cf.* Reisman, *supra* note 1, at 839 n. 6 and 849–50; Professor McDougal's introduction in J. N. Moore, Law and the Indo-China War viii–ix (1972); and his remarks in Paust and Blaustein, *supra* note 21, at 44, n. 95.

[26] *See* Reisman, *supra* note 1, at 836–51; and *infra* note 28.

and magnitude in that regard as to create the "condition of necessity" for a response under Article 51.[27] Although coercion not involving the use of armed force can violate Article 2(4) and result in UN action, it does not follow automatically that states may unilaterally respond as well under Article 51 of the Charter. Similarly, the reverse is true. Although a state may not properly respond under Article 51, this does not mean that Article 2(4) has not been violated.[28] It is by no means clear that the Arab coercive process does not also involve an armed attack and an intense coercion of the type contemplated under Article 51, for the oil "weapon" was employed in the context of an armed attack upon the state of Israel and its use was intended to supplement that effort.

In any event, Article 2(4) prohibits more than the threat or use of "armed" force.[29] This has been clearly articulated in a series of United Nations instruments supplementary to the Charter—documents which spell out the goal-values generally shared by the international community. Chronologically, they include:

(a) The Draft Declaration on Rights and Duties of States, 1949,[30]

(b) The Essentials of Peace resolution, 1949,[31]

(c) The Peace Through Deeds resolution, 1950,[32]

(d) The Draft Code of Offences Against the Peace and Security of Mankind, 1954,[33]

[27] *See* McDougal and Feliciano, *supra* note 12, at 179, 237, and 240. Nor must they constitute an "aggression" to be proscribed under Article 2(4). *See also* Reisman, *supra* note 1, at 838–39, 842–43 and 849–50.

[28] If coercive conduct is proscribed under Article 2(4) but does not reach levels of intensity and magnitude such as to justify responsive coercion under Article 51 (or even Article 52), the permissible response would be a community response within the relevant Charter provisions. For comment on the situation where the UN machinery is ineffective, *see, e.g.*, Paust and Blaustein, *supra* note 21, at 9 n. 22, 10–11 n. 25, 22–23, 25 n. 54, and 42–44: Moore, *supra* note 25, at viii–ix, 183, and 185, and authorities cited; J. Paust, remarks, Conference on The Legal Regulation of the Use of Force, 2 Ga. J. Int. & Comp. L., Supp. 1, at 121–22 (1972); Reisman, *supra* note 1, at 836–58; J. E. Bond, *A Survey of the Normative Rules of Intervention*, 52 Mil. L. Rev. 51, 59–63 (1971); R. Lillich, *Forcible Self-Help Under International Law*, 22 Naval War Coll. Rev. 56 (1970); R. Lillich, *Forcible Self-Help by States to Protect Human Rights*, 53 Iowa L. Rev. 325, 347–51 (1967); and B. Harlow, *The Legal Use of Force Short of War*, 1966 U.S. Naval Institute Proceedings 88 (Nov. 1966).

[29] *See, e.g.*, McDougal and Feliciano, *supra* note 12, at 178–79, 196 and 200. This was also the Egyptian position in the Committee on Friendly Relations. UN Doc. A/AC.125/SR.25, at 12 (1966).

[30] Report of the International Law Commission (ILC), 4 UN GAOR, Supp. 10, at 7–10, UN Doc. A/925 (June 9, 1949).

[31] UN G.A. Res. 290(IV), 4 UN GAOR, UN Doc. A/1251, at 13 (Dec. 1, 1949).

[32] UN G.A. Res. 380(V), 5 UN GAOR, Supp. 20, at 13–14, UN Doc. A/1775, (Nov. 17, 1950).

[33] Report of the ILC, 9 UN GAOR, Supp. 9, at 11–12, UN Doc. A/2693, (July 28, 1954).

(e) The Declaration on Inadmissibility of Intervention Into the Domestic Affairs of States, 1965,[34]

(f) The Declaration on Principles of International Law Concerning Friendly Relations and Co-Operation Among States in Accordance With the Charter of the United Nations, 1970,[35]

(g) The resolution on Permanent Sovereignty over Natural Resources, 1973,[36]

as further explained and supplemented by:

(h) The Report by the Secretary-General of the United Nations on the Question of Defining Aggression, 1952,[37]

(i) The Soviet draft resolution on the Definition of Aggression, 1954,[38] and

(j) The Vienna Convention on the Law of Treaties, 1969.[39]

The General Assembly, for example, has authoritatively declared in the Declaration on Friendly Relations that it is "the duty of states to refrain in their international relations from military, political, economic or any other form of coercion aimed against the political independenec or territorial integrity of any state . . ."[40] In its exegesis of Article 2(4), it has also declared that every state has a duty to refrain from "any forcible action" which deprives certain peoples of self-determination, equal rights, and freedom and independence. The Declaration further states that "armed intervention and all other forms of interference or attempted threats against the personality of the state or against its political, economic, and cultural elements, are in violation of international law." Additionally it has been declared that:

> No state may use or encourage the use of economic, political or any other type of measures to coerce[41] another state in order to obtain

[34] UN G.A. Res. 2131, 20 UN GAOR, Supp. 14, at 11–12, UN Doc. A/6014 (Dec. 21, 1965).

[35] *Supra* note 1.

[36] UN G.A. Res. 3171, 28 UN GAOR (Dec. 17, 1973) (vote: 108–1–16).

[37] UN Doc. A/2211 (Oct. 3, 1952).

[38] 9 UN GAOR, Annexes, 51, at 6–7, UN Doc. A/C.6/L.332/Rev. 1 (Oct. 18, 1954).

[39] UN Doc. A/CONF.39/27 (May 23, 1969), *reprinted* at 63 AJIL 875 (1969).

[40] *Supra note* 1. We say "authoritatively" because it may be assumed that a unanimous consensus of the voting state elites in the General Assembly adequately reflects the generally shared expectations of the peoples of the United Nations. Regarding primary and representative authority, *see* J. Paust, *An International Structure for Implementation of the 1949 Geneva Conventions: Needs and Function Analysis,* 1 Yale Studies in World Public Order (1974) and J. Paust, *Human Rights and the Ninth Amendment: A New Form of Guarantee,* forthcoming.

[41] This sweeping condemnation of coercion or interference is not very useful by itself for the clarification of criterial distinctions between permissible and impermissible coercion. *See, e.g.,* McDougal and Feliciano, *supra* note 12, at 197, *passim*; and S. Schwebel, *Aggression, Intervention and Self-Defense in Modern International Law,* 2 Rec. des Cours 413, 453–54 (1972). Since the use of economic sanctions is regulated under Chapter VII of the UN Charter, it is useful to consider restraints upon the use of economic coercion in that Chapter in interpreting restraints upon all types of coercion under Article 2(4) of the Charter. Moreover, the fact that economic

from it the subordination of the exercise of its sovereign rights and to secure from it advantages of any kind.

By interpreting the preamble and Articles 1 and 2 of the UN Charter in light of this recent authoritative expression of the General Assembly, we can identify and clarify the community expectation that a broad range of coercive conduct is impermissible. Through this clarified policy, it is now possible to see that the use of economic coercion can violate the Charter. A detailed study of trends in the Security Council and in other UN organs (not undertaken here) would also reinforce this expectancy. Moreover, UN decisions addressing questions of threats to the peace, breaches of the peace, and acts of aggression are relevant as indications of community expectations which are also useful for the interpretation of the dynamic content of Article 2(4) of the Charter.[42]

The General Assembly Declaration on the Inadmissibility of Intervention of 1965 [43] has articulated similar goals, including the free development of political status; the free pursuit of economic, social, and cultural development; the principle of "non-intervention" of states in the internal and external affairs of other states (declared to be "essential to the fulfillment of the purposes and principles of the United Nations"); and the interrelated ban on "economic, political or any other type of measures to coerce another State" from impermissible objectives of dominance or the extraction of "advantages." The final prohibition had also been incorporated in the Draft Code of Offences against the Peace and Security of Mankind of 1954 with respect to economic coercion which is utilized by a state or group against another state "in order to force its will and thereby obtain advantages of any kind." [44]

Even in the case where the objective of the initiator of coercion is couched in terms of permissible self-defense (or a claim is made on the basis of serving any other Charter policy), the international community has generally demanded and expected a proper deference to the two interrelated principles of *necessity* and *proportionality,* which seek to minimize coercion, violence, and the destruction of resource values, such as wealth, power, well-being, and skill. Both principles seek to minimize coercion in terms of permissible participants, arenas of interaction, inten-

---

forms of coercion are regulated under Chapter VII supplements the expectation that the term "force" in Article 2(4) includes measures of economic force. *See also infra* notes 43–47; and D. Bowett, *supra* note 11, at 2–3.

[42] The United Nations can respond to a "threat to the peace" (*e.g.,* under Article 39) which does not constitute a prohibited "threat or use of force" under Article 2(4). *See, e.g.,* M. McDougal, W. M. Reisman, *Rhodesia and the United Nations: The Lawfulness of International Concern,* 62 AJIL 1, 5–19 (1968). *See also,* McDougal and Feliciano, *supra* note 12, at 178–79 and 207 note 193, *passim.* Similarly, it is possible for the United Nations to respond to a "threat" of force prohibited under Article 2(4) which does not constitute, for example, an imminent armed attack within the broad meaning of Article 51 of the Charter which would justify a unilateral response.

[43] *Supra* note 34.

[44] Art. 2(9), *supra* note 33. *See also* UN Docs. cited *supra* notes 30–32. Similar prohibitory language appears in Art. 16 of the Charter of the OAS.

sities of coercion, and impacts. For example, the principle of proportionality requires that the use of coercion "be limited in intensity and magnitude to what is reasonably necessary promptly to secure the permissible objectives . . . under the established conditions of necessity." [45] And reasonableness should be tested by reference to the contextual features listed above with a view to minimizing coercion.

On a related point, some Arab spokesmen might put forth a claim that the oil found under Arab lands is their property and that it is their "right" to do whatever they wish with it. Although certain instruments adopted by the United Nations affirm the general community goal of allowing all states permanent control of their natural resources, recent General Assembly resolutions have reiterated the *priority* of other goals—that the natural resources be used or controlled in such a manner that international peace is served and the coercion of other states does not reach impermissible levels. A 1972 General Assembly resolution, adopted with nearly unanimous Arab approval, stated that states should control their natural resources, but then reaffirmed the Declaration on Principles of International Law Concerning Friendly Relations and Co-Operation Among States of 1970. It also expressly reiterated the prohibition on the use of "economic, political or any other type of measures to coerce another State" for impermissible objectives of dominance or "to secure from it advantages of any kind." [46] This seems sufficient in itself to make clear that the manipulation of natural resources is regulated by international law in certain cases. Natural resources are not always a matter of "domestic" concern or of complete "sovereignty," and a state cannot do whatever it wants with natural resources that happen to be under its control.[47] The 1972 resolution went on to declare "that actions, measures or legislative regulations by States aimed at coercing, directly or indirectly, other States engaged in . . . the exercise of *their* sovereign rights over *their* natural resources . . . are in violation of the Charter and of the Declaration contained in resolution 2625(XXV) and contradict the targets, objectives and policy measures of the International Strategy for Development for the Second United Nations Development Decade." [48] That strategy had

[45] *See* M. McDougal, *The Soviet-Cuban Quarantine and Self-Defense,* 57 AJIL 597, 598 (1963); and McDougal and Feliciano, *supra* note 12, at 241–44, *passim.*

[46] UN G.A. Res. 3016 (XXVII) (Dec. 18, 1972) (vote: 102–0–22).

[47] It also seems clear from Arts. 1(3) and 55(b), of the UN Charter that "international problems" of an economic nature can arise as matters of international concern. *See also* Washington Energy Conference Communique, 70 Dept. State Bull. 220 (1974); Secretary Kissinger's speech to the Conference, *id.,* 201; and his joint news conference with Federal Energy Administrator, William Simon, *id.,* 109. *See also* T. F. Bradshaw, *Keeping the Energy Peace,* Vista (Aug. 1973), at 20, predicting that an "inadequate flow of energy . . . can . . . provide more discord among nations than could all the ideological struggles of the past and present," and that developing countries stand to lose most. Professor R. N. Gardner, in testifying before the Subcommittee on International Economics of the Joint Economic Committee on December 13, 1973, disclosed an interesting anecdote in the remark of Cordell Hull: "if goods can't cross borders, armies will."

[48] *Supra* note 46 (emphasis added). UN G.A. Res. 2625, referred to in the resolu-

been charted with a UN proclamation that "[e]conomic and social progress is the common and shared responsibility of the entire international community," and that "[e]very country has the right and duty to develop its human and natural resources, but the full benefit of its efforts can be realized only with concomitant and effective international action." [49]

On December 17, 1973 (just after the initiation of the Arab oil "weapon"), an even stronger resolution (this time with full Arab approval), expressly reiterated each of these major expectations and added that the General Assembly:

> Deplores acts of States which use force, armed aggression, economic coercion or any other illegal or improper measures in resolving disputes concerning the exercise of the sovereign rights [over natural resources].[50]

The General Assembly has emphasized the need for an inclusive and peaceful approach to the overall problem of earth resource control and usage in this era of a greater interdependence of peoples and an increasing scarcity of resources, as well as the need for an inclusive regulation of the manipulation of resources for coercive impact. An inclusive approach, the General Assembly recognizes, is now necessary for the maximization of all interests or the "full benefit" of efforts to develop human and natural resources in the context of interdependence and scarcity. This critical recognition could be the beginning of an attempt by mankind to avoid a global "tragedy of the commons" or, what may be worse, a war for the "commons."

Secretary Kissinger has noted:

> If anything was needed to illustrate the interdependence of nations in this world, it is what has happened in the field of energy . . . It is a test of the proposition that the world has become truly interdependent, and that isolation and selfish approaches must be destructive for all concerned.[51]

---

tion, concerned the International Development Strategy. Here, the expectation seems to encompass, at least, an international reflection of the general policy behind the case of Rylands v. Fletcher, L.R. 3H.L. 330 (1868).

[49] *See International Development Strategy,* UN Doc. ST/ECA/139, at 3 (1970), reproducing UN G.A. Res. 2625(XXV). *See also* UN Charter, preamble and Arts. 1(3), 55, and 56; UN G.A. Res. 3172(XXVIII), Dec. 17, 1973 (vote: 123–0–0) concerning the growth of interdependence and the "urgent need for international co-operation"; UN G.A. Res. 3082(XXVIII) (Dec. 6, 1973), Charter of Economic Rights and Duties of States (adopted without objection); and R. FALK, C. BLACK, *eds.,* 2 THE FUTURE OF THE INTERNATIONAL LEGAL ORDER: WEALTH AND RESOURCES (1970).

[50] UN G.A. Res. 3171(XXVIII), Dec. 17, 1973 (vote: 108–1–16).

[51] 70 DEPT. STATE BULL. 109 (1974). *See also* H. Kissinger, *The Interrelationships of Society,* 1 THE INTERDEPENDENT (Apr., 1974) at 3.

Secretary-General Waldheim opened the sixth special session of the General Assembly on raw materials in April 1974 with the recognition of interdependence and the need for a "just apportionment of natural resources" and the "optimum use of the world's natural resources with the basic objective of securing better conditions of social justice throughout the world." UN Doc. A/PV 2207, Apr. 9, 1974. This necessarily infringes upon permanent control of resources by each individual state.

Implicit here is the recognition that, by the "free" use or control of one's own resources, an impermissible interference with the "free" use or control of resources of others can result, and that a balance must be struck that best serves all relevant community goals in view of the actual context and policies at stake. In no other way can an individual or group maximize the enjoyment of freedom from fear and want,[52] or "the full benefit of its efforts."

This also explains the expectation in Article 1(2) of the International Covenant on Economic, Social and Cultural Rights of 1966 that the "free" disposal of natural wealth and resources must not prejudice "any obligations arising out of international economic co-operation, based upon the principle of mutual benefit, and international law," and "[i]n no case may a people be deprived of its own means of subsistence."[53] Undoubtedly, this statement is in effectuation of the purpose, set forth in the UN Charter, of achieving "international co-operation in solving international problems of an economic, social, cultural, or humanitarian character."[54] This is likewise the expectation behind the statement in the preamble of the Covenant on Economic, Social, and Cultural Rights recognizing that the Charter goal of equal rights for "all members of the human family is the foundation of freedom, justice and peace in the world." And each of these expectations should be considered in a rational effort to maximize

---

A position contrary to the inclusive approaches of Secretary Kissinger or the Secretary-General was taken by the People's Republic of China as disclosed in an opening speech at the special session. UN Doc. A/PV 2209, Apr. 10, 1974.

See also UN G.A. Res. 3085(XXVIII), Dec. 6, 1973 (adopted without objection), wherein the Assembly took notice of the Declaration adopted by the Fourth Conference of Heads of State or Government of Non-Aligned Countries (Algiers, Sept. 9, 1973) in which they expressed the belief that "the multilateral trade negotiations will . . . help in the establishment of a new system of world economic relations based on equality and the common interests of all countries." It has also become increasingly apparent that U.S. interests are best served with a more inclusive approach to economic matters. *See also* testimony of Professor Gardner, *supra* note 47, pointing out that Roosevelt and Churchill's Atlantic Charter had proclaimed the principle of "access, on equal terms, to the trade and to the raw materials of the world."

[52] *See* International Covenant on Economic, Social and Cultural Rights, preamble; adopted by UN G.A. Res. 2200, 11 UN GAOR, SUPP. 16, at 49, UN Doc. A/6316 (Dec. 16, 1966). *See also* McDOUGAL and FELICIANO, *supra* note 12, at 376 (re: the maximization postulate); R. FALK, THIS ENDANGERED PLANET 247–49, 403–06, *passim* (1971) (offering an "ideology of economic humanism"); and W. Friedmann, *The Relevance of International Law to the Processes of Economic and Social Development*, 2 THE FUTURE OF THE INTERNATIONAL LEGAL ORDER 3 (Falk & Black *eds.*, 1970).

[53] *See also* preamble and Arts. 1(1), 1(3), 5, 24, 25. Withholding resources from another state in order to deprive its people of their own means of subsistence can constitute an egregious thwarting of these articulated policies and also constitute a threat to the peace as well as a violation of Article 2(4) of the Charter. *See also* UN G.A. Res. 3185(XXVIII) (Dec. 18, 1973) and Res. 3171(XXVIII) (Dec. 17, 1973).

[54] Art. 1(3), which is one of the "Purposes of the United Nations" that must not be thwarted by the threat or use of force against other states or peoples under Article 2(4). *See also* preamble and Arts. 55 and 56.

the serving of community policy, especially where freedom, justice, and peace are often interdependent.

International Trade Law.

The most important instrument governing international trade outside of the UN Charter itself is the General Agreement on Tariffs and Trade (GATT),[55] to which there are more than 76 parties, including Egypt,[56] Israel, Kuwait, Lebanon, and Syria. The purposes of the GATT include the raising of standards of living, provision of full employment, development of the full use of the resources of the world, and the elimination of discriminatory treatment in international commerce.[57]

Artcle 1 of the GATT provides for most-favored-nation treatment to assure the elimination of discriminatory measures (any "advantage, favour, privilege, or immunity granted") among the parties. Article 11 makes export prohibitions or restrictions unlawful; Article 13 prohibits discriminatory quantitative restrictions; and Article 20 lists certain general exceptions, but reiterates the basic denial of "arbitrary or unjustifiable discrimination" in the trade process.

Admittedly Article 21(b)(iii) of the GATT might seem to allow the Arab states at least a claim that the oil cuts were "necessary" measures to assure "essential security interests," taken in time of war or some other emergency in international relations. Such a claim, however, must be judged in terms of the general goals of the GATT and the UN Charter.[58]

[55] TIAS No. 1700; 55–61 UNTS.

[56] Egypt made a provisional accession in 1962 and a full accession in 1970. TIAS Nos. 5309 and 6916.

[57] Preamble and Arts. 1, 11, 13, and 20.

[58] UN Charter, Art. 103 and Vienna Convention on the Law of Treaties, Arts. 31(3)(c), 53, and 64, *supra* note 39.

The language in Article 21(b) of the GATT permitting a party to take "any action which it considers necessary for the protection of its essential security interests" should be interpreted as a recognition of that party's capacity for making an initial characterization of the matter, *i.e.* a provisional characterization. *See* McDougal and Feliciano, *supra* note 12, at 218–19 and M. McDougal, H. Lasswell, J. Miller, The Interpretation of Agreements and World Public Order (1967). Otherwise, the "obligations" of parties to the GATT would be meaningless for whatever the party "considers necessary" could not be questioned.

On this point, L. F. Ebb insightfully raised the question in 1964 whether the U.S. Supreme Court review of determinations of administrative agencies of "national security" factors, "in a purely domestic context . . . ," and its rationale does not "foreshadow any similar future exercise of judicial review of national security findings in the international sphere." L. F. Ebb, Regulation and Protection of International Business 816 (1964); and I.C.C. v. N.Y., N.H. & Hartford R.R., 372 U.S. 744, 761–64 (1963). For a recent questioning of the "necessity" of past U.S. restrictions of foreign oil imports which seems to rely upon the "rationale" referred to by Professor Ebb, *see* W. F. James, III, *The Mandatory Oil Import Program: A Review of Present Regulations and Proposals for Change in the 1970's*, 7 Tex. Int. L.J. 373, 391 and 410–11 (1972), *cf. id.* at 400–03.

On an interrelated point, the universally recognized principle of "good faith" would seem to require that a provisional characterization by one party to a treaty cannot stand in perpetuity after it has been questioned by other parties to the agreement. GATT, Arts. 22 and 23, require "sympathetic consideration" to counterassertions and

Moreover, the Arab statements that the oil would be restored to any country as soon as it complied with Arab demands appear to refute the basis in "necessity" for the claim, except possibly in relation to the overall effort to regain "Arab" territory.[59] Even then, it has never been convincingly argued by any Arab spokesman that use of the oil "weapon" was actually necessary, as opposed to being merely helpful, to regain "Arab" lands. There is no reason to assume that the use of the oil "weapon" against the United States, Japan, and the Netherlands, for example, was "necessary" in order to stimulate serious negotiations between Israel and the Arabs for the implementation of UN Security Council Resolution 242. Victories by the Arab armies seemed to have been sufficient for that purpose. Nor can it be assumed that use of the "oil weapon" has changed Israel's basic position.

For reasons discussed below, we have concluded that: (1) Arab reliance on this exception in the GATT must fail in view of the actual context and relevant provisions of the UN Charter, which must be utilized as a guide to rational, policy-serving interpretation. (2) The Arab oil cuts must be condemned as "arbitrary" in the sense of the purposes of the GATT and in light of the unilateral character of the Arab decisions. (3) The oil cuts are also "unjustifiable" (even if not arbitrary) in that a joint Arab committee decided upon them in terms of the pro-Arab or anti-Arab posture of other states. (4) The oil cuts are additionally "unjustifiable" in terms of serving the relevant goals of the international community as contained in the UN Charter.[60]

The bilateral trade agreements between the United States on the one hand, and Saudi Arabia, Oman, and Iraq, on the other contain most-favored-nation treatment clauses with respect to import, export, and other duties and charges affecting trade and similar principles with respect to any concession, regulation, advantage, prohibition, or restriction on imports or exports.[61]

No relevant exception appears in the Saudi Arabian agreement. The agreement with Iraq, however, would seem to permit some discriminatory

"adequate opportunity for consultation." The Arab threats against targeted countries which sought to stand up to the oil "weapon" or merely to meet for the formulation of joint approaches to the overall energy crisis were hardly conducive to an "adequate opportunity for consultation" and the actions of those Arab states parties to the GATT have, thus, also thwarted the goals contained in Articles 22 and 23.

[59] *See, e.g.,* "Arabs Set Terms for Dutch," N.Y. Times, Dec. 1, 1973, at 11, col. 3; "5 Arab Ministers Confront Common Market Meeting," N.Y. Times, Dec. 15, 1973, at 1, col. 6; and The League of Arab States, "A Message to the American People," N.Y. Times, Nov. 29, 1973, at 49, col. 2, stating that "when American action to this effect is taken, we will be glad to resume oil shipments."

[60] Since under Article 103, Charter "obligations" must prevail in case of any conflict, the GATT should be interpreted so as to avoid such conflict. Moreover, since there is no textual reference to the meaning of "unjustifiable," it is clear that general norms of international law shall apply to the full interpretation of the term. *See, e.g.,* Vienna Convention on the Law of Treaties, Art. 31(3)(c), *supra* note 39.

[61] 48 Stat. 1826; 142 LNTS 329, Art. 3 (Saudi Arabia). TIAS No. 4530, 11 UST 1835, Arts. 4, 6, 8 (Oman). 54 Stat. 1790; TS 960, 203 LNTS 107, Art. 4 (Iraq).

action relating to "the adoption or enforcement of measures relating to neutrality or to rights and obligations arising under the Covenant of the League of Nations." Nevertheless, it would seem that joint Arab coercion designed to impose a pro-Arab stance in the context of a joint Arab initiated attack on Israeli forces does not properly fit within the meaning of the phrase "measures relating to neutrality." Certainly, the use of force to coerce other states into a non-neutral stance or conduct as well as a pro-Arab position on a Middle East settlement (such as Security Council Resolution 242) relates to neutrality; but since it plays havoc with the goal-values that underlie the principle of neutrality and also impairs other fundamental goal-values promulgated to regulate the use of force and the self-determination of states, the Arab coercion should not go unnoticed in interpreting the trade agreement.

It hardly needs to be pointed out that fundamental community policies should be taken into account in the interpretation of an international agreement to the extent that its precise meaning is unclear, that there is a gap in the disclosed intention of the agreement, or that peremptory norms would be impaired by one or more of several possible interpretations.[62] Moreover, an opposite conclusion would permit a party to create the very condition—a "necessity" or "security interest"—which would permit a derogation from the agreement. This would be in conflict with the import of the concomitant language in this agreement (as in the GATT) relating to the effort to fulfil obligations under the League of Nations Covenant, now presumptively the UN Charter. To say today that a state or group of states can initiate an armed attack upon another state and thus set up the very condition which allows a departure from trade obligations would permit a state to suspend performance of its obligations at will. Even if the armed attack were justifiable under the Charter, it does not automatically follow that any means of supplementing the attack are permissible or that the stability of world trade patterns and the serving of other Charter policies can be disregarded. Indeed, the serving of all relevant legal policy should be maximized.

The United States agreement with Oman contains a provision, as in the GATT, which allows a state to adopt a measure which is "necessary to protect its essential security interests"; however, the agreement with Oman, like the GATT, also refers to the fulfillment of UN Charter obligations.[63] A coercive strategy that is impermissible under the UN Charter cannot justify an exception to both the GATT and a trade agreement, which themselves contain provisions designed to assure the implementation of the law of the Charter. Moreover, what constitutes a state's "essential security interest" must be determined with comprehensive reference to all relevant legal policies and actual features of context. More specifically, the primary exceptions in the GATT and relevant bilateral trade

[62] *See, e.g.*, Vienna Convention on the Law of Treaties, *supra* note 39, Arts. 31(3)(c), 53, and 64.

[63] *Supra* note 61, Art. 11(d). *See also* the GATT, Arts. 20(d), and 21(c).

agreements dealing with national "security interests" should be applied with reference to the full range of community policy to balance permissible national security interests with the UN Charter goals found in the preamble and Articles 1, 2, and 56. Moreover, Article 103 of the UN Charter clearly makes that instrument a peremptory set of norms which will prevail in case of any conflict between the obligations under the Charter and obligations under any other international agreement.

There is substantial authority to support this approach to interpretation.[64] The oil cuts are most assuredly discriminatory and contrary to the most-favored-nation treatment provisions of the GATT and the bilateral trade agreements.[65] Thus, the main remaining question of legal policy is whether the Arab oil "weapon" is permissible or impermissible under the UN Charter.

A Consideration of the Arab Strategy

For present purposes, Arab strategy need not be considered in depth; it seems sufficient merely to indicate some of the most important and disturbing aspects of Arab use of the oil "weapon" and impairments of community policy under headings which are useful for systematic description of the coercive process: participants, objectives, situation, base values, strategies, outcomes, and effects.

Participants

Nearly all of the Arab states were joint initiators of this form of coercion, and nearly every state has been affected by the coercive process as instrumental target, primary target, or spillover victim. Moreover, specific targets included Japan, Western Europe, and the United States. Even though, in the words of Secretary Kissinger, one can "understand" the reasons that led some oil producing states to impose an embargo against the United States "at a time when they perceived us to be taking sides in a military conflict . . ."[66] the targeting of other countries is not understandable except with reference to the proclaimed Arab objectives, discussed below. Moreover, within targeted states the targets included

[64] *See, e.g.*, Vienna Convention on the Law of Treaties, *supra* note 39, Arts. 31, 43, 53, and 64; M. McDougal, H. Lasswell, J. Miller, *supra* note 60 especially on supplemental means of interpretation. On the use of economic coercion as a means of imposing a treaty, *see also* Final Act, Vienna Convention, UN Doc. A/CONF.39/ii, add. 2, at 285. Although many articles of the Convention prohibit coercion during the formation (pre-outcome) stage of agreement, the policy throughout clearly seems to prohibit coercion to force interpretations or exceptions at all stages, *i.e.*, also during outcome and post-outcome stages. *See* McDougal, Lasswell, and Miller, *supra* and J. Stone, *supra* note 2, commenting on Art. 52 of the Convention.

[65] *See* "Saudi Oil Embargo Is Termed Breach of '33 Treaty With U.S.," N.Y. Times, Dec. 19, 1973, at 12, col. 4 (quoting Professor R. N. Gardner).

[66] Joint news conference of Jan. 10, 1974, *supra* note 47, at 115. He added that "it is inappropriate to maintain the postures of confrontation that existed before" in the light of the major U.S. efforts to promote a settlement.

both combatant and noncombatant types of participants. Indeed, there seemed to be indiscriminate targeting of governmental, nongovernmental, military, economic, diplomatic, and other types of persons and institutions without proper deference to the basic principles of necessity and proportionality and the effects that such a strategy would have upon peoples and resources around the world.

Objectives

The use of this oil strategy was deliberate.[67] The stated objectives of the initiators were couched for the most part in terms of an overall effort to regain "occupied territory." But other objectives were also articulated by Arab spokesmen:

(1) To force an overall settlement upon Israel on terms satisfactory to the Arabs through the coercion of Israel itself or through the use of force to make others pay more attention to Arab claims and demands; [68]

(2) To seek a continued embargo against any country supporting Israel in any manner, with each country classified as either friendly to the Arabs, neutral, or supporting Israel; [69]

(3) To force other states to sever diplomatic and trade relations with Israel; [70]

[67] On the importance of this factor *see, e.g.*, L. Chen, *supra* note 16, at 135–38.

[68] *See, e.g.*, N.Y. Times, Mar. 1, 1974, at 5, col. 1; Dec. 11, 1973, at 34, col. 3; Dec. 29, 1973, at 2, col. 1; *contra* N.Y. Times, Feb. 25, 1974, at 1, col. 3. *See also* Dec. 1, 1973, at 11, col. 3; Dec. 15, 1973, at 1, col. 6; Feb. 5, 1974, at 2, col. 1, citing a pledge by Saudi Arabia and Kuwait that there would be no let up on the embargo until an agreement was reached on "Syrian terms"; Mar. 17, 1974, at 15, col. 1; and Mar. 19, 1974, at 20, col. 2.

The Algerian Minister of Energy, Belaid Abdesselam, also claimed a right of necessity to use "our oil weapon" in order "to call the world's attention to the injustices of the situation." U.S. News & World Report (Dec. 31, 1973), at 21. Egyptian Ambassador Ghorbal claimed that the oil weapon was used to gain attention to 25 years of suffering and demanded that it continue until the Israelis committed themselves to "total withdrawal." N.Y. Times, Jan. 7, 1974, at 1, col. 2. The Saudi Arabian Minister of Foreign Affairs, Omar Sakkaf, claimed, among other things, a right to use the oil weapon to "put" the "case" to the American people. N.Y. Times, Dec. 31, 1973, at 5, col. 1. *See also* The League of Arab States, "A Message to the American People," *supra* note 59.

The coercion continued far beyond a calling of "attention" to Arab demands, and it did not cease even after serious negotiations. President Sadat later declared that the oil weapon "was not blackmail. It was only a message to show the whole world that the Arabs after the 6th of October deserve to take their place under the sun." N.Y. Times, Feb. 25, 1974, at 1, col. 3.

[69] *See* Text of the Declaration After the Arab Leaders' Summit Meeting, N.Y. Times, Nov. 29, 1973, at 16, cols. 1 and 6.

This broad Arab objective did not confine itself to traditional distinctions in the law of neutrality but, in a sweeping approach, equated political and military "support." Even in the Vietnamese conflict, the United States did not regard political support for North Vietnam as a violation of neutrality.

[70] *See supra* notes 68 and 69 and N.Y. Times, Jan. 15, 1974, at 4, col. 1 noting that "a shift in Japanese policy in the Middle East was followed by a decision by the Arab countries to reclassify Japan as a friendly nation." *See also* N.Y. Times, Dec.

(4) To compel other states to extend economic aid to the Arab nations; [71]
(5) To compel other states to extend military aid to the Arab nations.[72]

These are attempts to control the foreign policies and conduct (international and domestic) of other states and peoples and to affect the free choice of such states and peoples through a manipulation of resources. They constitute an interference in domestic affairs and a thwarting of fundamental community policy, as some Arab spokesmen have stated, in order to "shape events."

Further, these objectives were being pursued unilaterally, with no known attempt to forewarn the international community of impending action.[73] There were no efforts to work through the United Nations—specifically created to maintain international peace and security, with its own built-in coercive strategy. Likewise, there were no Arab efforts to use any other peaceful and cooperative means or machinery to settle the underlying disputes. In fact, as the coercive strategy continued for the first four months, there were continuing threats made against any inclusive response to the oil "weapon" or to the arrogated oil prices by consumers and/or other producers.[74] Similarly, the Arab states refused to seek inclusive measures for settlement of the world energy crisis. As if to underline the unilateral approach of the Arabs to this whole matter, the embargo was continued despite the January 18th and other agreements, the Israeli pull back from occupied Egyptian territory, active U.S. involvement in the negotiating process as an accepted intermediary, and some five months of attention to Arab demands.[75] Even President Sadat appealed to other Arab leaders at the end of January for an end to the oil embargo.[76] By March 4, Sheik Zaki al-Yamani of Saudi Arabia openly agreed that the embargo against the United States should be lifted, and Saudi Arabia and Egypt were apparently prepared to do so by March 10, although Arab

---

13, 1973, at 4, col. 4 and Secretary Kissinger's speech to the Washington Energy Conference in which he criticized "the manipulation of raw material supplies in order to prescribe the foreign policies of importing countres" *supra* note 47, at 202.

[71] *See* N.Y. Times, Dec. 30, 1973, at 3, col. 1; Jan. 18, 1974, at 12, col. 2; Jan. 28, 1974, at 1, col. 6; Feb. 9, 1974, at 11, col. 2; Feb. 26, 1974, at 27, col. 2.

[72] *See supra* notes 68 and 71 and N.Y. Times, Jan. 26, 1974, at 3, cols. 2 and 3.

[73] N.Y. Times, Feb. 22, 1974, at 13, col. 1. To a certain extent the West might have been "warned" by some threats by certain Arab states in 1972 to use oil as a political weapon, but the actual cuts were very sudden. *See* J. E. Akins, *supra* note 3, and Sheehan, *supra* note 2, at 50 and 54.

[74] *See* N.Y. Times, Feb. 5, 1974, at 2, col. 2; Nov. 23, 1973, at 1, col. 6; Jan. 13, 1974, at 14, col. 4. Joint energy talks on February 11, 1974 in an effort to reach an inclusive response to an even greater global energy threat than the use of the oil weapon itself. *See* text of the President's invitation, 70 Dept. State Bull. 123 (1974) and Secretary Kissinger's speech and news conferences, *supra* note 47.

[75] N.Y. Times, Jan. 28, 1974, at 19, col. 4; and Jan. 25, 1974, at 3, col. 1. The continuation of the embargo certainly leaves Arab claims of necessity in relation to *continued* use of the oil "weapon" in serious doubt. *See* Reisman, *supra* note 1, at 842–43. *See also* N.Y. Times, Feb. 7, 1974, at 1, col. 4.

[76] *See* N.Y. Times, Jan. 28, 1974, at 19, col. 4 and Jan. 30, 1974, at 3, col. 1.

solidarity on this point proved elusive.[77] In response, Secretary Kissinger warned as of early February that:

> Since October the United States first brought about the cease-fire, the six-point agreement, the disengagement between Israel and Egypt. To maintain an embargo now under these conditions must be construed as a form of blackmail, and would be considered highly inappropriate by the United States and cannot but affect the attitude with which we will have to pursue our diplomacy.[78]

These Arab actions are incompatible with the principles of the Charter which are designed to assure the adjustment or settlement of international disputes or situations that might lead to a breach of the peace by peaceful and inclusive means and the achievement of "international co-operation in solving international problems of an economic . . ." nature,[79] as recently supplemented by General Assembly resolution 3073(XXVIII). In that resolution the General Assembly reiterated:

> Its appeal to all Member States to take full advantage of the framework and means provided by the United Nations in order to prevent the perpetuation of situations of tension, crisis and conflict, avert the creation of such new situations which endanger international peace and security, and settle international problems exclusively by peaceful means.[80]

Again, we must emphasize the General Assembly's condemnation of "economic coercion or any other illegal or improper means in resolving disputes concerning the exercise of the sovereign rights" of others over natural resources.[81]

In addition to the lack of a cooperative and inclusive approach, there seems to have been no attempt to offer any formal argument in favor of the necessity or legality of such action under the UN Charter or other international instruments (including trade agreements). While we can appreciate and even applaud the new Arab confidence and solidarity,[82] the rise of this new confidence through the use of the oil "weapon" has tended to foster some of the very exclusive oriented perspectives that must be overcome if we are to have peace in the Middle East. What the Arab states have included as some of their objectives and their unilateral approach to matters of international concern are the most alarming features

[77] N.Y. Times, Mar. 5, 1974, at 6, col. 8, and Mar. 12, 1974, at 1, col. 5.

[78] N.Y. Times, Feb. 7, 1974, at 1, col. 4 and joint news conference, *supra* note 47, at 117–18.

[79] *See* UN Charter, preamble and Arts. 1, 2, 55, and 56.

[80] *See also* UN G.A. Res. 3185(XXVIII) (Dec. 18, 1973); Reisman, *supra* note 1, 842–43; McDougal and Feliciano, *supra* note 12, at 181–83; Bowett, *supra* note 11, at 11. It should be recalled that the GATT also seeks a more inclusive conciliatory approach. *See supra* note 58.

[81] UN G.A. Res. 3171(XXVIII) (Dec. 17, 1973) (vote: 108–1–16).

[82] For recent evidence of the new Arab confidence and sense of power, *see, e.g.*, "Arab Price and Power," Newsweek, Feb. 18, 1974, at 40. The article also explores certain psychological predispositions identified as "Arab traits." *See also* N.Y. Times, Feb. 28, 1974, at 1, col. 7.

of context. This has also prompted Professor Julius Stone to declare:

> Article 53 of the UN Charter expressly commands that "no enforcement action shall be taken under regional arrangements, or by regional agencies without the authorization of the Security Council." This is exactly what present Arab state oil measures against the U.S., Netherlands, Japan and other states amount to, even if their demands conformed (which they do not) to the Security Council resolutions involved . . . This kind of unauthorized concerted plan by a group of members to cripple the economies of other members for collateral political ends obviously flouts the "purpose" and "principles" of articles one and two of the Charter . . . .[83]

While we agree with much of what Professor Stone has written, the Arab embargo, properly speaking, cannot be considered as "enforcement action," for this implies a basic consistency between Arab objectives and community interest. The oil cuts are unilateral efforts at coercion which, even if claimed to be "enforcement action," are impermissible in terms of serving all relevant legal policies. Thus, there is no conformity with the basic requirements in Article 52 of the Charter. Moreover, the Arab strategy would not meet the test of Article 53 in the absence of authorization by the Security Council. We do not seek to argue the illegality of Arab actions against South Africa and the illegal regime of Southern Rhodesia, which have been the subjects of United Nations sanctions. Such action may constitute permissible self-help that seeks to serve overall community interest.[84]

[83] J. Stone, *supra* note 2.

[84] *See, e.g.,* UN Charter, Arts. 25 and 48–50; UN G.A. Res. 3055(XXVIII) (Oct. 28, 1973), 3115(XXVIII) (Dec. 12, 1973), and 3116 (XXVIII) (Dec. 12, 1973). *See also* J. Carey, UN Protection of Civil and Political Rights 23–26, *passim* (1971); Reisman, *supra* note 1, at 842–43; Bowett, *supra* note 11; and McDougal and Reisman, *supra* note 42.

A comprehensive policy and contextual analysis allows for a differentiation between the Arab use of the oil weapon against a state like Japan or the Netherlands, with global effects, from the selective use of trade measures against the emigration policies of the Soviet Union by the United States, as proposed in the Jackson amendment. The latter would promote a human rights objective and the fulfillment of Charter obligations under Article 56, would be a highly selective response, and would be far less coercive than in the case of the vital dependence of Japan and the Netherlands on Middle East oil. *See also* Reisman, *supra* note 1, at 836–39, 842–43, and 849–51.

It is not irrelevant to note that the Soviet Union advocated a continuation of the oil weapon against the United States despite several U.S. efforts to obtain a viable peace in the Middle East and almost in open defiance of norms on friendly relations, cooperative action, and the peaceful settlement of disputes. *See* N.Y. Times, Mar. 13, 1974, at 24, col. 4.

On the imperfect Arab attempts to place the Jackson amendment and an earlier "blockade" of Cuba in the same category as the Arab oil "weapon," *see* statement by Belaid Abdesselam, *supra* note 68. In the Cuban case the U.S. refusal to trade with Cuba was related to an OAS sanction against Cuban subversive activities in the hemisphere that were allegedly violative of the norms of Article 2(4) of the UN Charter. Moreover, the Cuban "blockade" has never cut off foreign trade. *See* N.Y. Times, Jan. 9, 1974, at 6, col. 4.

We conclude that the five types of Arab objectives outlined above (despite claims concerning the recapture of territory or the desires to aid the Palestinian people)[85] are inconsistent with the UN Charter. More specifically, there is an impairment of both the "political independence" of states and of the prohibition of the use of force which thwarts the "Purposes" of the United Nations contained in Article 2(4) of the Charter; there appear to be no exculpating claims that may tip the balance against that impairment. The Arab objectives outlined above certainly affront the Charter goals of tolerance, friendly relations, cooperative effort to solve international economic problems, and the peaceful settlement of disputes. The Arab economic coercion is in contradiction with the principle contained in the Declaration on Friendly Relations and Co-Operation of 1970 which prohibits the use of coercion to impair the sovereign rights of other states (such as the right to determine foreign or domestic policy and actions relatively free of coercion) or "to secure from" them "advantages of any kind." As regards the Arab purpose of regaining territory or of acquiring territory for the Palestinians, the principles of necessity and proportionality have not been observed and the use of the oil "weapon" seems a highly unnecessary and disproportionate response to continued Israeli control of some Arab lands.

Moreover, as recognized in the Report of the Secretary-General in 1952 on the Question of Defining Aggression,[86] impermissible intervention or interference in the affairs of another state "may assume the most varied forms: *e.g.*, encouraging a party, paying it funds, sending weapons, etc." Certainly the coercion of another state in an effort to force the payment of funds (*e.g.*, economic aid) or the shipment of weapons would fit within that sort of prohibition, and there seems little doubt that the use of the Arab oil "weapon" is rendered illegal on these grounds alone.

Related to these issues was the Syrian refusal to comply with the basic humanitarian provisions of the Geneva Conventions of 1949 which require, among other things, that a list be provided to Israel of captured prisoners of war and that the International Committee of the Red Cross be given access to captured persons in order to assure their humane treatment.[87] We would not mention this violation of international law here, except for the fact that it became a central issue in regard to Israeli and Syrian disengagement and was inextricably intertwined with the

[85] Professors Paust and Gardner addressed this and other issues at a board meeting of the International League for the Rights of Man (N.Y., Feb. 7, 1974). There, Professor Gardner cogently argued that the Arab claim to use the oil weapon for the promotion of human rights of the Palestinians is "nearly hollow" in view of their past lack of "support" of Palestinian refugees with oil profits. *See also* remarks of the U.S. Representative before ECOSOC, "Oil Nations Scored on Aid to Poor," N.Y. Times, Jan. 18, 1974, at 12, col. 2. [86]*Supra* note 37.

[87] *See* A. Blaustein and J. Paust, On POW's and War Crimes, 120 CONG. REC. E370 (Jan. 31, 1974). For text of two Israeli complaints submitted to the ICRC and the UN Secretary-General in December, *see* 119 CONG. REC. E8033–E8036 (Dec. 13, 1973). Complaints were also forwarded to the ICRC by Egypt and Syria of Israeli violations of the Geneva Conventions. N.Y. Times, Mar. 13, 1974, at 3, col. 6.

continuation of the Arab oil embargo even after repeated and generally effective U.S. efforts to bring about a peaceful settlement.[88] Egypt and other Arab states did not press the Syrians on this matter as they are required to do under Article 1 of the Geneva Conventions and Articles 1(3) and 56 of the UN Charter.[89] Other Arab states allowed this violation to continue for nearly five months. The oil embargo was extended, while Syria utilized prisoners of war as pawns in the negotiating process.[90]

Situation

The geographic area within which the Arabs utilized their oil strategy was global. There was no effort to minimize the destruction of values through a limitation of coercion to arenas of armed conflict between the Arab states and Israel, or even to arenas of active military involvement. Nor did the Arabs make the traditional criterial distinctions[91] between military and civilian objectives in their delineations of targets. The coercion was of substantial duration. Moreover, the continued use of the strategy long after agreements for military disengagement and the extensive efforts made by all parties to begin serious negotiations for an overall settlement plays even greater havoc with the principles of necessity and proportionality.

Bases of Power

The Arab states obviously possess ample resources of power and wealth to apply intense coercion through time and space. Saudi Arabia alone is thought to possess one quarter of the world's known oil resources and is the world's largest oil exporter.[92] Specific targets such as Japan, the Philippines, the Netherlands, and numerous Western European countries are extremely dependent upon oil and the maintenance of stable trade relations not only for wealth and well-being but for overall power, including the power to maintain their national defense and security. Japan, which is nearly 100 percent dependent upon oil imports, obtains some 88 percent of its oil from Arab states and Iran; Western European states in general depend on the Middle East for some 73 percent of their oil

[88] N.Y. Times, Feb. 25, 1974, at 1, col. 3.

[89] *See, e.g.*, Paust and Blaustein, *supra* note 21; and J. Paust, *My Lai and Vietnam: Norms, Myths and Leader Responsibility*, 57 Mil. L. Rev. 99, 118–23 (1972). Subsequently Egypt did make efforts ot comply with an ICRC initiative to establish a special commission to investigate charges and countercharges of violations of the Geneva Conventions. N.Y. Times, Mar. 13, 1974, at 3, col. 6.

[90] Finally, on February 27, 1974, Syria provided Secretary Kissinger and the ICRC with a list of 65 prisoners of war and opened the way toward a multilateral Geneva conference on the settlement of Middle East conflict.

[91] By "criterial distinctions" we mean distinctions based upon criteria which are formulated in order to facilitate rational, policy-serving decision. See McDougal and Feliciano, *supra* note 12, at 15, 56–59, 152 n. 88, 158, *passim*; H. Lasswell, M. McDougal, *Criteria For A Theory About Law*, 44 S. Cal. L. Rev. 362, 376, 384, *passim* (1971); H. Lasswell, A Pre-View of Policy Sciences 85–95 (1971).

[92] *See* N.Y. Times, Nov. 29, 1973, at 16, col. 1.

imports,[93] and are generally dependent upon foreign oil to make up about 98 percent of their needs.[94]

Strategies

While the primary strategy employed was economic, there was also a manipulation of the diplomatic and ideological instruments of corecion.[95] Diplomatic efforts included use of the economic instrument to communicate threats against "supporting Israel" and "joining the Americans" in any kind of countermeasures, "because your whole economy will definitely collapse all of a sudden."[96] The use of this particular strategy, the oil "weapon," involved a choice of the sort of weapon that is far less capable of discriminate application than, for example, the embargo of military arms to another country. It is the type of strategy which will necessarily have a great impact upon the civilian economy and civilian participants. Thus, its use would seem to require a very strong showing of necessity.

Outcomes

It is clear that the outcomes of the use of the oil weapon involved intense coercion on target governments and peoples. The coercion met with some notable successes. Some states have changed their official diplomatic posture toward Israel, and states have also begun to change their domestic and international policies with respect to trade, emigration of foreign nationals, the supply of arms to Arab states, economic programs for Arab development, a Middle East settlement, and other matters. In the first four months of the coercive process, new trade and development agreements were "negotiated" involving a total of some six billion dollars for the Arabs, while another five billion dollars of benefits was being actively considered.[97]

Effects

A particularly important effect was the sudden disruption of normal trade patterns, which threatened and still threatens the stability of the

[93] N.Y. Times, Dec. 24, 1973, at 1, col. 8. *See also* U.S. Dept. State, FOREIGN POLICY OUTLINES, "Oil and Energy," No. 33–99 (Nov. 1973); J. Dapray Muir, *Legal and Ecological Aspects of the International Energy Situation*, 8 INT. LAWYER 1, 2–4 (1974); and J. E. Akins, *supra* note 3.

[94] *See* chart, *"Dependence on Imported Oil,"* N.Y. Times, Feb. 10, 1974, Sec. 3, at 2, col. 1. Italy's Foreign Minister, Aldo Moro, has bluntly called for a pro-Arab policy and bilateral trade with oil exporters, adding: "The Arab peninsula and Iran are a complex that is essential to Italy and Europe." N.Y. Times, Mar. 1, 1974, at 5, col. 1.

[95] The President of Algeria, at a 38-nation Islamic Conference in February, defended the use of oil as a "political" weapon. *See* N.Y. Times, Feb. 24, 1974, at 1, col. 3. The text of the Arab statement in Vienna on the ending of the embargo declared that "its main objective" was to "draw the attention of the world to the Arab cause in order to create the suitable political climate . . ." *See supra* note 10, at 20, col. 5.

[96] *See* N.Y. Times, Nov. 23, 1973, at 1, col. 6.

[97] *See* N.Y. Times, Jan. 28, 1974, at 1, col. 6.

world economy.[98] There was also a threatened destruction of resource values throughout the globe which would be disproportionate to the claimed necessity for realizing Arab objectives (even assuming that all of these objectives are otherwise proper in terms of legal policy and contextual factors).[99]

More specifically, we list some of the "disproportionate" effects of this strategy in terms of certain specific values affected: [100]

(a) *Wealth*: We note here the deleterious effects upon jobs, balance of payments, worldwide trade patterns, incentives for new development programs (national and international), general economic development (if not survival) of the developing countries of the Third World, and recessionary trends.[101] The interrelated price increases for oil could also result in a deficit of $29 billion for developing countries.[102] And there is an

[98] On the importance of this factor *see, e.g.*, L. Chen, *supra* note 16, at 135–38 and 159 and Washington Energy Conference Communique, *supra* note 47.

[99] *See, e.g.*, N.Y. Times, Dec. 31, 1973, at 2, col. 1.

[100] We utilize the eight value categories adopted by Professors McDougal and Lasswell for a more comprehensive and rational appraisal of aggregate value consequences (*i.e.*, wealth, well-being, power, skill, enlightenment, respect, affection, rectitude). The reader should note that these may not have been intended results, but they are, nevertheless, direct effects. For references to value analysis *see, e.g.*, Lasswell and McDougal, *supra* note 91, at 388; M. McDougal, H. Lasswell, W. M. Reisman, *Theories about International Law: Prologue to a Configurative Jurisprudence*, 8 VA. J. INT. L. 188 (1968); and J. N. Moore, *Prolegomenon to the Jurisprudence of Myres McDougal and Harold Lasswell*, 54 VA. L. REV. 662 (1968).

[101] *See, e.g.*, Washington Energy Conference Communique and News Releases, *supra* note 47; N.Y. Times, Dec. 31, 1973, at 2, col. 1; Mar. 3, 1974, at 10, col. 1 and Mar. 4, 1974, at 1, col. 4; D. Ottaway, "Black Africa Feels Arab Oil Cuts a Threat to Solidarity," The Guardian, Dec. 13, 1973 (London); "Kicking the Poor," The Economist, Dec. 8, 1973 (London). Economic disruption became evident with the 25 percent cut in oil production and colossal price increases.

[102] *See* N.Y. Times, Feb. 7, 1974, at 1, col. 4. The Shah of Iran's pledge of $1 billion to the World Bank and the International Monetary Fund in this regard is commendable but insufficient, and some day the Third World may come to view such resource profits as "windfall" profits from the earth's resources (a chance national distribution) despite certain trends toward "permanent control" over natural resources. *See* N.Y. Times, Feb. 25, 1974, at 14, col. 3. *See also* E. M. Borgese, "Who Owns the Earth's Resources–," VISTA (Aug. 1973) at 12, 46 and *infra* note 110. Instead of new patterns of ownership, however, it seems more likely in the near future that international cooperation between producers and major consumers of oil will result in international commodity agreements. *See* R. C. Longworth, *The Ecopolitics of Oil*, SAT. REV., WORLD (Jan 26, 1974) at 25, 27. A supplemental suggestion has been made by Dr. Abbas Zaki, head of an Abu Dhabi foreign aid fund, that 20 percent of the oil profits should be paid for in certificates issued by the World Bank and the Fund so that some profits can be directed toward global development. *See* E. Sheehan, *supra* note 2, at 68. Whatever the Arabs devise to offset the effects of higher oil prices for the Third World, it is probable that there will be some Arab controls on the use of available funds. Other means of meeting the problem of resource allocation might include agreements and institutions for the greater stabilization of trade and equal access to resources and markets or a breakdown of cooperative patterns and a North-South war. *See* the dichotomy between annihilation and economic humanism offered in FALK, *supra* note 52, at 415–37. During a lecture at Yale Law School in

overall danger of world depression if inclusive measures are not soon taken. The resultant $6 billion development programs for the Arabs stand in sharp contrast.

(b) *Well-being*: There have been devasting effects upon fertilizer production and consequential cuts in food production which have emphasized the warning that as many as 20,000,000 people could die in the Third World as a result of such scarcities.[103] Noticeable cutbacks in the production of medicines could also result in health problems and more deaths around the globe. The poorest of the earth will be the most seriously affected "victims" of the scarcity of oil, food, and fertilizer, and it has been estimated that an additional $3 billion in aid will be needed to save them from "catastrophe."[104] The scarcity of fertilizer could result in a loss of some five million tons of food for India alone. Surely, the Arabs could have foreseen the disastrous effects upon food production. It is the ready foreseeability of such consequences that is one of the most alarming aspects of the matter. Given the fact that the United States and Japan produce much of the world's fertilizer and that North America and Australia are the only food grain exporters in the entire world, it is difficult to escape the fact of predictable food scarcity over an extended period and an extended area of the globe—an effect which was neither "necessary" nor "proportionate" in terms of "legitimate military objectives" or the maximizing of all relevant community goals of world public order and human dignity.[105]

March, 1974, Professor Falk outlined additional possibilities including a great politico-military power dominance system which would control the primary war, power, and media systems and/or a geo-economic dominance system which would encourage a "businessman's peace" and an alignment of the superpowers and certain natural resource "have" states for the stabilization of markets and the relative value position of the wealth and power elites. Both of these possibilities would favor detente and world trade over any attempt to share earth resources and technology with an outside Fourth World or any attempt to promote human rights within particular states.

[103] N.Y. Times, Jan. 26, 1974, at 1, col. 1, quoting Dr. N. E. Borlaug, Rockefeller Foundation, that as many as 20 million may die because of crop shortages which will result in part from climate changes, but primarily from fertilizer cut backs. *See also* N.Y. Times, Mar. 11, 1974, at 10, col. 3, citing a report by the World Bank and Mar. 10, 1974, at 13, col. 1, on an F.A.O. report disclosing a doubling and tripling in fertilizer costs. *See also* N.Y. Times, Dec. 31, 1973, at 2, col 1, and Feb. 28, 1974, at 20, col. 1, noting the known interdependency of "virtually all parts of the agriculture industry" on electricity or oil.

[104] *See* N.Y. Times, Feb. 9, 1974, at 10, col. 3 and Feb. 24, 1974, at 4, col. 4.

[105] On the principles of "proportionality" and "necessity" in the use of weapons, *see* Panel on Human Rights and Armed Conflict, PROC. AMER. SOC. OF INT. LAW, 67 AJIL (No. 4), 141–68 (1973); J. Paust, *My Lai and Vietnam: Norms, Myths and Leader Responsibility, supra* note 89, and *Command Responsibility and Military Necessity,* 26 NAVAL WAR COLL. REV. 103 (Feb. 1973); E. Rosenblad, *Starvation as a Method of Warfare—Conditions for Regulation by Convention,* 7 INT. LAWYER 252 (1973); and Mudge, *Starvation as a Means of Warfare,* 4 INT. LAWYER 228 (1970). On more recent efforts to proscribe starvation and the ruination of food supplies and patterns of distribution for noncombatants, *see* ICRC BASIC TEXTS, Protocol I, Arts. 40–51 (Geneva 1972); and UN G.A. Res. 3102 (XXVIII) (Dec. 12, 1973) (vote: 107–

Evidence has been made public showing that cuts in oil imports to the United States (presumably a legitimate target for some sort of Arab coercion in response to military aid of Israel) would not have a deleterious effect upon the military capability of the United States.[106] It has, however, had an effect upon fertilizer and food production in an "indiscriminate" and "uncontrollable" manner. Not only have noncombatants in the United States suffered, but noncombatants in the Third World will be the primary victims of the oil "weapon." Moreover, the complex interdependence of oil, fertilizer, and food patterns throughout the globe now accentuate the unworkability and "impossible rigidity" of old "rules" that allowed the embargo of oil as contraband of war as well as the infeasibility of any "list theory" for the regulation of weapons in times of armed conflict.[107]

The laws of armed conflict, however, are not the only community goals at stake where a possible and foreseeable effect of economic coercion is the death of some twenty million people—equivalent in terms of lives lost to deaths from World War II atrocities. Articles 25 and 28 of the Universal Declaration of Human Rights state that everyone is entitled to an international order in which adequate food and medical care can be provided.[108] There is a great deal of room for disagreement whether the

---

0–6). UN S.C. Res. 253 (1968) excepted from the sanctions against the illegal regime of Southern Rhodesia those medical and other supplies needed for humanitarian purposes. In marked contrast to humanitarian efforts to limit the usages and impacts of violence have been the Soviet assertions that the Arabs have a "legitimate, inalienable right to use *all effective means* for liberation" of territories (emphasis added). This approach to "law" and social order, though shared by certain totalitarian ideologists and self-appointed terrorist elites, is completely indifferent to the principles of necessity and proportionality, to the authority of shared perspective and praxis, and to the human values inherent in human rights law. The Soviet-Syrian communique is reported in N.Y. Times, Mar. 15, 1974, at 8, col. 4. *See also* J. Paust, *Terrorism and the International Law of War,* and *Some Terroristic Claims Arising From the Arab-Israeli Context, supra* note 17; J. Paust, *Law in a Guerrilla Conflict: Myths, Norms and Human Rights,* 3 ISRAEL Y.B. ON HUMAN RIGHTS (1974); Y. Dinstein, *Terrorism and Wars of Liberation Applied to the Arab-Israeli Conflict, id.,* 78.

[106] *See* W. F. James, III, *supra* note 58, at 388–91, and references cited. Thus, no direct detriment to the United States was engendered by the Arab cuts in oil production and exports. *Cf.* R. C. Longworth, *supra* note 102, at 25, 26, disclosing some fuel problems for the U.S. Sixth Fleet due to Italian cuts in available oil. Secretary of Defense Schlesinger also stated that "the immediate effect of the oil embargo was the cutting off of our overseas forces from local sources of fuel," but that "bulk fuels in support of the Mediterranean forces was quickly available." See *Report of the Secretary of Defense to the Congress on the FY 1975 Defense Budget and FY 1975–1979 Defense Program* 233 (Mar. 4, 1974). He also noted that the Defense Department consumes only 3.5 percent of "the national petroleum usage." Thus, presumably, the oil embargo affected primarily the civilian population and the "weapon" was indiscriminate in impact.

[107] *See* J. Paust, remarks, 67 AJIL, *supra* note 105, at 163; and MCDOUGAL and FELICIANO, *supra* note 12, at 479–80.

[108] UN G.A. Res. 217A, 3 GAOR, UN Doc. A/810, at 71 (1948). *See also* UN CHARTER, preamble and Arts. 1(3), 55(b), and 56; UN, THE UNITED NATIONS AND

actions of certain states sufficiently promote these goals "in such a way as to achieve the most efficient development and utilization of natural resources . . . [t]aking into account the problems of both food-importing and food-exporting countries, to ensure an equitable distribution of world food supplies in relation to need"—especially when equal distribution may not mean equal survival but equal starvation because there may not be enough to feed the present population of the globe.[109] But it seems obvious that the deliberate use of the oil "weapon" has substantially jeopardized the fulfillment of these policies. Because of the unnecessary, "disproportionate," and foreseeable effect of this economic form of coercion, it undermines any prospect of ensuring through cooperative action an equitable distribution of food and medicine to the world's needy. Moreover, this kind of effect will perpetuate, if not exacerbate, a general Third World inequality, perhaps as devastating to the Third World as Arab economic neglect has been to the Palestinian people.[110]

(c) *Power*: Commentators have stressed concern over the potential effect of the oil cuts on the combat capability of European allies of the

---

HUMAN RIGHTS 39–41 (1968); UN G.A. Res. 3121(XXVIII) (Dec. 13, 1973); and 3085(XXVIII) (Dec. 6, 1973).

[109] *See* International Covenant on Economic, Social, and Cultural Rights, preamble and Arts. 11 and 12; *cf. id.*, Art. 25. *See also* N.Y. Times, Feb. 17, 1974, at 13, col. 1; and R. FALK, *supra* note 52, at 177.

It has also been stated by Dr. J. Knowles, president of the Rockefeller Foundation, that among the 2½ billion people in less developed countries, 60 percent are malnourished and 20 percent (500 million people) are believed to be starving to death. *See* N.Y. Times, Mar. 15, 1974, at 34, col. 4. Certainly an important conditioning factor here is the population menace. *See, e.g.*, Falk, *supra*; and V. Nanda, *The Role of International Law and Institutions Toward Developing A Global Plan of Action on Population,* 3 DEN. J. INT. L. & POL. 1 (1973), and references cited.

[110] Exceptions might include increased economic strengths and dominance of certain Arab and other oil producers of the Third World such as Nigeria and Indonesia. *See* "Kicking the Poor," The Economist, Dec. 8, 1973 (London). The 1973 "Arab" contribution ($2.25 million) to the UN relief program for Palestinian refugees was only 9 percent of the U.S. pledge ($25 million), and the Arab contribution has been even smaller in proportion to the total contributed by the United States since 1950. With Saudi Arabia alone spending more than $1 billion on the 1973 Egyptian and Syrian war effort, one wonders why more Arab oil profits could not have gone to feed the Arab poor. Was the financing of peace and the greater well-being of other Arabs so significantly less desirable? And why did the Soviet Union, Eastern Europe, and the People's Republic of China (itself, the world's largest grain importer) contribute nothing to the UN relief efforts for the Palestinian people? *See Money to burn; time to kill,* THE INTERDEPENDENT (Apr. 1974) at 1, col. 3; and C. L. Cooper, N.Y. Times, Apr. 4, 1974, at 41, col. 1, pointing out that the United States and Western Europe have contributed nearly 66 percent of the aid to the starving people of the Sahelian area of Africa but the Arab oil exporters have, so far, contributed less than 1 percent. It hardly needs to be emphasized that an extremist policy of state control over national resources will exacerbate this situation; and, although it would allow a few of the "have" natural resource states to escape a Third World existence, it could entrench another group (some 30 states and one quarter of the earth's population at a minimum) into a permanent Fourth World status with the rather uncomforting and irrelevant "control" of nearly nothing.

United States and thus on detente in Europe.[111] Political analysts have already noted the effects of oil scarcity upon European unity.[112] The Arabs cannot be entirely blamed for the unilateral scrambling of others for oil but their strategy has certainly provoked a bilateralist approach and brought politico-economic turmoil to many European nations.

If there are threats to European unity, detente, and security, one can imagine the threats to the national security interests of the Third World countries that are hard hit by economic, food, and health problems. The effect on overall world peace could be substantial, as governmental elites face power depletions and their fellow countrymen face recession or depression.

(d) *Skill*: The economic, food, and health problems could reduce skill levels among all peoples either directly or through job training cuts and a lack of funds for general education programs. Unemployment has risen in the United States, Great Britain, and other countries and these types of deleterious impacts are likely to continue in European and Third World countries.

(e) *Respect*: Patterns of respect for international law and international institutions have been threatened.[113] If some organ of the United Nations does not inquire into the legality of the use of oil as a "weapon" by the Arabs, there may be not only a diminution of UN authority in general, but also an unregulated increase in the use of oil and numerous other resources as a "weapon" in international relations with, perhaps, a concomitant increase in military interventions.[114]

Conclusion

At stake are not only the Charter goals of tolerance, friendly relations, the peaceful settlement of disputes, cooperative effort to solve international economic and other problems, and peace in general, but also the relative independence of peoples and their own political, economic, and ideological self-determination (the full and free shaping and sharing of all values). Several declared objectives of the Arab states are incompatible with basic community goals and the actual use of the oil "weapon" was "unnecessary" and "disproportionate" in terms of legitimate objectives. Thus, both the scope and purpose of this coercive strategy were

[111] *See* R. C. Longworth, *supra* note 22, at 25, 27, disclosing the warning of British strategist Neville Brown and certain findings of a Princeton study for the U.S. Navy; N.Y. Times, Jan. 12, 1974; and S. M. Schwebel, *supra* note 23. *See also* N.Y. Times, Mar. 4, 1974, at 1, col. 4, on the European political crises.

[112] *See* N.Y. Times, Feb. 18, 1974, at 3, col. 4; C. L. Sulzberger, *id.*, Jan. 13, 1974, at E17, col. 8; and Washington Energy Conference Communique, *supra* note 47.

[113] *See, e.g.*, U. Scheuner, The German Tribune, Jan. 10, 1974, at 4, col. 1. Professor Gardner also noted that "not a single voice has been raised in the United Nations to cite" the 1970 Declaration On Friendly Relations and Co-Operation in response to the oil "weapon." N.Y. Times, Dec. 19, 1973, at 12, col. 4.

[114] *See* N.Y. Times, Jan. 27, 1974, at E3, col. 3; and C. L. Sulzberger, *id.*, Jan. 9, 1974, at 35, col. 5.

unreasonable under the actual circumstances. The impact of the use of this form of economic coercion has been substantial in terms of the persons affected and the goals impaired. It was a coercion that threatened and might still impair not only the general wealth, well-being, and power of numerous nation-states and peoples, but also, more specifically, their national defense and security. Thus, the coercion was of such mounting intensity and efficacy that it can be authoritatively proscribed as a violation of basic Charter goals and of Article 2(4).

A cooperative effort is called for to obtain a more inclusive regulation of the economic instrument of coercion and a more inclusive and policy-serving use of the earth's resources—not for war and unilateral dominance, but for peace and for mankind.

DESTINATION EMBARGO OF ARAB OIL: ITS LEGALITY UNDER INTERNATIONAL LAW

By Ibrahim F. I. Shihata *

I.

Measures Applied by Oil Exporting Arab States

The use of Arab oil as an instrument of pressure for the revival of dormant efforts to restore peace in the Middle East was already a popular demand in many Arab countries before the outbreak of Arab-Israeli hostilities in October 1973. The political argument was simple. Production of oil beyond certain limits did not make economic sense for many Arab countries. Their depleting crude was increasingly converted into depreciating dollars and pounds yielding in fact a lower economic return than that achieved by simply keeping it in the ground. Worse still, this conversion was taking place in countries with few alternative resources and with a rather limited absorption capacity for the generated funds. Unchecked production was thus an economic sacrifice that could only be interpreted as a political favor to the consuming countries. Instead of responding positively to such a favor, the United States and most of its Western allies continued to ignore the vital interests of the Arab states. In particular, they either acquiesced in or actually encouraged the continuation of Israel's territorial expansion at the expense of its neighboring Arab states,[1] and of its refusal to implement the United Nations resolutions on the rights of the Arab Palestinian people.[2] By continuing to extend its massive military, economic, and diplomatic support to Israel, the United States in particular opted for a partial position in the Middle East conflict

* Legal Advisor, Kuwait Fund for Arab Economic Development. Opinions expressed in this essay are those of the writer and do not necessarily represent the views of the Kuwait Fund.

[1] The "Jewish State" suggested in the Partition Plan of Palestine (adopted by the UN General Assembly by Resolution 181(II) Nov. 29, 1947, GAOR, 2nd Sess., Resolutions, 31–50, UN Doc. A/519) was to cover an area of about 5,655 sq. miles, compared to about 907 sq. m. owned by Jewish settlers and agencies at the time and to about 10,249 sq. m. which formed the total area of Palestine under British Mandate. Territories of Palestine controlled by Israel after the 1949 Armistice Agreements covered, however, 8,017 sq. m., while territories of Arab States occupied by Israel in June 1967 covered 26,476 sq. m., including 23,622 sq. m. in Egypt, 2,270 sq. m. in Jordan (other than the Arab city of Jerusalem) and 444 sq. m. in Syria. *See* The Middle East and North Africa 398 (19th ed., 1972).

[2] For a comprehensive list of these resolutions, *see* United Nations Resolutions on Palestine 1947–1972, at 176–79, 195–98 (Institute for Palestine Studies, Beirut & Center for Documentation and Studies, Abu Dhabi, 1973). These resolutions have affirmed, in particular, the right of the Palestinians to return to their homes, to compensation for those who opt not to return, to respect for their immovable properties in Palestine, for their human rights, self-determination, and the legitimacy of their struggle for it.

which was clearly anti-Arab. In such circumstances, Arab oil exporting countries had no reason to continue to do political favors for the Western consuming countries. It was time for them to act on the basis of economic rationality only and to cutback their production to the limits justified by their economic needs.

The weight of this simple argument carried its way after repeated warnings by Arab statesmen had proved futile. Shortly before the outbreak of hostilities in October, 1973, officials of Saudi Arabia, the largest Arab oil producer, were revealing plans to check the increase of their crude oil production if the United States did not take a more impartial position in the Middle East conflict.[3] With the outbreak of hostilities the argument unsurprisingly gained full momentum.[4] Less than 24 hours after the fighting started on October 6, the Executive Committee of the Palestine Liberation Organization called for an immediate halt of the pumping of all Arab oil.[5] The Iraqi Government responded on the same day by nationalizing the interests of two U.S. companies, Exxon and Mobil, in the Basrah Petroleum Company.[6] Amidst the warnings issued in various Arab oil producing countries, Kuwait took the initiative, on October 9, of calling for an emergency meeting of Arab Oil Ministers to discuss "the role of oil in the light of current developments."

Held in Kuwait on 17 October and attended by 10 Arab countries,[7] the meeting issued a communiqué[8] indicating that oil production would be reduced by not less than 5 percent of the September 1973 level of output in each Arab oil exporting country, with a similar reduction to be applied each successive month, until such time as total evacuation of Israeli forces from all Arab territory occupied during the June 1967 war is completed and the legitimate rights of the Palestinian people are restored.[9] The

[3] *See, e.g.*, statements of Saudi Arabia's Oil Minister Sheikh Zaki Yamani, Washington Post, April 17, 1973, at 1, confirmed by King Faisal, *id.*, July 6, 1973, at 1 and Newsweek, Sept. 10, 1973. In the latter magazine's interview, King Faisal explicitly explained that "cooperation requires action on both sides: not sacrifices on one side and negative, if not hostile attitudes on the other side."

[4] Ironically, however, the first cutback in Arab oil production was a direct result of Israeli military action. Two of the four East Mediterranean terminals—Banias and Tartus in Syria—were targets of Israeli air and sea raids which damaged considerably their loading facilities. A third terminal—Sidon in Lebanon—remained open but was not visited by tankers. As a result, throughput from Saudi Arabia and Iraq had to be reduced to a trickle before the cutback decisions on the Arab side were actually issued. *See* 17 MIDDLE EAST ECONOMIC SURVEY (MEES), No. 1, Oct. 26, 1973, at 2. Israel also suspended operations at the Ashkelon terminal as of Oct. 6, 1973 thus halting a potential 500,000 b/d of exports. *See Middle East Oil Emergency*, 40 PETROLEUM PRESS SERVICE, No. 11, at 407, 408 (Nov. 1973).

[5] 16 MEES, No. 51, Oct. 12, 1973, at 4.

[6] Law No. 70, Oct. 7, 1973. English translation in *id.*, at i–iii.

[7] Saudi Arabia, Kuwait, Iraq, Libya, Algeria, Egypt, Syria, Abu Dhabi, Bahrain, and Qatar.

[8] 16 MEES, No. 52, Oct. 19, 1973, at iii–iv. The communiqué was signed by all participants excepting the Oil Minister of Iraq.

[9] Coinciding with this step, a Ministerial Committee representing the six Gulf member states of OPEC (five Arab countries plus Iran) decided on October 16, 1973, to

meeting had in fact passed the following resolution which was unofficially released at a later date, and may be worth quoting here in full:

> *Considering* that the direct goal of the current battle is the liberation of the Arab territories occupied in the June 1967 war and the recovery of the legitimate rights of the Palestinian people in accordance with the United Nations resolutions;
>
> *Considering* that the United States is the principal and foremost source of the Israeli power which has resulted in the present Israeli arrogance and enabled the Israelis to continue to occupy our territories;
>
> *Recalling* that the big industrial nations help, in one way or another, to perpetuate the status quo, though they bear a common responsibility for implementing the United Nations resolutions;
>
> *Considering* that the economic situation of many Arab oil producing countries does not justify raising oil production, though they are ready to make such an increase in production to meet the requirements of major consumer industrial nations that commit themselves to cooperation with us for the purpose of liberating our territories;
>
> *Decided* that each Arab oil exporting country immediately cuts its oil production by a recurrent monthly rate of no less than 5% to be initially counted on the virtual production of September, and thenceforth on the last production figure until such a time as the international community compels Israel to relinquish our occupied territories or until the production of every individual country reaches the point where its economy does not permit of any further reduction without detriment to its national and Arab obligations.
>
> Nevertheless, the countries that support the Arabs actively and effectively or that take important measures against Israel to compel its withdrawal shall not be prejudiced by this production cut and shall continue to receive the same oil supplies that they used to receive prior to the reduction. Though the cut rate will be uniform in respect of every individual oil exporting country, the decrease in the supplies provided to the various consuming countries may well be aggravated proportionately with their support to and cooperation with the Israeli enemy.
>
> The Participants also recommend to the countries party to this resolution that the United States be subjected to the most severe cut proportionately with the quantities of crude oil, oil derivatives and hydrocarbons that it imports from every exporting country.
>
> The Participants also recommend that this progressive reduction lead to the total halt of oil supplies to the United States from every individual country party to the resolution.[10]

---

abandon negotiations with oil companies on the price of crude and announced new posting pricse adding about 70 percent to the posting for Arabian light crude. *Id.*, at (i). This measure was already under consideration before the flare-up of Arab-Israeli hostilities and was particularly espoused by Iran, a non-Arab country. The establishment of its legality is therefore beyond the scope of this paper.

[10] 17 MEES, No. 4, Nov. 16, 1973, at (iii). First published as an advertisement, in The Guardian (London), Nov. 10, 1973. The resolution was not signed by the Oil Minister of Iraq.

The communiqué and resolution defined their objective in no unclear terms,[11] combining escalating cutbacks in production with selective discrimination between friendly and unfriendly states. The "legitimacy" of such an objective was particularly emphasized, along with the concern of the participants for the economic welfare of the industrial world. Production of crude oil in the ten countries attending the meeting averaged in September 1973 around 19.5 million barrel/day. A 5–10 percent cut meant a reduction of 1 and 2 million, or roughly from 3 to 6 percent of the volume of oil exports then moving in world trade.[12]

On October 18, the Saudi Arabian Royal Cabinet decided to reduce oil production immediately (and until the end of November) by 10 percent and to continue reduction thereafter "month after month at a rate to be determined at the time in accordance with the [Arab Oil Minister's] decision." The Cabinet indicated also that efforts to get the U.S. Government to modify its stand vis-à-vis the on-going war and its military assistance to Israel were "currently in progress." It added the clear warning that "if these efforts do not produce tangible results soon, then the Kingdom will stop oil exports to the U.S." [13]

The embargo of Arab oil to the United States, already recommended at the October 17 meeting, was imposed unilaterally by Abu Dhabi on October 18, by Libya on October 19, by Saudi Arabia and Algeria on October 20, by Kuwait and Qatar on October 21 and by Oman on October 25.[14] On October 19, it should be noted, the U.S. involvement in the military conflict then going on between Arab and Israeli forces reached such a magnitude that President Nixon requested that Congress appropriate $2,200 million in the current financial year for military assistance to Israel.

On October 21 Iraq, which had not concurred in the cutback decision of October 17, announced the nationalization of the 60 percent Dutch holding in Shell's 23.75 percent interest in the Basra Petroleum Company as a "punitive measure against the Netherlands for its hostile stand towards the Arab Nation." [15] Two days later, Kuwait which had already adopted an

[11] *See also* the communiqué of Arab Oil Ministers dated March 18, 1974, where this objective is reiterated as quoted in note 30 *infra*. Other wild objectives propagated by the Western press and quoted in Paust and Blaustein, *The Arab Oil Weapon—A Threat to International Peace*, 68 AJIL 427ff. (1974) never figured in the original cutback decision or in subsequent official Arab joint statements.

[12] Estimates in 17 MEES, No. 4, Nov. 16, 1973, at 3–4.

[13] English translation of text in *id.*, at iv.

[14] For the attitude of each Arab country *see*, 17 MEES, No. 1, Oct. 26, 1973, at 3–7.

[15] Law No. 90, Oct. 21, 1973. For English translation of the text, *see id.*, at 12. The reasons stated by the Iraqi News Agency for this action include the use of Dutch territory as "a bridgehead for assistance sent to the enemy," the supply by the Netherlands to Israel of crude oil from its imported stock, the continuous flights of KLM to "transport mercenaries and assistance to the enemy," the initial opposition of the Netherlands to the issue of an unbiased communiqué by EEC members, the declaration of the Dutch Foreign Minister to Arab Ambassadors of his country's support for Israel, the personal participation of the Dutch Minister of Defense in a demonstration staged in the Dutch capital to express support for Israel during the war, and the participation of various Dutch establishments and companies in collecting contributions for the Israeli war effort. *Id.*, at 13.

immediate 10 percent cut in production on October 21, embargoed oil shipments to the Netherlands for "its hostile attitude towards Arab rights and its Pro-Israeli bias." [16] Oil exports to that country were also curtailed by Abu Dhabi, on October 23, by Qatar on October 24, by Oman on October 25, by Libya on October 30 and its curtailment was confirmed by Saudi Arabia on November 2.[17] With the beginning of November, oil production had already been cut back by at least 25 percent in Kuwait, 10 percent in Saudi Arabia, Algeria, and Qatar and by at least 5 percent in Libya, Bahrain, Dubai, and Oman.[18] Before the embargo went into effect, total U.S. imports of Arab oil averaged, according to reliable estimates, around 1.8–1.9 million b/d equivalent to 28 percent of aggregate U.S. oil imports and 10 percent of its total consumption.[19] Dutch imports of Arab oil reached, on the other hand, 1.47 million b/d or 71 percent of its overall oil imports.[20]

After the cessation of military operations, Arab Oil Ministers held their second meeting on November 4–5 in an attempt to enhance the use of oil for accelerating the process of reaching a peaceful settlement of the Arab-Israeli conflict. They decided on escalation in the initial percentage reduction to 25 percent below the September 1973 level, including the volumes deducted as a result of the embargo. At that time Saudi Arabia had already reached a staggering 31.7 percent drop in production and Kuwait 25 to 30 percent.[21] The decision was meant, however, to bring about a similar decrease in production in Libya, Abu Dhabi, Algeria, and Qatar. As a result, a total reduction of about 2,826,000 b/d or some 28.5 percent below the September average became effective.[22] The meeting decided also to send the Arab Oil Ministers of Algeria and Saudi Arabia to Western capitals "to explain the Arab point of view regarding the oil production cutback measures." As for future cutbacks, it was decided that a further reduction amounting to 5 percent of the November output should follow in December "provided that such reduction shall not affect the share that any friendly state was importing from any Arab exporting country during the first nine months of 1973." [23]

The trend towards escalation was soon to be reversed, however, partly in view of the less biased attitudes which gradually developed in Western Europe and Japan, and partly because of the relative success of the efforts for reaching a peaceful settlement in the area. On November 18, nine Arab Oil Ministers convening in Vienna decided not to implement the 5 percent reduction for the month of December with respect to European countries (meaning the nine EEC members with the exception of the

[16] *Id.*, at 5.

[17] *See id.*, at 6–7 and 17 *id.*, No. 2, Nov. 2, 1973, at 3–4. It was later explained however that the embargo did not cover oil shipped to Rotterdam for the purposes of refining and reexportation to nonembargoed countries.

[18] *Ibid.*

[19] *Id.*, 16, No. 52, Oct. 19, 1973, at 4, and 17 *id.*, No. 22, March 18, 1974, at 13.

[20] *Id.*, No. 2, Nov. 2, 1973, at 1.

[21] *Id.*, Supp. Nov. 6, 1973, at 2, 5.

[22] *Id.*, at 2.

[23] *Id.*, at 4.

Netherlands) "in appreciation of the political stand taken by the Common Market countries in their communiqué of 19 November, 1973 regarding the Middle East crisis."[24] The Sixth Summit Arab Conference held in Algiers from November 26 to 28 further exempted Japan and the Philippines from the effects of the 5 percent cutback scheduled for December. It also qualified the progressive monthly reduction formula by adopting a ceiling for reductions in production "to the extent that reduction in income should not exceed one quarter on the basis of the 1972 income level of each producing country."[25] Consuming countries were also to be classified in three categories: friendly, neutral, or "supporting the enemy." The classification was to be applied and reviewed by a committee of the Ministers of Foreign Affairs and Oil of the Arab oil producing states. Any neutral country reclassified as friendly would receive the same quantities of oil as it imported in 1972, while re-export of oil from any country to a hostile state should be guarded against. In response to a decision of the OAU Ministerial Council held in Addis Ababa on November 21 and attended by 42 African countries,[26] the Arab Summit Conference decided also to impose an oil embargo against Portugal, South Africa, and Rhodesia.[27]

Subsequent to the Sixth Arab Summit Conference, Arab Oil Ministers convened in Kuwait and expressed a greater measure of flexibility. In their communiqué of December 8 they agreed to lift the oil embargo against the United States with the beginning of the implementation of a schedule of withdrawal of Israeli forces from Arab territories occupied since 1967. Furthermore, they decided that once a withdrawal schedule was reached, a schedule for the gradual return of oil production to its September 1973 level would be drawn up to go with the implementation of the stages of withdrawal. Supply of oil to "African countries and friendly Islamic States" was also to continue uninterrupted "to the extent that they have valid contracts even if it means an increase in production." These latter countries either had never established diplomatic relations with Israel or had severed such relations before or during the hostilities of October 1973 as an expression of support for the legitimacy of the Arab cause. African countries had further called upon all countries, Arab and non-Arab, to impose a total economic embargo and in particular an oil embargo against Israel, in the abovementioned decision of the OAU Ministerial Council.

Emphasizing that the use of oil by Arab states was an instrument of flexible persuasion meant only to ensure respect for the rules of interna-

[24] *Id.*, No. 5, Nov. 23, 1973, at 5. Iraq did not attend the meeting.

[25] Considering that oil prices (excluding dollar depreciation adjustments) have risen by 70 percent since 1972, this ceiling meant that oil producing Arab states could in fact reduce output to some 45 percent of the 1972 level before reaching the minimum 75 percent of 1972 revenue level. 17 MEES, No. 6, Nov. 30, 1973, at 1.

[26] OAU Doc., ECM/RES 21 (viii) Nov. 21, 1973.

[27] For an English translation of the Conference "Resolution on Oil," *see* 17 MEES, No. 6, Nov. 30, 1973, at 9. The Conference was attended by Heads of States of 16 Arab countries. Iraq and Libya were not represented, while Jordan sent a lower level delegation.

tional order in the Middle East, Arab Oil Ministers took further steps in their meeting in Kuwait on December 24–25 for the relaxation of oil production cutbacks. The 25 percent cutback was eased down to 15 percent of the September 1973 level of production with effect from January 1, 1974, while the extra 5 percent originally scheduled for January was dispensed with altogether. Japan, which had already issued two Foreign Ministry statements endorsing UN Security Council resolutions on the Middle East conflict, was allowed a "special treatment which would not subject it to the full extent of the across-the-board cutback measures." This was explicitly justified not only by "the change in Japan's policy towards the Arab cause," but also by "the deteriorating economic situation in Japan." It was also decided to resume oil supply to Belgium via Rotterdam, (up to the level of September 1973 imports) and to supply "certain friendly countries," presumably France, Britain, and Spain, with all their actual oil requirements even in excess of that level.[28] The embargo imposed against the Netherlands remained intact however, despite the earlier declaration of the Dutch Government spokesman on December 4 to the effect that his government "considers that the Israeli presence in occupied territories is illegal." [29] As for the United States, the Ministers' communiqué made a conciliatory gesture by expressing the hope that the "desire of the U.S. Government to participate in the search for a just and peaceful settlement of the problem will be fruitful and will lead to results beneficial to the peoples of the world and in particular to bilateral relations between the Arab and the American peoples."

This gesture was later followed by the much argued decision of Arab Oil Ministers, taken in Vienna on March 18, 1974, to lift the embargo of Arab oil to the United States, to treat both Italy and West Germany as "friendly countries," and to increase oil production in each Arab country to the extent needed to enable it to carry out that decision.[30]

As a result of the above decisions, countries importing Arab oil are, at the time of writing (May, 1974), classified as follows: [31]

(1). The "friendly states" which are allowed to import all their actual requirements of Arab oil;

(2). the "neutral states," including the United States, which are allowed to import the equivalent of their average imports of Arab oil during the

[28] *Id.*, No. 11, Jan. 4, 1974, at 1. [29] *Id.*, No. 7, Dec. 7, 1973, at 13.

[30] *Id.*, No. 22, March 22, 1974, at 1, 6. The Ministers' communiqué reiterated the "basic objective" of the Arab oil measures which is "to draw world attention to the Arab question in order to create an atmosphere conducive to the implementation of UN Security Council Resolution 242 calling for total withdrawal from the occupied Arab territories and the restoration of the legitimate rights of the Palestinian people" and referred to "the new direction" in American official policy toward the Arab-Israeli conflict. The communiqué provided however that the decision would be subject to review on June 1, 1974. Algeria expressed the view that the lifting of the embargo was "provisional in nature and limited to the period expiring 1 June 1974." Syria and Libya dissented to the decision altogether. *See* a translation of the text of the communiqué in *Ibid.*

[31] *Compare* a quadripartite classification in 17 *id.*, No. 11, Jan. 4, 1974, at 1.

first nine months of 1973 or during the month of September 1973, whichever is greater; and

(3). "the embargoed States," the Netherlands, South Africa, Portugal, and Rhodesia, whose supplies of Arab oil are cut off completely, (although in the case of the Netherlands, supplies are allowed for purposes of refining and re-exportation to nonembargoed countries).

Measures applied by Arab oil producing countries have thus included nationalization of foreign assets (in Iraq), reduction of oil production, discrimination in oil exports, and embargo of oil shipments to certain countries. The arguments for and against the validity of discriminatory and politically motivated nationalizations are well known.[32] The imposition of limitations on the production of primary commodities is, on the other hand, obviously within the exclusive domestic jurisdiction of sovereign states. Such limitations have, at any rate, been imposed in the past by two Arab states [33] as a conservation measure in respect of oil production, without invoking any international legal controversy. The discussion in this article will therefore concentrate on the legality of the embargo of Arab oil shipments to certain foreign states and the politically motivated discrimination in the export of Arab oil. Since these measures are intrinsically tied to the Middle East conflict, a discussion of certain legal aspects of that conflict seems inescapable in this respect.

II.

Illegality of Armed Israeli Presence on Egyptian and Syrian Territories

The legal complexities of the Arab-Israeli conflict are many.[34] Although their details do not fall within the scope of this article, one issue has to be clearly established as a basis for the reasoning that follows: Israel has no legal right under contemporary international law to the occupation and, a fortiori, to the annexation of the territories of Egypt and Syria which it has occupied by force since June 1967.[35]

[32] *See, e.g.,* 8 Whiteman, Digest of International Law 376–82 (1967); 3 Hackworth, Digest of International Law 555, 645 (1943); Fatouros, Government Guarantees to Foreign Investors 249–51 (1962); S. Friedman, Expropriation in International Law 189–93 (1953); Charpentier, *De la non-discrimination dans les investissements,* 9 Annuaire Français de Droit International 35–63 (1963).

[33] Kuwait limited the annual production of its crude oil to 3 million b/d as from 1972 (15 MEES, No. 25, April 14, 1972, at 12), while Libya introduced several successive cutbacks on the production of oil companies operating in its territory beginning in 1968 (12 *id.*, No. 4, Nov. 22, 1968), and continuing in 1970 (13 *id.*, No. 33, June 12, 1970) and in 1972 (15 *id.*, No. 19, March 3, 1972).

[34] For enumeration of such legal issues, *see* Quincy Wright, The Middle East: Prospects for Peace (1969); Quincy Wright, *Legal Aspects of the Middle East Situation,* 33 L. & Contemp. Prob. 24 (1968). *And see* a comprehensive, but partisan, discussion of these issues, in Martin, Le Conflit Israelo-Arabe (1973).

[35] Occupied Jordanian territory and the Gaza Strip are excluded from discussion only because of their irrelevance to the topic of this article.

Israel has not denied the sovereignty of Egypt over the Sinai Peninsula [36] or that of Syria over the Golan Heights. Both territories were outside the international boundaries of "Palestine" before the establishment of Israel and have been part of the respective territories of Egypt and Syria since their independence. Israel's claim to their occupation has thus been "justified" only by alleged considerations of security and less overtly by the desire to gain territorial advantages in future negotiations.[37] Such considerations are obviously of a political, not legal, character. Foreign military occupation, which "cannot displace or transfer sovereignty," [38] may not be legally based on mere allegations by the occupying power of its self-appreciated security requirements. The prohibition of the use of force as a means for the settlement of international disputes and in particular for acquisition of territory, which seems to constitute the cornerstone of contemporary international law,[39] would otherwise be meaningless. Several partisan writers have attempted, however, to find legal bases for Israel's political claims to the occupation and even to the annexation of territories of neighboring Arab states. Four main arguments have been advanced in this respect: [40]

(1). Israel, it is alleged, was in a state of self-defense when it invaded Arab territories in June 1967.[41] This is based either on the assumption that

[36] The shaky arguments presented in L. M. BLOOMFIELD, EGYPT, ISRAEL AND THE GULF OF AQABA IN INTERNATIONAL LAW (1957) and reproduced in STONE, THE MIDDLE EAST UNDER CEASE FIRE 13 (1967) and in BLUM, SECURE BOUNDARIES AND MIDDLE EAST PEACE 8 (1971), disputing the long established Egyptian title over Sinai, were wisely not quoted by responsible Israeli officials.

[37] *See, e.g.*, Israel's statement dated April 2, 1969 on its conception of secure and recognized boundaries in answer to Question No. 5 submitted by the UN Secretary-General's Special Representative, Ambassador Jarring, in UN Doc. S/10070, Annex 1, at 6; and its statement of February 26, 1971 in response to Ambassador Jarring's proposal of withdrawal of Israeli forces beyond the international boundaries of Egypt in UN Doc. S/10070, Add. 2, at 4. *And see* BLUM, *supra* note 36, at 63–70.

[38] MCNAIR, LEGAL EFFECTS OF WAR 320 (3rd ed., 1958) where this doctrine is described as "the most important principle of law incident to belligerent occupation." *See also*, CASTREN, THE PRESENT LAW OF WAR AND NEUTRALITY 215–16 (1954); DEBBASCH, L'OCCUPATION MILITAIRE 10 (1962).

[39] *See* the first principle in the UN General Assembly Declaration of Principles of International Law concerning Friendly Relations and Co-operation among States in accordance with the Charter of the United Nations, GAOR, 25th Sess., SUPP. No. 28 (A/8028): Resolution 2625, Oct. 24, 1970. *And see, e.g.*, BROWNLIE, INTERNATIONAL LAW AND THE USE OF FORCE BY STATES 410–23 (1963); JENNINGS, THE ACQUISITION OF TERRITORY IN INTERNATIONAL LAW (1963); Garner, *Non-Recognition of Illegal Territorial Annexation and Claims to Sovereignty,* 30 AJIL 679–88 (1936).

For international documents establishing the principle, *see* 5 WHITEMAN, DIGEST OF INTERNATIONAL LAW 847–965 (1965).

[40] For a discussion and refutation of other minor arguments such as alleged "acquisitive prescription" or "general recognition" *see* WRIGHT, THE MIDDLE EAST, *supra* note 34, at 22–23. The argument that international practice knows precedents for annexation of territories for the purpose of guaranteeing the security of certain states, presented in particular by BLUM, *supra* note 36, at 24–45, simply ignores the development of international law under the UN system.

[41] *See e.g.*, Higgins, *The June War, the U.N. and Legal Background,* 3 JOURNAL OF CONTEMPORARY HISTORY 271 (1968); STONE, NO PEACE—NO WAR IN THE MIDDLE

the measures taken by Egypt before that date (mainly its declaration on May 23, 1967 of the closure of the Straits of Tiran to Israeli shipping and its request for withdrawal of UN troops from Sharm El Sheikh) amounted in fact to an "armed attack" against Israel in the sense of Article 51 of the UN Charter,[42] or on the basis of the controversial theories of "anticipatory" [43] or even "interceptive" [44] self-defense. If such a "legitimate" exercise of force was so successful as to enable Israel to occupy vast territories of other states, it conferred on it, in that view, a right to continue its occupation of such territories until adequate security measures are instituted, and further gives it a better title to these territories, against their prior holder, to the extent that the holder had itself seized them unlawfully.[45] Territorial change could therefore properly result from the "lawful use of force" which is said to have been exerted by Israel in its invasion of Arab territories in 1967.[46] The alleged objective territorial title which vested in Israel as a result is thus based on the twofold assumption that Israel was exercising self-defense against states whose previous territorial sovereignty over the conquered areas was doubtful.

Such subjective assertions are not adequately substantiated by factual evidence. Despite initial claims to the contrary, it is now established beyond doubt that Israel initially attacked Egypt on June 5, 1967, that it continued its invasion of Egyptian, Syrian, and Jordanian territory until it achieved its war aims notwithstanding earlier appeals by the Security Council for a cease-fire, and that it has since refused to withdraw to the pre-June 5 lines.[47] Similar acts have been cited elsewhere as appropriate criteria for defining aggression, not self-defense.[48] The earlier Egyptian

---

EAST 39–40 (1969); ELIHU LAUTERPACHT, JERUSALEM AND THE HOLY PLACES 46 (Anglo-Israeli Association, Pamphlet No. 19, 1968); Schwebel, *What Weight to Conquest* 64 AJIL 344–47 (1970); Shapira, *The Six Day War and the Right of Self Defence* 6 ISRAEL L. REV. 65–80 (1971); MARTIN, *supra* note 34, at 153–70.

[42] *Id.*, at 165; Dinstein, *The Legal Issues of Para-War and Peace in the Middle East*, 44 ST. JOHN'S L. REV. 466 (1969–70).

[43] Schwebel, *supra* note 41, at 346. For the refutation of the doctrine of anticipatory self-defense, *see*, 2 OPPENHEIM, INTERNATIONAL LAW 156 (H. Lauterpacht ed., 7th ed., 1952); KELSEN, THE LAW OF THE UNITED NATIONS 269, 787–89 (1950); JESSUP, A MODERN LAW OF NATIONS 165–68 (1948); BROWNLIE, *supra* note 39, at 278; Brownlie, *The Use of Force in Self Defence*, 28 BYIL 232–47 (1961). *Compare* Schwebel, *Aggression, Intervention and Self-Defence in Modern International Law*, RECUEIL DES COURS 413, 478–83 (II, 1972).

And see an early insistence, on another occasion, by Israel's representative to the United Nations on the argument that self-defense presupposes an actual armed attack. In UN Security Council, Official Records, 6th Year, 551st Meeting, 10.

[44] Dinstein, *supra* note 42, at 466, 468–70.

[45] Schwebel, *supra* note 41, at 345–46.

[46] E. Lauterpacht, *supra* note 41, at 52; MARTIN, *supra* note 34, at 263. *And see* MEYROWITZ, LE PRINCIPE DE L'EGALITÉ DES BELLIGERENTS DEVANT LE DROIT DE LA GUERRE 296 *et seq.* (1970).

[47] For these developments see *Report of the Secretary-General presented pursuant to Security Council Resolution 331 (1973) dated 20 April 1973*, in UN Doc. S/10929, May 10, 1973.

[48] *See Report by the Secretary-General of the United Nations on the Question of Defining Aggression*, submitted to the General Assembly pursuant to its Resolution 599

acts, even if considered unjustified when taken, could not reasonably be construed as an actual "armed attack" that would justify Israel's resort to self-defense.[49] If, *arguendo,* Article 51 of the UN Charter were to be construed as extending the exercise of self-defense to response to measures which do not constitute "armed attack" and the Egyptian measures were such as to justify Israel's right to "anticipatory self defense," the exercise of such a right would not at any rate give rise to a subsequent right to occupation or annexation.[50] As the UN resolutions on this very matter have indicated, international law prohibits acquisition and occupation of territory by "war,"[51] "force,"[52] or "military conquest,"[53] not only by "aggression" or "aggressive conquests." The General Assembly Declaration of the Principles of International Law concerning Friendly Relations and Co-operation among States,[54] as well as its subsequent Declaration on the Strengthening of International Security,[55] both declare that the forcible military occupation of the territory of any state is inconsistent with international law. The Security Council's declarations of the "invalidity" of Israel's annexation of Arab Jerusalem[56] and the deliberate abstention of all states from recognizing such annexation further confirm the weakness of the counterargument which was meant in particular to defend that step.

(2). The Armistice Demarcation Lines, agreed upon between Israel and its neighboring states in 1949, were provisional in character and did not prejudice the rights of the parties in respect of the ultimate peaceful settlement of the Palestine question.[57] This valid statement was construed in the pro-Israel literature to mean that the pre-June 5, 1967 lines were not "secure and recognized boundaries" for Israel and did not constitute polit-

(VI), Jan. 21, 1952, in GAOR, 7th Sess. Annex. Agenda Item 54 UN Doc. A/2211, at 17–86, Oct. 3, 1952. *And see,* 5 WHITEMAN, *supra* note 39, at 719–873; Wright, *The Concept of Aggression in International Law,* 29 AJIL 873 (1953).

[49] Wright, *Legal Aspects of the Middle East Situation, supra* note 34, at 27.

[50] *Accord.* Wright, *id.,* at 24. *See also,* Falk, *Quincy Wright on Legal Tests of Aggressive War,* 66 AJIL 560, 566 n. 22 (1972). *And see,* JENNINGS, *supra* note 39, at 52–67.

[51] *See,* Security Council Res. No. 242, Nov. 22, 1967, UN Security Council Official Records, 22nd Year, RESOLUTION AND DECISIONS, at 8.

[52] *See,* UN G.A. Res. 2628 (XXV), Nov. 4, 1970, GAOR, 25th Sess., SUPP. No. 28 (A/8028), at 5; Res. 2799 (XXVI), Dec. 13, 1971, *id.,* 26th Sess., SUPP. No. 29 (A/8429), at 82; Res. 2949 (XXVII), Dec. 8, 1972, *id.,* 27th Sess. (A/4548) Part I, at 24. In the three above resolutions the illegality of occupation is properly considered a corollary of the illegality of annexation as "the acquisition of territories by force is inadmissible and . . . consequently territories thus occupied must be restored."

[53] *See,* UN Security Council Res. 252, May 21, 1968, UN Security Council Official Records, 23rd Year, RESOLUTIONS AND DECISIONS, 8–12; Res. 267, July 3, 1969, *id.,* 24th Year, 4; Res. 271, Sept. 15, 1969, *id.,* 5; Res. 298, Sept. 25, 1971, *id.,* 26th year, 6.

[54] UN G.A. Res. 2625(XXV), Oct. 24, 1970, GAOR, 25th Sess., SUPP. No. 28 at 122–24 (A/8028).

[55] UN G.A. Res. 2734(XXV), Dec. 16, 1970, *id.,* at 22–24.

[56] Referred to in note 53 *supra.*

[57] *See,* The General Armistice Agreement between Israel and Egypt, Feb. 24, 1949 (Art. IV (3)), 42 UNTS 251; between Israel and Lebanon, March 23, 1949, *id.,* 287; between Israel and Jordan, April 3, 1949 (Art. II (2)), *id.,* 303; and between Israel and Syria, July 20, 1949 (Art. II (2)), *id.,* 327.

ical frontiers immune from alterations that "would render them more secure from a strategic viewpoint."[58] Such assertions are not only in contravention of earlier Israeli official positions[59] but also ignore the important fact that, with the exception of the lines separating Israeli and Jordanian forces, most of the armistice lines coincided with previously established international boundaries. The Armistice Agreements themselves distinguished between two such types of line and carefully described the pre-established boundaries by their proper name. The explicit provisions of these agreements on the right of each party to assert territorial claims in the ultimate settlement were confined to claims on the territory of Palestine. As envisaged in 1949, the settlement of the "Palestine question" could not have included, by any stretch of imagination, reallocation of sovereignty over the territory of *other* Arab states in favor of Israel. Article IV(3) of the Egypt-Israel Armistice Agreement leaves no doubt in this respect as it recognizes the right of the parties to assert rights, claims, or interests of a nonmilitary character only *"in the area of Palestine covered by this Agreement."* In fact, the only demarcation line under that agreement which was not part of the "Egyptian frontiers" was that which separated the Gaza Strip from the Israeli-held territory. That line was defined in the Agreement (Article VI(1)) in connection with "the Egyptian frontier." The delimitation of the demilitarized zone (Article VIII(2)) as well as the withdrawal of Egyptian forces from Al-Faluja area (Article III(2)) were also described in terms of "the Egypt-Palestine frontier." Likewise, Article V(3) of the Israel-Syria Armistice Agreement explicitly provided that "where the existing truce lines run along the international boundary between Syria and Palestine, the Armistice Demarcation Line shall follow the boundary line."

The provisional character of the armistice lines could not in any case have conferred on Israel lawful sovereignty over territories to which it was not otherwise legally entitled, even within the former boundaries of mandated Palestine. The boundaries of the "Jewish State" adopted by the UN General Assembly in 1947,[60] which are still "the only generally recognized boundaries for Israel,"[61] included in fact only about two-thirds of the area which became subject to Israel's control after the 1949 armistices. Israel's expansion beyond the 1947 lines was itself an incident of its military successes in the 1948 war. The provisional character of the armistice lines should therefore have inspired, as it did in 1949, a return to the lines of the 1947 Partition Plan, not further expansion beyond the armistice lines. State-

[58] BLUM, *supra* note 36, at 23. *See also* MARTIN, *supra* note 34, at 280–81.

[59] *See, e.g.,* Statements of Israel's Permanent Representative to United Nations before the Security Council during discussion of Israel's complaint concerning passage through the Suez Canal, UN Security Council Official Records, 6th Year, 549th Meeting, at 2–7 (July 23, 1951). *And see generally,* FEINBERG, THE LEGALITY OF A STATE OF WAR AFTER CESSATION OF HOSTILITIES 36 (1951).

[60] Resolution 81(II), Nov. 29, 1947, GAOR, 2nd Sess., RESOLUTIONS, 31–50, UN Doc. A/519.

[61] Wright, *The Middle East Problem,* 64 AJIL 270, 277 (1970).

ments of Israeli officials issued after the conclusion of the Armistice Agreements confirmed that understanding.[62] The Israeli Government also accepted, in the Protocol of Lausanne of May 12, 1949, the use of a map of Palestine identical to the UN Partition Plan as the "basis for discussion" of the ultimate settlement [63] on the recommendation of the UN Conciliation Commission.[64] Even when Israel changed its attitude during the Lausanne negotiations of 1949, it did not extend its ambitious territorial claims beyond the territory of mandated Palestine. It suggested, on the contrary, the exclusion of "the middle area of Palestine under Jordanian occupation," *i.e.*, the West Bank, from its immediate claims.[65] Israel's insistence at that time on new claims beyond the previously agreed-upon basis of the discussions was indeed the blow which brought negotiations to a halt. It was that attitude, perhaps more than any other factor, which reinforced the spirit of mistrust prompting Arab Governments to adopt in subsequent years a negative position towards further negotiations on the subject.

(3). Security Council Resolution 242 of 1967 [66] was repeatedly described by Israeli writers as merely a recommendation.[67] Doubts on the binding character of that resolution have probably been erased, however, by the text of Security Council Resolution 338 (1973) [68] which was equally "accepted" by Israel.

The meaning attributed to Resolution 242 in the standard pro-Israel argument is that it does not require withdrawal of Israeli forces from all Arab occupied territories but requires withdrawal only to such lines as would constitute "secure boundaries" for Israel.[69] Such an interpretation is based *first* on a certain reading of the English text of the resolution which affirmed that a just and lasting peace in the Middle East should include the application of the principle of "*withdrawal of Israeli forces from territories*

[62] *See, e.g.*, UN Doc. A/AC. 24/SR. 45–48, 50–51, May 5–9, 1949. And see earlier and more explicit statements of Israeli representatives in UN, GAOR, 3rd Sess., Pt. 1, 1st Comm., 640–43, 644–45, 832, 840–42.

[63] *See*, UN GAOR, 3rd Sess., Ad hoc Political Committee, Annex, vol. II, at 5, 8–9, UN Doc. A/927, June 21, 1949.

[64] *Ibid.*

[65] *Id.*, Supp. 18, at 3–4, 19–21, UN Doc. A/1367/Rev. 1 (1950).

[66] Res. No. 242, Nov. 22, 1967, UN Doc. S/PV 1382, at 36; UN Security Council Official Records, 22nd Year, Resolutions and Decisions at 8.

[67] *E.g.*, Blum, *supra* note 36, at 63, Dinstein, *supra* note 42, at 477, Shapira, *supra* note 41, at 235, 236; Rosenne, *Directions for a Middle East Settlement—Some Underlying Legal Problems*, 33 L. & Contem. Prob. 44, 57 (1968); Lapidoth, *La résolution du Conseil de Sécurité en date 22 Novembre 1967 au sujet du Moyen Orient*, 74 Rev. Gén. Dr. Int. Public 289, 292–4 (1970).

[68] S/Res./338 adopted by the Council in its 1747th Session, October 21/22, 1973. In paragraph 2, the Security Council "*calls* upon the parties concerned to start immediately after the cease-fire the implementation of Security Council Resolution 242 in all of its parts."

[69] *E.g.*, Blum, *supra* note 36, at 72–79; Lapidoth, *supra* note 67, at 300–01; Rosenne, *supra* note 67, at 60. *See also* Stone, *The "November Resolution" and Middle East Peace: Pitfall or Guidepost?*, University of Toledo L. Rev., Nos. 1 and 2, at 43 (1970); E. V. Rostow, *Legal Aspects of the Search for Peace in the Middle East*, Proc. Amer. Soc. Int. L., 64 AJIL, No. 4, 64, 69 (1970).

occupied in the recent conflict" (and not explicitly from *all the* said territories). It is based secondly on the resolution's provision for the right of each state in the area to live in peace *"within secure and recognized boundaries free from threats or acts of force,"* a description which could not apply—says the argument—to the pre-June 5, 1967 lines.

The resolution, it is true, does not use the definite article in the withdrawal paragraph, but it amply describes the territories from which withdrawal is required as being those "occupied in the recent conflict" without any exception. Insistence on the relevance of the absence of the definite article in this respect would lead to the absurd conclusion that some Israeli forces could be maintained in any territories from which withdrawal is accomplished, as the resolution fails also to provide for withdrawal of *"all the"* Israeli forces from such territories.

The United Nations itself has understood the resolution to mean withdrawal for *all* occupied territories, as is evident from the language of the other official texts of the resolution [70] and from the subsequent resolutions of the General Assembly on the subject.[71] Other states and international organizations have also expressed on several occasions their understanding that the resolution requires "total withdrawal" and have called upon Israel to withdraw accordingly. Not less than thirty-five states have in fact severed their diplomatic relations with Israel because of the latter's failure to conform to that understanding. Even the United States, the real power behind the failure of the Security Council to adopt a stronger decision against Israel,[72] has indicated, through its former Secretary of State, that any alterations in the former armistice lines "should not reflect the weight of conquest." [73] The absurdity of the counterargument is demonstrated in fact by its insistence, against the consensus of the international community, on tying the destiny of sovereign states, their history, and geography, to the absence of a definite article which is not even needed grammatically to convey the required comprehensive meaning.

[70] See, e.g., the French text: *"Retrait des forces armées israeliennes des territoires occupés lors du recent conflit;"* and the Spanish text *"Retiro des las fuerzas armadas isralies de los territorios que ocuparon durente el reciento conflicto,"* UN Doc. S/INF. 22/REV. 2, at 4. Since the English text does not mean partial withdrawal there is no room for the argument that in case of conflict between the texts in different languages the one which was submitted to the vote prevails, or for the argument, advanced by MARTIN, *supra* note 34, at 256, that partial withdrawal is the common meaning in all texts.

[71] *See* resolutions referred to in note 52, *supra*.

[72] For a detailed account, *see,* LALL, THE UN AND THE MIDDLE EAST CRISIS, 1967, at 230–73 (1968).

[73] Text of Address of Mr. William Rogers, Dec. 9, 1969, *U.S. Mission to the U.N., Press Release* 371, Dec. 9, 1969; 62 DEPT. STATE BULL. 7 (1970). Mr. Rogers indicated that only "insubstantial alterations" may be introduced to ensure mutual security. Such alterations would be based, however, on the acceptance of the parties, not merely on the language of the Security Council resolution. *See also,* Wright *Legal Aspects of the Middle East Situation, supra* note 34, at 24; Wright, *The Middle East Problem, supra* note 61, at 274–75; Falk, *The Beirut Raid and the International Law of Retaliation,* 63 AJIL 415, 435, n. 55 (1969).

Withdrawal from occupied territories should not at any rate be mixed with the establishment of secure boundaries. The resolution requires withdrawal *from* occupied territories and not *to* secure boundaries. The purpose of withdrawal is indeed the restoration of the *status quo ante,* while the establishment of secure and recognized boundaries aims at the creation of a *status juris* which understandably cannot admit the forcible acquisition by one party of territory over which it does not otherwise have a valid title. In this, the Security Council resolution may have been generous with Israel, as noted by Quincy Wright,[74] since it did not extend the withdrawal paragraph to all the territories over which Israel lacked an established legal title. The resolution indicates, however, in no less than four places, that the creation of secure boundaries cannot result in the forcible acquisition of territory. It emphasizes in its preamble "the inadmissibility of the acquisition of territory by war." It also emphasizes the commitment of all UN members to act in accordance with Article 2 of the Charter which recognizes the sovereign equality of states and prohibits the threat or the use of force in the settlement of international disputes. In its operative paragraphs the resolution calls for "the respect for and acknowledgment of the sovereignty, territorial integrity and political independence of every State in the area." It also affirms the necessity for guaranteeing "the territorial inviolability" of every state in the area. To say that the proper application of such language should result in the forcible occupation or annexation of Arab territories by Israel, because the pre-June 5 lines did not satisfy its self-appreciated security requirements, is, to say the least, an anomaly in reading the text which goes beyond a partisan *petiti principii.*

One may finally wonder, in the light of the more recent events of October 1973, whether the pre-June 5 lines were in fact less secure than any other possible frontiers for Israel. The lines, which were accused in the popular argument of failing to prevent three previous wars, did not exist in fact at the time of the first of these wars and were crossed and successfully conquered, in 1956 and 1967, by the Israeli, not the Arab, armed forces. Since their establishment in 1949, they have never been crossed in the opposite direction by regular forces under the authority of Arab states. When these lines were replaced by the "natural barriers" reached in 1967, Israel proved, despite its own security theories, less successful in "defending" the new lines. Once again the quest for secure boundaries seemed to require a search for proper guarantees and arrangements which would ensure their continuity and stability, instead of providing an excuse for geographical expansion.[75] The falsity of such an excuse, one may notice, is particularly

[74] Wright, *The Middle Eastern Crisis,* PROC. AMER. SOC. INT. L., 64 AJIL, No. 4, 71, 78 (1970).

[75] The history of Resolution 242 further confirms this truth. The phrase "secure and recognized boundaries" in the British draft was taken from the earlier U.S. draft submitted to the Security Council on November 7, 1967 (UN Doc., S/8229). Security in boundaries was envisaged by the sponsors of the latter draft as a condition in the *arrangements* to be adopted, not in the geographic location, as is evident in the draft resolution submitted by the United States on June 20, 1967 to the General Assembly

proved by the fact that the part of the occupied territories which has actually been annexed by Israel, *i.e.* Arab Jerusalem, is by no means an Israeli security issue.

(4). Some Israeli writers, while expressing respect for the principle of inadmissibility of acquisition of territory by war, have indicated that such a principle does not prohibit acquisition of territory by cession, *i.e.*, by an agreement between the victorious state and its occupied enemy.[76] In this argument, inadmissibility of annexation does not entail inadmissibility of occupation. On the contrary, it gives the victorious state the right to maintain control of the occupied territories until an agreement is reached with the former sovereign by means of which the latter relinquishes its rights and cedes them to the occupant power. In practical terms this view can have but one of two results: The occupant power may use its military occupation as an instrument of pressure and coercion to gain territorial concessions from the occupied country or, failing this, it may extend its occupation indefinitely. In both situations, the very principle of inadmissibility of acquisition of territory by war will definitely be sacrificed. The law which prohibits forcible annexation cannot therefore tolerate forcible occupation. Resolutions of the UN General Assembly have thus stipulated that the territory of a state should not be the object of *occupation or acquisition* by another state resulting from the threat or use of force,[77] and have explicitly considered the restoration of occupied territories a natural sequence of the inadmissibility of acquisition of territory by force.[78]

An agreement reached under alien military occupation through which an occupied sovereign state is forced to relinquish part of its territory is likely at any rate to be deemed null under modern international law. If not vitiated by coercion,[79] it would violate a *jus cogens* principle of the highest international order [80] and could be considered as inconsistent with the UN Charter and the Declaration of Principles of International Law concerning Friendly Relations and Co-operation among States.[81] The remote possibil-

---

(UN Doc., A/L 520). According to the last draft the proposed settlement was thus to include "recognized boundaries and *other arrangements that will give them security* against terror, destruction and war." (Emphasis added).

[76] *See, e.g.,* Blum, *supra* note 36, at 84, Rosenne, *supra* note 67, at 59; Lapidoth, *supra* note 67, at 295–96.

[77] *See* resolutions referred to in notes 52, 54, 55, *supra.*

[78] Res. 2628(XXV), Res. 2799 (XXVI), and Res. 2949(XXVII) referred to in note 52, *supra.*

[79] *Compare* Art. 52 of the Vienna Convention on the Law of Treaties opened for signature from May 23, 1969 until November 30, 1969 (UN Doc., A/CONF. 39/27, May 23, 1969). *And see,* 1 OPPENHEIM, *supra* note 43, at 891–92; MCNAIR, THE LAW OF TREATIES 213–17 (1961); H. LAUTERPACHT, RECOGNITION IN INTERNATIONAL LAW 426, 429 (1947).

[80] *Compare* Art. 53 of the Vienna Convention, *supra* note 79. *And see,* McNair, *supra* note 79, at 213–17; BROWNLIE, PRINCIPLES OF PUBLIC INTERNATIONAL LAW 417–18 (1966); Verdross, *Jus Dispositivum and Jus Cogens in International Law,* 60 AJIL 55, 60 (1966).

[81] *See* in particular Art. 2(4) of the UN Charter and Principle I of the abovementioned Declaration, Res. No. 2625(XXV), Annex.

ity of reaching such an agreement could not therefore provide a valid pretext for continuing the military occupation of a territory against the will of its proper sovereign.

The case for the legality of Israel's forcible occupation and annexation of territories of neighboring Arab states was obviously presented to promote the short term political ends of Israel without regard to the advancement of *lex lata* international law or the purposes of the United Nations. Such a case can hardly serve the legitimate interests of other members of the international community, and fails to promote a settlement of the Arab-Israeli conflict just to both sides. It remains therefore void of the moral value which may have otherwise justified it *de lege ferenda.*

Egypt and Syria as the states vested with sovereignty, but illegally deprived of actual control, over territories occupied by Israel were thus entitled to seek redress for the protection of their territorial integrity. Under the UN system they were probably under the obligation to resort first to peaceful methods. This they have done in vain for more than six years. Egypt, in particular, expressed officially [82] its readiness to enter into a peace agreement with Israel containing all the obligations provided for in Security Council Resolution 242(1967) as broadly elaborated by the Special Representative of the UN Secretary-General.[83] In response, Israel defiantly insisted on territorial expansion.[84]

With such an intransigent Israeli position, encouraged in fact by the near total support of the U.S. Government and by the acquiescence of most other Western powers, little choice was left for Arab states to regain control over their occupied territories. Egypt and Syria finally managed, in October 1973, to exercise their territorial jurisdiction by employing forcible measures limited respectively to Egyptian and Syrian territories and aimed solely at restoring control over such territories. Governmental action taken by a state within its own territory for the restoration of legal order disrupted by unauthorized acts of others certainly falls within the inherent territorial jurisdiction of each sovereign state. Although such action may be based on the exercise of the state's traditional right to self-help under customary international law [85] or under a broad reading of the UN Charter

[82] *See, Aide-Memoire presented to Ambassador Jarring by the United Arab Republic (now the Arab Republic of Egypt) on 15 February 1971,* UN Doc. S/10929, Annex III, at 1–2.

[83] *See, Aide-Memoire presented to Israel and the United Arab Republic by Ambassador Jarring on 8 February 1971, id.,* Annex II, at 1–2.

[84] *See, Communication presented to Ambassador Jarring by Israel on 26 February 1971, id.,* Annex IV, at 1–2. In item 4 of that communication, it is bluntly stated that "Israel will not withdraw to the pre-5 June 1967 lines."

[85] *See, e.g.,* Lillich, *Forcible Self-Help under International Law,* 22 NAVAL WAR COLL. REV. 56 (1970), where he refers also to a lecture given by Professor McDougal in 1968 in which the latter came to the conclusion that "in the absence of collective machinery to protect people against attack and deprivation . . . the principle of major purposes requires an interpretation which would honor self-help against a prior unlawfulness." *Id.,* at 65.

provisions on self-defense,[86] one need not argue the relevance of such concepts in regard to the Egyptian and Syrian measures. The denial to Egypt and Syria, in the particular circumstances of the situation, of the right to take individual or collective action would have resulted in fact in depriving them indefinitely of their essential right to territorial integrity, guaranteed by the UN Charter.[87] Without such a right, state jurisdiction, let alone sovereignty, would be nothing but a sham. This obviously explains the fact that not a single state or international organization has characterized the Egyptian and Syrian measures of October 1973 as illegal or even unwarranted.

Whether these two states and the other Arab states bound with them by regional arrangements including mutual defense pacts [88] were entitled to use against third states such economic measures as those explained in detail in the previous section of this paper is a different question, however. The fact that such measures were taken on the whole as a complementary step in the legitimate struggle of Arab states to regain control of occupied Arab territories and to reach a final peaceful settlement of the Middle East conflict is of great relevance. It remains to be proved, however, that the use of such measures by the Arab states applying them did not constitute a violation of general principles of customary international law or a breach of specific treaty commitments.

III.

Legality of Arab Oil Measures under Customary International Law

In applying the standards of customary international law to the measures adopted by Arab oil exporting countries the following points should be taken into consideration:

(1). The measures in question were initiated at a time when many of the states applying them were in an actual situation of war—Egypt and Syria as the major belligerents against Israel, with Iraq, Kuwait, and to a lesser extent, Algeria and Saudi Arabia as cobelligerents with them. This war situation was prompted, as shown above, by Israel's insistence on the forcible occupation of Egyptian and Syrian territories and the attempt by Egypt and Syria to regain control over their occupied territories after exhaustion of peaceful means to achieve that result.

[86] That is, a reading which considers a continued forcible occupation following an armed intervention a prolonged "armed attack" under Article 51 of the Charter.

[87] Using the above argument in what is submitted to be the wrong context, Elihu Lauterpacht adds: "For if force can never be used to effect lawful territorial change, then, if territory has once changed hands as a result of an unlawful use of force, the illegitimacy of the position thus established is sterilized by the prohibition upon the use of force to restore the lawful sovereign." E. Lauterpacht, *supra* note 41, at 52.

[88] All Arab states are members of the Joint Arab Defense Council, an organ of the Arab League. For an English translation of some relevant inter-Arab joint military pacts, *see*, 2 Khalil, The Arab States and the Arab League. A Documentary Record. International Affairs 101–05, 242–45, 250–53 (1962).

(2). The use of the measures was clearly tied, as shown above, to the achievement of the twofold objective of "withdrawal of Israeli forces from occupied Arab territories and restoration of the legitimate rights of the Palestinian people." They were aimed, in other words, at the establishment of two of the basic requirements of a lasting peace in the Middle East.

(3). The measures were also in complete conformity with the economic interests of the states applying them. As explained earlier, these measures meant, in fact, the termination by Arab oil exporting states of the practice of doing favors for countries whose foreign policy made them unworthy, in Arab eyes, of receiving such favors. Yet in taking these measures Arab states showed consideration for the welfare of the countries particularly affected, such as Japan, and modified their position towards them accordingly.

(4). The measures were taken, on the whole, pursuant to resolutions of the Oil Ministers of the states members of the Organization of Arab Petroleum Exporting Countries (OAPEC). With the exception of the "Resolution on Oil" issued by the Sixth Summit Arab Conference on 28 November, 1973,[89] such measures were adopted in meetings which were sponsored by OAPEC and were chaired in each case by the Minister from the country whose representative assumed chairmanship of the meetings of OAPEC's organs in each particular month. It is not clear, however, whether these resolutions should be treated as resolutions of OAPEC's Council of Ministers, or merely as the result of ad hoc meetings of the Ministers of Oil of member countries in their respective capacities. The OAPEC's Secretariat has not officially published them as resolutions of the organization. The "Resolution on Oil" issued by the Arab Summit Conference, on the other hand, is legally attributable to the League of Arab States. The Conference is the highest political organ of the League.

Identification of the standards of customary international law according to which the legality of the measures in question are to be tested requires a detailed scrutiny of state practice in the matter of the political uses of export controls. These standards will further be clarified by reference to the practice of those international organizations which have considered such uses, either by authorizing them in individual cases or by issuing general statements on the extent of their legitimacy.

A. STATE PRACTICE IN PEACETIME CONDITIONS

(1) *U.S. Practice.*

Special export controls over individual commodities have been long imposed by U.S. legislation for economic and strategic reasons.[90] General

[89] *See, supra,* note 27.

[90] *See,* e.g., The United States Shipping Act of 1916, as amended, 46 U.S.C. §808, 835, 46 C.F.R. §221.5 *et seq.* (sale and transfer to foreign registry of vessels owned by

U.S. export controls may be said to have begun, however, in 1940, as measures of national defense and economic warfare.[91] Such controls continued to apply after the termination of World War II, resulting in fact in the embargo on shipments of a great number of articles to a wide range of countries. Around the turn of the year 1947, the U.S. Administration began to revive some war regulations and to use them for control of exports to the Soviet bloc. By 1948 most exports to the Soviet Union and Eastern Europe were thus placed under control "in the interest of security." [92] This practice was further formalized in 1949 by the adoption of the Export Control Act which bluntly stated it to be U.S. policy to use export controls, *inter alia,* "to further the foreign policy of the United States." [93] According to that Act, the President of the United States was authorized to "prohibit or curtail the exportation from the United States, its territories and possessions of any articles, materials, or supplies . . . except under such rules and regulations as he shall prescribe." [94] Pursuant to the Act, such rules and regulations were to provide for the denial of any request for authority to export U.S. commodities "to any nation or combination of nations threatening the national security of the United States if the President shall determine that such exports make a significant contribution to the military or economic potential of such nation or nations which could prove detrimental to the national security and welfare of the United States." The Export Regulations actually issued under that Act had a wide extraterritorial effect.[95] They contained a detailed licensing system which required "validated licenses" for certain goods and "general licenses" for others and discriminated between different countries of destination.[96] A sophisticated system of discrimination developed accordingly, culminating in the classification of foreign destinations (excepting Canada) into eight

---

US citizens); the Act of October 6, 1917, 12 U.S.C. §95a, 95b; 31 C.F.R. §54.1 *et seq.* and the Gold Reserve Act of 1934, 31 U.S.C. §440 (export of gold); the Natural Gas Act of 1938, 15 U.S.C. §717b; 18 C.F.R. §153.1 *et seq.* (export of natural gas) The Tobacco Seed and Plant Exportation Act of 1940; 7 U.S.C. §576 (export of tobacco seed and live tobacco plants); the Agricultural Trade Development and Assistance Act of 1954, 7 U.S.C. §1691 *et seq.;* 68 Stat. 454 (export of subsidized U.S. agricultural commodities to the Sino-Soviet bloc); the Atomic Energy Act of 1954, 42 U.S.C. §2011 (export of atomic materials, facilities) etc.

[91] *See* Act of July 2, 1940, 54 Stat. 712, 714 (1940), as amended, 50 U.S.C. App. §701 (expired). For a historical account *see, Comment, Export Controls,* 58 YALE L.J. 1325 (1951).

[92] THE STRATEGIC TRADE CONTROL SYSTEM 1948–1956, Dept. of State, Ninth Report to Congress (1957) on Operations under the Mutual Defense Assistance Control Act of 1951, at 4–5 (excerpt republished in METZGER, LAW OF INTERNATIONAL TRADE. DOCUMENTS AND READINGS 1047, 1051 (1966)).

[93] The Export Control Act of 1949, Section 2, 19 U.S.C. §2021 (1949) as extended and amended by Public Law 89-63, 89th Cong.

[94] *Id.,* Sec. 3 (a).

[95] *See,* Silverstone, *The Export Control Act of 1949: Extraterritorial Enforcement,* 108 U.P.L.R. 337–43 (1959).

[96] *See,* SURREY AND SHAW (eds.), A LAWYER'S GUIDE TO INTERNATIONAL BUSINESS TRANSACTIONS 56–85 (1963).

groups, each with a different export control treatment.[97] A complete embargo of U.S. exports to the People's Republic of China, Hong Kong, and Macao was imposed on December 3, 1950 and continued in operation for over twenty years, while a similar embargo imposed on exports to Cuba on October 19, 1960 remains, with a few exceptions, in effect at the present time.[98]

Even when the Export Control Act of 1949 was finally replaced by the Export Administration Act of 1969 (in effect since January 1, 1970),[99] the latter Act, described as "the first significant trade liberalization measure passed by Congress since the end of World War II,"[100] maintained the President's power to prohibit the export of materials under such rules and regulations as he may prescribe. This extensive power was again based on the declared policy to preserve "the national security" and to "further significantly the foreign policy of the United States and to fulfil its international responsibilities." As a result, many of the regulations adopted under the 1949 Act, including the grouping of countries of destination, remain in full force.[101]

This discriminatory trade control system is further reinforced by the Mutual Defense Assistance Act of 1951, commonly called the Battle Act.[102] In this Act the policy of the United States is stated to include an embargo on the shipment of a host of strategic supplies, *including petroleum,* to "nations threatening United States security, including the USSR and all countries under its domination." Such a legislatively sanctioned embargo is unabashedly stated to be imposed in order to "(1) increase the material strength of the United States and of the cooperating nations; (2) impede the ability of nations threatening the security of the United States to conduct military operations, and (3) to assist the people of the nations under the domination of foreign aggressors to reestablish their freedom." A classified list of items embargoed under the provisions of Title I of the Act was thus established and remains, after many amendments, in force to this date. Further steps were also adopted under the Act to strengthen and adjust the control of the export of other commodities which called for a lesser degree of control than outright embargo.[103]

[97] For these groups, *see* EXPORT CONTROL, 99th Rep., 1st Quarter 1972, by the Secretary of Commerce to the President, the Senate and the House of Representatives, 2–3. *And see* a description of an earlier classification in Metzger, *Federal Regulation and Prohibition of Trade with Iron-Curtain Countries,* 29 LAW & CONTEM. PROB. 1000, 1001 (1964).

[98] For a critical detailed account of these measures, *see* ADLER-KARLSSON, WESTERN ECONOMIC WARFARE 1947–1967—A CASE STUDY IN FOREIGN ECONOMIC POLICY, particularly at 201, 210 (Stockholm Economic Studies, New Series IX, 1968).

[99] 50 U.S.C. App. §§2401 *et seq.* as extended by Senate Joint Resolution 218, April 29, 1972, Public Law 92–284, 92nd Congress.

[100] Statement of Senator Mondale of Minnesota as quoted in, Berman, *The Export Administration Act of 1969: Analysis and Appraisal,* 3 AMER. REV. OF EAST-WEST TRADE 19 (Jan., 1970).

[101] *See* EXPORT CONTROL, *supra* note 97, at 1.

[102] 22 U.S.C. S1611 *et seq.;* 65 Stat. 644 (1951), as amended by 75 Stat. 424, approved Sept. 4, 1961.

[103] See, THE STRATEGIC TRADE CONTROL SYSTEM 1948–1956, *supra* note 92, at 11–14.

(2) *Practice of other States, including the Netherlands.*

(a) *Multilateral measures: Internationalization of the U.S. discriminatory practice:* Since the beginning of the implementation of its export control system, the U.S. Government has attempted to increase its effectiveness by securing similar action by other countries. It has succeeded in achieving this objective by two means. First, the United States put economic pressure on the countries which received assistance from it by relating, in the Cannon Amendment,[104] the Kem Amendment[105] and the Battle Act,[106] American foreign aid to export control action by the recipient countries against the Sino-Soviet bloc.[107] Secondly, it negotiated with other Western countries, first on a bilateral basis, then multilaterally, the establishment of strategic export controls on the pattern of the U.S. system. Early in 1949 the United Kingdom and France formulated an Anglo-French list of strategic items which was similar to the U.S. lists prepared earlier for the same purpose. Later in November of that year a Consultative Group was founded in Paris by the United Kingdom, France, Italy, the Netherlands, Belgium, Luxembourg, and the United States which was joined on later dates by Norway, Denmark, Canada, the Federal Republic of Germany, Portugal, Greece, Turkey, and Japan. Members of the Group formulated three lists of controlled goods covering items for embargo, for quantitative control, and for exchange of information and surveillance.[108] Thus, a detailed multilateral export control program was developed by fifteen Western states with a permanent organization and agreed lists continually updated by the "Coordinating Committee" and the "China Committee" in accordance with criteria for adding, deleting, upgrading, and downgrading the items involved. The objectives of such a multilateral system were identical to those of the U.S. program and, as in that program, more restrictive controls were applied to exports to China, North Korea, and North Vietnam.[109]

It should be particularly recalled that the countries which were intended to be adversely affected by such multilateral measures in many cases maintained normal diplomatic relations with the states applying those measures. The countries affected have not helped directly or indirectly in maintaining forcible occupation of American or Western European territories. Nor have they been involved in any manner in depriving the peoples of the United States or of the other cooperating Western nations of their right to self-determination. Some of the affected countries were accused, however, at the time of the Korean War, (December 17, 1950) of providing military assistance to regimes with which U.S. forces were involved in armed hostilities. Only North Korea and North Vietnam could be said to have been

[104] Sec. 1304 of Public Law 843, effective Sept. 27, 1950.

[105] Sec. 1302 of Public Law 45, effective June 2, 1951.

[106] Sec. 103(b), 104 and 105, 202 and 203 of the Mutual Defense Assistance Control Act of 1951, *supra* note 102.

[107] For the effect on the 61 countries then receiving military, economic, or financial assistance from the United States, *see* METZGER, *supra* note 92, at 1066.

[108] *See, id.*, at 1064.

[109] For further details, *id.*, at 1066–79.

engaged in armed conflict with the United States during part of the period in which shipment of all American and West European strategic goods to these two countries was officially embargoed.

(b) *Domestic legislation:* The imposition of export control regulations and discrimination in their application to different countries of destination by no means constitute isolated instances in state practice. Although such regulations are often meant to serve economic purposes, they have been widely used as instruments of foreign policy to secure political advantages for the states applying them, such as the denial to unfriendly countries of badly needed strategic goods. Thus, the European countries cooperating with the United States in the implementation of the multilateral program met with no difficulty in finding a basis in their own domestic legal systems for such a practice. A report submitted to the U.S. Congress in 1962 on export controls in six European countries, including the Netherlands, found that each of the six countries "maintains substantially the same controls on strategic exports to countries of the Sino-Soviet bloc" as those imposed by the United States.[110] It further confirmed that "controls over exports of goods on the international embargo list . . . are carried out through their own laws and regulations." [111]

In the Netherlands, the embargo of strategic goods to such destinations as the Sino-Soviet bloc was executed under an export prohibition law issued in 1935 along with some other supporting wartime regulations.[112] In 1962 a new law on foreign trade [113] was issued and further formalized the Dutch participation in the Western embargo policy, which, it is reported, was never officially treated in the parliamentary debates required by that law as to all import and export regulations.[114]

The politically inspired export control of strategic goods may even be traced in such countries as Sweden and Switzerland.[115] It is, of course, a general practice in the Soviet Union [116] and, one may safely assume, in other Socialist countries where the government exercises a monopoly over foreign

[110] *See*, REPORT ON EXPORT CONTROLS IN THE U.K., FRANCE, ITALY, FEDERAL REPUBLIC OF GERMANY, BELGIUM AND THE NETHERLANDS, submitted by Senator Thomas J. Dodd and Senator Kenneth B. Keating to the Sub-Comm. to Investigate the Administration of the Internal Security Act and other Internal Security Laws of the Senate Comm. on the Judiciary. 87th Cong. 2nd Sess., April 4, 1962 at 12.

[111] *Ibid.* Reference in the Report is made in particular to Law of June 30, 1931, modified by Law of July 10, 1934, and Decree of January 17, 1955, in *Belgium;* Decree of November 30, 1944 in *France;* Foreign Trade Circular No. 89154 in *Germany;* and Tabella Esport dated July 22, 1957, amended on August 13, 1960, in *Italy.* No mention is made in the Report, however, of the *U.K.*'s Import, Export and Customs Powers (Defence) Act 1939 or, quite obviously, of the Export of Goods (Control) order 1967 which was issued pursuant to the 1939 Act after the date of the Report. For text *see* S.I. 1967 No. 675 reprinted in SCHMITTHOFF, THE EXPORT TRADE 429–33 (5th ed., 1969). The Dutch Laws of 1935 and 1962, referred to *infra,* are also not mentioned in the Report.

[112] *See,* ADLER-KARLSSON, *supra* note 98, at 68.

[113] STAATSBLAD, No. 295.

[114] *See* ADLER-KARLSSON, at 68.

[115] *Id.,* at 75–77.

[116] *See, e.g.,* ALLEN, SOVIET ECONOMIC WARFARE (1960).

trade. A list of the "Laws and Regulations relating to Control of Import and Export Trade in Member Countries" of the Asian-African Legal Consultative Committee also confirms that such restrictive practices have found their way into the legal systems of developing countries.[117] In short, as Adler-Karlsson concluded in his exhaustive study of the subject, "the embargo policy has been world-wide." [118]

B. STATE PRACTICE IN TIME OF WAR

The right of a belligerent state to resort to measures of economic warfare against its adversary and to apply economic sanctions against third states which violate their obligations of neutrality in this regard is so manifest that elaborate treatment is unnecessary. It should be pointed out, however, that neutral states (such as the United States and the Netherlands supposedly were during the Arab-Israeli hostilities of October 1973) are under the obligation of acting towards belligerents in accordance with their attitude of impartiality. This means, in particular, abstention from "the supply in any manner, directly or indirectly, by a neutral Power to a belligerent Power, of warships, ammunition or war material of any kind whatever." [119] It means also that a neutral power should not allow a belligerent to transport war materials or supplies over its territory.[120] As the Dutch Government itself admitted in the course of World War I, a neutral state is bound to prevent the transit of materials likely to strengthen a belligerent when such materials are connected with military operations.[121] A breach of such obligations of neutrality entitles affected belligerents to take retaliatory action in the nature of reprisals [122] (including maritime embargo in the technical sense). It enables them, a fortiori, to resort to retorsion against the delinquent neutral by taking unfriendly or unfair acts in its regard (such as the imposition of an embargo on shipment of strategic goods destined to its ports). Such measures of reprisal or retorsion [123] are

[117] [Asian-African Legal Consultative Committee], ECONOMIC LAWS SERIES NO. 1: LAWS AND REGULATIONS RELATING TO CONTROL OF IMPORT AND EXPORT TRADE IN MEMBER COUNTRIES, DECEMBER 1965.

[118] ADLER-KARLSSON, *supra* note 98, at 3.

[119] Art. 6 of Hague Convention XIII(1907) Respecting the Rights and Duties of Neutral Powers in Naval War. 36 Stat. 2415; TS 545; 1 BEVANS 723. *See also* Art. 44 of the "Rules of Aerial Warfare, 1923," drafted by a Commission of Jurists at The Hague, Dec. 1922–Feb. 1923, reproduced in GREENSPAN, THE LAW OF LAND WARFARE 650 (1959). For the general character of the international custom codified in these provisions *see*, 2 OPPENHEIM, *supra* note 43, at 686; Greenspan, *supra*, at 548.

[120] *See* Art. 2 of Hague Convention V(1907) concerning the Rights and Duties of Neutral Powers and Persons in Case of War on Land. 36 Stat. 2310; TS 540; 1 BEVANS 654. *And see* 2 OPPENHEIM, *supra* note 43, at 690.

[121] *See* the argument presented by the Netherlands in answer to Great Britain's protest over the transit of metals from occupied Belgium to Germany and of sand and gravel from Germany to Belgium during World War I, as reported in 2, OPPENHEIM, *supra* note 43, at 690–91.

[122] *Accord*, Greenspan, *supra* note 119, at 584.

[123] For a clear distinction between the two terms, as used in the above context, *see* 2 OPPENHEIM, *supra* note 43, at 136.

not merely punitive retaliatory acts, but must also be considered as instruments for discouraging the offending nonbelligerent from committing further violations of international law with regard to the injured party.

Under the controversial concept of differential or qualified neutrality in its modern sense, a neutral power might be able to discriminate against the belligerent whose recourse to war is unlawful.[124] Such a concept cannot therefore be cited in defense of a neutral state which supplies or helps in supplying war materials to a belligerent in order to enable it to maintain forcible control over territories of other states. This should be particularly so when the military operations during which the supply of such war materials takes place are restricted to the area of the illegally occupied territories, as was the case in the Arab-Israeli hostilities of 1973.

The practice of states, especially that of the United States, in the course of World War II reveals the extent of the use of economic warfare measures, not only among belligerents but also by or against neutrals. The oil policy adopted by the major powers during that war is particularly significant. "It was the general aim of British policy to create an oil famine in Europe."[125] In accordance with that policy, Great Britain requested the United States, early in 1940, and the latter agreed, to complete arrangements to ensure that no U.S. flag tankers would carry oil from the Americas to such "adjacent neutrals" in Europe as Spain and Portugal.[126] The U.S. Government went further by proposing to cutoff all supplies of oil to foreign countries including Japan.[127] A presidential order issued on July 25, 1940 extended the application of the Defense Act so that licences would be required for the export of petroleum and its products, and of scrap.[128] Six days later, the U.S. President ordered that export of aviation petrol should be restricted to the countries of the Western Hemisphere.[129] Meanwhile the Soviet and Japanese Ambassadors in Washington were informed that "it was the policy of the U.S. Government to give Great Britain every help short of war and that they intended to give licences for all British oil requirements."[130] As a result of such measures, Japan, which at the time was not at war with either the United States or Britain, and which was believed to be "very short of aviation oil," was deprived of American oil imports on which it was dependent for about two-thirds of its total import requirements.[131] Furthermore, on September 26, 1940, the United States, while still a "neutral" power, declared an embargo on the export of iron and steel scrap as from October 16, 1940 "except to countries of the Western Hemisphere and to Great Britain."[132]

The relevance of the above practice is clear. As explained earlier, Arab oil exporting countries were either cobelligerents against Israel in the hos-

[124] *See, e.g., id.*, at 651.

[125] I Medlicott, The Economic Blockade 474 (1952).

[126] *Id.*, at 476, Furthermore, Medlicott reports that, with a minor exception, "the British and American oil policies were virtually identical" even before the U.S. entered the war. *Id.*, at 481.

[127] *Id.*, at 477.

[128] *Id.*, at 478.

[129] *Id.*, at 479.

[130] *Ibid.*

[131] *Id.*, at 480.

[132] *Id.*, at 485.

tilities of October 1973 or were merely "nonbelligerents." Along with Egypt and Syria, Iraq, Kuwait, and to a lesser degree, Algeria and Saudi Arabia participated in the war. They were thus definitely entitled to take retaliatory measures against such neutral powers as the United States, which supplied Israel, in the course of operations, with massive quantities of war materials, some of which are reported to have been delivered directly in Arab occupied territories. Sanctions were also justified against such states as the Netherlands and Portugal, which allowed the use of their territory for the transit of some of these war materials to Israel. Other Arab oil exporting countries were following the example of the United States in 1940 by curtailing the exportation of their oil to unfriendly countries. A great many countries have taken similar steps even in peacetime conditions.

It is much too simple to dismiss such an impressive state practice and the special role of the United States in it, both in peacetime and in war conditions, by merely stating that "the United States itself has been one of the worst offenders in using trade controls in ways which have adversely affected other countries." [133] No general rule of international custom denying states the power to use export controls for political purposes could have developed against the overwhelming weight of such a state practice. The basic elements required for the emergence of such a general customary rule are not only absent, they are negated, as shown above, by impressive evidence to the contrary.

IV.

Legality of Arab Oil Measures Under Pertinent Resolutions of International Organizations:

A. UN DECLARATIONS

The UN General Assembly's Declaration of the Principles of International Law concerning Friendly Relations and Co-operation among States, which is generally treated as declaratory of contemporary international law, includes the following statement:

> No State may use or encourage the use of economic, political or any other type of measures to coerce another State in order to obtain from it the subordination of the exercise of its sovereign rights and to secure from it advantages of any kind.[134]

The seemingly general language of such a statement which has figured in

[133] Testimony of Professor Richard N. Gardner to the Sub-committee on International Economics of the Joint Economic Committee of the United States Congress, December 13, 1973, at 3. Professor Gardner admitted, however, that "the present state of international law in this area is most unsatisfactory" and that there was a clear need for "new rules."

[134] UN G.A. Res. 2625(XXV), Oct. 24, 1970, GAOR, 25th Sess., Supp. No. 28 at 122–24 (A/8028).

earlier UN declarations of a more political nature,[135] certainly represents a progressive development, not a mere codification of the international practice described above. It should be read in the light of the following considerations:

(1) The statement cannot be read in isolation from other parts of the Declaration. That instrument includes, in particular, the following principle:

> The territory of a State shall not be the object of military occupation resulting from the use of force in contravention of the provisions of the Charter. The territory of a State shall not be the object of acquisition by another State resulting from the threat or use of force. No territorial acquisition resulting from the threat or use of force shall be recognized as legal.[136]

The Declaration also states that subjection of peoples to alien domination is contrary to the Charter and that the peoples deprived by forcible action of their right to self-determination "are entitled to seek and to receive support in accordance with the purposes and principles of the Charter." When the principles embodied in the latter statements are violated in regard to a certain state, one may reasonably assume from the reading of the entire text of the Declaration that such a state will not be deprived of the right to resort to economic measures of self-defense or of reprisal [137] against the states responsible, directly or indirectly, for that violation.

(2) Prohibition of the use of economic measures to coerce another state in order to secure advantages from it cannot be absolute in any case. "[A] certain degree of coercion is inevitable in States' day-to-day interactions for values. Fundamental community policy does not seek to reach and prohibit this coercion. . . ." [138] It will be necessary, therefore, to characterize unlawful economic measures by their objective, not merely by their effect,[139] and to limit this characterization to measures involving the subordinating of sovereign rights of other states, and not merely seeking some advantage from them.

[135] *See, e.g.,* Declaration on the Inadmissibility of Intervention in Domestic Affairs of States and the Protection of their Independence and Sovereignty, UN G.A. Res. 2131, Feb. 21, 1965, GAOR, 20th Sess., Supp. No. 14 at 12 (A/6220), described by the U.S. representative to the General Assembly as "a political Declaration with a vital political message, not as a declaration or elaboration of the law governing non-intervention." *Id.*, 1st Committee, 143rd Meeting, A/C.1/PV.1422, at 12.

[136] *Supra* note 34.

[137] *Cf.*, Bowett, *Economic Coercion and Reprisals by States,* 13 Va. J. Int'l L. 1, 7–9 (1972). Mr. Bowett further maintains that "there has been no agreement within the United Nations that economic reprisals are illegal under the Charter. Indeed, given the rather low level of compliance accorded by States to the prohibition of armed reprisals (footnote omitted), *it would seem excessively optimistic to argue that economic reprisals are illegal per se*" (emphasis added).

[138] McDougal and Feliciano, Law and Minimum World Public Order 197 (1961).

[139] *Accord,* Bowett, *supra* note 137, at 5.

(3) The statement under consideration may not, at any rate, be interpreted as imposing an obligation on states to make economic sacrifices for the benefit of other states without receiving a proper consideration therefor. If a state chooses to do favors for other countries at the expense of its long term economic interests, it is for that state to decide what advantage it should receive in return, as long as the required consideration is permissible under international law. The legitimacy of the action of such a state becomes all the more evident, when the consideration required by it is simply the cooperation of the recipients in ensuring respect of international law in regard to itself or to other states.[140]

(4) Finally, the language of the above-quoted statement assumes normal peacetime conditions. It cannot apply in an actual war situation where belligerent states are ordinarily entitled, in accordance with the rules of the law of war, to use their economic power to coerce their adversaries and even to inflict damage on third parties violating their obligations of neutrality towards them.

The statement of the Friendly Relations Declaration should also be read in conjunction with other general UN declarations, especially the General Assembly's resolutions on state sovereignty over natural resources. In 1960, the Assembly upheld "the sovereign right of every State to dispose of its wealth and its natural resources." [141] Such a sovereign right to the free disposition of natural resources is confirmed by subsequent resolutions of the Assembly and of UNCTAD's Trade and Development Board.[142] It includes in particular the freedom of each state to develop rules and conditions which it considers "necessary or desirable with regard to the *authorization, restriction* or *prohibition*" of such activities as exploration, development, and disposition of natural resources.[143] More recently, the UN General Assembly deplored actions aimed at coercing states engaged in the exercise of their "sovereign rights over their natural resources" as violations of the Charter and of the Friendly Relations Declaration.[144]

[140] In the light of the above, one may differentiate between the U.S. practice under the Battle Act, where U.S. assistance is tied to the recipient's adoption of economic sanctions against third states which are not necessarily guilty of a breach of international law, and the Arab oil measures, which practically made the unlimited supply of oil dependent on the expression of friendly attitudes towards the Arabs' claim for the restoration of the *status juris* in the Middle East.

[141] UN G.A. Res. 1515(XV), GAOR, 15th Sess., Dec. 15, 1960.

[142] *See,* UNCTAD: Resolution on Permanent Sovereignty over Natural Resources, Oct. 19, 1972, UN Doc. TD/B/421 of Nov. 5, 1972 (335th meeting) where reference is made to all earlier UN General Assembly resolutions on this matter.

[143] *See,* e.g., UN G.A. Res. 1803(XVII), GAOR, 17th Sess., Dec. 14, 1962 (emphasis added). For a study of this and earlier UN resolutions in their application to Arab Oil, *see,* Mughraby, Permanent Sovereignty Over Oil Resources (1966).

[144] UN G.A. Res. 3016(XXVII), GAOR, 27th Sess., Dec. 18, 1972; Res. 3171 (XXVIII), GAOR, 28th Sess. Dec. 17, 1973. It is surprising therefore to see these two resolutions, which are obviously meant to strengthen the right of states over *their* natural resources against coercion from consuming countries, cited against Arab states, in Paust and Blaustein, *supra* note 11, at 420–21.

When Arab oil measures were in full force, the Assembly, far from condemning them, affirmed "the right of the Arab States and Peoples whose territories are under foreign occupation to permanent sovereignty over all their natural resources." [145]

The prohibition of "economic coercion" expressed in the Friendly Relations Declaration cannot therefore be an absolute injunction in the *lex lata* of international law. It is not a restatement of the wider and more controversial concept of "economic aggression." [146] The latter concept was found, early in 1952, to be "particularly liable to extend the concept of aggression almost indefinitely" [147]:

> The acts in question not only do not involve the use of force, but are usually carried out by a State by virtue of its sovereignty or discretionary power. Where there are no commitments a State is free to fix its customs tariff and to limit or prohibit exports and imports.[148]

In the above context, the prohibition of economic coercion should be realistically limited to the use by states of economic measures for achieving illegitimate purposes. According to this interpretation it is the objective of the measures that stands out as the most pertinent criterion for their legitimacy.

B. ACTION AUTHORIZED OR REQUESTED BY INTERNATIONAL ORGANIZATIONS

Economic coercion, including the embargo on shipments of strategic materials to countries in need of them, has also been stipulated by international organizations as an appropriate method for securing collective policy objectives of a noneconomic character. Sanctions of this type have by no means been confined to measures applied by the Security Council under Article 41 of the UN Charter or authorized by it for adoption by regional agencies, pursuant to Article 53(1) of the Charter.

The Security Council is certainly qualified, under these provisions, to employ coercive economic measures and to call upon states to apply them, as it has done in fact with regard to Rhodesia (general embargo on trade including specifically the supply of oil and oil products) [149] and to South

[145] UN G.A. Res. 3175(XXVIII), GAOR, 28th Sess., Dec. 17, 1973.

[146] Recent proposals in the United Nations on the definition of aggression seem content to leave out economic coercion at this stage at least. *See*, the USSR Draft in UN Doc. A/AC 134/L.12 (1969); Draft of the thirteen non-committed Powers in, *id.*, A/AC 134/L.16 (1969); and Add. 1 & 2; Draft of the eight Western Powers in, *id.* A/AC 134/L.17 (1969); and draft definition adopted by the Special Committee and forwarded to the General Assembly A/AC. 134/L.46 (1974).

[147] *See, Report by the Secretary-General of the United Nations on the Question of defining Aggression*, GAOR, 7th Sess., Agenda Item 54, UN Doc. A/2211, at 74.

[148] *Ibid. And see* Schwebel, *Aggression, Intervention and Self-Defence in Modern International Law*, RECUEIL DES COURS 413, 449–52 (II, 1972).

[149] *See*, S/Res/217 (1965), Nov. 20, 1965; S/Res/221 (1966), April 9, 1966; S/Res/232 (1966), Dec. 16, 1966; S/Res/253 (1968), May 29, 1968; S/Res/277 (1970), March 18, 1970; S/Res/314 (1972), Feb. 28, 1972; S/Res/318 (1972), July 28, 1972; S/Res/320 (1972), Sept. 29, 1972.

Africa (embargo on the supply of arms and ammunition).[150] Similar actions have also been authorized by the UN General Assembly. Early in 1951, the Assembly recommended that every state impose "an embargo on the shipment to areas under the control of the Central People's Government of the People's Republic of China and of the North Korean authorities" of many strategic materials including petroleum.[151] On other occasions, the Assembly has called upon states or Specialized Agencies to withhold financial, economic, and technical assistance from certain countries.[152] For instance, it has specifically invited "all States" to "avoid actions, including actions in the field of aid, that could constitute recognition of [Israel's] occupation" of Arab territories.[153]

Coercive economic measures were also authorized by the O.A.S. with regard to the Dominican Republic in 1961 and to Cuba in 1962 and 1964.[154] The O.A.U. has similarly assumed competence to authorize and request the adoption of such measures against such states as South Africa,[155] Portugal,[156] Rhodesia,[157] and, indeed, Israel.[158] The recent Resolution 21

[150] *See*, S/Res/181 (1963), Aug. 7, 1963; S/Res/182 (1963), Dec. 4, 1963; S/Res/191 (1964), June 18, 1964; S/Res/282 (1970), July 23, 1970; S/Res/311 (1972), Feb. 9, 1972.

[151] UN G.A. Res. 500(V), May 18, 1951, GAOR, 5th Sess., SUPP., No. 20A, A/1775/Add.1 (1951), at 2.

[152] *See, e.g.*, UN G.A., Res. 2107(XX), Dec. 21, 1965; UN G.A., Res. 2311(XXII), Dec. 14, 1967; UN G.A. Res. 2426(XXIII), Jan. 8, 1969 (with respect to South Africa and Portugal).

[153] UN G.A., Res. 2949(XXVIII), Dec. 8, 1972.

[154] *See* a discussion of these measures and of the question of the competence of a regional organization such as the O.A.S. to authorize them in the absence of a prior authorization from the Security Council in Claude, *The OAS, The UN and the United States*, 347 INT. CONCILIATION 1 (March 1964); Halderman, *Regional Enforcement Measures and the United Nations*, 52 GEORGIA L.J. 89 (1963).

[155] *See, e.g.*, OAU Doc. CIAS/Plen.2/Rev.2, May 25, 1963 in RESOLUTIONS ADOPTED BY THE CONFERENCE OF HEADS OF STATES AND GOVERNMENTS OF INDEPENDENT AFRICAN COUNTRIES 1963–1972 at 3, 5; AHG/Res. 5(1), 6(1), July 21, 1964, *id.*, 20, 21; AHG/Res/34(11), Oct. 25, 1965, *id.*, 49. Res. 6(1) of 1964 appealed to all oil producing countries to impose an embargo on shipment to South Africa of oil and oil products. *See also* the following resolutions of OAU Council of Ministers: CM/Res. 6(1), 11 August 1963, 1 RESOLUTIONS, RECOMMENDATIONS AND STATEMENTS ADOPTED BY THE ORDINARY AND EXTRAORDINARY SESSIONS OF THE COUNCIL OF MINISTERS 1963–1967 at 5 (May 1973); CM/Res. 31(III), July 17, 1964, *id.*, 29; CM/Res. 48(IV), March 9, 1965, *id.*, 50, CM/Res. 66(V), Oct. 21, 1965, *id.*, 74; CM/Res. 68(VII), Nov. 4, 1966, *id.*, 102; CM/Res. 102(IX), Sept. 10, 1967, *id.*, 122; CM/Res/138(X), Feb. 24, 1968, 2 *id.*, 1968–1973 at 7, CM/Res. 242/Rev. 1(XVII), June 19, 1971, *id.*, 141; CM/Res. 269(XIX), June 12, 1972, *id.*, 183.

[156] *See, e.g.*, OAU Doc. CIAS/Plen. 2/Rev. 2 *supra* note 155; AHG/Res. 9(1), July 24, 1964, *id.*, 26; AHG/Res. 35(11), Oct. 25, 1965, *id.*, 52. *And see*, CM/Res. 6(1), *supra* note 155; CM/Res. 83(VII), Nov. 4, 1966, *id.*, 99; CM/Res. 137(X), Feb. 24, 1968, 2 *id.*, 5; CM/Res. 268(XIX), June 12, 1972, *id.*, 178; CM/Res. 272(XIX), June 12, 1972, *id.*, 193.

[157] *See*, OAU Doc. CM/Res. 62(V), Oct. 21, 1965, *id.* 70, ECM/Res. 13(VI), Dec. 5, 1965, *id.* 86; CM/Res. 78(VII), Nov. 4, 1966, *id.* 94; CM/Res. 102(IX), Sept. 10, 1967,

(1973) of the Council of Ministers of that organization specifically calls upon states to "impose a total economic embargo, particularly on the supply of oil, against Israel, Portugal, South Africa and the racist minority regime of Southern Rhodesia." [159]

With the exception of the 1951 UN General Assembly resolution on China and North Korea, these measures were authorized in peacetime. The measures recommended in the latter resolution were to be taken, on the other hand, by "every State" including nonbelligerents and thus were not meant to be a mere exercise of the rights of belligerents under the law of war.

Such precedents may well be cited in support of the Arab oil measures as a supplementary basis for their lawfulness. On the one hand, they further prove the prevailing trend in international practice, whereby the application of coercive measures is clearly differentiated from the use of armed force, which is subject to a much more restrictive set of rules. On the other hand, they do explain a certain aspect of the legal background of Arab oil measures. These measures were not only sanctioned by the Summit Arab Conference, the highest organ of the League of Arab States; they were also taken in compliance with previous resolutions of other international organizations in so far as they applied to Rhodesia, South Africa, and Portugal. Furthermore, the embargo on the supply of oil to Rhodesia is a legal obligation incumbent on Arab states by virtue of binding decisions of the Security Council.

V.

Legality of Arab Oil Measures under Treaty Law

A. MULTILATERAL CONVENTIONS

Of all existing multilateral trade conventions, the General Agreement on Tariffs and Trade (GATT) [160] seems to be the only one that has some bearing on our discussion. Other multilateral trade conventions either do not regulate quantitative export controls, or do not include any of the Arab oil exporting countries among their parties. As for the GATT, Egypt and Kuwait are contracting parties to it while Algeria, Bahrain, and Qatar have accepted its *de facto* application to them.[161] These countries have participated, as shown above,[162] in the oil cutback and embargo resolutions.

---

id. 116; CM/Res/10(IX), Sept. 10, 1967, *id.* 133; CM/Res/207(XIV), March 6, 1970, 2 *id.* 86; CM/Res. 269(XVIII), Feb. 19, 1972, *id.* 164; CM/Res. 267(XIX), June 12, 1972, *id.* 175.

[158] *See,* OAU Doc., ECM/Res. 21(VIII), Nov. 21, 1973.

[159] *Ibid.,* para. 20.

[160] Signed at Geneva on Oct. 30, 1947, TIAS 1700; 55–61 UNTS.

[161] *See,* Treaties in Force. A list of Treaties and Other International Agreements of the United States in Force on January 1, 1974, at 330. (Dept. of State Pub. 8755).

[162] *See supra* note 7.

Article 11 of the GATT contains a general prohibition, subject to exceptions irrelevant to our discussion, on quantitative restrictions imposed on imports or exports "through quotas, import or export licences or other measures." Prohibition or restriction of imports and exports are also to be administered, pursuant to Article 13(1), without discrimination against "all third countries." Furthermore, Article 1, which is entitled "General Most-Favoured-Nation Treatment," provides for the automatic extension to like products imported from or exported to other parties, of any advantage granted by a party in respect of, *inter alia,* "all rules and formalities in connection with importation or exportation."

Such provisions, if read in isolation from other parts of the Agreement, may give the erroneous impression that contracting Arab states are under a general and absolute prohibition in the employment of discriminatory export controls against other contracting parties such as the United States and the Netherlands. The GATT, much like any other treaty, must, however, be read in its entirety.[163] Pursuant to other provisions of the GATT, the above-quoted general principles are subject to two types of exceptions. The "general exceptions" provided for in Article 20 include in particular the right of each party to take measures "relating to the conservation of exhaustible natural resources." Such measures must be made effective "in conjunction with restrictions on domestic production *or* consumption," and "should not apply in a manner which would constitute a means of arbitrary or unjustified discrimination between countries where the same conditions prevail or a disguised restriction on international trade . . ." These conditions obviously obtain in the case of production cutbacks employed for the purpose of conserving a depleting resource such as oil. More importantly, the "security exceptions" contained in Article 21 allow each contracting party to take "any action which *it considers* necessary for the protection of its essential security interests," if such an action is taken "in time of war or other emergency in international relations." It is significant to note that in the latter provision the Agreement maintains the freedom of each party to estimate the necessity of the action it takes in such exceptional circumstances. Even if necessity is to be judged by objective criteria, one may easily recognize its relevance in a wartime situation when the vital interests of the state are at stake. Discretion of the state in such matters is, indeed, a question of public policy,[164] which may restrict the application of the most favored-nation clause even in the absence of explicit provisions.[165]

It is true that Article 22(1) of the GATT requires each contracting party to accord "sympathetic consideration" to, and to afford "adequate opportu-

[163] *See,* H. Lauterpacht, *Restrictive Interpretation and the Principle of Effectiveness in the Interpretation of Treaties,* 26 BYIL 76 (1949). *And see* for possible exceptions, not warranted in the above context, McNair, *supra* note 79, at 474–84.

[164] *See,* T. Flory, Le G.A.T.T.—Droit International et Commerce Mondial 83 (1968), where the security exceptions in GATT's Article 21 are also described as constituting matters within the "domestic jurisdiction" of each party.

[165] *See,* a discussion of this point in relation to bilateral trade agreements, *infra* pp. 623–25.

nity for consultation" with other parties. However, such an obligation is incumbent upon a contracting party only after it receives "such representations as may be made by another contracting party with respect to any matter affecting the operation of this Agreement." Consultation cannot therefore be a precondition for taking measures, but is merely a procedure devised in the GATT to secure satisfaction to the injured party in cases of alleged violations.[166] None of the contracting parties affected by the Arab oil measures has submitted representations under Article 22 of the GATT; nor have they resorted to the nullification or impairment procedure provided for in Article 23 of that Agreement.

Article 35 of the Agreement provides, on the other hand, for its non-application between any two contracting parties which have not entered into tariff negotiations with each other. No such negotiations were entered into, however, between the State of Kuwait, which is the only Arab oil exporting contracting party, and any other party to the GATT. It may also be relevant to note that the United States had long implemented an oil import program which gave practical preferences to such states as its neighbor Canada,[167] notwithstanding the above-quoted general principles of the GATT. These points need not be over emphasized, however, in view of the fact that Arab oil measures are perfectly justified under Article 21 of the Agreement, which effectively suspends its operation under emergency conditions.[168]

B. BILATERAL TREATIES

The relevant bilateral trade agreements concluded between Arab oil exporting countries and countries affected by the Arab oil embargo seem to be limited to three agreements [169] concluded between the United States and Saudi Arabia, Iraq, and Oman, respectively, before any of these latter countries was significantly involved in the export of oil. None of these agreements, it is submitted, presented a legal barrier to the implementation of the Arab oil measures vis-a-vis the United States. Although all agreements include a most-favored-nation clause, the special wording used in each agreement warrants its independent examination.

The U.S.–Saudi Arabia Agreement of 1933 [170] confined the application of

[166] *Cf.*, Dam, The GATT, Law and International Economic Organization 221 (1970).

[167] *See* a description of U.S. practice in, James III, *Comment, The Mandatory Oil Import Program: A Review of Present Regulations and Proposals for Change in the 1970's*, 7 Tex. Int'l L.J. 373 (1972).

[168] *See also* the testimony of Prof. R. N. Gardner referred to in note 133 *supra*, where he emphatically states that all the GATT principles on discrimination are "effectively vitiated" by Article 21 thereof.

[169] The above statement is based on information obtained from some of the Foreign Offices of the Arab states involved, supported by the results of a review of the League of Nations Treaty Series, the United Nations Treaty Series, and the U.S. Treaties in Force referred to in note 161, *supra*.

[170] Provisional Agreement in regard to Diplomatic and Consular Representation, Judicial Protection, Commerce and Navigation, signed at London on Nov. 7, 1933, 48

the most-favored-nation clause included in its Article 3 to treatment "[i]n respect of import, export and other *duties* and *charges* affecting commerce and navigation, as well as in respect of *transit, warehousing* and *other facilities.*" Such a wording obviously excludes quantitative restrictions on exports from the scope of the clause. The same article mentions also "any . . . regulation affecting commerce or navigation," but this is only in stating that *concessions* with respect to them will be immediately reciprocated. Even if the oil measures applied by Saudi Arabia were to be characterized as involving "concessions," [171] a presumption in favor of an exception on grounds of national security interests can well be derived from a treaty of this type.[172] A similar presumption may also be established "in favor of the overriding character of exemptions on grounds of international public policy." [173] As explained earlier in this article, the Saudi oil embargo was applied in an attempt to secure an objective of the highest international order: The restoration to the lawful sovereigns of illegally occupied territories and the restoration of the rights of peoples deprived of self-determination.

The U.S.–Iraq Agreement of 1938 [174] explicitly provides, in Article 2, that "in all that concerns matters of prohibition or restrictions on importations and exportations each of the two countries will accord, whenever they may have recourse to the said prohibitions or restrictions, to the commerce of the other country, treatment equally favourable to that which is accorded to any other country . . ." Article 4 is equally explicit, however, in permitting exceptions relating to "the adoption or enforcement of measures relating to neutrality or to rights and obligations arising under the Covenant of the League of Nations." Such a codification of the "international public policy exception" could obviously be invoked by Iraq against the United States, which deviated from its obligations of neutrality in the course of the Arab-Israeli hostilities in which Iraqi forces were involved. It should be noted, however, that Iraq did not concur in the cutback and embargo resolutions of the Arab Oil Ministers, and that exportation of its oil through the East Mediterranean terminals was halted due to Israeli military action.[175]

Stat. 1826 (1933); 11 Bevans 5456; 142 LNTS 329. The Agreement does not extend, pursuant to Article (4) thereof, to the treatment which the United States accords to the commerce of Cuba and the Panama Canal zone.

[171] As is implied in the testimony of Professor R. N. Gardner referred to in note 133 *supra,* and in his statement quoted in "Saudi Oil Embargo Termed Breach of '33 Treaty with U.S.," N.Y. Times, Dec. 19, 1973, at 12, col. 4.

[172] *Accord,* Schwarzenberger, *The Most-Favoured-Nation Standard in British State Practice,* 22 BYIL 96, 110, 111 (1945).

[173] *Id.,* at 111, 120.

[174] Treaty of Commerce and Navigation, signed at Baghdad, Dec. 3, 1938, 54 Stat. 1790 (1940); TS960; 9 Bevans 7; 203 LNTS 107. According to the treaty, extension of advantages given by the United States does not include advantages accorded to Cuba, the Panama Canal Zone, border traffic zones, and states in Customs Unions (Art. 1).

[175] *See, supra* note 4.

Finally the trade agreement concluded in 1958 between the United States and the "Sultanate of Muscat and Oman and Dependencies" [176] prohibits, in Article 8, the imposition by either party of restrictions on the exportation of any product to the territories of the other party "unless the exportation of the like product to all third countries is similarly restricted or prohibited." Such a provision, which admittedly would preclude Oman under normal conditions from implementing discriminatory embargo measures on oil shipments to the United States, is restricted, however, by the text of Article 11(d) of the same Agreement. According to this latter article the agreement does not preclude the application of measures "necessary to fulfil the obligations of a Party for the maintenance or restoration of international peace and security, or necessary to protect its essential security interests." The internal security interests of that country would certainly have been further impaired had it deviated from the collective Arab stand adopted during the war crisis. It is unofficially reported, at any rate, that Oman, which is not an OAPEC member, has not participated in the meetings of Arab Oil Ministers, and was the last Arab country to declare an embargo on oil shipments to the United States, was quite lenient in applying that measure, and was the first to lift it.

It may be worth repeating in this respect that the United States has felt free in normal peacetime to impose a quota system for the import of oil, which discriminated in favor of oil imported from certain countries other than Saudi Arabia, Iraq, and Oman. The preferential treatment given under that system to certain countries, such as Canada, could hardly conform to the standards provided for in the above-mentioned agreements. It is not surprising, therefore, that the U.S. Government has not officially characterized the measures adopted by these Arab countries with respect to the export of their oil in a crisis situation as constituting a breach of treaty commitments on their part.

VI.

Conclusion

In the light of the above analysis, the destination embargo of Arab oil may now be viewed in its right perspective. Far from being a "weapon for blackmailing the West" or a "threat to international peace," it has been employed as an instrument for the respect and promotion of the rule of law in an area of international relations where such a rule has long been forsaken for the rule of superior military force. In their use of that instrument, Arab oil exporting countries were in fact following the steps of a great number of other states which have used their export regulations to

[176] Treaty of Amity, Economic Relations and Consular Rights (with Protocol) signed at Salalah on Dec. 20, 1958, 11 UST 1835; TIAS No. 4530; 380 UNTS 181. Each party reserved the right to accord special advantages to "adjacent countries" or by virtue of a customs union (Art VIII (4)). Application of the treaty does not extend to Cuba, the Philippines, trusteeship territories in the Pacific, and the Panama Canal Zone.

further their foreign policies. Only the objective of the Arab states seems to have been more legitimate. The Arab states took that measure not to weaken unfriendly countries but merely to discourage third countries from violating their obligations of neutrality toward them and from continuing their encouragement of, or their acquiescence in, an illegal situation. The Arab states have considered it their moral responsibility to keep the industrialized nations fueled with Arab exhaustible oil, in spite of their awareness that such a policy may not serve their best selfish economic interests. They were not to be expected, however, to do favors indefinitely for states which had refused to cooperate with them in putting an end to the illegal occupation and annexation of Arab territories and to the continuing denial of the right of the Palestinian people to self-determination.

The oil measures taken by the Arab states were the result of the exercise of their "sovereign right" to dispose of their natural resources in the manner which best suits their legitimate interests. In exercising that right, the Arab states have not violated any established rule of international custom or any prior treaty commitments. To accuse them of abuses in the exercise of that right by questioning its necessity and proportionality is to assume a simplistic wisdom that does not befit the circumstances of the case. After all other measures had been exhausted in vain, it could hardly have been deemed unnecessary for the Arab states to resort to economic pressure for the restoration of Arab occupied homeland. Such a pressure was readily available in the field of oil supply as the Arab states had little influence outside this field vis-a-vis the countries concerned. When the pressure proved to be particularly damaging to countries relatively remote from the dispute, as in the case of Japan, or when affected countries showed a slight concern for the legitimate demands of Arab states, the Arab oil measures were almost immediately lifted with regard to them. This is to be compared with the intransigent stand of Israel which—opposing the interests of the international community in the uninterrupted supply of Arab oil—has insisted in the face of these measures on the continuation of its forcible occupation of territories of Arab states.

A general and absolute prohibition on the use of economic measures for political purposes in the international sphere is still an idealist's dream. Before it hardens into a rule of international law, enforcement machinery must develop for the protection of the militarily weaker states, which may happen to have a relatively great economic power. Precluding such states from the use of their economic power in the settlement of political disputes before a general ban is imposed on armaments and in the absence of an effective collective security system could not serve the interests of international justice. It would only help the development of what President Roosevelt once described as "a one-way international law which lacks mutuality in its observance and therefore becomes an instrument of oppression." [177]

[177] The President's message to Congress of Jan. 6, 1941, cited in GREENSPAN, *supra* note 119, at 519.

In retrospect, the Arab oil measures have proved to be an effective instrument for reestablishing concern for the long-awaited peace in the Middle East. The new direction in the U.S. policy in that area has no doubt been influenced by the U.S. energy needs and its dependence on Arab oil for meeting them. Inasmuch as that new direction is characterized by evenhandedness, it is likely to serve the general interests of the international community for peace and justice in an area where both elements have long been lacking. It should also serve the best interests of the United States itself. Arab oil limitation will also probably turn out to have been a blessing in disguise for the United States in another sense, "for without it a crash alternative source program would have come later, if at all." [178] Arab oil measures may even prove, in a wider perspective, to have been a blessing for all parties to the Middle East conflict, including Israel. To the extent that the application of these measures was a major factor in the efforts presently being undertaken for reaching a lasting and just settlement of the Arab-Israeli dispute, they should be partially credited for the outstanding results. It is this settlement, not the forcible occupation and the arrogance of power practiced by Israel since 1967, which is the best guarantee for the security of all the states of the Middle East and for the long term interests of their peoples.

[178] W. E. Griffith, *The Fourth Middle East War, the Energy Crisis and U.S. Policy,* 17 Orbis 1161, 1185 n.23 (1974).

The Arab Oil Weapon: A Reply and Reaffirmation of Illegality

JORDAN J. PAUST* AND ALBERT P. BLAUSTEIN**

I. INTRODUCTION

On October 16, 1973, several Arab states began to employ an "oil weapon" against states and peoples which for various reasons had failed to take a pro-Arab stance with regard to the ongoing Mid-East conflict. Since that time, the use of Arab money has been discussed as a possible political weapon and Arab coercion as well as the concomitant surge in Arab wealth has been recognized as an omen of a new economic era.

Any speculation in regard to future interaction of global wealth and power is still too vague to afford an accurate prediction. The possibilities range from actual economic warfare, with sporadic military intervention, to lesser forms of economic confrontation mitigated by joint military policing of markets and resource centers. Exacerbation of continued world depression or recession appears just as likely as a radically new era of competitive but cooperative interdependence and growth. The forms which any of the above-mentioned phenomena might take are unknown. The amount of concern to be evidenced toward the scarcity of resources and the human death toll during the impending years of embargo and post-embargo wealth transfer is also unclear at present, particularly since such a transfer may be of a magnitude unprecedented in human history. Post-embargo blacklisting of pro-Israeli or even pro-Jewish business firms, Arab investment and practical control of several key industries, and overall problems involving the growing gap between developing and developed countries or the monopolistic economic tendencies exhibited by some nation-states may lead to results for which governments will be unequipped. It is unclear whether monopolies and resource cartels will aid the emergence of a new interdependence, or whether they will secure its downfall. Another question deserving

---

* Associate Professor of International Law, Bates College of Law, University of Houston.

** Professor of Law, School of Law, Rutgers University.

reflection is the influence of coercive cartels on the struggle for formal human rights to food, to a decent standard of living, and to self-determination.

As in the case of other significant human developments, future efforts to study and address world interdependence amid resource scarcity and growing starvation will strongly influence emerging patterns of law. Surprisingly, no Arab government which uses the "oil weapon" and blacklisting of foreign firms has yet expressed any legal justification for its actions. The authors' research has failed to uncover a typical "white paper" such as is frequently published by governments in eager attempts to justify significant political action. The only attempted legal justification offered for the use of oil as a political weapon appears in writing by Dr. Ibrahim Shihata,[1] which had been made in response to an article by the authors regarding the illegality of the oil weapon under international law.[2]

The present article will explore several aspects of Dr. Shihata's work so as to examine the application of relevant legal policy to the Arab oil weapon and to the emerging processes of economic interdependence and the control and politically-motivated manipulation of natural resources. The authors' first article discussed the factual background, the types of legal policy at stake, and actual outcomes and effects of the oil weapon, while formulating an approach for determining the legality or illegality of resource manipulation for political objectives. The article concluded that on the basis of legal policies and actual patterns of thought, action and effect, the Arab oil weapon violated article 2(4) of the United Nations Charter.[3] Although many forms and degrees of coercion are extant and permissible in day-to-day relations between states, a state's choice of coercive strategies is necessarily limited by the legitimacy of the goals pursued and actual effects in social process. In the authors' analysis, any attempted justification of the deliberate use of resources to secure even legitimate goals requires a consideration of the objectives sought, the actual patterns of interaction, the detrimental effects of the weapon, the legitimate goals of other states, available alternatives and universal legal policies at stake.

Dr. Shihata provides the only case to date for legality of the

---

1. Shihata, *Destination Embargo of Arab Oil: Its Legality Under International Law*, 68 AM. J. INT'L L. 591 (1974) [hereinafter cited as Shihata].

2. Paust & Blaustein, *The Arab Oil Weapon–A Threat to International Peace*, 68 AM. J. INT'L L. 410 (1974) [hereinafter cited as Paust & Blaustein].

3. Paust & Blaustein, *supra* note 2, at 439.

Arab oil weapon under customary law, the United Nations Charter and supplemental declarations, and trade agreements. His response, however, looks to "state practice"[4] rather than to the actual factual context and relevant legal policies, as illustrated by the characterization of the "unlimited" production of Arab oil as a "political favor"[5] which can be bartered legitimately in return for such concessions from consumer nations as "impartial attitudes"[6] toward the Middle East conflict or support for Arab objectives in a Middle East settlement. The oil weapon is viewed by Dr. Shihata as an "instrument of flexible persuasion"[7] complementing military and diplomatic measures in the struggle for a favorable settlement of Arab demands. Dr. Shinata's reporting of the factual background and his analyses, however, indirectly support the conclusions expressed in the authors' first article: for the most part, the factors of law and context which were analyzed in the original work and which demonstrated the international illegality of the oil weapon seem to have been left unchallenged. Certain assertions of law and fact, however, are erroneous.

The present article will address the theory of resource ownership and manipulation in two ways, by discussing Dr. Shihata's statements regarding coercive use, and then analyzing the broader question of ownership and control of natural resources. The three assertions to be rebutted are the following:

(1) That the world community cannot question either the necessity or the proportionality of Arab manipulation of resources;

(2) That the provisions of the United Nations Charter which were designed to regulate transnational coercion are inapplicable in time of war;

(3) That contracts and trade agreements concluded between Arab nations and other states are merely "political favors."

The present article does not attempt a response to the separate issue of legality or illegality of the Israeli occupation of Arab lands. Instead, discussion is confined to the use of economic coercion in the face of growing world economic interdependence.

---

4. Shihata, *supra* note 1, at 609 *et seq*.
5. *Id.* at 591-92, 609, 626. *See also id.* at 598, 618.
6. *Id.* at 592, 595-96, 609, 618 n.140.
7. *Id.* at 596. *See also id.* at 591, 627.

II. Questioning of the Necessity or Proportionality of Coercive Manipulation of Resources.

Dr. Shihata states that by questioning the "necessity and proportionality" of the coercive manipulation of oil, one would "assume a simplistic wisdom."[8] Yet it seems that ignoring the relationship of actual conditions, circumstances, outcomes and effects of the use of economic coercion would put creative and pragmatic policy-serving approaches into the realm of the impossible. Moreover, the United Nations Charter, the customary law of reprisal, and related norms governing "self-help" require that any strategy of coercion, economic or otherwise, be proportionate to the "necessity" of the situation.[9] Even in armed warfare, there are legal limits to competitive death, injury, and suffering.[10] A realistic and policy-serving approach to legal decision-making cannot avoid examination both of the necessity for coercive action and of the effects upon the shaping of legal policies concerning world public order and the sharing of earth resources. In fact, coercive measures identified as illegal by authoritative decision-makers have been categorized in terms of an unnecessary use of the strategy of coercion and disproportionate effects.[11]

---

8. *Id.* at 626. Dr. Shihata also does not raise the questions of necessity or proportionality in his listing of past economic reprisal actions. *See id.* at 614-16 *passim.*

9. *See* Paust & Blaustein, *supra* note 2, at 419-20. *See also* J. Brierly, The Law of Nations 316, 323-32 (5th ed. 1955); M. McDougal & F. Feliciano, Law and Minimum World Public Order 217-44 *passim* (1961); 2 L. Oppenheim's International Law 141-42 (H. Lauterpacht ed. 1952); W. Reisman, Nullity and Revision (1971); Bowett, *Economic Coercion and Reprisals by States*, 13 Va. J. Int'l L. 1, 7-11 (1972); Bowett, *Reprisals Involving Recourse to Armed Force*, 66 Am. J. Int'l L. 1, 7, 11-12, 16 (1972); Falk, *The Beirut Raid and the International Law*, 63 Am. J. Int'l L. 415 (1969); Falk, *The Cambodian Operation and the International Law*, 65 Am. J. Int'l L. 1, 14-15 (1971); Lillich, *Forcible Self-Help under International Law*, 22 Naval War Coll. Rev. 56, 58, 60 (1970); MacChesney, *Some Comments on the "Quarantine" of Cuba*, 57 Am. J. Int'l L. 592, 594-96 (1963). *Cf.* Baxter, *The Legal Consequences of the Unlawful Use of Force under the Charter*, 62 Am. Soc. Int'l L. Proc. 68, 69, 74 (1968).

10. *See, e.g.*, Hague Convention on Maritime War, July 29, 1899, 32 Stat. 1827, T.S. 396; Hague Convention on Laws of War on Land, July 29, 1899, 32 Stat. 1803, T.S. 403; Geneva Convention Relative to the Treatment of Prisoners of War, August 12, 1949, 6 U.S.T. 3317, T.I.A.S. 3364, 75 U.N.T.S. 135. *See also,* M. McDougal & F. Feliciano, *supra* note 9; J. Paust & A. Blaustein, War Crimes Jurisdiction and Due Process: A Case Study of Bangladesh (1974).

11. *See, e.g.*, J. Brierly, *supra* note 9; M. McDougal & F. Feliciano, *supra* note 9; Paust & Blaustein, *supra* note 2, at 419-20, 433-38; Lillich, *Economic Coercion and the International Legal Order*, Int'l Aff. 358 (July 1975).

As Dr. Shihata admits, not only were oil embargoes imposed upon states which had demonstrated a hostile attitude towards Arab rights or a pro-Israeli bias,[12] but even neutral states were not to receive the same quantities of oil as they imported in 1972.[13] A normal oil flow would be renewed only upon reclassification as "friendly" states.[14] Exclusive orientation toward objectives, without regard to necessity, proportionality, outcome, and effect, is particularly disturbing in light of the severe world shortages of energy, food, and fertilizer[15] and of relevant legal policies. Coercion directed toward proponents of what one group determines to be offensive attitudes is also particularly alarming when viewed as a foreshadowing of recurrence of totalitarian thought and the related use of terrorist strategy.[16]

III. Application of Article 2 of the United Nations Charter in Time of War

Dr. Shihata is probably the first jurist to argue that the language of a General Assembly resolution derived from article 2 of the United Nations Charter, which concerns the duty not to intervene in matters within the domestic jurisdiction of any state,[17] "as-

---

12. Shihata, *supra* note 1, at 595, 618 n.140. *See also* Al-Din Al-Bitar, *The Implications of the October War for the Arab World*, 3 J. Palestine Studies 34, 39 (1974); Itayim, *Arab Oil—The Political Dimension*, 3 J. Palestine Studies 84, 92-95 (1974); Paust & Blaustein, *supra* note 2, at 427-28; N.Y. Times, July 11, 1974, at 1, col. 3 (quoting the Saudi Arabian Oil Minister).

13. Shihata, *supra* note 1, at 596, 618 n.140. For other Arab writings on the restriction of the flow of oil to neutral states, see Itayim, *supra* note 12, at 92-95; Sus, *Western Europe and the October War*, 3 J. Palestine Studies 65, 75 (1974). Itayim states that "Iraq publicly dissociated itself from" the oil embargo and "criticized the Arab oil embargo and cutback measure, as counterproductive in that they tended to penalize friend and foe alike. . . ." Itayim, *supra* note 12, at 90 n.1. Dr. Shihata, however, states that the detailed and documented listings of proclaimed Arab objectives were "wild," and that they "never figured" in Arab decisions or statements. Shihata, *supra* note 1, at 594 n.11.

14. Shihata, *supra* note 1, at 596, 618 n.140. *See also*, Paust & Blaustein, *supra* note 2, at 411 (direct quote from Saudi Arabian Oil Minister).

15. *See* Paust & Blaustein, *supra* note 2, at 427-32.

16. *See* T. Gurr, Why Men Rebel 46-50, 63 *passim* (1970); Greer, *The Prophets of Gloom and Doom Are Not All Right*, N.Y. Times, Sept. 4, 1974, at 41, col. 2; Gwertzman, *Kissenger's View of the Oil Problem*, N.Y. Times, Oct. 3, 1974, at 2, col. 4; Reading, *Inflation's Ugly Question: Can Nations Survive It?*, N.Y. Times, Sept. 15, 1974, at 4, col. 3; N.Y. Times, Oct. 13, 1974, at 34, col. 4; N.Y. Times, Sept. 27, 1974, at 1, col. 6.

17. G.A. Res. 2625, 25 U.N. GAOR, Supp. 28 at 121, U.N. Doc. A/8018 (1970), reprinted at 65 Am. J. Int'l L. 243 (1974). *See also* U.N. Charter, art. 2, paras. 4, 7.

sumes normal peacetime conditions . . . [and] cannot apply in an actual war."[18] According to this view, a combatant state would be free to use intense economic coercion against any other state or people without violating article 2. Yet one of the purposes of the article is to regulate disorders and to prevent future occurrences of violence. There is no General Assembly declaration or charter provision which restricts such regulation to peacetime; in fact, the preamble to the charter expresses the common determination to save the peoples of the member nations "from the scourge of war . . . to unite our strength to maintain international peace and security, and to ensure, by the acceptance of principles and the institution of methods, that armed force shall not be used, save in the common interest." Article 1 addresses threats to the peace and "acts of agression or other breaches of the peace." Restriction exclusively to peace time of the charter's general advocacy of friendly relations, human rights, non-intervention, self-determination, and fundamental freedoms would be inimical to the goals of world public order as expressed in the charter.

IV. Contracts and Trade Agreements as "Favors"

Dr. Shihata asserts that contracts entered into by Arab states and agencies with non-Arab states, corporations, and nationals are mere "favors"[19] which may be withdrawn at any time. Such a theory not only seems to be contrary to Moslem law as well as to civil and common law contract principles,[20] but it also appears to rest solely on the basis of Arab economic needs as a justification for sharp unilateral production cuts and the coercive embargo of oil. With this sort of regard for contract and treaty law, it is clear why Dr. Shihata asserts an exclusively oriented approach to interpretation of the GATT provisions on national security exceptions to prohibitions of discriminatory trade measures,[21] apparently in disregard of points made in the first article concerning provisional

---

18. Shihata, *supra* note 1, at 618. This statement appears to contradict his earlier recognition that the "prohibition of the use of force as a means for the settlement of international disputes . . . seems to constitute the cornerstone of contemporary international law. . . ." *Id.* at 599.

19. Shihata, *supra* note 1.

20. *See, e.g.*, R. David & J. Brierly, Major Legal Systems in the World Today 398, 406-10 (1968); A. Larson & W. Jenks, Sovereignty within the Law 176-77 (1965); R. Schlesinger, Comparative Law 194-95 (1959); *Symposium on Muslim Law*, 22 Geo. Wash. L. Rev. 1 (1953); Arbitration between Saudi Arabia and ARAMCO, 27 Int'l. L. Rep. 117 (1963; award of Aug. 23, 1958).

21. Shihata, *supra* note 1, at 622.

characterization of security needs.[22] The statement that GATT allows a "freedom of each party to estimate the necessity"[23] of national security measures lacks textual support and is, in fact, contrary to the recognition by GATT that a more inclusive approach to trade problems is required in an era of interdependence and resource scarcity.[24] With regard to Dr. Shihata's approach to the obligation to consult, GATT expressly states that a contracting party must accord "sympathetic consideration" to, and shall afford "adequate opportunity for consultation."[25] The obligation to provide for consultation does not become inapplicable whenever a state is in the process of "taking measures" against opposing states.[26] Further, the denial of an opportunity for consultation to states deprived of fair economic treatment would be contrary to the policies of the United Nations Charter as identified in the General Assembly Resolution on Friendly Relations and Co-operation[27] and elsewhere.

The failure of affected nations to submit formal representations to the Arab states under article 22 of GATT is not surprising, since the intensity of the coercion employed and the Arab desire to decide alone upon oil allocations indicate that such action would have been futile.[28]

---

22. Paust & Blaustein, *supra* note 2, at 423-24.

23. Shihata, *supra* note 1, at 622.

24. *See* J. Jackson, World Trade and the Law of GATT 752 (1969); Paust & Blaustein, *supra* note 2, at 423-24 n.58.

25. General Agreement on Tariffs and Trade, Oct. 30, 1947, 61 Stat. (5), (6), T.I.A.S. 1700, 55 U.N.T.S. 188. *See also* Shihata, *supra* note 1, at 622-23.

26. Shihata, *supra* note 1, at 623. *Contra*, G. Curzon, Multilateral Commercial Diplomacy 42-44 (1965); J. Jackson, *supra* note 24, at 163 *et seq.*; K. Dam, The GATT, Law and International Organization 21, 221, 351 (1970); Bowett, *supra* note 9, at 11; Jackson, *GATT as an Instrument for the Settlement of Trade Disputes*, [1967] P.A.S.I.L. 114; Jackson, *The Puzzle of GATT*, 1 J. World Trade L. 131, 157 *et seq.* (1967). As Bowett states: "No unilateral resort to reprisals is permissible prior to the use of the pacific procedures." Bowett, *supra* note 9, at 11. This analysis also finds support in the Vienna Convention on the Law of Treaties, arts. 26, 27, 31, A/Conf. 39/27, May 23, 1969. The text of this Convention is reprinted at 63 Am. J. Int'l L. 875 (1969).

27. G.A. Res. 2625, 25 U.N. GAOR, Supp. 28, at 121, U.N. Doc. A/8018 (1970). The text of this resolution is reprinted at 65 Am. J. Int'l L. 243 (1971). *See also* Baxter, *supra* note 9, at 69; J. Moore, Law and the Indo-China War (1972); W. Reisman, *supra* note 9. Baxter notes: "If a State uses force after an armstice has once been concluded, it must be prepared to justify its conduct by reference to Article 51 of the Charter." *Id.* at 73. This reasoning is applicable to a long-term situation of "cease-fire" or cessation of armed hostilities, especially with regard to laws of neutrality when "states disagree about which nation is acting lawfully." *Id.*

28. *See* Paust & Blaustein, *supra* note 2, at 411. Perhaps in the future a formal

V. Ownership, Control, and Use of Earth Resources

The argument that the placing of "limitations on the production of primary commodities" is "within the exclusive domestic jurisdiction of sovereign states"[29] is an out-dated and now-discredited theory, since problems regarding natural resources merit international concern whenever outcomes and effects transcend national boundaries.[30] International concern is even more paramount when manipulation of resource production and allocation threatens international peace and the lives of millions of people throughout the globe. At a time of demonstrated interdependence amid resource scarcity, complete "sovereign control" over natural resources is, at best, a disagreeable delusion. The question is not whether there will be international effects, but how those effects should more rationally occur. With significant interconnection between energy, fertilizer, food and financial patterns, it is now far too clear that a "free," unrestrained nation-state determination of resource production and sharing would be inimical to the serving of fundamental human rights. Since freedom, in the new world, is relative, jurisdictional competence must reflect the new realities if attempts to serve national and international goals are to be realistic and effective.

Article 22 of the Universal Declaration of Human Rights recognizes that all persons are entitled to the realization of economic rights.[31] Article 25 of the declaration adds the right to an adequate

---

complaint will be lodged with the International Court of Justice, seeking monetary damages. *See, e.g.*, The Corfu Channel Case, [1949] I.C.J. 4. *See also* J. Brierly, *supra* note 9. The continuing lack of cooperation is forestalling the implementation of court or arbitration action.

29. Shihata, *supra* note 1, at 598. *See also* N.Y. Times, April 1, 1975, at 18, col. 1 (OPEC Declaration, March 4-6, 1975).

30. *See* Paust & Blaustein, *supra* note 2, at 420-23, 433-39; The Trail Smelter Case, *infra* note 38. Moreover, Shihata's assertion that the use of force to regain territory "falls within the inherent territorial jurisdiction of each sovereign state," Shihata, *supra* note 1, at 607, is incorrect. The Declaration on Friendly Relations and Co-Operation prohibits the use of force "as a means of solving international disputes, including territorial disputes and problems concerning frontiers of states" or "to violate international lines of demarcation, such as armistice lines. . . ." G.A. Res. 2625, 25 U.N. GAOR Supp. 28, at 122, U.N. Doc. A/8028 (1970). *See also* U.N. Charter, art. 1, paras. 1, 2, art. 2, paras. 3, 4.

31. The full text of article 22 states:

> Everyone, as a member of society, has the right to social security and is entitled to realization, through national effort and international co-operation and in accordance with the organization and resources of each State, of the economic, social and cultural rights indispensable for his dignity and the free development of his personality.

standard of living, including a right to adequate nourishment.[32] Article 28 states: "Everyone is entitled to a social and international order in which the rights and freedoms set forth in this Declaration can be fully realized."[33] An international "order" which recognizes the prerogative of producing states unilaterally to allocate scarce natural resources would hardly contribute to the realization of these rights in the context of the current energy and food shortages. Unilateral control over these matters would undermine the goal stated in article 1(3) of the United Nations Charter, *i.e.*, the achievement of "international cooperation in solving international problems of an economic, social, cultural, or humanitarian character, and in promoting and encouraging respect for human rights and for fundamental freedoms for all. . . ."

Patterns of production and distribution of energy and food sources are now subject to many state, regional, and international jurisdictions, and a more inclusive and rational exercise of international regulation is all the more essential at this time.[34] Such con-

---

G.A. Res. 217A, U.N. Doc. A/810 at 75 (1948) (vote: 48/0/8, with one Arab state abstaining—Saudi Arabia). The six abstaining socialist states as well as all Arab states have subsequently affirmed that the Universal Declaration is part of binding law. *See, e.g.*, International Convention on the Elimination of All Forms of Racial Discrimination, preamble and arts. 4 and 7, *opened for signature* Mar. 7, 1966, 660 U.N.T.S. 195; G.A. Res. 1904, 18 U.N. GAOR Supp. 15, at 35 U.N. Doc. A/5603 (1963); G.A. Res. 1514, 15 U.N. GAOR Supp. 16, at 66, U.N. Doc. A/L.323 and Add. 1-6 (1960); J. Carey, UN Protection of Civil and Political Rights 12-15 and 177-87 (1970); Contemporary International Law 235-37 (G. Tunkin ed. 1969); Bleicher, *The Legal Significance of Re-Citation of General Assembly Resolutions*, 63 Am. J. Int'l L. 444, 458-65 (1969).

See also International Covenant on Economic, Social, and Cultural Rights, adopted by G.A. Res. 2200, 21 U.N. GAOR Supp. 16, at 49, U.N. Doc. A/6316 (1966), art. 11 ("recognizing . . . the essential importance of international co-operation based on free consent," and stating: "The States Parties . . . shall take, individually and through international co-operation, the measures . . . which are needed"); and *International Development Strategy*, U.N. Doc. ST/ECA/139, at 3 (1970) ("Economic and social progress is the common and shared responsibility of the entire international community"), reproducing G.A. Res. 2625, 25 U.N. GAOR Supp. 28, at 121, U.N. Doc. A/8028 (1970).

32. G.A. Res. 217A, U.N. Doc. A/810 at 76 (1948).

33. *Id.*

34. Possibilities include: increased use of the U.N. Food and Agriculture Organization (FAO); creation of a new international oil, fertilizer, and food council; use of a new world food bank; and use of a new world oil bank. *See* address by Secretary of State Kissinger, Seventh Special United Nations Assembly, excerpts printed at N.Y. Times, Apr. 16, 1974, at 12, col. 1; and Figueres, *Some Economic Foundations of Human Rights*, U.N. Doc. A/CONF. 32/L.2, at 17-18 (1968), *reprinted at* Basic Documents on Human Rights 459, 508-09 (I. Brownlie ed. 1971). There

trol would be facilitated if the international community were prepared to renounce selfish national claims and recognized that vital earth resources are the property of all peoples. But this is not likely in the very near future. However, even the recognition of each state's right to ownership, exploitation, and pricing of its natural resources does not necessarily include the condoning of coordinate production cuts and sharp price increases used systematically to coerce other governments and peoples.

The 1974 Charter of Economic Rights and Duties of States[35] reiterates a general claim that every state "has and shall freely exercise full permanent sovereignty, including possession, use and disposal, over all its wealth, natural resources and economic activities."[36] The following provision, however, also appears in the charter:

> No state may use or encourage the use of economic, political or any other type of measure to coerce another State in order to obtain from it the subordination of the exercise of its sovereign rights.[37]

Thus, no sovereign may use its resources in any way it wants to use them—it must not use them so as to coerce other governments and peoples in an impermissible manner. This basic limitation on resource control and use is also recognizable in the sister and customary principle that "no State has the right to use or permit the use of its territory in such a manner as to cause injury . . . in or to the territory of another or the properties or persons therein. . . ."[38]

---

is already an agreement entered into by many oil importers to form a new International Energy Agency under the aegis of the twenty-four member O.E.C.D., which includes an agreement to build oil stockpiles and to share them in the event of another cut in supply.

35. G.A. Res. 3281, XII U.N. Monthly Chronicle, January 1975, at 108 (vote: 120/6/10 (U.S.)).

36. *Id.* art. 2 para. 1.

37. *Id.* art. 32. *See also id.* art. 30 (states have a "responsibility to ensure that activities within their jurisdiction or control do not cause damage" to other states). This basic expectation is substantially mirrored in the 1963 Declaration on Inadmissibility of Intervention, the 1970 Declaration on Principles of International Law Concerning Friendly Relations and Co-Operation, and General Assembly resolutions on resource use and control in 1972 and 1973, *see* Paust and Blaustein, *supra* note 2, at 420-22.

38. Trail Smelter Case, (United States v. Canada), 3 U.N.R.I.A.A. 1938, 1965 (decision of Mar. 11, 1941), utilizing several United States Supreme Court decisions held to be in conformity with the general rules of international law. *See also* Oster v. Dominion of Canada, 144 F. Supp. 746 (N.D.N.Y.), *aff'd sub nom.* Clay v.

The two international law principles are reflective of the principle of *sic utere tuo alienum non laedas,* and they emphasize the international responsibility included in territorial sovereignty. Judge Sir Hersch Lauterpacht writes:

> Like independence, territorial supremacy does not give an unlimited liberty of action. . . .A State, in spite of its own territorial supremacy, is not allowed to alter the natural conditions of its own territory to the disadvantage of the natural conditions of the territory of a neighboring State. . . . A State is bound to prevent such use of its territory as, having regard to the circumstances, is unduly injurious to the inhabitants of the neighboring State. . . ."[39]

While the natural resources of the earth remain divided among individual states, state decision-makers must avoid discriminatory practices of resource allocation, while striving instead to use natural wealth for the benefit of all peoples. There can be no doubt that the manipulation of natural resources is regulated by international law and that the control or use of natural resources is not always a matter of "domestic" concern. A state cannot do what-

---

Dominion of Canada, 238 F.2d 400 (2d Cir. 1956), *cert. denied*, 353 U.S. 936 (1957); Corfu Channel Case, [1949] I.C.J. 4, 22, applying the "well-recognized" principle that every state has an "obligation not to allow knowingly its territory to be used for acts contrary to the rights of other States." This doctrine is also reflected in the Treaty Between the United Arab Republic and Sudan, Nov. 8, 1959, 453 U.N.T.S. 51 (the Nile Waters Agreement); *see also* Nile Waters Agreement of 1929 Between the United Kingdom and Egypt, May 7, 1929, Brit. T.S., No. 17, at 2, 93 L.N.T.S. 44; F. BERBER, RIVERS IN INTERNATIONAL LAW 52-122 (1959).

39. 1 L. OPPENHEIM, INTERNATIONAL LAW 290-91 (8th ed. H. Lauterpacht 1955); *see id*. 346-47, 474-75. *See also Lac Lanoux* Arbitration (Spain v. France), 12 U.N.R.I.A.A. 281, 24 I.L.R. 101 (1957), excerpts in 53 AM. J. INT'L L. 44 (1959); Survey of International Law 34, U.N. Doc. A/CN.4/1/Rev. 1 (1949); J. BARROS & D. JOHNSTON, THE INTERNATIONAL LAW OF POLLUTION 74-82 (1974); J. BRIERLY, THE LAW OF NATIONS 231-32 (6th ed. 1963); A. LARSON & C. JENKS, SOVEREIGNTY WITHIN THE LAW 335-56, 377 *et seq*. (1965); Dickstein, *International Lake and River Pollution Control: Questions of Method*, 12 COLUM. J. TRANSNAT'L L. 487 (1973); Friedmann, *The Uses of "General Principles" in the Development of International Law*, 57 AM. J. INT'L L. 279, 287-90 (1963); Handl, *Territorial Sovereignty and the Problem of Transnational Pollution*, 69 AM. J. INT'L L. 50 (1975); Rubin, *Pollution by Analogy: The Trail Smelter Arbitration*, 50 ORE. L. REV. 259, 266 (1971); and notes 35-36 *supra*. "The emerging principle of *sic utere tuo ut alienum non laedas* constituted recognition of the fact that territorial sovereign rights in general were correlative and interdependent and were consequently subject to reciprocally operating limitations." Handl, *supra*, at 55.

ever it wishes with natural resources that happen to be under its control. Clearly, the free use or control of resources by one state or group of states can result in an impermissible interference with the free use of control of resources of others as well as an impermissible deprivation of basic human rights.

VI. A Limited Awareness of Actual "Practice"

Dr. Shihata's efforts to provide a "detailed scrutiny"[40] merely demonstrate the intellectual futility of trying to approach a serious problem in international law with a limited awareness of actual "practice" and contextual conditions. It is not surprising that an analysis of "practice" which is devoid of concern for the identification of the legal policies at stake in given interactions and which ignores any measurement of overall patterns of authority and actual outcomes and effects leads Dr. Shihata to a general conclusion that, after all, "[n]o general rule" actually exists to regulate the use of Arab oil "for political purposes."[41] And, not surprisingly, there is no consideration of actual contracts or trade agreements in Dr. Shihata's "detailed scrutiny," no consideration of coercive outcomes, and no consideration of actual effects. Contrary to implications evident in his approach, the simple fact that prior embargoes have occurred does not answer the question of legal permissibility or impermissibility, nor does it provide insight into the "basic elements" of customary law which condition its creation, change, or demise. Further, his lumping together of all sorts of domestic and international phenomena and claims does not facilitate awareness of actual trends in legal decision and the actual factors which have conditioned past decision. A detailed inquiry shows, instead, that there is no precedent for the actual use of Arab oil as a weapon and the actual outcomes and effects.

With regard to specific cases of prior economic coercion, nothing in Dr. Shihata's analysis of United States actions against the Soviet Union[42] and the action of the Organization of American States against Cuba[43] justifies the use of Arab oil as a destructive political weapon.[44] The rational serving of relevant legal policies in each of these situations is quite different and, in fact, Dr. Shihata seems to support the sort of differentiation that we would make

---

40. Shihata, *supra* note 1, at 609.
41. *Id.* at 616.
42. *Id.* at 610.
43. *Id.* at 620.
44. Paust & Blaustein, *supra* note 2, at 430 n.84.

with regard to Cuba.[45] Moreover, it is nowhere explained during Dr. Shihata's leaps in logic how the legality of certain sanctions by international organizations can lead to the conclusion that "[s]uch precedents may well be cited in support of the Arab oil measures."[46] We do not for an instant believe that the Arab community (as organized or disorganized as one chooses to believe) constitutes an "international organization," nor do the Arab states or their oil ministers constitute a "regional organization" within the meaning of articles 52 and 53 of the United Nations Charter.[47] Despite the assertion made, past practices of international or regional organizations exercising sanctions through use of economic instruments of coercion do not support the unilateral use of oil or money as a "political" weapon for exclusive demands.

VII. The Need to Address Actual Effects

The statement that in implementing the oil embargo the "Arab states showed consideration for the welfare of the countries particularly affected . . . and modified their position towards them accordingly,"[48] is actually belied by the experience of India, Bangladesh, Pakistan, Kenya, Tanzania, and much of the Third and Fourth Worlds. These countries suffered greatly from the indiscriminate effects of application of the oil weapon.[49] Additionally, while the embargo has ceased, the 400 per cent increase in oil prices still exists. It was even stated by President Sadat of Egypt that he believes "the time will come when Arab capital will be used as a weapon also."[50] To our survey of documented effects through June 1974, must be added the warning of Secretary General Waldheim in September 1974, that the world's 32 most impoverished nations are running out of food.[51] There is a unanimous consensus among the experts on food patterns that the present food crisis and the increasing danger of mass death by starvation stems from a severe shortage of fertilizer and oil, and that this in turn is primar-

45. *See Shihata*, *supra* note 1, at 620. *Cf*. The United Nations imposition of sanctions against South Africa, 18 U.N. SCOR, 1056th meeting, 5 (1963); Rhodesia, 20 U.N. SCOR, 1265th meeting, 3 (1965); North Korea and the Peoples Republic of China, G.A. Res. 500, 5 U.N. GAOR Supp. 20A, Add. 1, at 2, U.N. Doc. A/1775 (1951).

46. Shihata, *supra* note 1, at 621.

47. Paust & Blaustein, *supra* note 2, at 430.

48. Shihata, *supra* note 1, at 609.

49. Paust & Blaustein, *supra* note 2, at 434 n.101, 435 n.103.

50. The New Haven Register, Oct. 7, 1974, at 8, col. 2.

51. N.Y. Times, Sept. 28, 1974, at 3, col. 2.

ily the result of sudden and tremendous oil price increases.[52] Moreover, all agree that the most severe impact of these scarcities in the immediate future will be seen in India and Bangladesh. And, contrary to Dr. Shihata's statements,[53] the notorious lack of fertilizer for India's agricultural needs and the lack of fuel to run irrigation pumps, tractors and other farm equipment, food transportation equipment, and small industries did not prove a sufficient incentive for the Arabs to lower prices on oil sold to India.[54] Moreover, this sharp increase took place despite India's long support of Arab political objectives in the Middle East. The "consideration for the welfare" of India that has actually been demonstrated is itself an objective refutation of Dr. Shihata's proclaimed humanism.

The significant amount of monetary aid to developing countries which was provided in 1974 by OPEC producers failed to relieve the disastrous effects of oil prices and production cuts.[55] In fact, although it is estimated that OPEC had promised some ten billion dollars in aid, which nearly equalled the amount of increased prices paid by the Third World, the actual amount provided totaled less than three billion dollars.[56] Additionally, the distribution of aid apparently depended upon Arab-Moslem status, since Egypt, Syria, and Jordan received over 60 per cent of the funds, while Pakistan, Bangladesh, and the Sudan enjoyed a good portion of the remainder.[57] The 730 million dollars provided in 1974 to the poorest nations absorbed only half of the increased oil charges.[58]

---

52. *See, e.g.*, N.Y. Times, Nov. 5, 1974, at 1, col. 7; *id.*, Sept. 19, 1974, at 1, col. 6, and at 18, cols. 1-6; *id.*, Sept. 6, 1974, at 1, col. 4; *id.*, Sept. 1, 1974, at 1, col. 5; *id.*, July 26, 1974, at 31, col. 1. *See also* Mondale, *Beyond Detente: Toward International Economic Security*, 53 FOREIGN AFF. 7, 9 (1974); Mayer, *Coping With Famine*, *id.* at 98.

53. Shihata, *supra* note 1, at 430.

54. *See*, N.Y. Times, Sept. 6, 1974, at 1, col. 4. The economic difficulties encountered by India as a result of oil price increases has prompted sales of oil to India by Iran on a low interest concessional basis. N.Y. Times, Oct. 5, 1974, at 7, col. 1. But such aid and loan programs, although helpful, will not satisfy the needs of the poorest of the world who do not share in the increase of revenues enjoyed by Arab oil producing states. *See* U.S. Relations with Arabian Peninsula/Persian Gulf Countries, U.S. Dep't of State, Current Foreign Policy, no. 8777, (Sept. 1974).

55. *Id.*

56. Power, *Cranking Up Oil Producers' Aid-Giving Machine*, N.Y. Times, Mar. 15, 1975, at 27, col. 3.

57. *See id.* Houston Chronicle, Mar. 9, 1975, at 27, col. 3.

58. N.Y. Times, Mar. 15, 1975, at 27, col. 3.

The combination of oil and fertilizer shortages plus increased oil prices indicate that possibilities of industrial and agricultural development are, in the words of one observer, "in pawn to the oil exporting nations."[59] The growing awareness that a "common pool of food-producing resources"[60] exists and that energy, fertilizer, and food production are interdependent has prompted many to seek a rational solution through global cooperation.[61] There are ample warnings that unless there is more energy, fertilizer, and food available to the peoples of the developing nations there is a real danger of social instability and violence if not, as others now add to our warning, a danger of wars for scarce resources and of increasing deference to totalitarian thinking.[62] We are clearly at a crossroad. Destructive confrontations will, as President Ford has pointed out, bring "unacceptable risks for all mankind."[63] Moreover, few would disagree with the President that with an increased interdependence in patterns of food, fertilizer, and energy, "[f]ailure to cooperate on oil and food and inflation could spell disaster for every nation. . . . A global strategy for food and energy is urgently required."[64]

VIII. A New and Interrelated Coercive Boycott

Underscoring the threat of President Sadat to use Arab money as a political weapon[65] are recent Arab efforts to blacklist business entities of the developed countries in order to coerce those who

---

59. McElheny, *Rising World Fertilizer Scarcity Threatens Famine for Millions*, N.Y. Times, Sept. 1, 1974, at 1, col. 5, 34, col. 4.

60. *See* N.Y. Times, Sept. 19, 1974, at 1, col. 6.

61. *See* President Ford, Energy: A Global Strategy, U.S. Dep't of State, News Release, Sept. 23, 1974; President Ford, A Framework of International Cooperation, U.S. Dep't of State, News Release, Sept. 18, 1974 (address before the U.N. General Assembly), address by E. Martin, U.S. Dep't of State, News Release, June 18, 1974; N.Y. Times, Sept. 19, 1974, at 1, col. 6; *id.*, July 26, 1974, at 31, col. 1; N.Y. Times, April 10, 1974, at 12, col. 4 (address by Secretary General Waldheim to the General Assembly of the U.N.); and, N.Y. Times, May 13, 1974, at 11, col. 1. *See also* U.S. Dep't of State, Special Report, no. 3, World Food Situation, pub. no. 8769, Int'l Org. and Conf. Ser. 114 (July, 1974).

62. *See, e.g.*, N.Y. Times, July 26, 1974, at 31, col. 1; U.S. Dep't of State, Foreign Policy Outlines, Interdependence: Population Growth (June, 1974). *See also*, N.Y. Times, Sept. 27, 1974, at 1, col. 6; N.Y. Times, Oct. 4, 1974, at 3, col. 1, (concerning the Saudi Arabian Minister of Petroleum's recognition of the dangers to the political systems of Italy, France and Japan which have resulted from the sudden rise in oil prices).

63. Energy: A Global Strategy, *supra* note 61, at 2.

64. A Framework of International Cooperation, *supra* note 60.

65. Houston Chronicle, Mar. 5, 1975, at 1, col. 2.

allegedly are aiding Israel.[66] Partially blacklisted companies such as Sony and Leyland were informed that blacklisting would cease upon the conclusion of pending agreements to establish operations in Arab countries.[67] This strategy, which is contrary to the "free consent" provisions of contract law and the Vienna Convention on the Law of Treaties,[68] is reminiscent of the differentiation among neutral and friendly countries in the application of the oil embargo.[69] Such distinctions, we aver, are in fact unrelated to the war against Israel and are being made only to acquire the best results for Arab states that a self-oriented coercive strategy will produce.

As further support for our assertion of true motivational concerns, we note that pressure has caused many business firms to exclude Jews and persons of Jewish ancestry from travel to certain Arab countries, whether or not the Jews are Israelis or pro-Israel in their outlook.[70] Further, the United States Department of Defense has been charged with the violation of domestic civil rights and international human rights laws by conceding to Arab pressure to exclude American Jews from American military groups sent to Saudi Arabia.[71]

The use of economic coercion against Jews as an ethnic group, without regard to their actual aiding of the Israeli war effort, con-

---

66. N.Y. Times, Feb. 13, 1975, at 1, col. 5.

67. N.Y. Times, Mar. 3, 1975, at 3, col. 2.

68. Vienna Convention on the Law of Treaties, U.N. Doc. A/Conf. 39/27 (1969).

69. See note 13 *supra*.

70. *Id.* Companies which comply with Arab blacklists, apart from their failure to respect U.S. civil rights and international human rights relating to freedom from racial, religious, or ethnic discrimination may also be engaged in a conspiracy in restraint of trade in violation of federal anti-trust law. *See* N.Y. Times, Mar. 3, 1975, at 3, col. 4; *id.*, Feb. 28, 1975, at 8, col. 1. *See also* Paust & Blaustein, at 411 n.7. 15 U.S.C. §§1-2, might provide a jurisdictional basis for the sanctioning of deprivations of civil and human rights, under the Ninth Amendment to the United States Constitution as well as 42 U.S.C. §§ 1981-1988; 18 U.S.C. §§ 241 and 242 *et seq. See also* United States v. Imperial Chemical Industries, 100 F. Supp. 504 (S.D.N.Y. 1951) (violation of the Sherman Act); Banco Nacional de Cuba v. Farr, Whitlock & Co., 383 F.2d 166, *cert. denied* 390 U.S. 956 (1968) (nonapplication of act of state doctrine to violations of international law); Paust, *Human Rights and the Ninth Amendment: A New Form of Guarantee*, 60 CORNELL L. REV. 231 (1975) (protection from human right deprivations under the ninth amendment); N.Y. Times, Jan. 17, 1976, at 5, col. 3 (concerning recent U.S. sanction efforts).

71. *See* N.Y. Times, Mar. 17, 1975, at 30, col. 7; N.Y. Times, Feb. 28, 1975, at 8, col. 1.

stitutes a violation of articles 55(c) and 56 of the United Nations Charter. The boycott of pro-Israeli and pro-Jewish firms emphasizes the critical need for concerted action by the United Nations to oppose the coercive use of natural resources, wealth, and power in any manner inconsistent with the purposes of the United Nations.

IX. Conclusion

This critique of Dr. Shihata's response to our original article, which asserts the permissibility of the Arab use of oil as a "political weapon,"[72] reemphasizes the need for an awareness of legal policies and contextual features conditioning the acceptability of particular strategies in given situations. The failure to question the necessity and proportionality of economic coercion, and the assertion of the irrelevance of contracts and trade agreements, fail to serve present law and to foster the development of common legal policies which are necessary in an increasingly interdependent world. The present era demands awareness of actual patterns of interaction and a cooperative effort toward more inclusive regulation of economic coercion, so as to insure a more rational, fair, and policy-serving utilization of the earth resources for all peoples.

---

72. Shihata, *supra* note 1, at 594.

ECONOMIC COERCION AND THE INTERNATIONAL LEGAL ORDER

Richard B. Lillich

NOW as never before economic considerations dominate the international as well as the domestic political scene. The claims of the developing countries to a fairer share of the world's economic pie are being heard—and are often being followed by co-ordinated action by groups of these countries to back up such claims. The Arab oil embargo of 1973–74, which turned OPEC from a paper tiger into a permanent force to be reckoned with internationally, was merely the first indication of what the future holds in store. Subsequent collective action by the International Association of Producers of Bauxite has succeeded in boosting the price of that mineral, albeit nowhere near so spectacularly as in the case of oil,[1] and the recent decision of the Intergovernmental Council of Copper Exporting Countries to cut shipment by 10 per cent in an effort to shore up the price of copper, while so far having little effect, may cause further economic difficulties for the industrial countries in the not too distant future.[2]

Reaction to the above developments, especially the traumatic oil embargo, has been swift and predictable. Calling it 'blackmail', a phrase later used by the US Secretary of State, Henry Kissinger, the columnist William Buckley contended in November 1973 that '[i]t is both a moral and a legal question whether the Arab embargo has reached the point of asphyxiation that warrants belligerent reprisals'.[3] Although with the easing of the embargo last summer this crisis atmosphere passed, in September the US Secretary of Defense, James R. Schlesinger, was still explaining that the United States was 'not contemplating' any military action against the Arab oil producers,[4] and in late November *The Times* reported the study of the Stockholm International Peace Research Institute on 'Oil and Security' under the headline: 'Military action against oil nations deemed unlikely'.[5]

1 *New York Times*, Mar. 7, 1974, p. 55, col. 2.

2 *The Times*, Nov. 20, 1974, p. 21, col. 8.

3 See his syndicated column of Nov. 10, 1973, reprinted in the *New York Times*, Nov. 14, 1973, p. 10, col. 1. Compare text at notes 6 and 30 below.

4 *The Times*, Sept. 26, 1974, p. 6, col. 2.

5 *Ibid.*, Nov. 20, 1974, p. 10, cols. 5–6. The article acknowledged, however, that '[t]he possibility of outside military intervention in the oil-rich Middle East cannot be lightly dismissed . . .'. See text at and accompanying note 7 below.

While such action currently appears out of the question, as indicated by Dr. Kissinger's remark last January that it would be considered only if 'there is some actual strangulation of the industrialised world',[6] the increasing pressure which last year's fivefold increase in the price of oil has put on the balance-of-payments problems of many industrialised countries, as well as on the world's monetary system generally, may some day produce a military response, conceivably in conjunction with another round of the Arab-Israeli war.[7]

Perhaps more realistic, and certainly more hopeful, has been the attempt, led by the United States, to establish in advance patterns of response to any future oil boycott. The newly-created 18-nation International Energy Agency is an historic attempt to co-ordinate the actions of Western countries should another energy crisis erupt. Under the agreement establishing IEA, the member states in effect surrender much of their freedom of action—their so-called 'sovereignty'—should such an emergency arise, since mandatory cuts in consumption and a formula for sharing during shortages have been predetermined.[8] Laudable as this approach is, however, it does not come to grips with the continuing high price of oil. Nor, of course, does it provide more than a guideline—and perhaps an unsuitable one at that—for how to structure a response to the claims of the bauxite, copper and other raw material producing countries. Indeed, from the viewpoint of the ideal international economic order, the formation of groups like OPEC, on the one hand, and IEA, on the other, seems as undesirable as it is understandable. It is ironic, to say the least, that laissez-faire economics,

[6] See his *Business Week* interview of Jan. 13, 1975, reprinted in 72 Dept. State Bull. 97, 101 (1975). Compare text at note 3 above. He added, 'I want to make clear . . . that the use of force would be considered only in the gravest emergency'. *Ibid.* President Ford subsequently endorsed these remarks. *The Times*, Jan. 25, 1975, p. 4, col. 2. For clarifying comments by the Secretary of State, see *ibid.* Jan. 17, 1975, p. 7, col. 5; *Int. Herald-Tribune*, Jan. 29, 1975, p. 2, col. 5.

[7] Such a war presumably would trigger another oil embargo, which the US Secretary of Commerce, Frederick B. Dent, has stated 'would strangle us, because we have become even more dependent on Mid-East oil than we were in 1973.' *The Times*, Feb. 14, 1975, p. 6, col. 7. See also the Assistant Secretary of State, Thomas Ender's remarks that a total embargo 'would be something very close to nuclear warfare. That would be as big a threat as could come to the industrialised nations.' *Int. Herald-Tribune*, Feb. 15–16, 1975, p. 1, col. 5. Compare text at note 6 above.

For a strong critique of the United States' virtual foreclosure of military action, see Tucker, 'Oil: The Issue of American Intervention', *Commentary*, Jan. 1975, p. 21. Compare Middleton, 'Taking Over Arab Oil Fields Held Possible but Dangerous', *Int. Herald-Tribune*, Jan. 13, 1975, p. 2, cols. 1–2 (pro-Tucker), with Lewis, 'Thinking the Unthinkable', *ibid.*, Dec. 31, 1974, p. 6, cols. 3–6 (anti-Tucker). An even stronger plea for such a response, with a complete intervention scenario, may be found in Ignotus (pseudonym), 'Seizing Arab Oil', *Harper's Mag.*, Mar. 1975, p. 45. This article, it is said, accurately describes a Department of Defense contingency plan 'to invade Saudi Arabian oilfields in the event of another Middle East war and a further Arab oil embargo'. Aris, 'How US troops would seize Saudi oil wells', *The Sunday Times*, Feb. 9, 1975, p. 8, col. 3.

[8] Crawford, 'Oil: Sharing It,' *ibid.*, Nov. 24, 1974, p. 62, cols. 5–8.

so generally discredited domestically, has made such a significant comeback internationally.

Basic to the creation of a 'new international economic order'—an objective receiving near-unanimous support at the Sixth Special Session of the UN General Assembly held in the spring of 1974[9]—is international law. Surprisingly, in the welter of economic, social and political claims during the past year, legal considerations have had little impact. What does international law say about economic coercion? What substantive norms and procedural devices can it recommend as models for the restructuring process now going on so haphazardly and at such cost? Does it have any role to play at all?

International law and economic coercion: past trends

Traditional international law allowed states almost unfettered discretion with respect to the use of force. War being a legitimate tool of foreign policy, obviously economic coercion, which is not even a breach of the peace, was deemed permissible. With the coming of the United Nations in 1945, however, the international community adopted an entirely different approach, at least insofar as military coercion was concerned. Article 2 (4) of the UN Charter requires that member states 'shall refrain in their international relations from the threat or use of force against the territorial integrity or political independence of any state . . .'. Thus, save for collective or individual self-defence against an aggressor, international law now forbids the use of forceful measures. But Article 2 (4) is silent on the question of economic coercion, presumably because the framers of the Charter believed, as was quickly shown, that the organisation would have its hands full stamping out coercion of the military type.

Over the years, however, it has been argued with growing conviction that the 'threat or use of force' proscribed by Article 2 (4) should be construed to cover acts of an economic nature by a state when directed against another state's 'territorial integrity or political independence . . .'. Thus, in a recent article entitled 'The Arab Oil Weapon—A Threat to International Peace', Professors Paust and Blaustein contend that Article 2 (4) 'prohibits more than the threat or use of "armed" force'.[10] In their gloss of the article, heavily influenced by the policy-science approach to international law made

[9] See 'Declaration on the Establishment of a New International Economic Order', U.N. Doc. A/RES/3201 (S-VI) (1974), reprinted in 13 *International Legal Materials* 715 (1974) and 68 *American Journal of International Law* 798 (1974).

[10] Paust and Blaustein, 'The Arab Oil Weapon—A Threat to International Peace', 68 (AJIL) 410, 417 (1974). For a reply to this article, see Shihata, 'Destination Embargo of Arab Oil: Its Legality Under International Law', 68 (AJIL) 591 (1974).

popular by Professor McDougal of Yale, coercion—economic as well as military—may be forbidden. Thus they conclude, after a lengthy survey of Charter policies, that 'the substantial impairment of goals of the international community as articulated in the Charter through the deliberate use of coercion against other states, not counterbalanced by complementary policies relating to legitimate self-defense or the sanctioning of UN decisions, constitutes a violation of Article 2 (4) as well as of other provisions of the Charter '.[11]

It would be easy to discount their construction of the Charter as the knee-jerk response of Western international lawyers to the Arab oil embargo were it not for the fact that, somewhat ironically, most African, Asian and other Third World spokesmen actively advocated such an interpretation throughout the 1960s and, indeed, up until October 1973. Thus, in the UN debate on the General Assembly's Declaration on Friendly Relations,[12] about which more later, Mr. El Reedy of the United Arab Republic maintained that in construing Article 2 (4) it was 'essential to include economic and political pressure as an illegal use of force because, in view of the present political and economic interdependence of States, powerful States could strangle weaker States with pressures of that kind to the point of threatening their political independence and territorial integrity '.[13] The Western states, although generally opposed to what they then considered a rewriting of the Charter, nevertheless left open the possibility that certain types of economic coercion might violate international law. To confine Article 2 (4) to military coercion, stated Mr. Sinclair of the United Kingdom, 'was not to say that all forms of economic and political pressure which threatened the territorial integrity and political independence of another State were permissible: they might well constitute illegal intervention '.[14]

Indeed, even a cursory survey of UN declarations during the past decade reveals strong support for the proposition that at least certain types of economic coercion now violate international law. Thus the UN General Assembly's Declaration on Non-Intervention,[15] adopted by a 109–0–1 vote in 1965, after condemning not only armed intervention but also 'all other forms of interference or attempted threats against the personality of the State or against its political, economic and cultural elements ', goes on to state specifically that '[n]o State may use or encourage the use of economic, political or any other type of

[11] Paust and Blaustein, note 10 above, p. 415.

[12] G.A.Res. 2625, 25 UN GAOR, Supp. 28, p. 121, UN Doc. A/8028 (1970), reprinted in 65 (AJIL) 243 (1971).

[13] UN Doc. A/AC.125/SR.25, p. 12, para. 23 (1966).

[14] *Ibid.*, p. 16, para. 39.

[15] G.A.Res. 2131, 20 UN GAOR, Supp. 14, p. 11, UN Doc. A/6014 (1965), reprinted in 60 (AJIL), p. 662 (1966).

measures to coerce another State in order to obtain from it the subordination of the exercise of its sovereign rights or to secure from it advantages of any kind '.[16] Among the oil-producing states supporting the Declaration were Algeria, Iran, Iraq, Kuwait, Libya, Saudi Arabia, Syria and the UAR. Needless to say, after the imposition of the oil embargo, with the shoe on the other foot, nothing was heard about this document from the above states.

The UN General Assembly's Declaration on Friendly Relations also is squarely to the point. Unanimously adopted in 1970 as the authoritative interpretation of the UN Charter, it begins by stating that it is 'the duty of States to refrain in their international relations from military, political, economic or any other form of coercion aimed against the political independence or territorial integrity of any State', and then, using language taken from the Declaration on Non-Intervention, proceeds to declare such economic measures to be in violation of international law.[17] Once again, despite the fact that the oil-producing states were among the group pressing hardest for this principle, and indeed for the proposition that it already was part of international law, nothing has been heard from them about its applicability to the oil embargo. As Professor Gardner notes caustically, '[n]ot a single voice has been raised in the United Nations to cite the relevance of this authoritative declaration to the Arab oil embargo—which is typical of the "double standard" that currently prevails in the world organisation and accounts for much of the scepticism about the integrity of its decision-making process'.[18] Even the United States failed to make the point, presumably because it thought to do so would be counterproductive. This decision, undoubtedly part of Dr. Kissinger's short-lived strategy to lower the price of oil by placating the Arabs, has been roundly criticised by the Joint Economic Committee of the US Congress, which has recommended that '[t]o discourage further economic warfare, the United States should ask the Secretary General of the United Nations to serve notice on the Arab oil producers that their actions violate the UN Resolution . . . limiting the use of economic and political pressure'.[19] The Administration completely ignored this recommendation.

Finally, in a classic case of adding insult to injury, when the UN General Assembly adopted its latest resolution on Permanent Sovereignty Over Natural Resources on December 17, 1973,[20] two

[16] *Ibid.*, Arts. 1, 2, p. 12, 60 (AJIL), p. 663.
[17] Note 12 above, pp. 122, 123; 65 (AJIL), pp. 244–45, 248.
[18] Gardner, 'The Hard Road to World Order', 52 *Foreign Affairs*, pp. 556, 567 (1974).
[19] Joint Economic Comm., *The 1974 Joint Economic Report*, H.R.Rep. No. 93–927, 93d Cong., 2d Sess., p. 17 (1974).
[20] UN Doc. A/RES/3171 (XXVIII) (1974), reprinted in 68 (AJIL), p. 381 (1974).

months after the imposition of the oil embargo and one month after the Arab leaders had adopted a joint resolution calling for the continued use of oil as an 'economic weapon',[21] Paragraph 4 thereof specifically deplored 'acts of States which use force, armed aggression, *economic coercion* or any other illegal or improper means in resolving disputes', while Paragraph 6 emphasised 'the duty of all States to refrain in their international relations from military, political, *economic or any other form of coercion* aimed against the territorial integrity of any State . . .'.[22] Apparently the Arab oil producers saw no inconsistency in supporting this resolution while simultaneously maintaining their 25 per cent reduction in oil shipments to the Common Market countries and Japan, plus their total embargo on shipments to the United States and the Netherlands, actions which Paust and Blaustein contend 'can be authoritatively proscribed as a violation of basic Charter goals and of Article 2 (4)'.[23] Moreover, they recently compounded this inconsistency by unanimously supporting the Charter of Economic Rights and Duties of States adopted by the UN General Assembly on December 12, 1974, Article 32 of which contains once again an authoritative condemnation of economic coercion.[24]

One final legal point generally has been overlooked. Even if one ignores the UN Charter and the above documents adopted under it, the actions of the various oil-producing states may still run foul of international law if they violate prior treaty commitments entered into by such states. Under a little-known bilateral treaty between the United States and Saudi Arabia, for instance, both states guarantee each other 'most-favoured-nation' treatment.[25] This clause clearly prevents discriminatory actions by both states, including actions such as the oil embargo, which bore harder on the United States than, say, on

[21] *New York Times*, Nov. 29, 1973, p. 16, col. 6.

[22] 68 (AJIL), p. 38 (author's italics).

[23] Paust and Blaustein, note 10 above, p. 439. 'The Arab strategy constitutes the deliberate employment of an economic instrument of coercion . . . against other states and peoples in order to place intense pressure upon their freedom of choice. . . . As such, the Arab oil embargo is in violation of international law, as formulated in the United Nations Charter and key supporting documents'. *Ibid.*, p. 412.

[24] UN Doc. A/RES/3281 (XXIX) (1974), reprinted in 72 Dept. State Bull. 147 (1975). Article 32 provides: 'No State may use or encourage the use of economic, political or any other type of measures to coerce another State in order to obtain from it the subordination of the exercise of its sovereign rights'. *Ibid.*, p. 153.

President Echeverría of Mexico, the prime mover behind the Charter, has claimed that it will be 'frequently invoked in defence of countries threatened by economic pressures or injured by foreign intervention in their economic affairs'. *The Times*, Feb. 19, 1975, Mexican Section, p. VIII, col. 5. One wonders whether he had the industrial countries in mind. Compare text following note 32 below.

[25] Treaty with Saudi Arabia on Diplomatic and Consular Representation, Judicial Protection, Commerce and Navigation, Nov. 7, 1933, 48 Stat. 1826 (1933), 11 C. Bevans, *Treaties and Other International Agreements of the United States of America 1776–1949*, US GPO, p. 456 (1974).

France.[26] Similar treaties are in force between the United States and Iraq and the United States and Oman.[27] In addition, Kuwait and the UAR are both parties to the General Agreement on Tariffs and Trade,[28] the multilateral treaty which is aimed at eliminating discriminatory treatment in international commerce. Articles 1, 11, 13 and 20 of GATT also preclude actions such as the oil embargo.[29] Once again, both in the case of the bilateral treaties and GATT, neither the United States nor its European allies thought it wise to raise these legal points for fear of offending the Arab states. While efforts to avoid confrontation in international relations are generally laudable, this refusal to demand compliance with the relevant legal norms obviously gained the Western states little in the short-term. It also contributed nothing to the long-term clarification of the norms of international law governing economic coercion.

International law and economic coercion: future developments

If, as the above survey reveals, there are now some restraints, however nebulous, upon a state's unilateral resort to economic coercion, what are they and how can they be enforced? Before exploring these questions it is perhaps worth emphasising that, while the discussion necessarily must focus on the Arab oil embargo, the Arab states certainly have no monopoly on the use or abuse of economic coercion. In response to Dr. Kissinger's characterisation of the embargo as 'blackmail',[30] George Ball, former Under Secretary of State in the Kennedy and Johnson Administrations, noted in the *New York Times* that it 'has the sour sound of sanctimony in the chancelleries of other nations. We Americans, after all, have been leading practitioners of economic sanctions to advance our own political—and even moral—policies, and if those sanctions have rarely, if ever, achieved the intended result, that has not deterred us'.[31]

More detailed criticism has come from Gardner, who, warning against 'an unduly self-righteous attitude on these matters', points out that

[26] 'The export embargo on oil was applied selectively to the U.S. and the Netherlands, and thus clearly violated the most-favored-nation provisions in the bilateral agreements'. Gardner, note 18 above, p. 566, n. 3. *Contra* Shihata, note 10 above, pp. 623–24.

[27] Shihata, pp. 624–25. See text at and accompanying note 26 above.

[28] General Agreement on Tariffs and Trade, Oct. 30, 1947, T.I.A.S. No. 1700, 4 C. Bevans, *Treaties and Other International Agreements of the United States of America 1776–1949*, p. 639 (1970).

[29] Paust and Blaustein, note 10 above, pp. 423–24. *Contra* Shihata, note 10 above, pp. 621–23.

[30] *New York Times*, Feb. 7, 1974, p. 1, col. 4. See text at note 3 above.

[31] Ball, 'Your Evil Embargo; Our Purity of Purpose', *New York Times*, Mar. 21, 1974, p. 41, col. 7.

> the United States itself has been one of the worst offenders in using trade controls in ways which have adversely affected other countries. As a result of congressional pressures, the President was given the authority to cut off aid to countries trading with Cuba or North Vietnam. Last summer we unilaterally cut off exports of soybeans and other agricultural products to our trading partners in Europe at the very time we were pressing them to modify policies of agricultural self-sufficiency and become dependent on our production. And the House of Representatives only recently adopted amendments to the trade bill denying most-favored-nation treatment and trade credits to the Soviet Union and other 'non-market economy' countries until they grant free emigration to their citizens.[32]

Thus, in recommending normative guidelines and procedural sanctions in this area of international law, as in all areas of law generally, the 'mirror image' principle must be kept in mind: namely, that the claims one projects against others inevitably will be reflected in similar claims against oneself.

Keeping the above in mind, in the first place it is desirable, and indeed mandatory if any real progress is to take place, to eliminate the military overtones in the rhetoric employed by both sides. Thus Dr. Kissinger's reference to economic 'blackmail'[33] and the Arab leaders' reference to oil being used as an 'economic weapon'[34] shed more heat than light. Similarly, Gardner's use of the phrase 'economic warfare',[35] and Hobart Rowen's invocation of the term 'economic aggression'[36] in a *Washington Post* column, add little to the debate. Indeed, the use of such language necessarily raises expectations about the possibility of a military response, expectations hardly conducive to the short-term settlement of disputes or the long-term maintenance of peace and security. Moreover, as Paust and Blaustein rightly observe, '[n]ot only are these terms generally too confining for a proper focus, but some are merely conclusions that may be attached to a particular coercive process after fact and law have been fully considered.'[37] To use them initially, in short, is to prejudge the case.

32 Gardner, note 18 above, p. 567. Compare text at notes 51–53 below.
33 See note 30 above.
34 See note 21 above.
35 Gardner, 'Economic Warfare: "All Can Play"', *Washington Post*, Dec. 14, 1973, p. A30, col. 5.
36 Rowen, 'The "Economic Aggression" of the Arabs', *ibid*., Dec. 6, 1973, p. A31, cols. 3–5. 'The extraordinary thing about the Arab oil boycott is the refusal of the Western World to recognise it for what it is—economic warfare—and to deal with it in those terms. Economic aggression is no less a hostile act than military aggression.' *Ibid*. at col. 3. For evidence that this fact finally has been recognised, see text at and accompanying notes 6 and 7 above.
37 Paust and Blaustein, note 10 above, pp. 412–13.

Secondly, it needs stressing that economic coercion, even of the most blatant type, is permissible when undertaken pursuant to internationally-authorised measures. Thus, in the case of UN sanctions against Rhodesia, not only is the economic coercion involved obviously compatible with world community policy, but it actually is made legal by the UN Charter itself.[38] For this reason, there can be no objection to the Arab oil embargo insofar as it may have affected Rhodesia, or for that matter perhaps even South Africa. What is at issue is only the unilateral use of economic coercion by a state or group of states without colour of international authorisation.

Thirdly, assuming unilateral acts of economic coercion may violate international law norms, what criteria should be applied to determine whether they do or do not? Here there is little, if any, precedent upon which to rely. Dr. Derek Bowett, in a prophetic article published three years ago, observed that 'it will require a great deal of practice, of "case-law", to give the concept of illegal economic coercion substance and definition.'[39] To illustrate the difficulties involved in determining what measures of coercion should be deemed illegal, he cited the American withdrawal of financial support for the Aswan Dam in 1956. 'Was the United States free to do this', he asks, 'or was the action illegal because it was "coercive" and aimed at the subordination of Egypt or securing advantages from Egypt?'[40] Similarly, what about the United States cutting Cuba's sugar quota in 1960? 'Was this', he asks, 'an attempt to coerce the Cuban Government into less antagonistic policies, and therefore illegal?'[41] Or, to raise an issue from the 1970s, is the so-called Jackson Amendment to the Trade Reform Act of 1974, making extension by the United States of most-favoured-nation treatment to the Soviet Union dependent upon that country's relaxation of its emigration policy with respect to its Jewish population, illegal because it admittedly is aimed at changing Soviet domestic law?

One cannot answer these questions definitively, but one can sketch out an approach based upon the general principle that serious and sustained economic coercion should be accepted as a form of permissible self-help only when it is also compatible with the overall interests of the world community, as manifested in the principles of the UN Charter or in decisions taken or documents promulgated there-

[38] UN Charter art. 41. On the lawfulness of UN sanctions against Rhodesia, see, for example, McDougal and Reisman, 'Rhodesia and the United Nations: The Lawfulness of International Concern', 62 (AJIL) 1 (1968).

[39] Bowett, 'Economic Coercion and Reprisals by States', 13 *Virginia Journal of International Law* 1, 4 (1972).

[40] *Ibid.* p. 3.

[41] *Ibid.* p. 4.

under. This approach, like the determination of many other issues in international law, rests more upon subjective than objective standards, a point well made by Bowett.

> Much of State economic activity is harmful to other States for the very obvious reason that State economies are competitive and that promoting one's own economy may well be injurious to others. This suggests that it will be necessary to characterise unlawful economic measures by their intent rather than their effect. In other words, measures not illegal *per se* may become illegal only upon proof of an improper motive or purpose.[42]

Lawyers, of course, are quite familiar with this approach in the context of domestic law. Indeed, as Bowett explains, '[t]his idea is found in the English common law. For example, the tort of conspiracy evolved to cover the situation in which two or more persons conspire to commit acts which are lawful *per se* but are motivated predominantly by the desire to injure the economic interests of the plaintiff rather than to protect the interests of the defendants.'[43] Since the proof of any doctrinal approach rests with its success when applied to concrete situations, what results flow from the application of the above approach to recent situations involving economic coercion? Two examples will suffice for present purposes.

In the case of the Arab oil embargo, it is apparent from the very words of the Arab leaders that, apart from obtaining a tremendous increase in the price of crude oil, its prime objective was to weaken the economies of the major Western countries, plus Japan, to the extent that ultimately they would, in Rowen's words, 'swallow hard and dump the Jewish state'.[44] Withdrawal of support for Israel, plus tangible support of the Arab cause, was the articulated demand upon which cessation of the oil weapon's use depended. Thus Japan, almost wholly dependent upon Arab oil, undertook the most humiliating reversal of policy. Suddenly, after a meeting on December 18, 1973 with President Sadat of the UAR, the then Deputy Premier, Takeo Miki, found himself announcing Tokyo's eagerness to extend to Cairo a 25-year loan of $140 million to widen and deepen the Suez Canal. Mr. Miki also indicated that Japan was prepared to participate in a wide range of joint economic and industrial projects, concluding that Japan was 'determined to do as much as possible to assist Egypt'.[45] Other states also shifted their positions vis-à-vis the Arab states in less dramatic fashion.

42 *Ibid.* p. 5.
43 *Ibid.*
44 Rowen, note 36 above, p. A31, col. 5.
45 *New York Times*, Dec. 19, 1973, p. 11, col. 1.

The argument has been made, of course, that harmful as the oil embargo admittedly was, the Arab states had no other recourse in their attempt to secure justice for their Palestinian brethren.[46] It will not wash. During 1973 the combined contributions of the Arab states to the UN relief programme for Palestinian refugees was only $2.25 million, just 9 per cent. of the American pledge of $25 million. Moreover, Arab contributions have been even smaller over the time span since 1950. 'With Saudi Arabia alone spending more than $1 billion on the 1973 Egyptian and Syrian war effort', Paust and Blaustein remark, 'one wonders why more Arab oil profits could not have gone to feed the Arab poor'.[47] Certainly the Arab states' concern has been selective, to say the least, when it comes to the Palestinians.

When it comes to the poor and hungry of other lands, though, until recently it has been almost non-existent.[48] Dr. Borlaug of the Rockefeller Foundation has estimated that as many as 20 million people may die because of crop shortages caused primarily by the lack of fertiliser due to the oil embargo.[49] Developing countries heavily dependent upon oil imports, such as Brazil, India, Singapore and South Korea, are running up staggering balance-of-payments deficits.[50] Another thirty of the poorest states, with over a quarter of the world's population, are witnessing the complete undercutting of their development programmes by the fivefold increase in the price of oil over the past year and a half, an increase which may well consign them to permanent 'Fourth World' status. The poorest lands, Bangladesh being the classic case, will simply be driven bankrupt. Viewing these consequences of the oil embargo and its aftermath, including the current oil-fueled inflation, it can hardly be argued that it has served the overall interests of the world community.

In the case of the Soviet Jews, however, a different situation existed. Under the Trade Reform Act of 1974, the United States did not suddenly deny the Soviet Union access to a vital commodity, but merely refused to bestow financial and trade benefits long sought by

[46] See Shihata, note 10 above.

[47] Paust and Blaustein, note 10 above, p. 437, n. 110.

[48] This attitude may be changing. See 'Petro-aid takes off', *The Economist*, Feb. 15, 1975, p. 72. During 1974, for instance, OPEC countries apparently committed $9.6 billion to foreign aid projects. Monroe, 'Petro-dollars and Petro-aid', *The Times*, Mar. 20, 1975, Arab Renaissance Section, p. V, col. 2. Yet 'OPEC aid is not quite as simple as these bald figures suggest. First, the actual delivery of the aid is lagging quite a way behind the promises to give it—only roughly $2.6 billion was actually handed out in 1974. Secondly, although the spread of aid is increasing fast, it is still highly concentrated'. Power, 'OPEC as an Aid-Giver', *Int. Herald-Tribune*, Mar. 5, 1975, p. 6, col. 3.

[49] *New York Times*, Jan. 26, 1974, p. 1, col. 1.

[50] 'The World Bank estimates that the increased cost of the current volume of oil imports for the non-oil-producing developing countries is $10 billion. This is equivalent to 15 per cent of their total import bill. For India it is roughly the same as two-thirds of its entire foreign-exchange reserves and over 25 per cent of its total exports.' Power, note 48 above.

that country. This action was taken not to achieve financial or trade advantages for the United States, or indeed for its allies, but to bestow human rights upon thousands of persons who have no effective means of achieving them without external assistance. Human rights, after all, are one of the two major purposes of the United Nations, and the Universal Declaration of Human Rights,[51] unanimously adopted by the General Assembly in 1948, provides in Article 13 (2) that 'everyone has the right to leave any country, including his own . . .'. More recently, the UN Covenant on Civil and Political Rights,[52] to which the Soviet Union became a party in 1973, contains almost identical language in Article 12 (2): 'Everyone shall be free to leave any country, including his own.' In the absence of international procedures to assist persons in the Soviet Union wishing to exercise this right, action by individual states to achieve such ends surely is and should remain permissible. Whatever economic coercion is involved, which admittedly is aimed at changing Soviet law and policy, is designed only to secure compliance with international law. Not only does it not adversely affect other states, but it actually supports their shared objectives in the human rights area. Thus, just as with the UN sanctions against Rhodesia,[53] the US stand on Soviet Jews serves the overall interests of the world community.

Conclusion

In an attempt to forge a constructive approach to the problems occasioned by the Arab oil embargo, it is necessary to go well beyond the present state of international law and even beyond the creation of special interest agencies like IEA to counter the special interest activities of groups like OPEC.[54] What is needed, as Gardner has

[51] G.A.Res. 217, UN Doc. A/810, p. 71 (1948).

[52] G.A.Res. 2200, 21 UN GAOR Supp. 16, p. 49, UN Doc. A/6316 (1967).

[53] See note 38 above.

[54] According to OPEC, interestingly enough, what is sauce for the goose is not sauce for the gander. In a 'Solemn Declaration' issued at the end of their Algiers conference in March 1975, the OPEC member countries denounced 'any grouping of consumer nations with the aim of confrontation, and condemn[ed] any plan of strategy designed for aggression, economic or military, by such grouping or otherwise against any OPEC Member Country.' *The Times*, Mar. 18, 1975, p. 9, col. 2. The target of this denunciation obviously was IEA.

Such utterances not only are one-sided, ignoring the 'mirror image' principle, but they are myopic as well. If, as will be argued in the text that follows, international stabilising commodity agreements provide the best solution to current problems, then groups like OPEC and IEA are inevitable, and indeed necessary, adjuncts to the negotiating process, as are unions and business groups to industry-wide collective bargaining in the United States. For an imaginative article along the above lines, suggesting that '[t]he price and production negotiations of the future, in a growing range of items, will be systematic arms-length bargaining sessions at which exporter and importer governments will face each other as equals to hammer out agreements that will constitute

suggested, is the writing of new rules of international law providing for equal access to raw materials and the use of international sanctions against states violating such rules. Authority to do so surely may be found in the UN Charter and the numerous documents adopted during the past decade. Indeed, Professor Rostow of Yale, seeing Article 2 (4) as a possible 'Sherman Act in disguise', has argued for world community regulation of any coercive and monopolistic manipulation of resources.[55] Any such effort at 'collective economic security' would have to be a two-way street, however, for as Gardner notes it 'could degenerate into a North-South economic war unless it is based on principles that are acceptable to a substantial number of developed and developing countries.'[56] If laissez-faire is to be abandoned to the extent of guaranteeing equal access to commodities, the quid pro quo obviously must be its abandonment insofar as prices for such commodities are concerned too. They must be guaranteed, as they rarely have in the past, by international stabilising commodity agreements.[57]

Writing a dozen years ago about the International Coffee Agreement, under which countries importing coffee assumed a number of obligations to make the agreement possible, Professor Bilder observed that 'their interest in the coffee problem is . . . primarily an indirect interest in the achievement of a stable and healthy world economy. Their co-operation thus demonstrates a growing international recognition of the fact that no one nation or group of nations can effectively insulate itself from the poverty and problems of others, and that in this interdependent modern world, the solution of such major problems has very much become every country's business and responsibility.'[58]

the international economic order of the future', see Franck and Chesler, '"At Arms' Length": The Coming Law of Collective Bargaining in International Relations Between Equilibriated States', 15 (VA. JIL) (forthcoming) (1975).

[55] See Paust and Blaustein, note 10 above, p. 411, n. 7.

[56] Gardner, note 35 above.

[57] The Soviet Union evidently supports such an approach, albeit in the context of UNCTAD-sponsored agreements, which most industrialised countries would regard less favourably than agreements concluded bilaterally between organised groups of producers and consumers (the OPEC-IEA model). See letter from B. Rachkov to *The Times*, Dec. 19, 1973, p. 15, cols. 4–5, 'Only the establishment of mutually beneficial relations between the oil-producing and oil-buying countries can guarantee a normal, uninterrupted supply to all nations. What are these relations? In the present-day world they could develop within the framework of international stabilising commodity agreements drawn up, as is generally known, under the auspices of the United Nations, or to be more precise, UNCTAD.

An agreement on one or another commodity envisages the involvement in it of both exporters and importers of the item. It does not take the property right to a commodity away from those to whom it belongs. It only periodically, on a long-term basis, determines the quantities and prices of deliveries acceptable to all.

Such agreements can, to some degree, guaranteee the world market against sharp rises and falls or prices, against a sharp change of abundance on the market to acute shortage. In UNCTAD, the idea of concluding such an agreement on oil is also supported by the Soviet Union, along with the oil-rich developing countries and dozens of other states.'

[58] Bilder, 'The International Coffee Agreement', 57 (AJIL), pp. 888, 891 (1963).

That this responsibility has now been recognised by most countries is shown by Article 6 of the Charter of Economic Rights and Duties of States, which categorically states that ' [i]t is the duty of States to contribute to the development of international trade of goods particularly by means of arrangements and by the conclusion of long-term multilateral commodity agreements, where appropriate, and taking into account the interests of producers and consumers.' [59]

Today the price of oil is too high, yet according to the World Bank it will go still higher by 1980. On the other hand, the price of commodities such as sugar and wheat, which has risen spectacularly in recent years, may well fall between now and then.[60] Speculating about future price trends, however, is not the best approach to achieving the ' stable and healthy world economy ' to which Bilder refers. Putting aside international laissez-faire, therefore, together with periodic bouts of economic coercion and reprisals, the producing and consuming countries of oil and other commodities need to hammer out new and mutually beneficial rules and agreements which, if subsequently broken, can be enforced automatically and effectively by international sanctions. ' A co-operative effort ', Paust and Blaustein conclude, ' is called for to obtain a more inclusive regulation of the economic instrument of coercion and a more inclusive and policy-serving use of the earth's resources—not for war and unilateral dominance, but for peace and mankind.' [61] Surely this goal must be shared by reasonable men everywhere. If so, it is high time their leaders, elected and otherwise, demonstrated more determination to achieve it.

[59] See note 24 above. Despite its participation in the International Coffee Agreement, ' [t]he United States historically has opposed price agreements, preferring to let the market forces work. Last month [February 1975], Thomas Enders, Assistant US Secretary of State, indicated that Washington still opposed such accords. Washington prefers aid to trade, notwithstanding that the recipients nearly always prefer trade.' Goldsborough, ' U.S. and Oil-Price Accords ', *Int. Herald-Tribune*, Mar. 7, 1975, p. 4, col. 4.

[60] *Ibid.*, Apr. 5–6, 1975, p. 9, col. 1. But see a CIA research report indicating that world grain shortages are likely to increase in the near future, giving the United States ' a measure of power it had never had before—possibly an economic and political dominance greater than that of the immediate post-World War II years '. Weinstein, ' CIA Study Says Food Crisis Could Increase U.S. Power ', *ibid.*, Mar. 18, 1975, p. 3, col. 1. Should such a situation materialise, presumably current apologists for the Arab oil embargo would be singing a different tune.

[61] Paust and Blaustein, note 10 above, p. 439.

SOME POLITICO-LEGAL ASPECTS OF RESOURCE SCARCITY

Timothy Stanley

Recently, one of my colleagues in the International Economic Policy Association's study of natural resources came up with a quotation from Lord Balfour which seems especially appropriate for this conference. Balfour (who, incidentally, died when gasoline was about six gallons for a dollar) gloomily predicted that the day would come when "the energies of our system will decay, the glory of the sun will be dimmed, and the earth, tideless and inert, will no longer tolerate the race which has for a moment disturbed its solitude . . . ."[1] His prediction sums up the long term resources problem. Hopefully, however, we do have a medium term of several millennia, at least, during which we must grapple with what the recent Academy of Sciences study[2] called "a series of shocks of varying severity as shortages occur in one material after another." At this time, I would attempt to sift out some of what might be called the "politico-legal" aspects of our enormous resources problem and to suggest some approaches which may offer promise.

Let me begin with a provocative note. If purely economic or "market" forces were the only ones at work in the world, then I believe that the problem of resource scarcity might not be worth the attention of this distinguished assemblage. In other words, if the world economy had a single political and legal system, and a classical free market, the forces of supply and demand could operate on the scarcity. The forces would develop the technology of alternatives and substitutes, promote new discoveries, advance the science of conservation, and evolve recycling techniques. We could then adjust to the

1. A. Balfour, The Foundations of Belief 31 (1895).

2. National Academy of Sciences, *Mineral Resources and the Environment*, N.Y. Times, Feb. 12, 1975, at 1, col. 1.

problem of absolute shortages (and its effects on trade, investment, and consumption) fairly smoothly.

It is not necessary to accept the Malthusian mathematics of the Club of Rome to recognize that we may indeed see the exhaustion of one or more vital resources within our lifetime. But even if it came to that, both producers and consumers, left to act in their own economic self-interest, could ensure that some form of substitution for depleted resources was developed. For the present, however, the scarcities are manipulated, rather than real. Even oil is in worldwide surplus.

It would be a gross understatement to note that such global adjustment mechanisms are non-existent today and unlikely to appear in the near future. There is no world legislature, nor does the United Nations General Assembly appear capable of becoming one. But this is exactly the point, for as it has been said, "Politics and economics are the seamy sides of one another." Because the initial impact of resources shortages or cartel actions is primarily economic, the political "underside" is rarely considered.

Consider, for example, petroleum and the world economic crisis. Bankers tend to view this as the technical problem of "recycling" the "petrodollars" accumulated by the oil producers. Economists see OPEC as a classical oligopoly or cartel, and speak of shifts in the "terms of trade." The man or woman in the street worries mainly about the price of gasoline at the pump, and the unemployment coupled with inflation with which they are now burdened. So does their elected representative in Congress. The political scientists tend to see the situation, more accurately perhaps, as a struggle for power among disparate groups of actors. Yet when two former academic colleagues of mine who are political scientists—one from Harvard who is now the Secretary of State and one from Johns Hopkins who was a critic of the Vietnam War—have the temerity to say publicly that the application of military force is not excluded, they are roundly denounced for thinking out loud about the unthinkable.[3] If we are playing an international poker game for virtually unlimited stakes, it seems entirely reasonable to ask why the rules allow the "one-eyed jacks" of oil, bauxite, or other resources to be "wild," while the traditional "aces" of military and political-economic power are unplayable.

It is the question of the rules of the game which I propose to

---

3. *See Kissinger on Oil, Food and Trade,* Bus. Week, Jan. 13, 1975, at 69; Tucker, *Oil: The Issue of American Intervention*, 59 Commentary 21 (Jan. 1975).

explore. The analogy that politics and economics are the opposite and "seamy" sides of the same coin is a good one, but not complete. For the faces of politics and economics are held together, and sometimes usefully "buffered" by another layer. This ingredient, which also helps set the rules under which the political and economic games are played, might be called "juris" for lack of a better word.

"Juris" is, of course, the genitive of the Latin "jus", which the dictionary defines as "law; laws, collectively; a rule or principle of law; also legal right; legal power," and by extension, "justice." Let me here use the term in the broadest possible sense so as to embrace not only contract and other legal doctrines covering the rights and duties with respect to property, but also the moral, political, and legal constraints which mankind has evolved over several millennia. That evolution has had the desirable purpose of limiting the law of the jungle, the "survival of the fittest," through which we have ultimately emerged as masters of the planet.

Many lawyers regard the genius of the Anglo-Saxon common law to be its recognition that the necessarily inflexible rules of "law" were capable of working severe *injustices* when applied to particular cases, even if they were founded on the very best of principles. Out of that recognition came the British courts of chancery and the concept of "equity" which developed alongside the law itself.[4] The other great contribution of the common law is its capacity for adaptation to new circumstances, without total dependence on new legislation, by judicial reinterpretation of the fundamental principles of law as applied to contemporary cases and controversies. While other legal systems have various means of accommodating this concept, the element of basic fairness, common to most systems, must be included in the "juris" layer that separates, and links, politics and economics. Even the Eastern civilizations have evolved analogous systems from theological teachings and doctrines of state and property.

Other participants in this Meeting will treat both the economic and the political aspects of the effects of resource scarcity on trade and investment. My thesis is that these effects, however they are assessed, may be overshadowed in the long term by the political reactions to, and efforts to capitalize on, scarcities, with a resulting erosion of the spirit of "juris." International intercourse is often suspended altogether in times of war, but until now it has rarely, if ever, been so threatened during peacetime.

---

4. *See generally* H. Hanbury, English Courts of Law (4th ed. 1960).

Except in the most primitive barter systems, it is difficult to conceive of how any economic or financial activity can take place across the boundaries of different politico-legal systems without a substantial degree of confidence by all parties that certain norms of commercial and legal behavior will be observed. Buyers simply must expect sellers to deliver on roughly the agreed terms; sellers must expect buyers to pay. Investors—whether of money or management or technology—must expect that contracts covering their investment will be treated with reasonable sanctity. Financiers, shippers, and insurance brokers must be able to count on payments being made in the currency and at the time specified.

All of this is self-evident. Also self-evident is the need for adjustment to special circumstances like devaluation, *force majeure*,[5] and many other legitimate grounds for contractual nonperformance. Indeed, the increasing use of renegotiations in contracts, of escalator clauses in pricing, and provisions for arbitration of differences, reflect the need to accommodate change, while still retaining the basic sanctity of the contract as a legal obligation, both within and among nations.

As any student of contract law knows, there are limits to the enforceability of contracts, for example, when they are undertaken contrary to public purposes or under duress. The common law has built into its doctrines the basic element of fairness, or justice, through the requirement that a contract be based on a valid "consideration," which can, however, include reliance on someone else's promise—perhaps by analogy to the economic concept of "opportunity cost."

The international applications of such doctrines are, of course, complicated by the principles of sovereign immunity, by various conflicts of laws principles, and by the practical difficulties of obtaining jurisdiction. There is, nevertheless, a very substantial body of both private and public international law dealing with contracts, expropriations, compensation, and arbitration, which makes this point relevant to the subject of natural resources and the various rights and obligations with respect to them. Even the Soviets accept the general body of law in this area, although naturally they apply it in terms of their own economic and judicial system.

Even sovereignty has its limitations. Generally states are held responsible for injuries to aliens, breaches of treaties, unlawful acts

5. In the law of insurance, *force majeure* connotes a superior or irresistible force. BLACK'S LAW DICTIONARY 774 (4th rev. ed. 1968).

of force, and violations of international law. To quote one international arbitral award, "Nothing can prevent a State, in the exercise of its sovereignty, from binding itself irrevocably by the provisions of a concession and from granting to the concessionaire irretractable rights."[6]

If I seem to be restating the obvious, it is only to highlight recent experiences with natural resources in a number of so-called developing countries. Consider the case of Jamaica's actions on bauxite. Six North American companies had invested close to one billion dollars in Jamaican bauxite extraction under contracts setting tax and price levels, signed for the most part since Jamaica became an independent nation, and running for 20 years. Jamaica found it necessary to increase its bauxite revenues, and the companies agreed to renegotiate. When these efforts reached an impasse (despite an industry offer to triple Jamaican revenues), the Jamaican Government unilaterally set a far higher tax and levy rate. Whatever the merits of the particular case, it is noteworthy that several of the contracts cancelled unilaterally by the Jamaican Government called for the arbitration of any disagreements by the International Centre for the Settlement of Investment Disputes,[7] a World Bank affiliate established precisely to provide an impartial forum for cases of this type. Jamaica, however, claimed that it "withdrew" from the arbitration agreement. The Centre courageously replied that consent cannot be unilaterally withdrawn,[8] but the outcome of this particular conflict of sovereignty versus international obligation is still unclear.

Consider further the case of oil. Early in 1974, following a period in which "long term" contracts were torn up in a matter of months, Libya nationalized three American producers; Kuwait unilaterally abrogated agreements with an Anglo-American oil consortium; and

6. Saudi Arabia—ARAMCO Arbitral Awards (1958), *quoted in* 8 M. WHITEMAN, INTERNATIONAL LAW 912 (1967).

7. In 1966, the International Centre for the Settlement of Investment Disputes was established in order to encourage international investment by providing a body to remove some of the uncertainties inherent in world-wide investment practices. The Centre was to provide the services of conciliation and arbitration to members of the world community. 1 CONVENTION ON THE SETTLEMENT OF INVESTMENT DISPUTES BETWEEN STATES AND NATIONALS OF OTHER STATES 2—21 (International Centre for the Settlement of Investment Disputes, 1970).

8. *See generally* INTERNATIONAL ECONOMIC POLICY ASS'N, INTERIM REPORT OF THE STUDY ON U.S. NATURAL RESOURCE REQUIREMENTS AND FOREIGN ECONOMIC POLICY 70—73 (1974) [hereinafter cited as IEPA INTERIM REPORT].

Saudi Arabia, Iran, and the smaller Persian Gulf states were not slow to follow suit. New participation shares were forced on investors in Nigerian oil, and Venezuela announced plans to speed up the reversion of all foreign-held "hydrocarbons" which were not due to revert to Venezuela until 1983. The actions of Peru, Chile, Zambia, and Zaire with regard to copper and iron ore are also analogous.[9]

The oil producers had conspired to apply a selective embargo which, it can be credibly argued, was a violation of the principles of the UN Charter. Their actions also conflicted with a UN resolution prohibiting the "coercive" use of economic power[10] (which the developing countries themselves had pushed through the General Assembly) and of the GATT,[11] to which at least some OPEC mem-

---

9. During the summer of 1974, four countries which account for over 70 percent of the world's production of copper met to determine their future role in international trade. The delegates from Chile, Peru, Zambia, and Zaire vowed "to completely coordinate the policy to be followed in the world copper market." N.Y. Times, June 29, 1974 at 65, col. 5.

By the end of October, the world's major consuming nations learned the meaning of that somewhat ambiguous statement. On October 30, 1974 it was announced that the copper cartel, following the example of OPEC, had agreed to set the price for copper. This announcement followed a year in which the world's consumption of copper had decreased markedly due to the oil shortage. N.Y. Times, Oct. 31, 1974 at 65, col. 4.

10. U.N. Resolution 2625 of The 1970 General Assembly expressly prohibits the use of "economic, political or any other type of measures to coerce another state in order to obtain from it the subordination of the exercise of its sovereign rights and to secure from it advantages of any kind," which was exactly what the Arab states sought to do in using their "oil weapon" against Israel. *See* G.A. Res. 2625, 25 U.N. GAOR Supp. 28, at 121, U.N. Doc. A/8028 (1970). For discussion of GATT applicability see IEPA INTERIM REPORT, *supra* note 4, at 29—32. The cases for and against the legality of the oil embargo are argued, respectively, in Shihata, *Destination Embargo of Arab Oil: Its Legality Under International Law*, 68 AM. J. INT'L L. 591 (1974) and Paust & Blaustein, *The Arab Oil Weapon—A Threat to International Peace*, 68 AM. J. INT'L L. 410 (1974).

11. The General Agreement of Tariffs and Trade (GATT) was formed as an acknowledgement by the world community that free international trade and investment is beneficial to every nation. This concept was embodied in the preamble to the General Agreement:

> [The contracting parties, r]ecognizing that their relations in the field of trade and economic endeavour should be conducted with a view to raising standards of living, ensuring full employment and a large and steadily growing volume of real income and effective demand, developing the full use of the resources of the world and expanding the production and exchange of goods.
>
> Being desirous of contributing to these objectives by entering into reciprocal and mutually advantageous arrangements directed to the substantial

bers have subscribed. The Arabs' anti-Jewish black list is also open to objections, especially as applied to force secondary and tertiary boycotts.

Extractive industries have always been particularly vulnerable to nationalism and xenophobia around the globe for allegedly removing a country's "patrimony," often at unfair prices or with unfair contracts.[12] One can challenge this underlying philosophy of nationalization, however, by asking whether the host country which agreed to the original arrangements would have been better off if no one had developed its resources, or if it had waited until it could develop its resources without outside help. If at the time the host country's "opportunity cost" dictated acceptance—indeed, if not active solicitation—of the foreign investment in question, is it entitled to renege the first time its bargaining power permits?

Not only investments are at stake; a recent news item indicated that some communist countries had rather cavalierly cancelled orders for wheat, purchased at a time of great world shortage, for future delivery. Another news story reported the dispatch of a United States mission to several countries in Asia and elsewhere to protest the unilateral abrogation of contracts for other commodities.

Before arriving at a scientific conclusion that "the rule of law," and/or the concept of "international due process" are in grave danger, however they are defined, one would have to compare systematically the contracts and investment agreements more or less honored with those violated. Such a project might be extremely worthwhile for someone able to undertake the necessary comprehensive re-

---

> reduction of tariffs and other barriers to trade and to the elimination of discriminatory treatment in international commerce,
>
> Have through their Representatives agreed [to the terms of the General Agreement] . . . .

61 Stat. (pt. 5) A 11 (1947).

12. A recent U.N. study, for example, counts a total of 875 expropriations; and forthcoming research by the Center for Multinational Studies counts 41 percent of the 170 expropriations of United States investments studied between 1946 and 1973 in the extractive industries. Permanent Sovereignty Over Natural Resources, Report to the Economic and Social Council by the Secretary General, Annex *A Profile of Recent Cases of Nationalization or Takeover of Foreign Enterprises*, New York, U.N. Doc. A/9716 (1974). *See also* Hawkins, Mintz, & Provissiero, Governmental Takeovers of U.S. Foreign Affiliates: A Post-War Profile, Occasional Paper No. 7 Center for Multinational Studies, Washington, (1975). In that survey, takeovers of financial affiliates accounted for 19 percent of the expropriations, manufacturing for 30 percent, and utilities for 10 percent, compared with the 41 percent for the extractive field.

search. Pending the availability of detailed analysis, one can only make the tentative observation that the petroleum and other resource crises appear to have accelerated the tendency toward disregard of international legal norms and obligations, thereby posing major problems for long term stability in the world's political economy.

Let us now look at the problem as it is perceived by the Third World. Its inhabitants, incidentally, have subdivided into "fourth" and "fifth" worlds. In contrast to the *nouveau riche* of the producers of oil and other resources, which I would like to term the "third" world, there is a "fourth" world of countries like Korea and Taiwan whose industrial development has progressed to a point of significance in international trade and investment, and whose future prospects are now greatly clouded. Additionally, there is a "fifth" world of desperately poor countries like Bangladesh which lack both resources and hope.

A political scientist might be struck by the failure of the "fourth" and "fifth" worlds, despite the damage to their own economies to condemn the oil producers. Is this passivity due to the strength of the rhetoric of third world solidarity, non-alignment, underdevelopment, anti-imperialism, and the rest? Or are the oil producers "buying" political support from the desperate with promises of loans, gifts, concessionary prices, and help to other cartels?

Venezuela has announced that it will sell oil to its Central American neighbors at about six dollars a barrel, but will require them to establish counterpart funds for the difference, available for Venezuelan use in their own countries—an idea obviously borrowed from the American P.L. 480 food programs.[13] The Shah of Iran is known to be helping the Pakistanis with both arms and credit; Abu Dhabi is reported to be financing numerous Arab causes; and India is thought to be receiving oil at discounted prices, as low as three and one-half dollars per barrel.[14] There is a good deal of talk—most recently at the February 1975 Senegal Conference of 110 non-aligned nations—about using OPEC surpluses to help other commodity producers establish cartel-type arrangements for such items as copper, coffee, and bananas. It has been rumored that the high price of sugar, for example, is partly due to large Arab purchases of speculative futures. These activities may help explain why the oil produ-

13. Agricultural Trade Development and Assistance Act, 7 U.S.C. §§ 1691 *et seq.* (1970).

14. *See* Bus. Week, Feb. 24, 1975, at 44.

cers' expected surplus is now being revised downward in some calculations, but they are hardly a cause for much comfort in the industrial oil consuming countries.[15]

The majority of the United Nations Assembly members, which United States Ambassador Scali called the "tyranny of the majority," make a simple case. It is reflected in part in the "Declaration on the Establishment of a New International Economic Order" and the "Charter of Economic Rights and Duties of States."[16] The latter deals in part with the "permanent sovereignty" over natural resources, and the right of producers to establish commodity cartels, with all other states "having the duty to respect that right by refraining from applying economic and political measures that would limit it."[17] But it omits any reference to the corresponding legal obligations to fulfill international agreements, including, if applicable, adequate, prompt, and effective compensation under international law in the event of nationalization for public purposes. This notion that certain nations, because of their "developing" status, have many rights but almost no duties was the reason why the United States and several other industrial countries found themselves obliged to vote against the so-called Charter, which of course has no binding effect. The United Nations debates on the subject, as well as the non-debates on the oil embargo, suggest the development of a double standard which represents a potentially serious erosion in international law, as Professor Gardner has pointed out in his article which appeared in *Foreign Affairs* last year.[18]

Thus, there exists a challenge by the underdeveloped countries to the otherwise accepted rules of international law. Many such countries claim not to be bound by the principles established while they were colonies and not yet sovereign members of the international

---

15. OPEC sources claim that its member countries committed five million dollars to underdeveloped countries in the forms of investments and humanitarian aid development loans during 1974. N.Y. Times, Jan. 18, 1975, at 1, col. 1.

16. "Declaration on the Establishment of a New International Economic Order," Resolution 3201 (S-VI) adopted without vote May 1, 1974, U.N. Report A/9556 (Part II).

17. "Charter of Economic Rights and Duties of States" adopted December 12, 1974 by a vote of 120 to 6 (10 abstentions), U.N. Report A/9946.

18. Gardner, *The Hard Road to World Order*, 52 FOREIGN AFFAIRS 556 (April 1974).

In another article, the same author has pointed out that the industrial countries can also claim "permanent sovereignty" over their capital, technology, and markets—to which the LDC's claim access, often on privileged terms.

system. Others argue that the rules were established and sometimes breached by the colonial countries to protect their own interests, and are no longer applicable in the "new" international economic order. But, whatever the rationale, such countries may really be rejecting the underlying concepts of "juris." What is evolving, I believe, is a non-legal or "revolutionary" approach to changing the economic relationships among states, based on the notion of historical injustice or inalienable rights without much regard for the rights of others, or for the stake of all in a viable international legal system. If there were an international political system which could engage in law- and rule-making, then any necessary adjustments could perhaps be made relatively peacefully, even as the United States adjusted to the rise of organized labor in the 1930s,[19] or to the civil rights challenges of the 1960s.[20] But in the absence of an international political system, even international agreements among the world's seven-score sovereign entities rest for their enforcement upon acceptance of international legal principles and obligations.

One is reminded by some of the United Nations rhetoric of the communist doctrine of "just" wars, promulgated during the 1960s. "Just wars" (which, not surprisingly, were usually promoted or supported by communist governments) could claim, in this view, a moral legitimacy whereby anyone resisting an attack in such a war became an aggressor. Indeed, whether it comes from left or right, the writ of both revolution and reaction tends to establish the "law of the ruler" rather than the "rule of law." Fortunately, the writ does not run to all the world, notwithstanding the "new economic order" arguments to the contrary. There exists a very interesting body of international law which derived from the Russian Revolution's effects on the property and rights of various claimants in the 1920s and 1930s. Most courts, caught between two innocent parties, simply found a procedural way out. But a few, in different countries, held that the *force majeure*[21] and *rebus sic stantibus*[22] escape clauses did not override the applicability of customary international law.

I recently had the occasion to review this issue with a distin-

---

19. *See* Jackson, pp. 1154—64 *infra*.

20. For a discussion of the legislative response to discriminatory practices see 2 B. SCHWARTZ, STATUTORY HISTORY OF THE UNITED STATES 935—1816 (1970).

21. *See* note 5 *supra*.

22. *Rebus sic stantibus* is a tacit condition attaching to all treaties which means that a treaty will no longer be obligatory whenever the conditions upon which it was based cease to exist. BLACK'S LAW DICTIONARY 1432 (4th rev. ed. 1968).

guished European scholar. He wryly observed, "It is very difficult to discuss the finer points of international law with a blackmailer, especially when he has the goods on you." The "goods" in this case are the foreign oil imports which Western Europe and Japan desperately need, and which even the United States cannot seem to make up its mind to do without. Of course he is quite right as to the economics and perhaps even the politics of the matter, but that hardly affects the legal principles involved for the symbolic figure of "justice" is blindfolded for the very reason that she cannot see the weights on the scales.

With regard to the oil embargo, whether it be the 1973 anti-Israel version, or any embargo which might be organized in the future, it is important to recognize that an embargo has sometimes been considered under international neutrality law to be an act of belligerence. It could be construed so as to entitle the countries affected to apply military force against it by claiming co-belligerent status. But let us admit here, since we have talked about equity, that in view of its history, the United States cannot claim "clean hands" in the use of big stick diplomacy, or even in the application of embargoes. Certainly, it is ironic that some of our worst examples are being emulated, and exceeded, even as we are becoming our own severest critics in trying to move toward a genuine rule of law.

As for the abrogations of private agreements between oil companies and producer nations, there has surely been some "shotgun acquiescence" by the companies affected. Confronted with carefully calculated "salami tactics" by sovereign political powers, the companies had in most cases very little backing from their own governments. They became, in effect, hostages to host country threats to expropriate their investments completely (and deny them access to the oil on which their vital "downstream" operations depend) if they used agreed contractual or other legal rights to fight a partial expropriation.

If, as a result of the oil crisis, the Western world recession becomes a depression with ensuing political or social cataclysms, future historians may assign the root failure to the inability of Western governments to recognize how much their own vital *national* interests were at stake in the relations between their resource companies, and the resource power of host countries. The superficial answer—to involve consumer governments in all critical commodity negotiations—has far-reaching implications for international relations (through the greater probability of confrontations between states), for the basic existence of the market system, and for overall business-government relationships in the industrial world. Yet, movement in this direction seems inescapable if the interests of consumers (and the multinational companies which in effect act as their wholesale purchasing agents) cannot be protected by international political agreements and legal principles against capricious or unjust treatment by foreign sovereignties.

Rhetoric about the new international economic "order" and cartelization of the world economy is one thing in the abstract, and another when backed by the political-economic-technological and military purchasing power of hundreds of billions of dollars, with little or no acknowledgement of the legal and other obligations of that power, or the harm its acquisition has caused others.[23]

These developments lead me to postulate four conclusions to this very brief review of a complex subject.

First: The erosion of the "juris" buffer between politics and economics already appears to be serious; if it continues, it may ultimately prove the most harmful consequence of the "scarcity" of primary resources. The harm is twofold: developed countries will lose income and access to resources, with resulting high inflation and unemployment, and the LDC's may face not only analogous civil behavior in their own countries, but a possible resort to force by the industrial countries, especially if the power of OPEC and its emulators becomes too great to tolerate. Alternatively, if commodity prices decline over time, can developing producer countries rely on consumers to honor any stabilization agreements or long term price contracts reached while prices were higher, once the underlying legal obligations have become depreciated? And can they safely place their investments in countries whose citizens have had their holdings expropriated by these very investors? Whatever the short term gains to some parties, everyone loses in the long run if anarchy substitutes for the rule of law. For example, as the world economy seeks to adjust the demand of the LDC's for contractual relationships—management contracts, technology purchases, minority investment, and the like—instead of foreign ownership of resources,

23. One international magazine has invented a new petro-currency, the "COPEC," which is defined as one year's oil surplus for OPEC, or $60 million. According to this calculation, for example, a Lockheed C-5A can be bought with eight COPEC hours; the Exxon Corporation in 79 COPEC days; and all of Britain's industrial assets in six COPEC years. *The Defi OPEC,* THE ECONOMIST, Dec. 7, 1974 at 85.

even greater assurances will be needed that the legal obligations of international contracts can be relied upon over time. Consequently, the legal aspects of international economic relations deserve far more attention than they have previously received. The simplistic comment that no one can deny the right of raw material producers to sell their resources at whatever price they can command ignores the fact that in the case of oil, prices were raised by political, not economic, means to something like 10,000 percent of the actual costs of production[24] through an embargo of highly questionable legality, and through the abrogation of contracts carefully entered into just a year previously. Also, the question of "whose" resources they are must take account of the money, technology, and management which discovered, developed, transported, and marketed these raw materials, and enhanced their economic value by developing the demand.

Second: On the other hand, it is difficult to deny that history dealt the cards unfairly when the ingredients of economic development were passed out, and that the advanced countries have taken due advantage of the allocation.

The idea of a planetary government which might impose international order remains a distant vision. The real world consists of multiple sovereignties in widely differing stages of strength and development, some impoverished and some in a better position to help themselves.

Americans like to encourage self-help by the able, at least up to a point, and that concept is included in our foreign development aid policy. But "self-help" needs some boundaries. Piracy, colonial exploitation, and price-gouging monopolies belong to more primitive times and should never again be practiced. A world that is permissive about expropriations, abrogations of contract, and cartel conspiracies encourages the spread of economic warfare and enhances the danger of armed conflict. A world of that kind moves backward.

Third: The weak, even more than the strong, are protected by

24. This figure is based on published estimates of 12 cents per barrel production cost in Saudi Arabia and the post-embargo world price of over $12.00 a barrel. The claim that the increase in oil prices merely compensates for the inflation in goods sold to the producing countries is specious. The index of U.S. consumer prices rose from 100 in 1955 to 187 in August, 1974; the index of Iran's petroleum prices rose from 100 to 621—three times as high—in the same period. Moreover, the total value of all Iranian imports from 1955 to 1972, not just the inflation component, is likely to be recouped in two or three years at present oil prices.

adherence to accepted legal norms. Some of the newly-rich may eventually come to share the developed world's concern for international disciplines in order to inhibit seizure of *their* assets, but we cannot afford to wait for this transformation of attitudes to occur. Instead, the United States should place much greater emphasis than it has so far on the legal aspects of the oil and other resource crises.

The United States and other affected consuming countries might do well to seek the advisory opinions of a specially instituted panel of distinguished and impartial international jurists on the legal aspects of world resources and cartel questions. Admittedly, the determinations of such a council would not be binding. Lacking jurisdiction, its findings and opinions would have only moral and perhaps some political force. Nonetheless, that would be a good way to start. The findings could be a useful nucleus for developing new or adapted rules of international commerce through normal multinational diplomacy. Countries which evidence a willingness to accept the basic legitimacy of such impartial opinions might be treated differently in United States economic policy and foreign relations than those who do not. Countries accepting compulsory jurisdiction of the World Court, it may be noted, have a different status than those who maintain a reservation, which would appear to argue, incidentally, for repeal of America's own "Connally Amendment" reservation.[25] Greater use can also be made of international arbitration machinery, both that already existing, and new mechanisms to be established in bilateral, "umbrella" trade agreements. For example, the "Gonzalez Amendment" to foreign aid and trade legislation, is, in my judgment, an improvement over the so-called "Hickenlooper" approach[26] because it does not require denial

25. The Connally Amendment provides that the International Court of Justice shall not have jurisdiction over "disputes with regard to matters which are essentially within the domestic jurisdiction of the United States as determined by the United States of America . . . ." International Court of Justice: United States Recognition of Compulsory Jurisdiction, Aug. 14, 1946, 61 Stat. 1218 (1946), T.I.A.S. No. 1598.

26. In international law parlance, the Hickenlooper Amendment, 22 U.S.C. § 2370(e)(2) (1964) is considered an exception to the Act of State doctrine which prohibits courts of the United States from reviewing acts of a foreign government within its own territory. Comment, *International Law—The Interaction of the Hickenlooper Amendment and Bernstein Exception with the Act of State Doctrine*, 2 LOYOLA U. (CHI.) L.J. 184, 187—193 (1972). The Hickenlooper Amendment provides that:

of benefits where countries have agreed to submit expropriation issues to the World Bank's Centre for the Settlement of Investment Disputes.[27] The legislation proposed by the State and Justice Departments to clarify the question of the limits to sovereign immunity of foreign governments in commercial matters is still another promising approach.[28]

At the outset, it was postulated that economic forces could provide the needed adjustments if left to themselves. But the political environment at home and abroad obviously will not let them. Yet, if a combination of extreme autarky and international economic anarchy continues to develop, it could lead either to successful American-Soviet spheres of influence—or even joint condominiums—or, alternatively, to the constant danger of nuclear superpower conflicts. Obviously, some international rules of economic law must be re-established, and the sooner the better.

Fourth: Those rules must embrace the broad concept of equity included in the term "juris." They must take into account both legitimate aspirations and claims of injustice in the developing countries. Further, the legitimate interests and rights of the more richly endowed countries must also be respected in any such concept. In the long run, conflicts are most likely to be avoided, and international cooperation and comity best encouraged, through attention to transnational legal processes, including arbitration and conciliation.

Some historians believe that the end of five centuries of Western pre-eminence has been hastened by the current "resources revolution." However, the prosperity of the West does not rest on technol-

---

> Notwithstanding any other provision of law, no court in the United States shall decline on the ground of the federal act of state doctrine to make a determination on the merits giving effect to the principles of international law in a case in which a claim of title or other right to property is asserted by any party including a foreign state (or party claiming through such state) based on (or traced through) a confiscation or other taking after January 1, 1959, by an act of that state in violation of the principles of international law, including the principles of compensation and the other standards set out in this subsection: Provided that this subparagraph shall not be applicable . . . (2) in any case with respect to which the President determines that application of the act of state doctrine is required in that particular case by the foreign policy interest of the United States and a suggestion to this effect is filed on his behalf in that case with the court.

22 U.S.C. § 2370(e)(2) (1970).

27. *See* note 7 *supra*.

28. H.R. 3493, 93d Cong., 1st Sess. (introduced on January 31, 1973).

ogical, economic, or military power alone. It owes a great deal to the development of the concepts of law and equity which guide its political and social systems. The contemporary world is at best a difficult and dangerous place. But it seems clearly preferable to struggle with its economic confrontations in a modern politico-legal framework, drawing on these concepts, than to revert to either the naked or covert application of national power, which should be limited to a remedy of last resort.

OPEC In The Context Of The Global Power Equation

Jahangir Amuzegar*

I. Introduction

The name of the Organization of Petroleum Exporting Countries has been on thousands of lips around the globe in recent months. The Organization's initials—OPEC—have filled thousands of newspaper pages the world over. To the people in the oil-importing countries, the word OPEC is a frightening one, reminding them of high oil prices, gas station lines and fuel shortages. OPEC has been called many names, the nicest of them being "international cartel;" it has been accused of many things, the mildest of them being "monopoly pricing."[1] Yet few of OPEC's critics, and fewer of its followers, know what OPEC really is or what its purposes are. Briefly, OPEC is an association of twelve full-member plus one associate-member countries, dedicated to the protection of their national interests in the production and export of oil. OPEC was originally established by five oil-producing countries as a "mouvement de resistance" (defense league) against arbitrary and unilateral decisions of the major oil companies.

At this point, a bit of oil price history is highly illuminating. In 1947 the "posted price," or the price on which royalties and taxes are based, of a barrel of Persian crude was $2.17. During the 1950's, while other prices were rising, the oil price was stable or on the decline. In February 1959, the "posted price" of Persian Gulf crude was officially lowered by the major oil companies, who gave as their reason a glut in world oil supply, to $1.90 a barrel. The oil exporters, who were economically poor and politically divided, could not and did not do anything to stop these losses per barrel. Instead, the exporters strove for increased output to maintain their total income. The companies, in turn, lowered the price to $1.80 in August 1960. Of this, 80 cents was the exporter's share.[2] Since most of the exporters were depending principally on oil income for their foreign exchange needs, the companies' disregard of these needs and the exporters' other aspirations resulting from repeated reduction of oil prices served as the turning point in the history of OPEC.

---

* Ambassador-at-Large and Chief of the Iranian Economic Mission in Washington, D.C.

1. For the history and background of OPEC see Z. Mikdashi, The Community of Oil Exporting Countries (1972).

2. *Hearings on S. Res. 40 Before the Senate Subcomm. on Antitrust and Monopoly*, 91st Cong., 1st Sess., pt.1, at 437 (1969). Another source puts oil prices at $2.22 per barrel for 1947. H. Frank, Crude Oil Prices In The Middle East 30 (1966).

The five countries involved (Iran, Iraq, Kuwait, Saudi Arabia and Venezuela) formed OPEC in September 1960. Later, Algeria, Ecuador, Indonesia, Libya, Nigeria, Qatar and the United Arab Emirates joined the group. Gabon was recently accepted as an associate member. OPEC's victories were hard and long in coming. Despite the members' resolve to prevent an oil price decline, the countries' policy of unrestrained production to obtain larger revenues and foreign exchange kept pushing prices down. These policies were imposed on the countries by the companies against the exporters long-term interests, and against technical requirements for prudent and efficient exploitation. Although the official posted price, under OPEC pressure, remained at $1.80 a barrel throughout the 1960's, significant discounts (of 40 cents to 55 cents a barrel from the posted price on the producers' own offtake) were not unusual. A barrel of offtake crude was often sold by the Persian Gulf producers at $1.25 in the world markets—with the prospects of the blissful "$1.00 a barrel" gleefully contemplated by the companies and net oil-importers.[3]

Then, success came suddenly. Following the Caracas Resolution of December 1970,[4] a conference was held in Tehran between OPEC representatives and those of the oil majors in February 1971. After a series of long and difficult negotiations, an agreement was reached whereby the posted price was increased to $2.30, and provisions were made for (a) small annual increases in that price, and (b) allowance for inflation in the major oil importing countries.[5] With this significant triumph in hand, other successes followed. In January 1972, a new concession was obtained by the oil exporters in terms of adjustment allowances in their incomes (received in U.S. dollars) against dollar devaluations.[6] In March 1972, the principle of "participation" by producer-governments in the operation of the oil companies was accepted.[7] In October 1973, after weeks of unsuccessful negotiations with the companies, the oil-exporting governments declared their intention to establish oil prices among themselves, free from the obstructionist tactics of the companies in bilateral bargaining.[8] The

3. FRANK, *supra* note 2, at 116.

4. OPEC Resolution XXI. 120 Calling for Negotiations and Forming Three-Member Negotiating Committees, Dec. 1970, 10 INT'L LEGAL MATERIALS 240-42 (1971).

5. Tehran Agreement Between Six Gulf States and Oil Companies Operating in Their Territories, Feb. 14, 1971, 10 INT'L LEGAL MATERIALS 247-54 (1971). Thus between 1947 and 1972 the posted price of crude oil in the Middle East rose only from $2.17 to $2.30. When inflation is taken into account, the real price was actually fifteen percent lower over twenty-five years.

6. Organization of Petroleum Exporting Countries: Agreement Between Oil Companies and Six Persian Gulf States on Increased Payments, Jan. 20, 1972, 11 INT'L LEGAL MATERIALS 554-60 (1972).

7. *See* L. MOSLEY, POWER PLAY: OIL IN THE MIDDLE EAST 388-411 (1973).

8. N. Y. Times, Oct. 17, 1973, at 16, col. 1.

posted price was raised to $5.11,[9] and finally, in December 1973, when the crude oil auction price in the free market had risen to over $22 a barrel, the posted price in the Persian Gulf was raised to $11.65 a barrel.[10]

II. Reasons for the Rise of OPEC

The intriguing question is: How could OPEC, which for ten long years had been largely helpless in promoting the interests of its members, suddenly succeed in bringing the oil majors to their senses, so to speak, and in making the whole world take notice of the Organization's aims and strengths? The answer lies in a multitude of forces, long in the making, which have suddenly converged on the scene. Eight interrelated factors can be distinguished as contributing to OPEC's recent rise in prominence.

The first factor relates to a change in the world's basic balance of politico-economic power. The nature and source of OPEC's bargaining strength in dealing with the major oil consuming nations and the oil majors are a part of this change in the global power equation—a reflection of the growing power and independence of the Third World. The essence of world power in the last two decades has undergone two fundamental changes: (a) away from originally bipolar, and later triangular, hegemony of the Super Powers; and (b) in favor of the less-developed countries (LDC's). International bargaining, a dynamic process, has thus undergone significant changes in its participants, its scope, and its dimensions. The bargaining leverage possessed by OPEC is a manifestation of the emergence of the Third World as a Third Force.[11]

Several basic features of this new global power equation can be easily underlined. The new U.S.-U.S.S.R. detente, for example, has ushered in greater tolerance by both major powers of neutralism, nonalignment, and the pursuit of political independence; non-alignment no longer necessarily connotes hostility toward the left or the right. Then, there has been a multilateralization of power bases, following the rise of Japan and the EEC to the position of Super Powers in the world. Furthermore, new international politico-economic alliances have been formed on the basis of functional and geographical rather than political and ideological considerations. For example, the Soviet Union and the United States have entered into a number of technical, cultural, scientific and even economic treaties and relationships with countries possessing different political ideologies. The membership

---

9. N. Y. Times, Oct. 19, 1973, at 61, col. 1.

10. N. Y. Times, Dec. 24, 1973, at 1, col. 8.

11. For a succinct analysis of the new developments see S. Brown, The Changing Essence of Power (1973) and G. Bergsten, The Threat From the Third World (1973).

composition of such international bodies as UNCTAD, GATT, the Arab League, and the Organization of African States, groupings in the International Monetary Fund and the World Bank, and other similar mixtures present vivid examples of pragmatic and apolitical coalitions.

These criss-cross coalitions have been stimulated and fostered by the Super Powers' need for votes in various international forums which, in turn, have stimulated and nurtured the emergence of the Third World as a significant force favoring cooperation rather than coercion in international relations. "Gunboat diplomacy" has been gradually replaced by relatively polite official debates and skillful informal lobbying in the corridors of international agencies. Finally, the emergence of the People's Republic of China as the new champion of the Third World has significantly strengthened the LDC's hand in their bargaining with the richer countries.

The second factor responsible for OPEC's rising power and influence has been the geopolitical strength of the OPEC members. For example, six major OPEC countries are located around the Persian Gulf, a strategic area for all Super Powers. The Soviet Union's historic desire for access to the warm waters of the Gulf and the Indian Ocean,[12] the United States' special commitments to the State of Israel plus her vast investments in the Middle East oil fields, and Sino-Soviet rivalry in this part of the world for its own sake and as a gateway to Africa—all have given the Persian Gulf region its geopolitical significance.

The third factor operating in OPEC's favor has been the Organization's control over oil reserves and exports on the one hand, and the industrial countries' dependence upon imported petroleum on the other. By 1985, more than half of world energy consumption (estimated at 145 million b/d of oil equivalent) will be supplied by crude petroleum. Considering that more than sixty per cent of the world's proven oil reserves and about eighty-five per cent of world oil exports are in OPEC's hands, the Organization's actual and potential clout is not difficult to recognize.[13]

The fourth factor accounting for OPEC's mounting significance and power is solidarity among the exporting countries. History records many exporting organizations of bygone days which faded away in a short span of time due to short-sightedness, secretive competition, and the pursuit of "beggar-my-neighbor" policies. In the case of OPEC, however, in spite of differences in ideology and political

12. In this connection see L. Landis, Politics and Oil: Moscow in the Middle East (1973).

13. R. Miller, The Economics of Energy: What Went Wrong and How We Can Fix It (1974).

philosophy among member countries, there has been a strong harmony of economic action among members, a harmony which has remained largely immune to countervailing maneuvers of both the big oil companies and the consuming nations.[14] Above all, OPEC's leadership has remained in the hands of moderate countries which have succeeded in avoiding useless and unproductive confrontations with the consuming nations.

The fifth element underlying OPEC's success has been the existence of conflicting interests among certain major consuming countries, despite their similar political philosophies and orientations. OPEC members, notwithstanding their dissimilar political regimes, have found it advantageous to follow certain common economic goals. Western Europe, the United States, and Japan, on the other hand, continue to follow what they themselves call "cannibalistic competition" in the economic arena. The United States, primarily relying on its own relatively rich domestic oil resources,[15] has recently vowed to follow a policy aimed at self-sufficiency by 1980. The United States' policies and prospects are thus vastly different from Japan's, a country which is totally dependent on foreign oil. In case of an emergency, the United States can maintain her levels of employment, income, and living reasonably well by adopting energy-saving policies which might necessitate only small sacrifices on the part of her people. But without foreign oil the Japanese economy would be in total chaos. The economic interests of EEC members also vary. England hopes to attain self-sufficiency and an exporting position in oil by 1980, a hope which cannot be shared by her other partners in the Community. Italy, France and Germany have thus found it necessary to follow their own national self-interest in attempting to obtain long-term supplies of foreign petroleum.[16]

The sixth element contributing to OPEC's strength has been the greater self-confidence among members as a result of a series of consecutive successes in the international economic scene. The expression "nothing succeeds like success" has never been more clearly manifested than in this case. OPEC members had endeavored to

---

14. *See* Mosley, *supra* note 7, at 388-411; Mikdashi, *Cooperation Among Oil Exporting Countries with Special Reference to Arab Countries*, 28 Int'l Org. 1, 9-10 (1974). For examples of discord among OPEC countries see Mikdashi, *supra* note 1, at 12-17 and Note, *From Concession to Participation: Restricting the Middle East Oil Industry*, 48 N. Y. U. L. Rev. 774, 791-93 (1973).

15. Even during the economic boom of 1972-73, only one-third of the United States' oil consumption was imported, but the figure for Japan was close to 100 percent.

16. The virtual abandonment of the Netherlands by other EEC countries in the face of the Arab oil embargo after October 1973 is another example of European disunity when national interests are at stake.

obtain their due shares since 1960, but their early setbacks in negotiations with oil companies repeatedly weakened their hand. Then they had their first success in February 1971 under the guidance and leadership of Iran's Shahanshah. From then on, one success led to another. The 1971 victory provided not only the psychological self-confidence needed by OPEC negotiators, but also the politico-economic underpinnings for future bargains. Once assured of their annual foreign exchange needs, the oil producers could negotiate from a position of financial strength and ultimately political power.

The seventh factor leading to OPEC's successful negotiations with the oil companies' skilled and sophisticated negotiators has been the ample supply of indigenous talent from the oil-producing countries. The exporter's representatives today are a group of well-informed and experienced individuals who fully match their Western counterparts in political skill and bargaining ability. They are equipped not only with their own courage and their governments' full support, but with reams of statistics and a number of arguments carefully selected and meticulously worked out by their technical and professional deputies. Oil bargaining sessions are no longer an exercise in favors humbly requested by the producers and magnanimously bestowed on them by the oil majors. The relationships are now conditioned by sovereign states bent on optimizing returns from their exhaustible resources and their customers. The West and the oil companies have come to understand these facts, and their relations with the Third World and the oil producers have significantly changed.[17]

The eighth factor responsible for OPEC's remarkable recent achievements has been the developing governments' success in following independent national policies free from the insidious influences of the oil companies or their governments. The majority of the people in the Third World have obtained greater confidence in their leaders now, and are willing to endure greater sacrifices to ensure the attainment of their national goals. At the same time, the political and administrative influence of the oil majors over both their own governments and those of the producing countries has considerably diminished.[18]

The success in oil negotiations and the acquisition of substantially vast sums of revenues have enabled national leaders in the oil-producing nations not only to give their people greater material amenities and increased economic welfare, but to prove to them their leadership ability and governing capacity. The rank and file, in turn, have not only become relatively more comfortable and thus more

---

17. R. Vicker, The Kingdom of Oil/The Middle East: Its People and Its Power (1974).

18. Mosley, *supra* note 7.

content; they have come to believe, more and more, their leaders' promises of higher material standards of living and enhanced national political prestige for their countries. This increased popular support has, in turn, strengthened the leadership's hand, allowing them to stand up to foreign politico-economic pressures and to resist oil company dictates.

III. The Weapons of OPEC

Having discussed the foundations of OPEC's economic strength and political power, we may consider the means through which this politico-economic power can be used in negotiating with international oil companies and Western consuming countries. The so-called "weapons" in OPEC's hands can be classified into two categories: (1) negative sanctions, and (2) positive stiumuli, which can be used alternatively vis-a-vis foreign interests. In resisting intolerable demands or intransigences of the oil-importing countries or companies, OPEC members may retaliate by resorting to such negative sanctions as:

1. Withholding part or all of the oil supply from all or selected customers through (a) nationalization or threat of take-over of oil and/or other foreign investments, and (b) temporary embargoes on exports;
2. Using its "embargo" power to demand and receive increasingly higher prices for crude oil—naturally to the extent that consumer resistance, the development of substitutes, and retaliatory measures by the oil importing countries (e.g., import quotas, foreign investment restrictions, denial of aid, and other retaliation) may permit;
3. Regulating domestic operation by foreign oil companies through such requirements as greater local participation in production and/or distribution; further changes in internal "value-added" in oil production and marketing; and increased local purchases, restricted company imports, etc.;
4. Switching huge export earnings from some foreign currencies and countries to others depending on type of cooperation and attitude, or denying foreign investment in "hostile" countries;
5. Making discriminatory price concessions, or engaging in unfavorable price discrimination vis-a-vis selected customers, or dumping other export products in "unfriendly" countries;
6. Retaliating against industrialized creditors by the repudiation or re-scheduling of foreign debts; and
7. Shifting alliances and coalitions in trade, investment and military agreements between cooperative and

non-cooperative nations (including threats of withdrawing from membership of regional pacts or closing military bases).

The possibility of using these negative sanctions is only part of OPEC's strength. Part of its power also resides in the offer of positive stimuli or incentives for cooperation. These incentives may include such things as:

1. Giving special concessions to foreign private investors for the purpose of exploiting domestic national resources which are outside the scope of existing contracts;
2. Promising cooperation in the reform of international monetary, fiscal and trade systems; and
3. Investing in joint ventures for the development of energy sources and/or other investment projects with cooperative and accommodating partners.

These positive and negative "weapons" have been used in the past and are more likely to be used in the future when circumstances warrant. Like all destructive weapons, however, the significance of the negative sanctions lies, partly at least, in their potential deterrence rather than actual use.

IV. Conclusion

In the final analysis, the very existence and occasional use of these weapons—even those which are retaliatory in nature—are not only in the interest of the Third World, but also to the advantage of the whole international community. The possibility of using the negative weapons will ensure greater economic justice among the rich and poor; reduce inferiority complexes of the developing nations (particularly the previous colonies) when dealing with the industrial countries; enhance their self-reliance and self-confidence; narrow existing political, psychological and economic gaps between the large and small countries; and pave the way for a better world. The productivity and beneficial prospects of the positive stimuli, in turn, open up vast horizons of cooperative endeavors between oil producers and oil consumers in efficient use of fuel supplies and in the search for newer sources of energy.

PART II
THE RESPONSE

P R E S I D E N T I A L   S T A T E M E N T S

PRESIDENT JIMMY CARTER

IN SECOND FORD-CARTER TV DEBATE

October 6, 1976

Would you be willing to risk an oil embargo in order to promote human rights in Iran and Saudi Arabia, withhold arms from Saudi Arabia for the same purpose, or -- I think, as a matter of fact, you have perhaps answered this final part, but would you withhold grain from the Soviet Union in order to promote civil rights in the Soviet Union?

GOVERNOR CARTER: I would never single out food as a trade embargo item. If I ever decided to impose an embargo because of a crisis in international relationships, it would include all shipments of all equipment.

For instance, if the Arab countries ever again declare an embargo against our nation on oil, I would consider that, not a military but an economic declaration of war, and I would respond instantly and in kind. I would not ship that Arab country anything. No weapons, no spare parts for weapons, no oil drilling rigs, no oil pipe, no nothing. I wouldn't single out just food.

PRESIDENT GERALD FORD

PRESS CONFERENCE

October 20, 1976

Q. Mr. President, during your last debate with Jimmy Carter Mr. Carter stated that if there was another Arab oil boycott and he was President of the United States he would break that boycott by countering it with a boycott of our own. Mr. President, do you think this is a realistic possibility? Could the United States break down an Arab oil boycott or embargo by penalizing them by refusing to sell materials to them? And secondly, even if it is realistic, would it be in the best interests of the United States?

A. My answer would be that I would not tolerate an Arab oil embargo. But I add very quickly, in the current atmosphere, because of the leadership of the Ford Administration, you aren't going to have an Arab oil embargo.

PRESIDENT JIMMY CARTER

PRESS CONFERENCE

MAY 28, 1976

Q. Governor, on another foreign policy - national security issue: In the event of renewed Middle East hostilities and a resulting Arab oil embargo, you have called for a tough counter-boycott this time, in essence restricting all Western goods and services to the Arab world.

A. That's right.

Q. Such a posture was considered in 1973 but it was considered futile because there were so many markets, East and West, to which Arab nations could turn. I am wondering what makes you think such a tough line would be effective this time around, if there is another time.

A. I think that is getting the cart before the horse. I think if we as a nation take the position ahead of time and the President expresses a position, which I have as a candidate, that if there is another embargo, if there is another attempt at blackmail, which was successful in 1973, that we would instantly consider it a declaration of economic war; and we would respond accordingly, with an embargo against the Arab countries who declared an embargo against us and that we under those circumstances would not ship them any food, weapons, spare parts for weapons, no oil drilling rigs, no oil pipes, no nothing. I think that is the best way to prevent another attempt at blackmail or another oil embargo. I don't think the advisable thing would be to wait until an embargo occurred and then to respond. I would do it if I said I was going to. But I think this is a good way to prevent an embargo, and I would carry this out.

Q. Another foreign policy statement you have made is that you would encourage better consultation with our allies overseas.

A. Yes.

Q. Now, in the situation we have just been discussing, a potential oil embargo, would not our allies react the same way they did in 1973 and go their own way with the Arabs, and therefore would not our counter-embargo fail for that reason?

A. It may or may not. I have never tried to speak for all our allies on the response to an Arab embargo that I have just described. We can get along without oil from Arab nations in an emergency if we have to. Some of our allies cannot. Japan could not. They import about 98 percent of their total energy needs, and I would not try to make the allies be compatible with us by force or heavy persuasion. But I think it would be very good for them to know what our position would be if an embargo was declared against our country. This is a serious thing that I would like to avoid. We are now importing between 40 and 50 percent of our total oil needs. But that doesn't mean that all that import comes from Arab countries, and I think it would be good for us and for the Arabs as well to know that it would be a very serious thing for them economically to declare another embargo against our country.

The Energy Crisis: Strategy for Cooperative Action

Address by Secretary Kissinger [1]

A generation ago the Western world faced a historic crisis—the breakdown of international order in the wake of world war. Threatened by economic chaos and political upheaval, the nations of the West built a system of security relations and cooperative institutions that have nourished our safety, our prosperity, and our freedom ever since. A moment of grave crisis was transformed into an act of lasting creativity.

We face another such moment today. The stakes are as high as they were 25 years ago. The challenge to our courage, our vision, and our will is as profound. And our opportunity is as great.

What will be our response?

I speak, of course, of the energy crisis. Tonight I want to discuss how the administration views this problem, what we have been doing about it, and where we must now go. I will stress two themes that this government has emphasized for a year and a half:

—First, the problem is grave but it is soluble.

—Second, international collaboration, particularly among the industrial nations of North America, Western Europe, and Japan, is an inescapable necessity.

The economic facts are stark. By 1973, worldwide industrial expansion was outstripping energy supply; the threat of shortages was already real. Then, without warn-

[1] Made before a University of Chicago Board of Trustees banquet at Chicago, Ill., on Nov. 14 (text from press release 500).

ing, we were faced first with a political embargo, followed quickly by massive increases in the price of oil. In the course of a single year the price of the world's most strategic commodity was raised 400 percent. The impact has been drastic and global:

—The industrial nations now face a collective payments deficit of $40 billion, the largest in history and beyond the experience or capacity of our financial institutions. We suffer simultaneously a slowdown of production and a speedup of an inflation that was already straining the ability of governments to control.

—The nations of the developing world face a collective yearly deficit of $20 billion, over half of which is due to increases in oil prices. The rise in energy costs in fact roughly equals the total flow of external aid. In other words, the new oil bill threatens hopes for progress and advancement and renders problematical the ability to finance even basic human needs such as food.

—The oil producers now enjoy a surplus of $60 billion, far beyond their payments or development needs and manifestly more than they can invest. Enormous unabsorbed surplus revenues now jeopardize the very functioning of the international monetary system.

Yet this is only the first year of inflated oil prices. The full brunt of the petrodollar flood is yet to come. If current economic trends continue, we face further and mounting worldwide shortages, unemployment, poverty, and hunger. No nation, East or West, North or South, consumer or producer, will be spared the consequences.

An economic crisis of such magnitude would inevitably produce dangerous political consequences. Mounting inflation and recession—brought on by remote decisions over which consumers have no influence—will fuel the frustration of all whose hopes for economic progress are suddenly and cruelly rebuffed. This is fertile ground for social conflict and political turmoil. Moderate governments and moderate solutions will be under severe attack. Democratic societies could become vulnerable to extremist pressures from right or left to a degree not experienced since the twenties and thirties. The great achievements of this generation in preserving our institutions and constructing an international order will be imperiled.

The destinies of consumers and producers are joined in the same global economic system, on which the progress of both depends. If either attempts to wield economic power aggressively, both run grave risks. Political cooperation, the prerequisite of a thriving international economy, is shattered. New tensions will engulf the world just when the antagonisms of two decades of the cold war have begun to diminish.

The potentially most serious international consequences could occur in relations between North America, Europe, and Japan. If the energy crisis is permitted to continue unchecked, some countries will be tempted to secure unilateral benefit through separate arrangements with producers at the expense of the collaboration that offers the only hope for survival over the long term. Such unilateral arrangements are guaranteed to enshrine inflated prices, dilute the bargaining power of the consumers, and perpetuate the economic burden for all. The political consequences of disarray would be pervasive. Traditional patterns of policy may be abandoned because of dependence on a strategic commodity. Even the hopeful process of easing tensions with our adversaries could suffer, because it has always presupposed the political unity of the Atlantic nations and Japan.

The Need for Consumer Cooperation

This need not be our fate. On the contrary, the energy crisis should summon once again the cooperative effort which sustained the policies of North America, Western Europe, and Japan for a quarter century.

The Atlantic nations and Japan have the ability, if we have the will, not only to master the energy crisis but to shape from it a new era of creativity and common progress.

In fact we have no other alternative. The energy crisis is not a problem of transitional adjustment. Our financial institutions and mechanisms of cooperation were never designed to handle so abrupt and artificially sustained a price rise of so essential a commodity with such massive economic and political ramifications. We face a long-term drain which challenges us to common action or dooms us to perpetual crisis.

The problem will not go away by permitting inflation to proceed to redress the balance between oil producers and producers of other goods. Inflation is the most grotesque kind of adjustment, in which all other elements in the domestic structure are upset in an attempt to balance one—the oil bill. In any event, the producers could and would respond by raising prices, thereby accelerating all the political and social dangers I have described.

Nor can consumers finance their oil bill by going into debt to the producers without making their domestic structure hostage to the decisions of others. Already, producers have the power to cause major financial upheavals simply by shifting investment funds from one country to another or even from one institution to another. The political implications are ominous and unpredictable. Those who wield financial power would sooner or later seek to dictate the political terms of the new relationships.

Finally, price reductions will not be brought about by consumer-producer dialogue alone. The price of oil will come down only when objective conditions for a reduction are created, and not before. Today the producers are able to manipulate prices at will and with apparent impunity. They are not persuaded by our protestations of damage to our societies and economies, because we have taken scant action to defend them ourselves. They are not moved by our alarms about the health of the Western world, which never included and sometimes exploited them. And even if the producers learn eventually that their long-term interest requires a cooperative adjustment of the price structure, it would be foolhardy to count on it or passively wait for it.

We agree that a consumer-producer dialogue is essential. But it must be accompanied by the elaboration of greater consumer solidarity. The heart of our approach must be collaboration among the consuming nations. No one else will do the job for us.

Blueprint for Consumer Cooperation

Consumer cooperation has been the central element of U.S. policy for the past year and a half.

In April 1973 the United States warned that energy was becoming a problem of unprecedented proportions and that collaboration among the nations of the West and Japan was essential. In December of the same year, we proposed a program of collective action. This led to the Washington Energy Conference in February 1974, at which the major consumers established new machinery for consultation with a mandate to create, as soon as possible, institutions for the pooling of effort, risk, and technology.

In April 1974 and then again this fall before the U.N. General Assembly, President Ford and I reiterated the American philosophy that global cooperation offered the only long-term solution and that our efforts with fellow consumers were designed to pave the way for constructive dialogue with the producers. In September 1974 we convened a meeting of the Foreign and Finance Ministers of the United Kingdom, Japan, the Federal Republic of Germany, France, and the United States to consider further measures of consumer cooperation. And last month President Ford announced a long-term national policy of conservation and development to reinforce our international efforts to meet the energy challenge.

In our view, a concerted consumer strategy has two basic elements:

—First, we must create the objective conditions necessary to bring about lower oil prices. Since the industrialized nations are the principal consumers, their actions can have a decisive impact. Determined national action, reinforced by collective efforts, can transform the market by reducing our consumption of oil and accelerating development of new sources of energy. Over time this will create a powerful pressure on prices.

—Second, in the interim we must protect the vitality of our economies. Effective action on conservation will require months; development of alternative sources will take years. In the meantime, we will face two great dangers. One is the threat of a new embargo. The other is that our financial system may be unable to manage chronic deficits and to recycle the huge flows of oil dollars that producers will invest each year in our economies. A financial collapse—or the threat of it—somewhere in the system could result in restrictive monetary, fiscal, and trade measures and a downward spiral of income and jobs.

The consumers have taken two major steps to safeguard themselves against these dangers by collaborative action.

One of the results of the Washington Energy Conference was a new permanent institution for consumer energy cooperation —the International Energy Agency (IEA). This agency will oversee a comprehensive common effort—in conservation, cooperative research and development, broad new action in nuclear enrichment, investment in new energy supplies, and the elaboration of consumer positions for the consumer-producer dialogue.

Equally significant is the unprecedented agreement to share oil supplies among principal consumers in the event of another crisis. The International Energy Program that grew out of the Washington Energy Conference and that we shall formally adopt next week is a historic step toward consumer solidarity. It provides a detailed blueprint for common action should either a general or selective embargo occur. It is a defensive arrangement, not a challenge to producers. But producing countries must know that it expresses the determination of the consumers to shape their own future and not to remain vulnerable to outside pressures.

The International Energy Agency and the International Energy Program are the first fruits of our efforts. But they are only foundations. We must now bring our blueprint to life.

To carry through the overall design, the consuming countries must act in five interrelated areas:

—First, we must accelerate our national programs of energy conservation, and we must coordinate them to insure their effectiveness.

—Second, we must press on with the development of new supplies of oil and alternative sources of energy.

—Third, we must strengthen economic security—to protect against oil emergencies and to safeguard the international financial system.

—Fourth, we must assist the poor nations whose hopes and efforts for progress have been cruelly blunted by the oil price rises of the past year.

—Fifth, on the basis of consumer solidarity we should enter a dialogue with the producers to establish a fair and durable long-term relationship.

Let me deal with each of these points in turn.

Coordination of Conservation Programs

Conservation and the development of new sources of energy are basic to the solution.

The industrialized countries as a whole now import nearly two-thirds of their oil and over one-third of their total energy. Over the next decade, we must conserve enough oil and develop sufficient alternative supplies to reduce these imports to no more than one-fifth of the total energy consumption. This requires that the industrialized countries manage the growth of their economies without increasing the volume of their oil imports.

The effect of this reduced dependence will be crucial. If it succeeds, the demand of the industrialized countries for imported oil will remain static while new sources of energy will become available both inside and outside of OPEC [Organization of Petroleum Exporting Countries]. OPEC may attempt to offset efforts to strengthen conservation and develop alternative sources by deeper and deeper cuts in production, reducing the income of producers who seek greater revenues for their development. The majority of producers will then see their interest in expanding supply and seeking a new equilibrium between supply and demand at a fair price.

Limiting oil imports into industrial countries to a roughly constant figure is an extremely demanding goal requiring discipline for conservation and investment for the development of new energy sources. The United States, which now imports a third of its oil and a sixth of its total energy, will have to become largely self-sufficient. Specifically, we shall set as a target that we reduce our imports over the next decade from 7 million barrels a day to no more than 1 million barrels, or less than 2 percent of our total energy consumption.

Conservation is of course the most immediate road to relief. President Ford has stated that the United States will reduce oil imports by 1 million barrels per day by the end of 1975—a 15 percent reduction.

But one country's reduction in consumption can be negated if other major consumers do not follow suit. Fortunately, other nations have begun conservation programs of their own. What is needed now is to relate these programs to common goals and an overall design. Therefore, the United States proposes an international agreement to set consumption goals. The United States is prepared to join an international conservation agreement that would lead to systematic and long-term savings on an equitable basis.

As part of such a program, we propose that by the end of 1975 the industrialized countries reduce their consumption of oil by 3 million barrels a day over what it would be otherwise—a reduction of approximately 10 percent of the total imports of the group. This reduction can be carried out without prejudice to economic growth and jobs by cutting back on wasteful and inefficient uses of energy both in personal consumption and in industry. The United States is prepared to assume a fair share of the total reduction.

The principal consumer nations should meet each year to determine appropriate annual targets.

Development of Alternative Energy Sources

Conservation measures will be effective to the extent that they are part of a dynamic program for the development of alternative energy sources. All countries must make a major shift toward nuclear power, coal, gas, and other sources. If we are to assure substantial amounts of new energy in the 1980's, we must start now. If the industrialized nations take the steps which are within their power, they will be able to transform energy shortages into energy surpluses by the 1980's.

Project Independence is the American contribution to this effort. It represents the investment of hundreds of billions of dollars, public and private—dwarfing our moon-landing program and the Manhattan Project, two previous examples of American technology mobilized for a great goal. Project Independence demonstrates that the United States will never permit itself to be held hostage to a strategic commodity.

Project Independence will be complemented by an active policy of supporting cooperative projects with other consumers. The International Energy Agency to be established next week is well designed to launch and coordinate such programs. Plans are already drawn up for joint projects in coal technology and solar energy. The United States is prepared to expand these collective activities substantially to include such fields as uranium enrichment.

The area of controlled thermonuclear fusion is particularly promising for joint ventures, for it would make available abundant energy from virtually inexhaustible resources. The United States is prepared to join with other IEA members in a broad program of joint planning, exchange of scientific personnel, shared use of national facilities, and the development of joint facilities to accelerate the advent of fusion power.

Finally, we shall recommend to the IEA that it create a common fund to finance or guarantee investment in promising energy projects in participating countries and in those ready to cooperate with the IEA on a long-term basis.

Financial Solidarity

The most serious immediate problem facing the consuming countries is the economic and financial strain resulting from high oil prices. Producer revenues will inevitably be reinvested in the industrialized world; there is no other outlet. But they will not necessarily flow back to the countries whose balance of payments problems are most acute. Thus many countries will remain unable to finance their deficits and all will be vulnerable to massive sudden withdrawals.

The industrialized nations, acting together, can correct this imbalance and reduce their vulnerability. Just as producers are free to choose where they place their funds, so the consumers must be free to redistribute these funds to meet their own needs and those of the developing countries.

Private financial institutions are already deeply involved in this process. To buttress their efforts, central banks are assuring that necessary support is available to the private institutions, particularly since so much of the oil money has been invested in relatively short-term obligations. Private institutions should not bear all the risks indefinitely, however. We cannot afford to test the limits of their capacity.

Therefore the governments of Western Europe, North America, and Japan should move now to put in place a system of mutual support that will augment and buttress private channels whenever necessary. The United States proposes that a common loan and guarantee facility be created to provide for redistributing up to $25 billion in 1975, and as much again the next year if necessary.

The facility will not be a new aid institution to be funded by additional taxes. It will be a mechanism for recycling, at commercial interest rates, funds flowing back to the industrial world from the oil producers. Support from the facility would not be automatic, but contingent on full resort to private financing and on reasonable self-help measures. No country should expect financial assistance that is not moving effectively to lessen its dependence on imported oil.

Such a facility will help assure the stability of the entire financial system and the credit-worthiness of participating governments; in the long run it would reduce the need for official financing. If implemented rapidly it would:

—Protect financial institutions from the excessive risks posed by an enormous volume of funds beyond their control or capacity;

—Insure that no nation is forced to pursue disruptive and restrictive policies for lack of adequate financing;

—Assure that no consuming country will be compelled to accept financing on intolerable political or economic terms; and

—Enable each participating country to demonstrate to people that efforts and sacrifices are being shared equitably—that the national survival is buttressed by consumer solidarity.

We have already begun discussion of this proposal; it was a principal focus of the meeting of the Foreign and Finance Ministers of the Federal Republic of Germany, the United States, Japan, the United Kingdom, and France in September in Washington.

Easing the Plight of Developing Countries

The strategy I have outlined here is also essential to ease the serious plight of many developing countries. All consuming nations are in need of relief from excessive oil prices, but the developing world cannot wait for the process to unfold. For them, the oil crisis has already produced an emergency. The oil bill has wiped out the external assistance of the poorer developing countries, halted agricultural and industrial development, and inflated the prices for their most fundamental needs, including food. Unlike the industrial nations, developing countries do not have many options of self-help; their margin for reducing energy consumption is limited; they have little capacity to develop alternative sources.

For both moral and practical reasons, we cannot permit hopes for development to die or cut ourselves off from the political and economic needs of so great a part of mankind. At the very least, the industrial nations must maintain the present level of their aid to the developing world and take special account of its needs in the multilateral trade negotiations.

We must also look for ways to help in the critical area of food. At the World Food Conference, I outlined a strategy for meeting the food and agricultural needs of the least developed countries. The United States is uniquely equipped to make a contribution in this field and will make a contribution worthy of its special strength.

A major responsibility must rest with those oil producers whose actions aggravated the problems of the developing countries and who, because of their new-found wealth, now have greatly increased resources for assistance.

But even after all presently available resources have been drawn upon, an unfinanced payments deficit of between $1 and $2 billion will remain for the 25 or 30 countries most seriously affected by high oil prices. It could grow in 1976.

We need new international mechanisms to meet this deficit. One possibility would be to supplement regular International Monetary Fund facilities by the creation of a separate trust fund managed by the IMF to lend at interest rates recipient countries could afford. Funds would be provided by national contributions from interested countries, including especially oil producers. The IMF itself could contribute the profits from IMF gold sales undertaken for this purpose. We urge the Interim Committee of the IMF and the joint IMF–IBRD [International Bank for Reconstruction and Development] Development Committee to examine this proposal on an urgent basis.

Constructive Dialogue With Producers

When the consumers have taken some collective steps toward a durable solution—that is, measures to further conservation and the development of new supplies—and for our interim protection through emergency planning and financial solidarity, the conditions for a constructive dialogue with producers will have been created.

We do not see consumer cooperation as antagonistic to consumer-producer cooperation. Rather we view it as a necessary prerequisite to a constructive dialogue, as do many of the producers themselves, who have urged the consumers to curb inflation, conserve energy, and preserve international financial stability.

A dialogue that is not carefully prepared will compound the problems which it is supposed to solve. Until the consumers develop a coherent approach to their own problems, discussions with the producers will only repeat in a multilateral forum the many bilateral exchanges which are already taking place. When consumer solidarity has been developed and there are realistic prospects for significant progress, the United States is prepared to participate in a consumer-producer meeting.

The main subject of such a dialogue must inevitably be price. Clearly the stability of the system on which the economic health of even the producers depends requires a price reduction. But an equitable solution must also take account of the producers' need for long-term income security and economic growth. This we are prepared to discuss sympathetically.

In the meantime the producers must recognize that further increases in the prices while this dialogue is being prepared and when the system has not even absorbed the previous price rises would be disruptive and dangerous.

On this basis—consumer solidarity in conservation, the development of alternative supplies, and financial security; producer policies of restraint and responsibility; and a mutual recognition of interdependence and a long-term common interest—there can be justifiable hope that a consumer-producer dialogue will bring an end to the crisis that has shaken the world to its economic foundations.

The Next Step

It is now a year and a month since the oil crisis began. We have made a good beginning, but the major test is still ahead.

The United States in the immediate future intends to make further proposals to implement the program I have outlined.

Next week, we will propose to the new International Energy Agency a specific program for cooperative action in conservation, the development of new supplies, nuclear enrichment, and the preparation of consumer positions for the eventual consumer-producer dialogue.

Simultaneously, Secretary [of the Treasury William E.] Simon will spell out our ideas for financial solidarity in detail, and our representative at the Group of Ten will present them to his colleagues.

We will, as well, ask the Chairman of the Interim Committee of the IMF as well as the new joint IMF–IBRD Development Committee to consider an urgent program for concessional assistance to the poorest countries.

Yesterday, Secretary [of the Interior Rogers C. B.] Morton announced an accelerated program for domestic oil exploration and exploitation.

President Ford will submit a detailed and comprehensive energy program to the new Congress.

Let there be no doubt, the energy problem is soluble. It will overwhelm us only if we retreat from its reality. But there can be no solution without the collective efforts of the nations of North America, Western Europe, and Japan—the very nations whose cooperation over the course of more than two decades has brought prosperity and peace to the postwar world. Nor, in the last analysis, can there be a solution without a dialogue with the producers carried on in a spirit of reconciliation and compromise.

A great responsibility rests upon America, for without our dedication and leadership no progress is possible. This nation for many years has carried the major responsibility for maintaining the peace, feeding the hungry, sustaining international economic growth, and inspiring those who would be free. We did not seek this heavy burden, and we have often been tempted to put it down. But we have never done so, and we cannot afford to do so now—or the generations that follow us will pay the price for our self-indulgence.

For more than a decade America has been torn by war, social and generational turbulence, and constitutional crisis. Yet the most striking lesson from these events is our fundamental stability and strength. During our upheavals, we still managed to ease tensions around the globe. Our people and our institutions have come through our domestic travails with an extraordinary resiliency. And now, once again, our leadership in technology, agriculture, industry, and communications has become vital to the world's recovery.

Woodrow Wilson once remarked that "wrapped up with the liberty of the world is the continuous perfection of that liberty by the concerted powers of all civilized people." That, in the last analysis, is what the energy crisis is all about. For it is our liberty that in the end is at stake and it is only through the concerted action of the industrial democracies that it will be maintained.

The dangers that Woodrow Wilson and his generation faced were, by today's standards, relatively simple and straightforward. The dangers we face now are more subtle and more profound. The context in which we act is more complex than even the period following the Second World War. Then we drew inspiration from stewardship; now we must find it in partnership. Then we and our allies were brought together by an external threat, now we must find it in our devotion to the political and economic institutions of free peoples working together for a common goal. Our challenge is to maintain the cooperative spirit among like-minded nations that has served us so well for a generation and to prove, as Woodrow Wilson said in another time and place, that "The highest and best form of efficiency is the spontaneous cooperation of a free people."

94th Congress } 1st Session } COMMITTEE PRINT

OIL FIELDS AS MILITARY OBJECTIVES
A Feasibility Study

PREPARED FOR THE

SPECIAL SUBCOMMITTEE ON INVESTIGATIONS

OF THE

COMMITTEE ON INTERNATIONAL RELATIONS

BY THE

CONGRESSIONAL RESEARCH SERVICE
LIBRARY OF CONGRESS

AUGUST 21, 1975

U.S. GOVERNMENT PRINTING OFFICE
56-520 WASHINGTON : 1975

CONTENTS

ABSTRACT

The possible use of U.S. military force to occupy foreign oil fields in exigency first surfaced as a serious issue in January 1975. This paper provides perspective, so that the Congress if need be could participate most meaningfully in deliberations to determine the *desirability* and *feasibility* of any such action.

Analysis indicates that sustained sanctions by all or most of OPEC's members would disrupt America's fundamental lifestyle and degrade U.S. security, although survival would never be at stake. By way of contrast, the vital interests of our major allies could quickly be compromised.

Any decision to ease agonies at home and (if need be) assist allies would be conditioned by political, economic, social, legal, and moral factors, but if nonmilitary facets were entirely favorable, successful operations would be assured *only* if this country could satisfy all aspects of a five-part mission:

—Seize required oil installations intact.
—Secure them for weeks, months, or years.
—Restore wrecked assets rapidly.
—Operate all installations without the owner's assistance.
—Guarantee safe overseas passage for supplies and petroleum products.

American abilities to cope with steps one through four would be suspect if sabotage were the only serious threat. U.S. parachute assault forces are too few to cover all objectives quickly. Amphibious forces are too slow. Skilled teams could wreak havoc before we arrived.

Presuming sufficient assets remained intact to serve U.S. interests, long-term security would remain a challenge. Two to four divisions plus substantial support would be tied down for a protracted period.

Shortages in specialized manpower and materials would make damaged facilities hard to repair or replace. Indeed, drafting U.S. civilian workers to supplant foreign counterparts might be mandatory.

Direct intervention by Soviet air/ground forces, a distinct possibility considering the strategic nuclear standoff, might make our mission impossible if we hit in the Middle East. Other areas would be mainly immune from such perils, but Soviet submarines would pose a serious problem if they struck in force—U.S. escort vessels are insufficient to insure safe passage for tankers and supply ships in any area, except the Caribbean.

In short, success would largely depend on two prerequisites:

—Slight damage to key installations.
—Soviet abstinence from armed intervention.

Since neither essential could be assured, military operations to rescue the United States (much less its key allies) from an airtight oil embargo would combine high costs with high risks. U.S. strategic reserves would be stripped. Prospects would be poor, and plights of far-reaching political, economic, social, psychological, and perhaps military consequence the penalty for failure.

OIL FIELDS AS MILITARY OBJECTIVES

A Feasibility Study

Question. Mr. President, both you and Secretary Kissinger have said that in case of strangulation of the West by the oil producers, you would use military force. * * * The American people would like to know whether you would require a congressional declaration of war or whether you would bypass that constitutional process, as some of your predecessors have done?

Answer. I can assure you on any occasion where there was any commitment of U.S. military personnel to any engagement we would use the complete constitutional process that is required of the President.

—President GERALD R. FORD,
Press Conference,
January 21, 1975.

BACKGROUND, PURPOSE, AND SCOPE

The possible use of U.S. military force to seize foreign oil fields if the "industrialized world" were being economically "strangled" by any combination of petroleum exporting countries first surfaced as a serious issue in January 1975.[1] The President, Secretary of State, and Secretary of Defense all addressed that subject.[2] Influential periodicals simultaneously began printing a spate of unofficial studies, speculation, and scenarios.[3] Interest in the subject continues.[4]

All public pronouncements pertain to hypothetical propositions. The Chief Executive and key Cabinet members identify armed intervention as a last resort, after all other efforts have been exhausted and survival is at issue. However, the fact that they hold military options open creates a need to separate fact from fantasy in ways that facilitate sound decisionmaking.

The purpose of this paper is to provide perspective, so that Congress could participate most meaningfully in deliberations to determine:

—Whether we should go to war to excise the effects of any given oil embargo against the United States and/or its allies.

—What strategic and tactical objectives would best serve U.S. purposes if the answer were affirmative.

—What forces would be essential.

---

[1] For an introductory chronology see Helms, Jesse A. "Misjudgments in the Middle East," Remarks in the Senate, *Congressional Record*, Jan. 23, 1975, pp. S791–S792.

[2] See annex A for selected quotations.

[3] For the seminal study, see Tucker, Robert W. "Oil: The Issue of American Intervention." Commentary, January 1975, pp. 21–31. Among succeeding essays, the most noted thus far has been Ignotus, Miles (a pseudonym, reportedly for "a Washington-based professor"), "Seizing Arab Oil," Harper's, March 1975, pp. 45–62. Rebuttals are found in Ravenal, Earl C., "The Oil-Grab Scenario," The New Republic, Jan. 18, 1975, pp. 14–16 and Stone, I. F., "War For Oil?", The New York Review, Feb. 6, 1975, pp. 7–8, 10.

[4] J. William Fulbright, former Chairman of the Senate Committee on Foreign Relations, most recently theorized on this subject. See Fulbright's 1980 Middle East Scenario (which actually commences with an oil embargo and U.S. military counteractions in 1976), Washington Star-News, July 13, 1975, pp. E–1, E–4.

—What special expenditures could be expected.
—What risks would be entailed.
—What benefits could accrue.

The resultant survey covers the immediate future only, through the 1970's. Thereafter, new United States and allied sources of energy could make armed intervention against petroleum producers an irrelevant act. However, the principles discussed herein could be applied to potential crises concerning other critical resources later in this century.

Petroleum statistics were drawn from authoritative public documents. Military data were derived from the best available open sources. Many figures are in flux. Some conflict with those in other publications, but discrepancies are matters of minor detail, which in no way invalidate basic conclusions.

The end product is not a brief for or against U.S. military operations to seize OPEC oilfields. Neither is it a contingency plan. It simply is a feasibility study that probes problems "in the round," with full recognition that any decision to condone the use of force would be conditioned by a spectrum of political, economic, social, legal, and moral factors that transcend purely military matters.[5]

---

[5] See annex B for a glossary of special terms. Annex C contains abbreviations.

PART I: PRIMAL PROBLEMS

VITAL INTERESTS RELATED TO OIL

The only vital national interest, by definition, is survival. States cease to exist if they fail to safeguard that essential. Threats to survival thus warrant severe countermeasures.

Less crucial interests include national security, freedom of action, fundamental lifestyles, vigor, and values. Life goes on if those elements are undercut, but conflicts often occur when people find physical and/or psychological pains intolerable.

Economic warfare, most notably oil embargoes, currently could threaten most modern societies just as surely as nuclear weapons. Degrees of vulnerability depend on relationships between each country's requirements on one hand and its resources plus stockpiled reserves on the other.

U.S. INTERESTS

Oil provides 46 percent of all energy consumed in the United States—almost half.[1] Domestic production supplied about 63 percent of the petroleum consumed in 1974. The rest had to be imported. (Data displayed in tables 1 and 2 at the end of this section include some months affected by the Arab oil embargo of 1973–74, but are reasonably representative.)

The importance of imports

The brief embargo from mid-October 1973 through mid-March 1974 was sponsored solely by Arab States and allowed considerable leakage. Some tankers with false manifests found their way directly from the Persian Gulf to U.S. ports. Others took devious routes with full Arab knowledge.[2] Nevertheless, that restrained effort showed how susceptible this country would be to renewed pressures.[3]

The United States could absorb a new Arab boycott by reducing consumption slightly. (See table 3.) However, our troubles would intensify tremendously if the entire Organization of Petroleum Exporting Countries (OPEC) imposed airtight sanctions, which someday could be the case. That cartel recently confirmed its readiness to "counteract * * * threats with a unified response whenever the need arises."[4]

---

[1] MacDonald, David R., "Report of Investigation of Effect of Petroleum Imports and Petroleum Products on the National Security Pursuant to sec. 232 of the Trade Expansion Act, as amended." Department of the Treasury, Jan. 13, 1975, annex E. (no pagination).

[2] Testimony of William Simon before the Permanent Subcommittee on Investigations of the Senate Committee on Government Operations, Jan. 25, 1974, printed in: U.S. Senate. Committee on Interior and Insular Affairs. "Current Analysis of Petroleum Supplies for 1st Quarter 1974." Committee print, serial No. 93-30 (92-65), 93d Cong., 2d Sess. Washington, U.S. Government Printing Office, 1974, p. 1. The Dec. 15, 1973 issue of the National Journal reported that the Cabinet-level Emergency Energy Action Group had decided on Nov. 19, 1973, not to disclose the sources of imported oil during the embargo to protect countries "leaking" oil to the United States. A Department of Commerce report released on Apr. 8, 1974 (Washington Post, Apr. 9, 1974: A-12) confirmed that oil from Arab countries continued to flow to the United States despite the embargo.

[3] The Arab oil embargo was only one of several factors that contributed to U.S. oil shortages in the winter of 1973-74, but it was the most conspicuous. Mark, Clyde, "The Arab Oil Embargo and U.S. Oil Shortages: October 1973 to March 1974." Washington, Congressional Research Service, May 3, 1974, (press release of Congressman Dante Fascell, May 27, 1974). 16 pp.

[4] "Conference of the Sovereigns and Heads of State of the OPEC Member Countries: Solemn Declaration." New York Times, Apr. 1, 1975, p. 18C.

Neither Canada nor friendly Caribbean states (now major U.S. suppliers) could help take up the slack, even if they wanted to.[5] OPEC provides almost half of Canada's petroleum. Refineries in Trinidad and Tobago, the Bahamas, and Netherlands Antilles also depend on OPEC oil. Crude oil sources would dry up if any of those parties transshipped to the United States during an embargo.

Consequently, it is realistically possible to postulate a worst case condition depriving the United States of most imports. If so, an energy shortage approximating 13 percent of current consumption could be expected.

Short-term conservation measures

Should serious shortages occur as a result of economic sanctions by unfriendly States, three domestic courses of action in combination would be open to U.S. decisionmakers: use stockpiles to take up the slack; augment U.S. output; reduce the rate of consumption.

Stockpile figures fluctuate. The Defense Department maintains modest inventories (exact sizes are classified). Current civilian crude oil stockpiles could match demands for about 65 days if necessary. Separate caches of refined products ostensibly could extend that time limit, but substantial stocks likely would be shifted to military channels in emergency.[6] Such transfers in fact took place in November 1973, during the Arab oil embargo, as authorized by the Defense Production Act of 1950.[7] Consequently, little relief is likely from that quarter.

Steps to increase U.S. production would bring forth few immediate benefits. Naval Petroleum Reserve No. 1 (NPR–1) at Elk Hills, Calif. reportedly would take months to prime. Activating NPR–4 in Alaska would take much longer, since its assets still await full exploration and development.[8] Technical adjustments to amplify the output of U.S. fields now in operation would also be protracted projects. Outer Continental Shelf (OCS) development will take at least 5 years.[9]

Cutting consumption using techniques outlined in table 4 could create quick and sizable savings approximating 1 million barrels a day (6 percent of current consumption), according to administration authorities.[10]

Thereafter, the law of diminishing returns would take over. U.S. Armed Forces, for example, already have severely curtailed maneuvers, other training exercises, flight schedules, and ship steaming time for Reserves as well as active elements.[11] Additional restrictions would

---

[5] Canada, which presently supplies 17 percent of all U.S. petroleum imports, plans to cut off that source shortly, since it needs more oil itself. See statement of Donald S. MacDonald, Canadian Minister of Energy, to the House of Commons, Nov. 22, 1974. Printed in U.S. Congress. House. "Energy From U.S. and Canadian Tar Sands: Technical, Environmental, Economic, Legislative, and Policy Aspects." Report prepared for the Subcommittee on Energy of the Committee on Science and Astronautics. 93d Cong., 2d sess. Washington, U.S. Government Printing Office, December 1974, pp. 87–90.

[6] U.S. stocks of crude oil for civilian use totaled 225 million barrels in October 1974. Imports that month were 3.9 million barrels a day. Reserves would last 65 days if all imports ceased. Monthly Energy Review, Federal Energy Administration, National Energy Information Center, December 1974.

[7] Cooper, Bert H., "Oil Shortages and the U.S. Armed Forces." Washington, Congressional Research Service, Apr. 16, 1974, p. 24.

[8] Fact Sheet, The President's state of the Union message. Washington, Office of the White House Press Secretary, Jan. 15, 1975. Question and answer section.

[9] Kash, Don E., White, Irvin L., et al., "Energy Under the Oceans: A Technological Assessment of Outer Continental Shelf Oil and Gas Operations." Norman, University of Oklahoma Press, 1973, 378 pp.

[10] MacDonald, David R., "Report of Investigation of Effect of Petroleum Imports and Petroleum Products on the National Security." Cover Memo, p. 2.

[11] Cooper, Bert H., "Oil Shortages and the U.S. Armed Forces," p. 12.

affect operational readiness adversely. Sharp cutbacks in defense and some segments of the civil economy could cause chain reactions, resulting in recession, unemployment, and other problems.

Mid- and long-range conservation measures, combined with accelerated efforts to enhance U.S. self-sufficiency in forthcoming decades, might stimulate the economy, but could not forestall immediate crises.[12] Neither could oil shales, nuclear fission, or futuristic fuels such as solar and fusion energy.

Consequences assessed

Sustained sanctions by the Arab States, perhaps abetted by Iran, would disrupt this country domestically and degrade U.S. security, but not even a full scale OPEC oil embargo would threaten U.S. survival, our only vital interest. Energy shortages averaging 10–15 percent could be tolerated until permanent adjustments were made.

In the process, however, severe economic and social problems probably would alter America's fundamental lifestyle. Oil shortages up to 50 percent, for example, could be expected in New England and some Middle Atlantic States. Shifting essential oil supplies from west to east would be a slow, laborious process. Pipelines are few and capacities low. Tankers would have to transit the Panama Canal, which excludes all such ships larger than 65,000 deadweight tons.

ALLIED INTERESTS

Serious oil embargoes would shatter Western Europe and Japan, whose current dependence on petroleum greatly exceeds our own (table 5). Their sources are almost exclusively external. Britain and Norway should improve their position when North Sea fields go into full production, in 1980 and 1975 respectively, but the rest of NATO and Japan will be at OPEC's mercy until other energy sources emerge.[13]

Severe sanctions by oil producing countries thus would involve vital interests at a very early stage, "strangling" Nippon and NATO in every sense of that word. Political, military, economic, and social interests in America would suffer accordingly.

TABLE 1.—U.S. OIL CONSUMPTION, 1974

	Million barrels per day	Percentage
Domestic crude production	8.4	63
Natural gas liquids, etc	2.1	
Imports (crude plus refined)	6.1	37
Total domestic supply for consumption	16.6	100

Source: American Petroleum Institute. "Annual Statistical Review, Petroleum Industry Statistics, 1965–74," Washington, May 1975, p. 13.

[12] For a representative sample, see U.S. Congress. House. Hearings Before the Subcommittee on Foreign Economic Policy of the Foreign Affairs Committee on Foreign Policy Implications of the Energy Crises. Washington, U.S. Govt. Print. Off., 1972, pp. 179–181.

[13] Highly industrialized Japan is even more dependent on foreign oil today than it was during World War II, when allied embargoes and blockades effectively "strangled" that country. For a detailed account see Cohen, Jerome B., "Japan's Economy in War and Reconstruction," Minneapolis, University of Minnesota Press, 1949. 545 pp.

TABLE 2.—CURRENT SOURCES OF U.S. OIL IMPORTS

[Direct shipments of crude and refined products, 1974]

	1,000 barrels per day	Percentage
OPEC:		
Venezuela	980	16.1
Arab OPEC members	748	12.3
Nigeria	713	11.7
Iran	469	7.7
Indonesia	300	4.9
Other OPEC members	65	1.1
Total, OPEC	3,275	53.8
Non-OPEC:		
Bahamas/Caribbean [1]	1,396	22.9
Canada	1,067	17.5
Other Arab States	34	.6
All others	316	5.2
Total, non-OPEC	2,813	46.2
Grand total	6,088	100.0

[1] Includes Virgin Islands and Puerto Rico.

Source: American Petroleum Institute. "Annual Statistical Review: Petroleum industry statistics, 1965–74," Washington May 1975, p. 10–11.

TABLE 3.—U.S. SHORTAGES IF THE ARAB STATES OR OPEC CEASED ALL EXPORTS TO THE UNITED STATES AND CANADA

U.S. ENERGY CONSUMPTION, 1974

U.S. energy consumption 1974	Oil or oil equivalent (thousands of barrels per day)	As percent of— Total energy	Total oil	Total imports
Total energy	36,150	100		
Total oil	16,629	46	100	
Total oil imports	6,088	17	37	100
OPEC	3,275	9	20	54
Caribbean [1]	1,396	4	8	23
Canada	1,067	3	6	18
All Arab	782	2	5	13

U.S. VULNERABILITY TO EMBARGO, 1974

[In percent]

Sources lost	Impact on United States: Shortage without conservation — Total oil	Total energy	Shortage if conserve 1,000,000 barrels a day [2] — Total oil	Total energy
All Arab	5	2	0	0
OPEC	20	9	15	6
OPEC, Canada	26	12	21	10
OPEC, Canada, Caribbean [1]	35	16	30	13

[1] Caribbean includes Trinidad and Tobago, Bahamas, Leeward-Windward Islands, Netherlands Antilles, Puerto Rico, and Virgin Islands.

[2] Calculate as 1,000,000 barrel per day reduction in total energy, total oil, and total imports.

Source: American Petroleum Institute. "Annual Statistical Review: Petroleum Industry Statistics, 1965–74." Washington, May 1975. p. 10–11, 45.

TABLE 4.—SELECTED SHORT-TERM OIL CONSERVATION MEASURES

National defense: Limit aircraft flying hours. Limit ship steaming time. Reduce training exercises. Electric utilities: Brown-out (reduce voltage). Reduce air conditioning. Eliminate lights for advertising. Motor transportation: Stress mass transit, car pools. Ban driving nights and Sundays. Increase fuel taxes sharply.	Industry/commerce: Convert from oil to coal (if facilities already installed). Restrict nonessential production. Eliminate nonessential travel. Residential: Restrict services (trash pickup, etc.). Turn off selected street lights. Increase utility taxes sharply.

TABLE 5.—PETROLEUM IMPORTS AND CONSUMPTION IN SELECTED NATO COUNTRIES AND JAPAN

	Oil as percent total energy consumption	Imported oil as percent of total oil requirements
United States	46	37
Canada	44	[1] 0
NATO Europe:		
Belgium	60	100
Denmark	98	100
France	66	99
Germany	55	95
Italy	85	100
Netherlands	46	96
Norway	45	[2] 70
United Kingdom	46	[2] 100
Japan	75	100

[1] Canada currently imports about half of its domestic needs, but exports about the same amount to the United States.
[2] Norway should become self-sufficient in oil when North Sea fields reach planned production in 1975. Britain, which began producing on June 18, 1975, will lag by about 5 years.

Source: "The Relationship of Oil Companies and Foreign Governments." Federal Energy Administration, Internal Energy Affairs, Feb. 15, 1975.

Dominant Decisions

U.S. DECISIONS

Decision No. 1: Is force justified?

This country could survive full-scale OPEC sanctions, as the foregoing treatise indicates. Indeed, one sizable school of thought suggests that a severe oil embargo could be a blessing in disguise if it compelled the United States to mend its immoderate ways at the fastest possible pace.[14] Many reputable men who subscribe to that sentiment find military solutions iniquitous and inappropriate. As alternatives, they advocate bilateral negotiations, international arbitration by the

[14] Charles J. DiBono, then the President's consultant on energy matters, believed that an extended embargo "might well be in our long-run best interest", because it would "stimulate intense public efforts to increase supply and reduce demand." "Calling the Oil Bluff," The Wall Street Journal, Oct. 16, 1973, p. 22. Some noted journalists concur. Anthony Lewis, for example, advocates adjusting "to the reality of scarcer and more expensive energy", and admonishes that "far from encouraging * * * adjustment, dreams of gunboat diplomacy will foster the dangerous illusion that * * * linear growth based on cheap energy can go on forever." "Thinking the Unthinkable," New York Times, Dec. 30, 1974, p. 30.

United Nations or disinterested third parties, and counterembargoes that cut off U.S. military aid and trade to intransigent States or freeze their financial assets and investment opportunities in America.

Proponents at the opposite pole lack the patience or proclivity to abide OPEC-induced adversity for long. In their opinion, it would be immoral to make the American people pay a high price in money and misery over many months (or years) if U.S. persuasion and other pressures failed to lift the embargo quickly. Robert Tucker, a spokesman for that group, put it this way: "It is excessive to insist that before using force one must exhaust all other remedies," if the consequences would create economic "chaos." [15]

The key question, then, is: "At what juncture (if any) would the United States be justified in using armed force to relieve pressures such as OPEC could impose?"

There are no easy answers.

From the standpoint of Congress, three salient considerations condition this stage of the decisionmaking process: [16]

—International law.
—Constitutional responsibilities.
—Public opinion at home and abroad.

International law

The conduct of U.S. foreign affairs is governed in part by treaties. Official pronouncements of international organs like the United Nations also are influential. So is customary law, which helps establish guidelines for our dealings with the global community. However, which sources are pertinent and which are inapplicable is open to interpretation. (See annex C for verbatim extracts from selected documents.)

Take the matter of "aggression" as a case in point. Simply defining that term is a contentious matter, since international law lags in economic and ideological fields, where nonviolent actions supplement or supplant armed combat.[17]

"Intervention of an economic nature becomes aggression if it jeopardizes essential rights of a state which are requisites to its security," according to some authorities.[18] Others see economic aggression simply as steps that "endanger (a state's) basic economy." [19] Attempts to differentiate between "illegal" and "legitimate" means are unfortunately fuzzy.

The United Nations takes a far narrower tack. Its Charter of Economic Rights and Duties unequivocally defends every country's "full permanent sovereignty including possession, use, and disposal, over its wealth, natural resources, and economic activities." [20] States

---

[15] Estimating the economic and social impact of an oil embargo is an inexact endeavor in which neither optimists nor pessimists can prove their case. The Federation of American Scientists, speaking only of Arab input, indicates that "cutoffs could cause * * * [a] world-wide depression." "The Arab Oil Boycott: A Blessing in Disguise?" F.A.S. Public Interest Report, Special Issue on Oil, January 1974, p. 1. By way of contrast, the Federal Energy Administration finds "that we know little about the long run implications of the [1973] embargo," much less any future boycott. "The Economic Impact of the Oil Embargo on The American Economy," Washington, Federal Energy Administration, Aug. 8, 1974, p. 12.

[16] Subsequent sections address risk-versus-gain ratios.

[17] Bowett, D. W., "Self-Defense in International Law," Manchester (United Kingdom), Manchester University Press, 1958, p. 107.

[18] Ibid. "Essential rights" are widely construed to include political independence, territorial integrity, security on the high seas, prerogatives to protect the state's citizens abroad, and the defense of economic interests. Bowett covers each in turn, pp. 29–114. See especially pp. 106–114 on economic interests.

[19] Several definitions are found in Thomas, A. V. W. and Thomas A. J., Jr.; "The Concept of Aggression in International Law," Dallas, Tex., Southern Methodist University Press, 1972, pp. 90–92.

[20] United Nations General Assembly Resolution 3281 (XXIX), Charter of Economic Rights and Duties of States, ch. II, art. 2, Jan. 15, 1975.

are forbidden to use such capital for coercive purposes,[21] but if they do, "no consideration of whatever nature * * * may serve as a justification for aggression," which the United Nations defines solely as "the first use of armed force." [22]

America's allies might invoke the principle of self-preservation to override the U.N. edict and break an embargo by force,[23] but no equivalent avenue would be available to the United States, which could survive OPEC sanctions. At best, we might cite blameless self-defense (a less compelling claim) as our best legal excuse.[24]

Possible U.S. precedents that might favor armed actions to alleviate economic afflictions appear only in the distant past, simply because this country's abundant natural resources until recently ruled out effective enemy embargoes. Even the War of 1812 is an indistinct instance, because the British employed blockades instead of boycotts to aim "a destructive blow * * * against our agricultural and maritime interests." [25]

Negative precedents are easier to come by. The United States condemned Japan for using armed force to improve its economic position, which suffered severely from American and allied embargoes before Pearl Harbor.[26] Authorizing U.S. armed force to offset an OPEC oil embargo thus might be awkward for Congress to approve.

In short, the legal implications of any U.S. determination to violate the sovereignty of foreign States in response to economic injuries are inconclusive. Decisionmakers who demand irreproachable authority before approving such steps may well withhold approval. Those who view laws as flexible instruments may find rationalizations.

Constitutional responsibilities

Those prescient statesmen who framed our Constitution were resolved that no one man should commit this country to war. The separation of powers consequently reserves for Congress the exclusive right to declare wars, although most constitutional scholars recognize that the Chief Executive must be able to respond rapidly in emergency. (See annex C for verbatim tracts from the Constitution and other pertinent documents.)

The President, in his oath of office on inauguration day, swears or affirms that he "will to the best of [his] ability, preserve, protect, and defend the Constitution of the United States," whose preamble includes a prescription to "provide for the common defense [and] promote the general Welfare." [27] Article II, section 3 further directs

---

[21] Ibid., ch. IV, art. 32.

[22] United Nations General Assembly Resolution 3314 (XXIX), Definition of Aggression, Annex, art. 2 and 5, Dec. 14, 1974.

[23] "The principle of self-preservation * * * is so fundamental that no system or law can possibly ignore it." Whiteman, Marjorie, Digest of International Law, Vol. 5, Washington, U.S. Govt. Print. Off., 1965, p. 975. Corroborating views are summarized in Stowell, Ellery C., "Intervention in International Law," John Byrne & Co., 1921 pp. 393–397.

[24] "When the delict does not involve force or the threat of force, it would * * * seem arbitrary to deny the defending state the right to use force in the defense of its rights as a matter of fixed principle." Whiteman, Marjorie, Digest of International Law, Vol. 12, 1971, p. 26.

[25] Blockades and embargoes both seek to impose economic sanctions, but there are sharp distinctions. International law is specific regarding blockades, which are backed up by force or threats of force. Laws are inconclusive concerning the use of embargoes as coercive instruments. The quotation is from President Madison's War Message to the Congress on June 1, 1812.

[26] To say that Japan's great offensive in December 1941 was generated exclusively by economic concerns (including embargoes) would grossly oversimplify the issues. However, economic warfare played a salient part, and the illustration provides some insight.

[27] The Preamble to the Constitution, unlike the articles, is not legally binding, but it does state basic interests. Art. I, Sec. 8, for example, charges the Congress with particular responsibilities related to promoting the general welfare, but philosophy in the Preamble nonetheless alerts the President to that requirement in its broadest context.

him to "take care that the laws be faithfully executed." Said laws implicitly include "treaty obligations; any obligation *inferable* from the Constitution; and the rights, duties, and obligations growing out of the Constitution itself, international relations and all the protection implied by the nature of government under the Constitution" [emphasis added].[28]

Presidential responsibilities in that amorphous context are rather elastic. Ostensibly, they would allow the President to commit U.S. Armed Forces without congressional concurrence—as often occurred in our history—if, in his judgment, military power provided the most appropriate reaction to an oil embargo.[29]

Congress, however, would have recourse if it disagreed.

The War Powers Resolution of 1973, vetoed by President Nixon as "clearly unconstitutional," was written into law when Congress disregarded his contention (see annex C for full text). Section 1 expressly stipulates that "collective judgment * * * will apply to the introduction of U.S. Armed Forces into hostilities, or into situations where imminent involvement in hostilities is clearly indicated." If the President dispatches armed elements in emergency, they must withdraw within 60 days unless Congress acquiesces, according to section 5. That short period, even augmented by the 30-day extension authorized under extenuating circumstances, would of course preclude lengthy operations. "Forces shall be removed [even earlier] by the President if the Congress so directs by concurrent resolution."

The War Powers Resolution in itself is not conclusive. Its legality has never been tested in the courts. Nevertheless, Congress does have a very sharp tool at its disposal with which to shape such decisions: appropriations powers under article I, section 8 of the Constitution, which in the past have effectively forestalled the use of U.S. Armed Forces abroad.[30]

The President, therefore, would be most likely to collaborate closely with the Congress, as the quote which opens this study suggests.

The role of public opinion

World public opinion is rarely pervasive. Most often, it reflects reactions by the masters (rather than the masses) of States that share common interests at specific instants.[31]

Neither does world public opinion exert persistent pressures. The Soviet savaging of Czechoslovakia that caused so much commotion in 1968 was quickly forgotten by all but the principals. Some cynics, exaggerating to emphasize that point, cite 6 weeks or so as the limit

---

[28] Taft, William Howard, "Our Chief Magistrate and His Powers," New York, Columbia University Press, 1925, pp. 87, 88, 91, citing In re Neagle (1899, 135 U.S. 1; *U.S.* v. *Logan* (1892), 144 U.S. 263.

[29] The Congress has declared war only five times: the War of 1812, the Mexican War, the Spanish-American War, World War I, and World War II. Five congressional joint resolutions have authorized the use of U.S. armed forces overseas since 1945: Formosa resolution, Public Law 84-4, H.J. Res. 159, approved Jan. 29, 1955; Middle East resolution, Public Law 85-7, H.J. Res. 117, approved Mar. 9, 1957; Cuban resolution, Public Law 87-733, S.J. Res. 230, approved Oct. 3, 1962; Berlin resolution, House Con. Res. 570, concurred in on Oct. 10, 1962; Gulf of Tonkin resolution, Public Law 88-408, H.J. Res. 1145, approved Aug. 10, 1964. In addition, U.S. Armed Forces have been committed many times without congressional concurrence of any kind.

[30] An amendment to the Defense Appropriations Act of 1970 (Public Law 91-171, Dec. 29, 1969), for example, stipulates that "none of the funds appropriated by this act shall be used to finance the introduction of American ground combat troops into Laos or Thailand." Public Law 91-652 applied similar proscriptions to Cambodia on Jan. 5, 1971. Public Law 93-50 extended such restrictions to all of Indochina and adjacent waters on July 1, 1973.

[31] Source materials on this subject cover both theory and practice. See for example Lippman, Walter, "Public Opinion," New York, Harcourt, Brace & Co., 1922. 427 pp.; and Harris, Louis, "The Anguish of Change," New York, W. W. Norton & Co., 1973, 306 pp.

of sustained emotion by observers (as opposed to participants). A pendulum effect frequently is evident—witness the dispassion with which much of the world viewed the war in Vietnam during the early 1960's; active support for U.S. involvement in the mid-1960's; disillusioned indignation in the late 1960's; active calls for U.S. disengagement in the early 1970's; and the subsequent drift toward indifference, despite continued conflict.

Allied approval of American actions to seize foreign oilfields almost certainly would reflect the respective attitudes of specific countries and coalitions, not U.S. cohorts en masse. Those whose interests were surely served as well as our own probably would ratify U.S. decisions. Those who perceived ill-starred prospects likely would oppose, as would the so-called Third World, which presently presents a unified front on many issues in the United Nations and other forums.

The practical consequences would be inconsiderable if rhetoric were the only weapon outraged countries wield.[32] However, this country's global reputation for decency conceivably could be diminished. Reprisals could range from political, economic, and psychological punishment to armed combat. U.S. diplomatic relations, installations and citizens overseas, trade, and commerce—including traffic in critical items other than oil—all could suffer from calculated or spontaneous acts intended to change our course. Terrorism could not be ruled out. Soviet military options would be particularly pertinent.

Neither Congress nor the executive branch could count on apathy to soften adverse opinion abroad. The probable predilections of foreign powers thus would have to be appraised accurately and consequences weighed before, not after, decisions were taken.

Moods in America would be even more important. Perhaps the most pointed lesson U.S. leaders learned in Vietnam was that national decisions, however desirable they may otherwise seem, must be acceptable to the people.

No great problems would surface if U.S. survival were at stake and the public knew it. War would be acceptable to most "hawks" and "doves" alike if we faced fatal strangulation by OPEC—there would be nothing to lose. In this case, however, controversy could be anticipated, since vital interests would not be at issue. Impatient men might well insist on military action to seek quick relief. Stoics likely would stress long-term solutions. Congress, with its thumb on the public pulse, would be best prepared to detect the predominant viewpoint. Indeed, that contribution to the decisionmaking process would be critical.[33]

The administration, Congress, or both—assisted by the mass media—could take steps to sway public opinion one way or another if they believed it advisable, although success would not be assured. In the final analysis, decisions that avoided war at all costs could be just as disastrous as those that initiated invasions if official judgment and the national consensus failed to coincide.

---

[32] Stalin, for one, found supplications unpersuasive, unless backed by force of arms, as evidenced by his disparaging remark to Pierre Laval in May 1935: "The Pope! How many divisions has he got?"

[33] Fifty-eight percent of the American people in April 1975 disapproved hypothetical proposals to seize Arab oilfields, according to a Harris survey. An even quarter then assented. Those figures could shift suddenly if an airtight embargo struck. Harris, Louis, "Oil or Israel?" New York Times Magazine, Apr. 6 1975, p. 34.

Decision No. 2: Whose interests to safeguard?

Decision No. 1 is comparatively uncomplicated. American interests alone would be involved. Two other contingencies could call for far more complex decisions:

—Should we safeguard allied interests as well as our own if embargoes engulfed us all simultaneously?

—Should we safeguard allies if they were faced with fatal embargoes that did not touch this country?

Honest men approach those propositions from sundry directions. Divisions thus are diverse and deep.

Influential factions, for example, contend that this country is responsible only for itself.[34] The slogan "Come Home, America" was coined to serve a special purpose, but it still appeals to a substantial slice of the U.S. population, which opines that outsiders should solve their own problems—we have enough to keep ourselves well occupied in the United States. Sad experiences in Southeast Asia currently strengthen such conclusions.

Others infer that U.S. interests are inseparable from those of NATO Europe, and probably Japan. Robert Tucker, who recently wrote "A New Isolationism: Threat or Promise?", seems a curious champion for interdependency, but he spells out the case for succoring allies quite succinctly:

> Even the few among us who have argued for a radical contraction of America's interests and commitments have done so on the assumption that the consequences of an American withdrawal would not be a world in which America's political and economic frontiers were coterminous with her territorial frontiers, and in which societies that share our cultures, institutions, and values might very possibly disappear.[35]

Deliberations in the clutch would be conditioned by strong emotions on both sides. Many elements in the decisionmaking matrix, including those already discussed, would be magnified.

U.S. treaty commitments would offer scant encouragement to U.S. leaders probing for legal permission to employ troops. The North Atlantic Treaty specifies that "an *armed attack* against one or more [members] * * * shall be considered an attack against them all", obligating the United States to take "such action as it deems necessary, including the use of armed force" (emphasis added). Military reprisals in response to economic aggression, however defined, are nowhere mentioned.[36] In the Treaty of Mutual Cooperation and Security between the United States and Japan, both States agree "to refrain in their international relations from the threat or use of force against the territorial integrity * * * of any State, or in any other manner inconsistent with the purposes of the United Nations"—which brands the first use of armed force as aggression.[37]

Constitutional constraints would be identical with those surveyed in the previous section.

Public opinion once again could be expected to provide key input to any "go-no go" decision.

---

[34] For recent discussions see Russett, Bruce, "The American's Retreat From World Power," Political Science Quarterly, Spring 1975, pp. 1–21; and Roskin, Michael, "From Pearl Harbor to Vietnam: Shifting Generational Paradigms and Foreign Policy," Political Science Quarterly, Fall 1974, pp. 563–588.

[35] Tucker, Robert W. "Oil: The Issue of American Intervention," p. 28. President Ford and Secretary Kissinger lean toward support for allies in their public statements. Both speak of "strangulation" that affects the "entire industrialized world," not just the United States.

[36] Treaties and Other International Agreements of the United States of America, 1776–1949. Compiled by Charles I. Bevans. vol. 4, Multilateral, 1946–49. Washington, U.S. Govt. Print. Off., 1970, pp. 828–831.

[37] United States Treaties and Other International Agreements. Vol. 11, pt. 2, 1960. Washington, U.S. Govt. Print. Off., 1961, pp. 1632–1635.

OPEC Decisions

Most discourse in open print dwells on the gravity of potential U.S. decisions to seize OPEC oilfields, but overlooks difficulties that would plague opponents before they chose to scourge the United States.

A few words provide perspective.

OPEC's members, especially prime movers astride the Persian Gulf in Iran and Arab States, have been free from foreign occupation or "oppressive" foreign influence for only a few years. An American invasion would cut short their freedom of action, which they cherish above all else.

Those same countries depend almost entirely on oil revenues to fund fabulous development programs and underpin their new-found status as world powers. Both benefits would be abridged for a protracted period if the United States seized their oil fields.[38] Significantly, the Arabs States also would lose financial resources that currently fuel the fight against Israel.

OPEC countries could not function in accustomed fashions if oil commerce were cut off. The spectre of "leftist radicals" replacing the ruling order in disrupted States could be cause for concern.

OPEC countries in the Middle East depend heavily on U.S. arms for psychological and practical purposes. Existing inventories would be depleted quickly if the United States canceled further shipments including spare parts, and terminated training programs, together with technical assistance.

OPEC's principal recourse in such circumstances would be appeals for greater support from the Soviet Union, which orthodox Moslems especially fear and distrust.

Consequently, considerable leeway for serious negotiation seems to exist, with realistic possibilities for concessions by all parties concerned. OPEC would have everything to lose and little to gain by any embargo that invited armed reprisals by the United States.

---

[38] OPEC would abridge its financial assets and freedom of action simply by invoking an embargo, but would control the degree and duration of its own duress. If U.S. troops occupied oilfields, this country could deny them the luxury of choice.

PART II: GLOBAL PERSPECTIVE

Mandatory Missions

Political, economic, social, legal, and moral issues just outlined deal with the desirability of seizing OPEC oil fields to crush severe embargoes. However, if all such facets were favorable, armed force would be appropriate only if achievability seemed assured.

Step one in testing for military feasibility is to sort out mandatory missions, both military and civilian. The irreducible minimum follows:

—Seize sufficient oil fields and facilities intact.

—Secure them for a protracted period.

—Restore wrecked assets rapidly.

—Operate installations without OPEC's assistance.

—Guarantee safe overseas passage for supplies and products.

Successful U.S. operations would be possible only if this country had the power to satisfy all five elements. Succeeding sections of this study examine prospects.

Counterintervention Threats

American aims just mentioned would by no means be self-fulfilling. OPEC and its sympathizers pose present and potential threats. (See table 6 at the end of this section for force summaries.)

In each instance, these threats comprise capabilities tempered by intentions.[1] This brief discourse outlines both.

OPEC THREATS

OPEC countries have few capabilities beyond their own frontiers. Terror tactics against the United States, NATO Europe, and/or Japan constitute the sole exceptions.

Capabilities

OPEC capabilities outlined below could be administered singly or in various mixtures:

—Surrender preemptively; negotiate a settlement.

—Oppose United States/allied assaults with forces shown in table 6.

—Interdict United States/allied shipping locally.

—Conduct guerrilla warfare.

—Sabotage ports and airfields.

—Sabotage oil installations.

—Conduct terror campaigns abroad.

---

[1] Capabilities constitute the ability of countries or coalitions to execute specific courses of action at specific times and places. Fundamental components can be quantified and compared objectively—so many tanks, ships, and planes. Time, space, climate, and terrain are also easy to calculate. Best of all, capabilities rarely are subject to rapid change.

Intentions deal with the determination of countries or coalitions to use their capabilities in specific ways at specific times and places. Interests, objectives, policies, principles, and commitments all play important roles. National will is the integrating factor. Intentions are very tricky to deal with, since they are subjective states of mind.

Still, some feel for friendly capabilities and determination plus enemy capabilities and intentions is imperative for decisionmakers who hope to design sound strategies.

Intentions

Any OPEC countries invaded by embargoed States would have a lot to lose (see p. 13). Preemptive surrender thus would be a practical possibility.

Current statements of intention, however, reject that course of action. Specifically, OPEC sovereigns and heads of State "declare their readiness * * * to counteract [U.S./allied] threats with a unified response whenever the need arises, notably in the case of aggression."[2]

Discussion

The regular Armed Forces of OPEC countries, singly or in combination, are quantitatively and qualitatively inferior, when compared with those of great powers. They could be swiftly crushed.[3] Iran, a future exception, is still far more fearsome on paper than in practice, despite U.S. arms, equipment, and training. At best, Iran's Army, Navy, and Air Force could compel us to pay a price in battle, but could not bar U.S. landings.[4]

OPEC forces have minimal capabilities to interdict U.S. merchant shipping by military means, even in their own coastal waters. They lack requisite air and naval power or, in the case of Iran, could be contained in cul-de-sacs.

Neither are most OPEC areas suitable for blockades. The Strait of Hormuz is a salient exception. Iran's military forces could seed that passage with mines if this country hit Persian Gulf States. Presuming such efforts succeeded, we would be hard pressed to convey petroleum promptly from the Persian Gulf to consumers.[5] That strategy, however, would keep all OPEC countries in the Middle East from shipping products to neutral states.[6] The Shah thus would likely be reluctant to take such steps, unless Iran itself were invaded.

Guerrilla warfare in conjunction with or as a substitute for conventional defense would be a credible OPEC option in Nigeria's jungles, marshes around Maracaibo, and Iran's rough terrain, where raiders would find sustenance and shelter. Commandos, operating from Omani coves, conceivably could stick limpet mines on supertankers that traverse the Strait of Hormuz at night. Conversely, scant cover, combined with comprehensive U.S. air/ground surveillance and sophisticated sensors, would inhibit enemy irregulars elsewhere in the Middle East and much of North Africa. Popski's private army, David Stirling's Special Air Service, and Lawrence's Arab radicals, who once ran rings around rivals in the desert, would find it difficult to

---

[2] "Conference of the Sovereigns and Heads of State of the OPEC Member Countries Solemn Declaration." New York Times, Apr. 1, 1975, p. 18C.

[3] OPEC's abilities to interfere with air strikes, parachute assaults, and airmobile operations could be increased quickly and effectively if outsiders supplied large stocks of antiaircraft weapons, especially small, mobile surface-to-air missiles such as SA–6 and SA–7, which are easily concealed. No such support is now evident.

[4] Dr. Alvin J. Cottrell, of the Georgetown Institute for Strategic and International Studies, published the following evaluation after a recent inspection tour in Iran and interview with the Shah. "[One] point * * * often is overlooked in superficial assessments of Iran's current military power and its allegedly grandiose ambitions. The Shah has made an investment in the sophisticated instruments of military power, but the investment is likely to bear fruit only some years in the future. The leadtime is conditioned not only by stretched out delivery schedules * * * but also by the infrastructure and training requirements to absorb [his] purchases." "Iran: Diplomacy in a Regional and Global Context," Washington (Privately published), 1975, p. 12.

[5] Admiral Elmo R. Zumwalt, Jr., when he was Chief of Naval Operations, identified the Strait of Hormuz as a critical choke point which is "relatively easy to mine or block", and concluded that "there is little the United States could do militarily to forestall this possibility." U.S. Congress. Senate. "Oil and Gas Imports Issues." Hearings before the Committee on Interior and Insular Affairs, pt. 3, 93d Cong., 1st Sess., Washington, U.S. Govt. Print. Off., 1973, pp. 764–765.

[6] Except Iraq, whose petroleum is pumped to Mediterranean ports.

duplicate their daring deeds under current conditions.[7] Standoff attacks and sapper strikes in open areas therefore would constitute annoyances, rather than serious threats to United States/allied activities.

Saboteurs, however, could play hob if they hit ports, airfields, and oil facilities before our landings. Wells, pipelines, pumping stations, powerplants, storage tanks, refineries, and loading installations all are vulnerable.

Wherever wells flow spontaneously, as they do in much of the Middle East, gases could be ignited easily, and flames being constantly fed would be hard to extinguish. Even one well blazing out of control could endanger entire fields by decreasing subterranean pressures. This country has the world's greatest talent for fighting oil fires, but if several flared concurrently, we would lack enough teams to cope.[8]

Destroying wells, of course, would be counterproductive for OPEC if a settlement were reached quickly—rejuvenation times would be tremendous. However, attacks on ancillary installations could cripple local oil industries without endangering basic resources. Terminals, for example include a range of lucrative targets: tanks, pumps, pipes, piers—all in a compact complex. Power supplies are very susceptible to sabotage.[9] Saudi Arabia's machinery presents special problems, being the biggest in the world: the biggest gas separators (50 of them); the biggest pumping stations (2 million barrels each per day); the biggest water-injection plants (400 million cubic feet daily from Abqaiq field alone); the biggest storage tanks, biggest oil port, biggest desalinization plant. One-of-a-kind items like that would be time consuming and expensive to replace. Frank Jungers, Aramco's chairman, estimates that "a quarter of the world's exports * * * would be out of commission for at least 2 years" if the infrastructure were wrecked.[10]

Jungers' prediction may be overly pessimistic, given related facts. Not many OPEC members manifest the Teutonic thoroughness that made German sabotage so successful at Cherbourg in 1944.[11] No preparations are presently evident in Persian Gulf oilfields,[12] despite proclamations that "mines [have] been planted * * * and would be set off at moment's notice", if necessary.[13] In fact, prepositioning explosives could cause all sorts of problems with potentially dissident elements, like displaced Palestinians. Non-Arab States, such as Nigeria and Venezuela, sense no significant threat, and thus have little incentive to plan sabotage operations, without which damage expectations would be poor from OPEC's perspective.

---

7 Accounts of those exploits are found in Peniakoff, Vladimir, "Popski's Private Army," New York, Crowell, 1950, 369 pp.; Cowles, Virginia S., "The Phantom Major: the Story of David Stirling and the S.A.S. Regiment," London, Collins, 1958, 320 pp.; and Lawrence, T. E., "Seven Pillars of Wisdom: A Triumph," Garden City, New York, 1966, 622 pp.

8 Letters from readers: "Oil and Force," Commentary, April 1975, p. 15. Quotes a petroleum engineer; and Mosley, Leonard, "Power Play: Oil in the Middle East," New York, Random House, 1973, pp. 137–141.

9 Venezuelan insurgents, who short-circuited four offshore transformers in 1962, shut down 600 wells for a short time. Professional planning would have produced superior results. "The Sovereign Puppet," Time, Nov. 9, 1962, p. 41.

10 Borchgrave, Arnaud de, "Intervention Wouldn't Work," Newsweek, Mar. 31, 1975, p. 48.
The Arabian American Oil Co. (ARAMCO) operates most petroleum concessions in Saudi Arabia.

11 U.S. forces landed in Normandy on June 6, 1944. Cherbourg fell on June 29. Before withdrawing, German defenders completed what one source called "the most complete, intensive, and best-planned demolition in history." All basins were blocked by sunken ships. 20,000 cubic yards of masonry were blown into berths, Ninety-five percent of the deep-draft quays were destroyed. Breakwaters were cratered, cranes crumpled, power and heating plants destroyed. Wholesale mining was accomplished. Bridges and buildings were blasted along with clearance facilities. Serious problems were still experienced in October. Ruppenthal, Ronald G. "Logistical Support of the Armies". Vol. II, September 1944–May 1945. Washington, Office of the Chief of Military History, Department of the Army, 1959, pp. 62–89.

12 Borchgrave, Arnaud de, Newsweek, March 31, 1975, p. 48.

13 "Kuwait Threatens Oilfield Destruction Should U.S. Step In," New York Times, Jan. 10, 1974, p. 17.

OPEC sabotage efforts could well be extended to United States and/or allied territory, where oil installations would be especially tempting targets in event of an oil embargo. Instability would be intense, especially if attacks on economic assets were combined with worldwide terror tactics.

Soviet Threats

OPEC's military threats to United States/allied operations are meaningful only on or near their own territories. Many of Moscow's capabilities have global implications.

Capabilities

Soviet counterintervention capabilities, listed below in rough order of priority, comprise an escalation ladder: [14]

—Conduct propaganda offensives.
—Increase military support to OPEC countries.
—Conduct shows of force:
 —Near United States/allied areas of operation; and/or
 —Elsewhere.
—Conduct diversions
—Conduct harassing operations:
 —In United States/allied areas of operation; and/or
—En route.
—Blockade the area of operations.
—Interdict United States/allied shipping.
—Conduct air strikes against oil installations, if the area of operations is in the Middle East or eastern Mediterranean.
—Conduct air/naval strikes against U.S. assault forces, if the area of operations in the Middle East or eastern Mediterranean.
—Engage in ground combat, if the area of operations is in the Middle East.
—Employ tactical nuclear weapons.
 —Employ strategic nuclear weapons selectively.
—Initiate a general nuclear war.

Intentions

Soviet intentions are less transparent than OPEC's.

Some commentators surmise that the Kremlin would choose to stand aside, or intervene indirectly at the very worst. Tucker believes that "the balance of perceived interest, as distinguished from the balance of military forces, is certainly against the Russians." [15] Ignotus concurs. As he sees it, assuring ample oil imports during an OPEC embargo would involve crucial United States and/or allied concerns. "Denial would merely be a desirable bonus for the Soviet Union." Direct counterintervention thus "need barely be considered."[16]

Some skeptics strongly challenge those assumptions. "We are talking about a chain of events," said one, "that, with a small but appreciable probability, would lead to a nuclear confrontation. We therefore have a right to require higher standards of proof from the proponents than from the critics of such an operation." [17]

---

[14] The conflict spectrum is a continuum of hostilities that ranges from subcrisis confrontation to spasmic nuclear war. Successive increases in scope or intensity constitute escalation. Levels of escalation are like the rungs of a ladder, which may be climbed in sequence or by skipping selected steps. Deescalation reverses that process. For a detailed discussion, see Kahn, Herman, "On Escalation: Metaphors and Scenarios," New York, Praeger, 1965, pp. 3-51.
[15] Tucker, Robert W., "Oil: The Issue of American Intervention," pp. 26-27;
[16] Ignotus, "Seizing Arab Oil," p. 58.
[17] Ravenal, Earl C., "The Oil-Grab Scenario," The New Republic, Jan. 18, 1975, p. 16.

That is easier said than done, since Soviet statements thus far furnish few clues to true intentions. Pravda, for example, recently decried the "defenders of monopoly interests" in the West who reputedly resort to "military blackmail" against OPEC by hinting at armed action—but muted conclusions merely stated that "gun boat politics" were "doomed to failure." [18]

Soviet decisions, taken at the time, would depend on circumstances at home and abroad. Moscow's military machine already rivals our own in most respects, and surpasses us in some. Threats thus far have been mitigated, for several reasons. Members of Moscow's ruling hierarchy are essentially conservative, despite their revolutionary records. National character, Communist doctrine, and unshakable convictions that time is on their side currently repress impulses to confront this country directly.

That situation, however, could change if U.S. economic strains caused by an oil embargo crucially undercut our diminishing military capabilities.[19] Divisiveness in U.S. ranks would further strengthen Soviet confidence, if the American people disapproved any decision to seize OPEC oilfields. The Kremlin then might consider a policy of opportunity, characterized by reduced constraint and greater proclivities for risk-taking.[20] Such prospects may seem remote, but potential Soviet threats clearly should be counted.

Discussion

What courses the Soviets would select from the smorgasbord of possibilities is open to speculation. It is one thing to "fish in troubled waters", but quite another to "fight foreign fishermen."

In some respects, however, the Kremlin enjoys an enormous advantage: its capabilities to interfere anywhere outside objective areas would be low cost, low risk operations with relatively high effectiveness.

Most such options listed above are self-explanatory, but one needs elaboration.

America and its allies would have little leeway to counter Soviet campaigns against shipping on the high seas. Threats of massive retaliation would be impotent in an atmosphere marked by mutual assured destruction and the absence of defense. Restrained nuclear reprisals against selected targets in the Soviet Union would be indecisive, and provoke unpredictable responses. Risking national suicide would be rational only if our survival were directly at stake, which would not be the case.

Threats projecting U.S. general purpose power would also lack credibility. With this country's existing complement of conventional

[18] Wren, Christopher, "Soviet Sees Military Blackmail by West Against Oil-Producing Countries," New York Times, Jan. 8, 1975, p. 2.

[19] The U.S. Army has been cut in half since 1970. Air Force and Navy personnel strengths have been cut by about a third. The intent was to constitute smaller forces which modernization measures would endow with greater capabilities than their predecessors. However, retraction began well before refurbishment could take place. Size, therefore, was reduced without concomitant improvements in combat power. Collins, John M. "Defense Trends in the United States, 1952–1973." Washington, Congressional Research Service, May 14, 1974, pp. 80–83.

[20] William R. Kintner and Robert L. Pfaltzgraff, Jr. spelled out three possible Soviet foreign policies in a pamphlet entitled "Soviet Military Trends: Implications for U.S. Security," Washington, American Enterprise Institute, 1971, pp. 9–12. A basic policy of condominium, which dominated the 1960's after the Cuban missile crisis, stressed "peaceful coexistence." It was (and is) paralleled in some areas by a policy of caution, predicated on Soviet reluctance to run serious risks, but reflecting greater willingness to stimulate rivalry that avoids compromising U.S. vital or compelling interests. A policy of opportunity would involve increased Soviet competition in arenas where U.S. interests are intense.

forces already committed against OPEC, ready reserves would be much reduced. Mobilizing, equipping, training, deploying, and sustaining requisite reinforcements would be a tremendous, costly, time-consuming task. Even if sufficient forces were available to challenge the Soviets on their home soil, insurmountable problems probably would remain—the only lucrative invasion avenues lead through NATO territory and the Baltic Straits, both of which could be banned.

A naval war of attrition thus remains our major reaction to attacks by Soviet submarines. Since shore installations on both sides might be fair game, stringent controls would be required to restrict escalation. Maintaining open sea lines of communication under restrictive conditions could provide a real challenge until protracted antisubmarine warfare operations reduced losses to "manageable proportions." Success would not be assured. Failure would separate committed U.S. forces from supplies and shortstop petroleum shipments.[21]

Soviet intervention capabilities ashore would be more inhibited.

To begin with, the Kremlin could bring only part of its power to bear. China and NATO pose competing threats. Rigid geographic restrictions further reduce the range of options. Probabilities that the Soviets might intervene in objective areas thus decrease in direct proportion to distances from their own periphery.

Backfire, Bear, and Badger bombers, for example, could easily close the Persian Gulf with mines before U.S. airpower was in place. Parachute assaults, airlandings, and other airmobile maneuvers could be completed unopposed. Thereafter, the Soviets would find such ploys perilous. Middle East oilfields, including most of those in Iran, are beyond the combat radii of Mig fighters based within their own borders. Missions would be minus escorts unless Moscow made use of fields in Arab States or Iran (map 8).[22]

Moreover, Soviet airpower unaided could neither position standard ground forces nor sustain them. Armor and other heavy, outsize items, plus nearly all supplies, would have to move overland via one of two tortuous routes. The western access, which crosses 2,000 miles from the Balkans to Basra by way of the Bosporus and Baghdad, seems most improbable. Ankara might authorize overflights if sympathies for OPEC were strong,[23] but likely would be reluctant to

[21] Data drawn from the following documents describe NATO reinforcement problems, but they are applicable. U.S. Congress. Senate. Hearings Before the Committee on Armed Services on fiscal year 1973 Authorization for Military Procurement [etc.]. Part 2. 92d Cong. 2d Sess. Washington, U.S. Govt. Print. Off., 1972, pp. 658, 1069. Also U.S. Congress. House. Hearings Before the Special Subcommittee on North Atlantic Treaty Organization Commitments, Committee on Armed Services. 92d Cong., 1st and 2d Sess. Washington, U.S. Govt. Print. Off., 1972, pp. 13006–13008.

[22] The approximate combat radius of Mig-21s is 350 miles; Mig-25s 700 miles; SU-7s 200–300 miles.

An extended review of Soviet capabilities in the Persian Gulf area is contained in Blechman, Barry M. and Kuzmack, Arnold M., "Oil and National Security," Naval War College Review, May–June 1974, pp. 10–13.

[23] A widely-quoted source states that "the Montreux Convention * * * establishes freedom of air passage for the Russians through a North-South corridor. The Soviets thus [have] no need to ask for authority to overfly Turkey—and according to the Convention they [are] not even obliged to communicate the fact that they [wish] to do so." "Letters to the Editor," International Defense Review, April 1974, p. 240.

That assertion apparently is false. Art. 23 of the Montreux Convention obliges Turkey to specify corridors for civil aircraft and permit them free passage, "provided that they give the Turkish Government, as regards occasional flights, a notification of three days." Military overflights are not addressed.

allow Moscow's armies to cross Turkish soil. The only alternative leads 1,000 miles from the Caucasus to Kuwait through Iran's mountain wall.

Roads in both regions are rudimentary at best. The rail "net" is nominal in most locales. Water is scarce. Intermediate way stations, supply points, and maintenance shops are nearly nonexistent. Wear and tear on men and materiel thus would be immense.

Prepositioned stocks would alleviate initial problems. Some arms and equipment conceivably could be commandeered from Syria and Iraq (especially tanks, artillery, armored personnel carriers, and motor transports). Long run troubles, however, still would remain.

In short, Soviet air-ground capabilities are circumscribed in the closest area. In remote regions, such as West Africa and Venezuela, they would be insignificant.

TABLE 6.—COMBAT FORCES, SELECTED OPEC COUNTRIES, OPEC SYMPATHIZERS, SOVIET UNION

OPEC forces listed below are widely deployed in their respective countries. Some are stationed in outside states (15 percent of Saudi Arabia's army, for example, is in Jordan and Syria). Oil producing regions could be reinforced in emergency, but sizable elements would have to remain elsewhere. Armed forces not shown are negligible.

GROUND FORCES

		Divisions			Brigade/Regiment			
	Strength	Armor	Airborne	Other	Armor	Other	Battalion	Tanks
Mid East:								
Egypt	280,000	3	----------	8	2	5	26	2,000
Iran	175,000	3	----------	2	0	3	0	1,160
Iraq	100,000	2	----------	3	1	0	0	1,390
Kuwait	8,000	0	----------	0	1	2	0	100
Saudi Arabia	36,000	0	----------	0	0	4	5	115
Syria	125,000	2	----------	3	4	0	8	1,670
Africa:								
Algeria	55,000	0	----------	0	1	4	54	450
Libya	25,000	0	----------	0	3	1	1	271
Nigeria	200,000	0	----------	3	0	0	0	0
Venezuela[1]	24,000	0	----------	0	1	1	24	31
Indonesia	200,000	0	----------	0	0	19	8	UNK
Soviet Union[2]		3	7	20	----------	----------	----------	----------

[1] Venezuela's army is being reorganized. 31 light and medium tanks are on order.

[2] Except for airborne divisions, Soviet forces shown are in the southern U.S.S.R. A few are at full strength. Most are about evenly divided between category 2 (½ to ¾ strength) and category 3 (⅓ strength). Full strength armored divisions have 325 medium tanks; mechanized divisions have 255. Reinforcements in European Russia are readily available.

TACTICAL AIR COMBAT UNITS

	Strength	Light, medium bombers	Fighter bombers	Fighter, air defense	Combat aircraft	Other
Middle East:						
Egypt	28,000	25 TU-16, 5 IL-28.	38 Mirage V, 100 SU-7, 100 Mig-17.	200 Mig-21	468	
Iran [1]	50,000	0	902F-4D, E, 100 F-5A.	0	196	
Iraq	10,500	8 TU-16	60 SU-7, 20 Hunter 57.	30 Mig-17, 100 Mig-21.	218	
Kuwait	2,000	0	4 Hunter 57, 112 BAC-167.	12 F-53	28	
Saudi Arabia [2]	5,500	0	34 F-5B, E, 21 BAC-167.	35 F-52, 53	90	
Syria	10,000	Some IL-28	60 Mig-17, 30 SU-7.	Some Mig-23, 200 Mig-21.	About 300.	
Africa:						
Algeria	4,500	30 IL-28	20 SU-7, 70 Mig-17, 25 Mig-15, 26 Magister.	35 Mig-21	206	
Libya	5,000	0	20 Mirage V	32 Mirage III	55	
Nigeria	5,000	6 IL2-8	21 Mig-15, Mig-17, 15 L-29.	0	42	
Venezuela	8,000	26 B-2	20 CF-5A, D, 10 OV-10 E.	F286K, 13 Mirage III.	About 90	
Indonesia	30,000	22 TU-16, 10 IL-28, 2 B 26.	II F-51D, 17 CA-27, 17 T-33.	4 Mig-15, 8 Mig-17, 15 Mig-21.	106	
Soviet Union [3]		[4] 500 TU-16, 200 TU-22.				800 Mig-17, 1,350 Mig-21, 300 Mig-23, 500 SU-7.

[1] 80 F-14, 70 F-4E, 141 F-5E, 4 F-28 on order.
[2] 126 F-5E/B, 38 Mirage III, 9 BAC-167 on order.
[3] Soviet medium bombers have strategic nuclear capabilities. 1 TU-22 squadron is based in Iraq. About half of all Soviet tactical aircraft are oriented toward NATO, a fourth toward China.
[4] Medium bombers.

NAVY COMBATANTS

	Destroyer Frigate Corvette	Submarine	Subchaser	Patrol boat	Guided missile boat	Torpedo boat
Middle East:						
Egypt	5	12	12	29	8	0
Iran [1]	11	0	0	10	0	0
Iraq	0	0	3	6	3	12
Kuwait [2]	0	0	0	10	0	0
Saudi Arabia	0	0	0	24	0	0
Syria	0	0	0	2	6	12
Africa:						
Algeria	0	0	6	0	9	12
Libya	2	0	0	8	3	0
Nigeria	3	0	0	9	0	0
Venezuela [3]	10	2	0	13	3	0
Indonesia	9	5	0	30	9	0

	Submarines: Attack		Submarines: Cruise missile	
	Nuclear	Diesel	Nuclear	Diesel
Soviet Union [4]	30	140	40	25

[1] 10 hovercraft in active inventory, 2 on order, together with 6 fast patrol boats.
[2] 8 hovercraft in active inventory.
[3] 2 submarines on order. Destroyer figure includes 6 destroyer escorts.
[4] Soviet cruisers and destroyers with surface-to-surface missiles also pose a threat to tankers and logistic shipping.

Source: Mainly "The Military Balance, 1974-75," London, International Institute for Strategic Studies, 1974, p. 8--10, 32-37, 43, 68.

Map 1.

SOVIET APPROACHES TO THE PERSIAN GULF

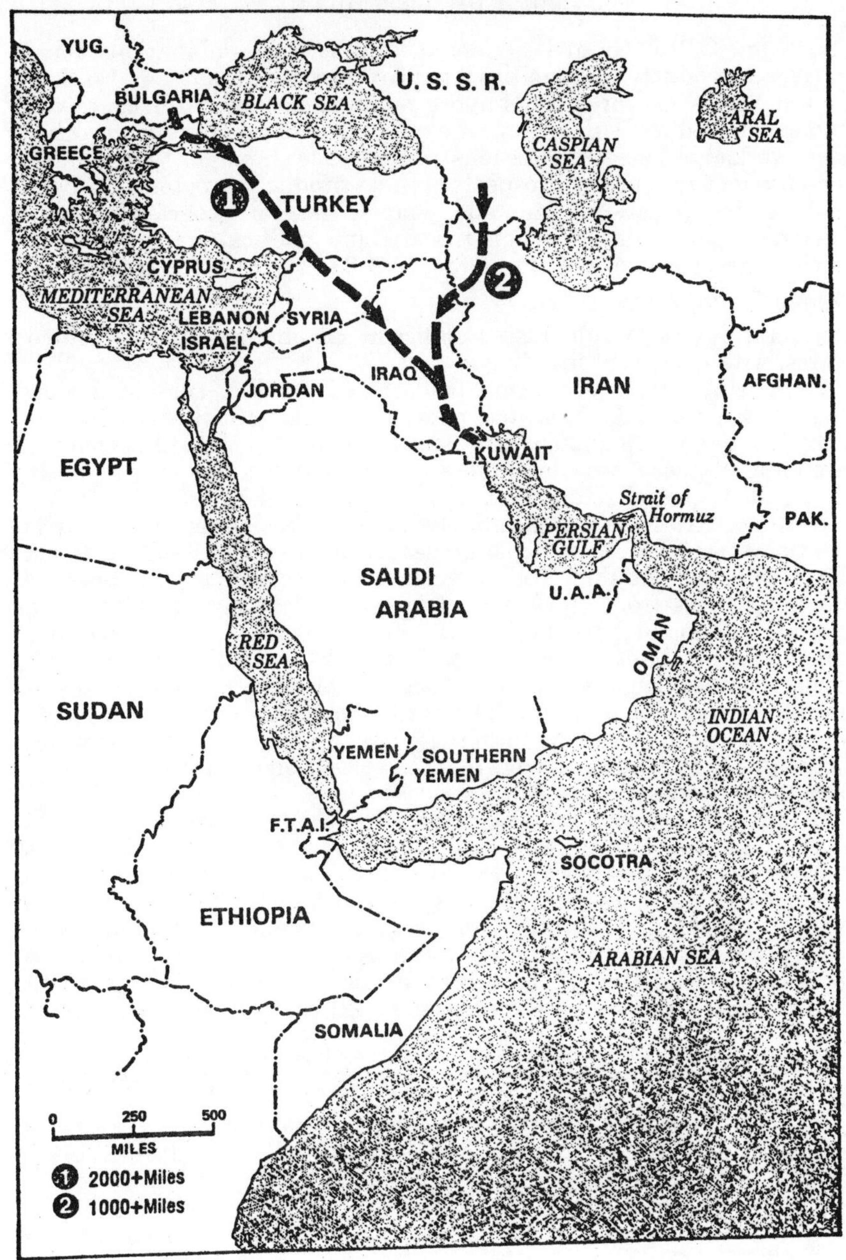

Selecting Areas of Operation and Outlying Objectives

The five-part mission previewed on page 15 merely prescribes what Armed Forces would have to do if ordered to obtain United States and/or allied oil imports by military means against all opposition. This section concerns the question "where?"

AREAS OF OPERATION

Very few OPEC countries, alone or in practical combinations, have petroleum production capacities and proven reserves that could satisfy United States and/or allied import requirements until all aggrieved states achieved self-sufficiency in energy, converted from oil to other fuels, worked out accommodations, or broke the embargo.[24] The following survey of prominent prospects stresses production potential, space relationships (location, size, and shape), general geographic characteristics, counterintervention threats, and political implications in special cases. (See tables 7–11 and maps 2–8 at the end of this chapter.)

Supply United States

Several options would insure sufficient oil imports for the United States, without regard for allies.

Venezuela's major producing fields at Maracaibo, combined with those in Nigeria, fall somewhat short of matching U.S. daily import demands, but pump enough petroleum to maintain the U.S. economy at a reduced pace if we conserved a million barrels a day as previously discussed. Essential refinery capacities also would be available.[25]

Both countries are comparatively close to the United States. It is five times farther from our eastern seaboard to Persian Gulf ports via the Mediterranean than to Maracaibo, just across the Caribbean.[26] Steaming times from Norfolk to Nigeria are less than half those to Persian Gulf loading points.[27] No terrain bottlenecks, such as the Suez Canal and Strait of Hormuz, interfere with traffic flow from either locale. Neither Nigeria nor Venezuela could offer more than token resistance to a U.S. invasion. Threats by Soviet air and ground forces would be nonexistent—no otherwise acceptable areas of operation duplicate that desirable attribute. (See section on counterintervention threats for details.)

Liabilities, however, are also impressive. Separate operations 4,500 miles apart would cause force requirements and costs to soar. Wells under water produce most of Maracaibo's petroleum. Such structures would be much more difficult to seize and secure than installations ashore. Parachute assaults, for example, would be impractical. Nigeria's fields are in mangrove swamps and rain forests similar to those that frustrated U.S. forces in Southeast Asia. Population patterns there are among the densest in Africa. Special tactics, tools,

[24] There is no consensus among authorities concerning just what it would take to "break" an embargo. OPEC's determination might actually be strengthened if this country seized a small fraction of that cartel's total production facilities, say enough to satisfy modest U.S. import requirements alone. Much greater pressures might have to be applied before OPEC's members cracked.

[25] The United States operates sufficient refineries to process domestic production, plus about half its imports. The residue amounts to roughly 3 million barrels a day. Venezuela could handle 1.2 million in the Maracaibo area. Facilities in the Dutch Antilles, Virgin Islands, Bahamas, Trinidad and Tobago, which are outside OPEC, could refine the remainder, if they chose to cooperate. International Economic Report of the President, Washington, U.S. Govt. Print. Off., March 1975, p. 154.

[26] The Suez Canal reopened on June 5, 1975, but prospects are poor that it would remain active in event of an OPEC embargo.

[27] Norfolk arbitrarily serves as a median point, although it is a naval base, not a petroleum port. Tankers actually discharge cargo at terminii from Texas to Massachusetts.

and techniques would be essential in both countries. Last, but perhaps not least, all Latin America likely would censure U.S. actions if we seized oilfields in Venezuela, which is our official ally in the Organization of American States (OAS).

Maracaibo might also be linked with Libya, whose potential gross production is a third greater than Nigeria's. The distance from Norfolk to Brega, south of Benghazi, is about the same as to Bonny, on the Bight of Biafra. Beyond that, however, debits would outweigh credits.

Most Libyan oil is pumped to loading points on the Gulf of Sirte, but petroleum from the Sarir field empties out near Tobruk, 300 airline miles northeast. Substantial reinforcements would be required to secure the extra pipeline and associated installations. More importantly, Sarir crude oil has a high paraffin content, and therefore must be heated in transit. If pumps shut down from sabotage or other causes, the conduit would turn into a giant "candle." This study therefore arbitrarily excludes Sarir's 200,000 barrels a day from U.S. options shown on table 10, but includes them with NATO options, where every drop would count.

Landings in Libya almost certainly would cause serious rifts between this country and its European allies if seizing oil installations served U.S. interests, but not NATO's. Worse yet, Soviet Armed Forces, especially naval elements, are better placed to meddle in the Mediterranean than in the Gulf of Guinea.[28] U.S. lines of communication, for example, would be very vulnerable at Gibraltar and near the Sicilian narrows.

OPEC's greatest producers, of course, are in the Middle East.

There would be little to recommend Iraq, even if its 2 million barrels a day matched the 6.2 million U.S. import demand and refineries were sufficient, which they are not. Most fields, which center on Kirkuk, are 400–500 miles from Persian Gulf ports, quite isolated from other Middle East assets. Consequently, they pump petroleum to a pair of loading points along the Mediterranean. Neither pipelines nor ports could be secured unless U.S. troops were physically deployed over huge portions of Iraq, Syria, and Lebanon.

Counterintervention threats would be less crucial in countries at the southern end of the Persian Gulf, where four states straggle along a 600-mile littoral arc from Bahrain and Qatar through the United Arab Amirates (UAA) to Oman. However, their combined production falls 40 percent short of U.S. requirements, and many wells are offshore.

Kuwait, in the center, is a more compact package. Its fields are within easy reach of the Persian Gulf coast. Most installations are onshore. Refinery capacity ranks with the best in the Middle East. Loading facilities are more than adequate. Daily petroleum production of 3.5 million barrels is almost 80 percent of Iraq and the UAA combined, but still scarcely more than half of America's current imports.

By way of contrast, either Iran or Saudi Arabia alone could supply U.S. needs for crude petroleum. Unfortunately, the former shares

[28] Admiral Thomas H. Moorer, former Chairman of the Joint Chiefs of Staff, and Admiral Elmo R. Zumwalt, Jr., for example, both warned that "it is dangerous for the United States now to deploy, in a bilateral confrontation with the Soviet Union in the Eastern Mediterranean, its fleet because the odds are that the fleet would be defeated in a conventional war." NBC radio and television program, "Meet the Press," June 30, 1974 (transcript p. 6).

Other authorities assert that the foregoing case is overstated, but nearly all concede that the danger would be considerable.

some of Iraq's most serious shortcomings. The latter is unnecessarily expansive.

Iranian oil fields, for example, are scattered for 300 miles north-to-south in rough, arid foothills of the sawtoothed Zagros range. Land routes in the region are poor. Loading facilities at Kharg Island would be easy to isolate and secure once in U.S. possession, but the Abadan refinery complex near Iraq's frontier lies on exposed flats that invite counteractions from both sides of the border.

Iranian Armed Forces, which feature the finest U.S. fighter aircraft and a consequential navy, are the strongest of any OPEC member. Iraq's military machine is less pretentious, but poses potential threats that could not be ignored. The Tigris-Euphrates confluence and swampy delta (commonly called the Shatt-al-Arab), together with built-up areas, would afford an infinite number of safe havens from which irregulars could mount incursions. Most important of all, U.S. intrusions might incite the Shah to seek assistance from the Soviet Union, which could interfere in force from the Caucasus.[29]

Selected Iranian oilfields (2.7 million barrels a day) could be combined with those in Kuwait (3.5 million) to meet U.S. import needs, but that course would do little to downgrade threats, and would add some difficulties. Iran likely would fight as hard for half its holdings as for all. Possible Soviet responses would remain essentially constant. U.S. forces would have to seize and secure oilfield and terminal facilities in two dissimilar, noncontiguous areas.

Tailor-made amalgams involving Saudi Arabia appear more promising, since that country is less exposed to Soviet air-ground strikes and its armed forces are small.

Kuwait, for example, combined with Saudi coastal fields, might prove manageable, although focal points are 250 miles apart and half the output comes from offshore.

All Saudi onshore assets currently operated by Aramco [30] would suffice, but they stretch for 300 miles across sere, sandy landscape, from the neutral zone to the edge of Rub al-Khali, Arabia's empty quarter.

South Saudi onshore holdings, plus Qatar and Bahrain, are less elongated, but comprise three disconnected areas that would complicate control.

The Saudi core's great Ghawar field alone could furnish 75 percent of the full U.S. requirement.[31] Tanker turnaround times to Ras Tanura would be a day less than those to Kuwait City, 250 miles farther north.[32] Precious fuel could be conserved. That extra distance could also constrain Soviet airpower.

Offshore loading facilities at Ras Tanura and Juaymah are among the best in the Middle East, but refinery capacities would fall short by half a million barrels per day, even if all installations were seized intact, a dubious assumption.[33] Sizable amounts therefore would

---

[29] One school of thought suggests that the Shah, recalling Soviet steps to unseat his father, would never traffic that way with the Kremlin. Others conclude he would have little choice if this country occupied Iranian oilfields, his chief source of power.

[30] Negotiations for the full nationalization of Aramco assets are presently in progress.

[31] Production from fields at Qatif and Dammam would be surplus to our stated needs, but distribution and terminal facilities in those locations would have to be secured in any case.

[32] Petroleum tankers average about 15 knots per hour. That translates into 33 hours steaming time to cover 500 miles round trip.

[33] Production in the Saudi core is 6.5 million barrels a day. Refinery capacity on site is 0.7 million. The United States could handle 3.5 million over and above domestic production, if "sweet" and "sour" problems were solved (see discussion with table 9). Roughly 1.7 million barrels a day would have to be refined elsewhere. Caribbean States (less Venezuela) might handle 1.1 million, while Europe processed the rest.

have to be refined in NATO Europe and the Caribbean. That course would be practical only if the countries concerned approved the forceable U.S. occupation of foreign oil fields. Concurrence could not be taken for granted, since operations to supply the United States alone could be inimical to NATO's interests.

Supply United States plus Japan

Demands for crude petroleum would nearly double (from 6.2 to 11.6 million barrels a day) if Japanese requirements were added to our own, but Japan's capacities for self-help in case of embargo would be very slim.[34] Its armed forces lack adequate mobility means and staying power to strike unaided in the Middle East, the only area with oil concentrations large enough to satisfy Nippon's full need. Japan thus would collapse economically if America were unwilling or unable to take up the slack.

Should this country elect to assist, two alternatives could be explored.

The United States perhaps could help Japan to help itself by furnishing sealift and logistic support for use by Japanese forces. If this country sought to satisfy its own import needs in Latin America and Africa, south Saudi onshore production could supply Japan's daily requirement of 5.4 million barrels (Ghawar, 4.7 million; Abqaiq, 0.9; Qatif and Dammam 0.1). If U.S. forces chose to hit the Saudi core, Japan's best targets would be Indonesia (1.4) and Kuwait (3.5) in combination. Offshore wells at Safaniyah, the northernmost Saudi field, could furnish most of the difference, should that seem desirable.[35] Terminal facilities in Kuwait, including a refinery, would facilitate service.

Alternatively, the United States could expand its areas of operation to compensate for shortages remaining after Japan seized oil installations in Indonesia. Maracaibo, Nigeria, and Libya in aggregate would be unable to satisfy the residual United States/Japanese requirement of 10.2 million barrels, even if U.S. forces could cope simultaneously with three separate theaters. This country thus would have to confine efforts to the Middle East, where the Saudi core and nearly contiguous Kuwait would suffice.

Supply United States plus NATO Europe

Supplying this country plus NATO would be far more difficult. No choice is encouraging.

This country's European allies, like Japan, have strictly circumscribed capabilities. French and Italian air/ground forces are relatively free, but other NATO countries, including Germany, are constricted by current commitments or simply lack abilities to project a potent punch much beyond their borders. Consequently, NATO's self-help program, carried out by a small segment of the Atlantic Alliance, would at best be limited to occupying oil installations in Libya and Algeria, which could cover 4.3 million of the 15.2 million barrel NATO requirement. Sufficient allied sea power is available to support such endeavors, but complications ashore could be expected, since some Algerian fields are 600 miles south in the Sahara, and part of Algeria's oil is pumped through Tunisia.

---

[34] It seems inconceivable that this country would rescue allies that failed to help themselves. The remainder of this section therefore addresses combined efforts to offset embargoes directed against America and its major allies, or exclusively against allies.

[35] Forty percent of Safaniyah's 1 million barrels daily output is from offshore wells, total about 400,000 barrels.

NATO shortages of 10.9 million barrels a day (almost double U.S. import requirements) could be alleviated only if America took action to seize all assets in Saudi Arabia and Kuwait, along with most of Iran's petroleum. Iran's contribution could be reduced to 55 percent if U.S. forces took all odds and bods from Bahrain to Oman, but the territory would then be tremendous—perhaps 1,000 straight line miles north to south, an expanse equal to that between Washington and mid-Missouri. Manpower and materiel requirements would be immense.

The OPEC cartel might break if United States and NATO elements seized a smaller package, but planners could not depend on it.

Supply United States plus Europe and Japan

Insuperable problems emerge at this stage. Assets in all the Middle East (less Iraq) and North Africa would be adequate to supply this country and its major allies at reduced rates of oil consumption, but military impediments would be inhibitive.

Supply Allies alone

This country and 15 of the world's largest oil consumers (including most NATO nations and Japan) signed an agreement on an International Energy Program late in 1974. In essence, that pact promotes "secure oil supplies on reasonable and equitable terms" by developing standby stocks within each member state, restraining demand, and allocating imports among members so as to ease shortages during "oil supply emergencies." [36]

The stipulated share of petroleum resources would avert or attenuate crises caused by embargoes, if no complications arose. However, OPEC conceivably could use selective boycotts against our foremost allies to drive a wedge between them and the United States. Should that contingency occur, neither NATO nor Japan could seize sufficient oil supplies to satisfy minimal import requirements.

The United States could choose to assist. If so, sanctions against NATO would demand direct military operations by this country in the Middle East, since allied capabilities are inadequate, and no other area could satisfy Europe's oil import requirements. Should OPEC's embargo strike solely at Japan, U.S. assistance might be confined to material support, as suggested earlier. Conversely, American and Japanese Armed Forces could be committed in any one of several oil producing areas whose output is sufficient to satisfy current needs.

OUTLYING OBJECTIVES

Some potential areas of operation, such as Venezuela and Nigeria, are isolated. Outsiders would find it difficult or impossible to oppose U.S. actions. No intervening obstacles impede passage from those oil producers to the United States or its principal allies.

Not so in other locales. Several OPEC countries adjoin in the Middle East, where coordinated military actions by members and/or sympathizers (especially the Soviet Union) are conceivable. Blocking positions well beyond the oilfields might prove essential. At the very least, U.S. units would need to oversee the Strait of Hormuz, probably from both shores—a sensitive proposition, should the Shah resist.

[36] France, Greece, Iceland, Norway, and Portugal are NATO's nonparticipants. U.S. Congress, Senate. International Energy Program. Hearings Before the Committee on Interior and Insular Affairs on a Plan for Sharing Energy Imports in Time of Emergency and Cooperating on Other Energy Programs. 93d Congress, 2d session. Washington, U.S. Govt. Print. Off., 1975, 213 pp. See pp. 72–96 of that document for verbatim text of Agreement on an International Energy Program.

Japan might have to hold Malacca. If Saudi areas were occupied, U.S. forces might need to control Riyadh, a possible hotbed of resistance. Extensive perimeters thus could be expected.

TABLE 7.—UNITED STATES, ALLIED OIL IMPORTS COMPARED WITH OPEC PRODUCTION

OPEC producing regions and states	Total 1973 crude and refined exports To:[1] (MMb/d)			Current normal crude production rate[2] (MMb/d)	Crude oil reserves[3] (billion barrels)	Approximate number of years production at normal rate
	United States	Western Europe	Japan			
Middle East:						
Saudi Arabia[4]	0.590	4.000	1.240	8.6	164.5	53
Iran	.420	1.900	1.730	6.1	66.0	30
Kuwait[4]	.160	1.750	.540	3.5	72.8	56
Iraq	.050	1.220	negl	2.0	35.0	50
United Arab Amirates[5]	.160	.600	.430	1.9	33.9	55
Qatar	negl	.400	nil	.5	6.0	32
Oman[6]	NA	NA	NA	.3	6.0	54
Bahrain[6]	NA	NA	NA	.1	.3	12
Africa:						
Libya	.350	1.590	.020	3.3	26.6	22
Algeria	.140	.670	nil	1.0	7.7	23
Nigeria	.550	1.130	.100	2.3	20.9	25
Gabon	NA	NA	NA	.2	1.8	24
Latin America:						
Venezuela	1.840	.440	.010	3.0	15.0	14
Equador	.052	nil	nil	.2	2.5	35
Indonesia	.250	negl	.840	1.4	15.0	29
United States/allies total imports all sources, 1973	6.2	15.2	5.4			
United States/allies domestic production, 1973	11.1	.2	negl			
United States/allies total consumption, 1973	17.3	15.4	5.4			

Note: MMb/d=Million barrels per day; negl=Negligible; nil=None; NA=Not available.

[1] 1973 is used as a representative, or normal, year to show export patterns. Data for 1974 was distorted by (1) the impact of the Arab oil embargo and production cutbacks of October 1973–March 1974 (full effects of the Arab action were not felt until December 1973); (2) the world oil surplus caused by conservation programs in industrialized countries; (3) oil production cutbacks instituted by producing states to meet lower world demands; (4) disrupted trade patterns caused by a tanker glut; and (5) further unsettling of the world market caused by the pricing changes which came into effect in January 1974 and December 1974. Data taken from: International Economic Report of the President. Washington, U.S. Government Printing Office, March 1975. p. 154.

[2] Normal production rate is maximum production capacity under current technological limitations, without political restrictions. For example, Kuwait's production rate for 1974 was about 2.2 MMb/d and Libya's was about 1.7 MMb/d. Both states have reduced their production for political reasons. Saudi Arabia has a potential rate of about 20.0 MMb/d, but only after extensive and expensive technological improvements.

[3] Reserve figures vary greatly from source to source. For example, DeGolyer and MacNaughton's Twentieth Century Petroleum Statistics lists Saudi reserves at 96.9 billion barrels. The International Petroleum Encyclopedia lists 132 billion barrels. Statistics in this study were taken from: Oil and Gas Journal, Dec. 30, 1974, p. 108–109. They do not include tar sands, heavy oils, or oil shales.

[4] Neutral zone production divided between Kuwait and Saudi Arabia.

[5] Of the 7 member states of the United Arab Amirates, Abu Dhabi, Dubai, and Sharjah are oil producers. The latter began production in 1974.

[6] Not an OPEC member, but an OPEC sympathizer.

TABLE 8.—OPEC PRODUCTION BY REGIONS AND MAJOR OIL FIELDS

	Million barrels per day	Percent offshore
Middle East:		
Iran:		
Offshore	0.3	
Onshore	5.8	
Total	6.1	0.5
Saudi Arabia:		
All Saudi onshore:		
Ghawar	4.7	0
Abqaiq	.9	0
Harmaliyah	.1	0
Khursaniyah	.1	0
Qatif	.1	0
Dammam, Fadhili, Khurais	.1	0
Total	6.0	0

TABLE 8.—OPEC PRODUCTION BY REGIONS AND MAJOR OIL FIELDS—Continued

	Million barrels per day	Percent offshore
Middle East—Continued		
Saudi coastal:		
Safaniyah	1.0	60.0
Zuluf	.2	100.0
Marjan	<.1	100.0
Khursaniyah	.1	0
Abu Hadriya, Fadhili, Qatif, Dammam	.2	0
Abqaiq	.9	0
Berri	.8	92.0
Total	3.3	50.0
South Saudi onshore:		
Ghawar	4.7	0
Abqaiq	.9	0
Qatif, Dammam	.1	0
Total	5.7	0
Saudi core:		
Ghawar	4.7	0
Abqaiq	.9	0
Berri	.8	92.0
Qatif, Dammam	.1	0
Total	6.5	11.0
Kuwait [1]	3.5	10.0
Bahrain [2]	.07	0
Qatar	.5	40.0
United Arab Amirates:		
Abu Dhabi:		
Murban, Bu Hasa	1.2	0
Mubarras, Umm Shaif, Zakum	.5	100.0
Dubai	.2	100.0
Sharjah	.05	0
Total	1.9	38.0
Oman [2]	.3	0
Africa:		
Algeria:		
Hassi Massoud (Trias Basin, north complex)	.7	------------
Edjeleh (Polignac Basin, south complex)	.2	------------
Other areas	.1	------------
Total	1.0	0
Libya:		
Sirte Basin	3.1	0
Sarir	.2	0
Total	3.3	0
Nigeria	2.3	27.0
South America:		
Venezuela:		
Zulia State (Maracaibo region)	2.5	85.0
Anzoategui/Monagas States (eastern onshore)	.5	0
Guarico/Barinas (central onshore)	.06	0
Total	3.0	75.0
Southeast Asia:		
Indonesia:		
Sumatra	1.0	0
Java	.2	(3)
Kalimantan	.1	(3)
Others	.1	------------
Total	1.4	17.0

1 Includes Khafji and Hout offshore in the Neutral Zone.
2 Not an OPEC member, but an OPEC sympathizer.
3 Some.

Note: All figures are approximate. Sums of subtotals do not coincide with associated grand totals where fields are included under more than 1 heading.

Sources: Oil and Gas Journal, Dec. 30, 1974, May 6, 1974; International Petroleum Encyclopedia, Tulsa, Petroleum Publishing Co., 1974. Data on Berri fields derived from Aramco Houston Office on May 22, 1975.

TABLE 9.—SELECTED REFINERY STATISTICS

[In millions of barrels per day]

Region or country	Domestic consumption 1973[1]	Refinery capacity 1974[2]	Refinery capacity shortage/excess
United States	17.3	14.8	−2.5
Japan	5.4	5.1	−.3
Western Europe	15.4	18.7	+3.3
Venezuela	.2	1.5	+1.3
Caribbean	.1	1.9	+1.8
Netherlands Antilles	(3)	(.9)	
Trinidad and Tobago	(3)	(.5)	
Bahamas	(3)	(.5)	
Middle East	.8	2.4	+1.6
Kuwait	(.1)	(.6)	
Saudi Arabia	(.3)	(.7)	
Bahrain	(3)	(.3)	
Iran	(.4)	(.8)	
Africa	.1	2.0	+1.9
Algeria	(3)	(.1)	
Libya	(3)	(3)	
Nigeria	(3)	(3)	

[1] Puerto Rico and Virgin Islands included in U.S. total.

[2] Capacities shown above reflect full utilization, and discount "sweet"/"sour" relationships, which could play important roles in contingency planning. Most U.S. refineries, for example, are designed to process "sweet" oil. Venezuela, Saudi Arabia, and Iran produce "sour" oil in the main. Kuwait is more or less "neutral." We could refine "sour" and "neutral" shipments in emergency, but at reduced efficiency and considerable risk to facilities. Converting equipment to handle "sour" and "neutral" oil on a routine basis would be costly and time-consuming. Other countries, most notably in Europe and the Caribbean, would have to process such products for the United States if we seized oil fields in "sour" oil areas. If they failed to do so, we would face serious problems. See glossary for "sweet" and "sour" oil.

[3] Less than 100,000 barrels per day.

Sources: Primarily the International Petroleum Encyclopedia, 1974. Tulsa, Oklahoma, Petroleum Publishing Co., 1974, and the International Economic Report to the President, Washington, U.S. Government Printing Office, March 1975, p. 154

TABLE 10.—SAMPLE OBJECTIVE AREAS: RELATED TO REQUIREMENTS

[Millions of barrels per day]

Selected combinations[1]	Crude oil[2] imports, 1973	Normal crude oil production
Supply United States	6.2	
Maracaibo, Nigeria		4.8
Maracaibo, Libya less Sarir		5.6
Iran		6.1
44 percent Iran, Kuwait		6.2
Saudi Coastal, Kuwait		6.8
All Saudi Onshore		6.0
South Saudi Onshore, Qatar, Bahrain		6.3
Saudi Core		6.5
Supply United States plus Japan	11.6	
Maracaibo, Nigeria (United States)		10.5
South Saudi Onshore (Japan)		
Maracaibo, Libya less Sarir (United States)		11.3
South Saudi Onshore (Japan)		
Saudi Core (United States)		11.4
Indonesia, Kuwait (Japan)		
Supply United States plus NATO Europe	21.4	
All Saudi, Kuwait, 82 percent Iran (United States)		21.4
Algeria, Libya (NATO)		
All Saudi, Kuwait, Bahrain to Oman, 55 percent Iran (United States)		21.4
Algeria, Libya (NATO)		
Supply United States plus Europe/Japan	26.8	
All Persian Gulf less Iraq (United States)		26.6
North Africa (NATO)		
Indonesia (Japan)		

[1] See table 8 for OPEC production by regions and major oil fields.

[2] U.S. petroleum imports could be cut in emergency, but this table reflects full demands to compensate for OPEC sabotage efforts, which could substantially reduce production in objective areas. Note 1, table, 7 explains why 1973 was used as a base.

TABLE 11.—KEY PRODUCING AREAS: COMPARATIVE CHARACTERISTICS

GENERAL GEOGRAPHY

	Terrain	Climate	Vegetation	Population	Size of area [1]	Distance from United States [2]
Middle East:						
Iran	Mountains	Arid	Scrub	Sparse	300×100	6,650
Iraq	Hills	do	do	do	500×100	6,200
Kuwait	Plain	do	Desert	do	100×50	6,700
Saudi Arabia	do	do	do	do	300×100	6,950
Bahrain	Island	do	do	do	20×10	7,000
Qatar	Plain	do	Steppe	do	120×35	7,100
United Arab Amirates	do	do	Desert	do	100×25	7,200
Oman	Hills	do	do	do	175×25	7,450
Africa:						
Algeria	Rough	do	Sparse	do	650×200	4,300
Libya	Plain	do	do	do	350×250	5,300
Nigeria	Delta	Wet	Rain forest	Dense	220×100	5,700
Latin America: Maracaibo	Lake	Moist	do	Moderate	100×50	1,850
Southeast Asia: Indonesia	Plain	Tropical	do	do	Fields on 5 islands	10,600

[1] Size of area indicates maximum length and width in statute miles.
[2] Airline distance from Norfolk, Va. to: Abadan, Iran; Kirkuk, Iraq; Dhahran, Saudi Arabia; Kuwait City, Bahrain; Umm Bab, Qatar; Abu Dhabi, UAA; Muscat, Oman; Algiers, Algeria; Sirte, Libya; Port Harcourt, Nigeria; Maracaibo, Venezuela; Djakarta, Indonesia.

PETROLEUM PRODUCTION PLANT

	Oil fields [1]	Active oil wells [1]	Shut-in oil wells [1]	Pipeline mileage [2]	Refinery capacity [3]	Oi port
Middle East:						
Iran	29	378	12	795	0.789	5
Iraq	8+	156	234	2,466	.169	2
Kuwait	8	692	Unknown	451	.566	3
Saudi Arabia	24	670	134	2,655	.690	3
Bahrain	1	211	33	Unknown	.250	1
Qatar	4	81	9	311	.001	2
United Arab Amirates	11	208	36	390	0	3
Oman	4	160	30	Unknown	0	1
Africa:						
Algeria	23+	826	294	2,522	.115	2
Libya	39	979	507	2,250	.016	5
Nigeria	98+	1,088	103	328	.060	5
Latin America: Venezuela [4]	73+	12,379	7,176	1,951	1.532	22
Southeast Asia: Indonesia	77+	2,707	6,788	361	.428	5

[1] Oil and Gas Journal, Dec. 30, 1974, pp. 129–148.
[2] Major trunk lines only. OPEC Annual Statistics, 1973, pp. 99–105.
[3] Refinery capacities in millions of barrels daily. International Economic Report of the President, March 1975, p. 154; American Petroleum Institute, Annual Statistical Review, May 1975, pp. 65–66.
[4] Includes all of Venezuela. Most statistics do not separate Maracaibo.

Map 2.

SEA ROUTES TO SELECTED OIL FIELDS

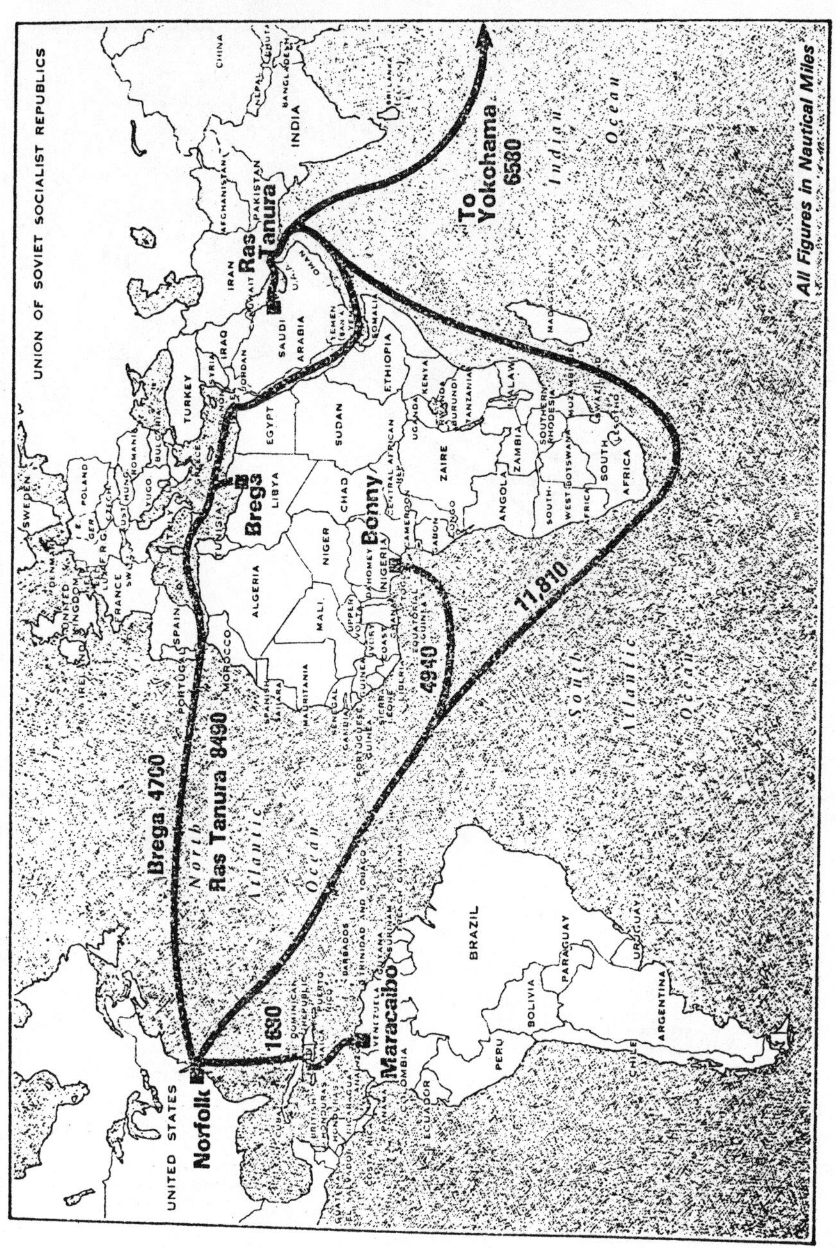

Map 3.

MARACAIBO OIL FIELDS

Map 4.

NIGERIAN OIL FIELDS

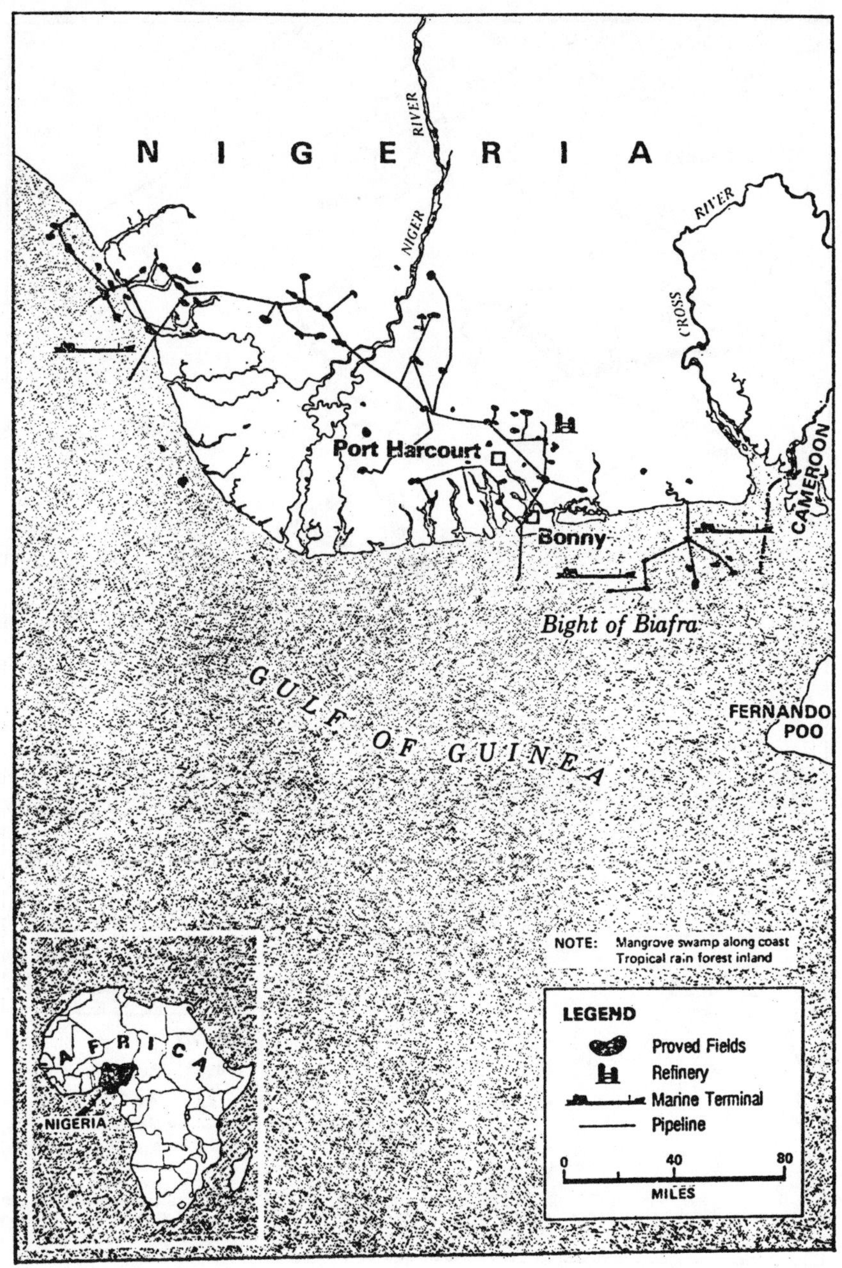

Map 5.

MIDDLE EAST OIL FIELDS

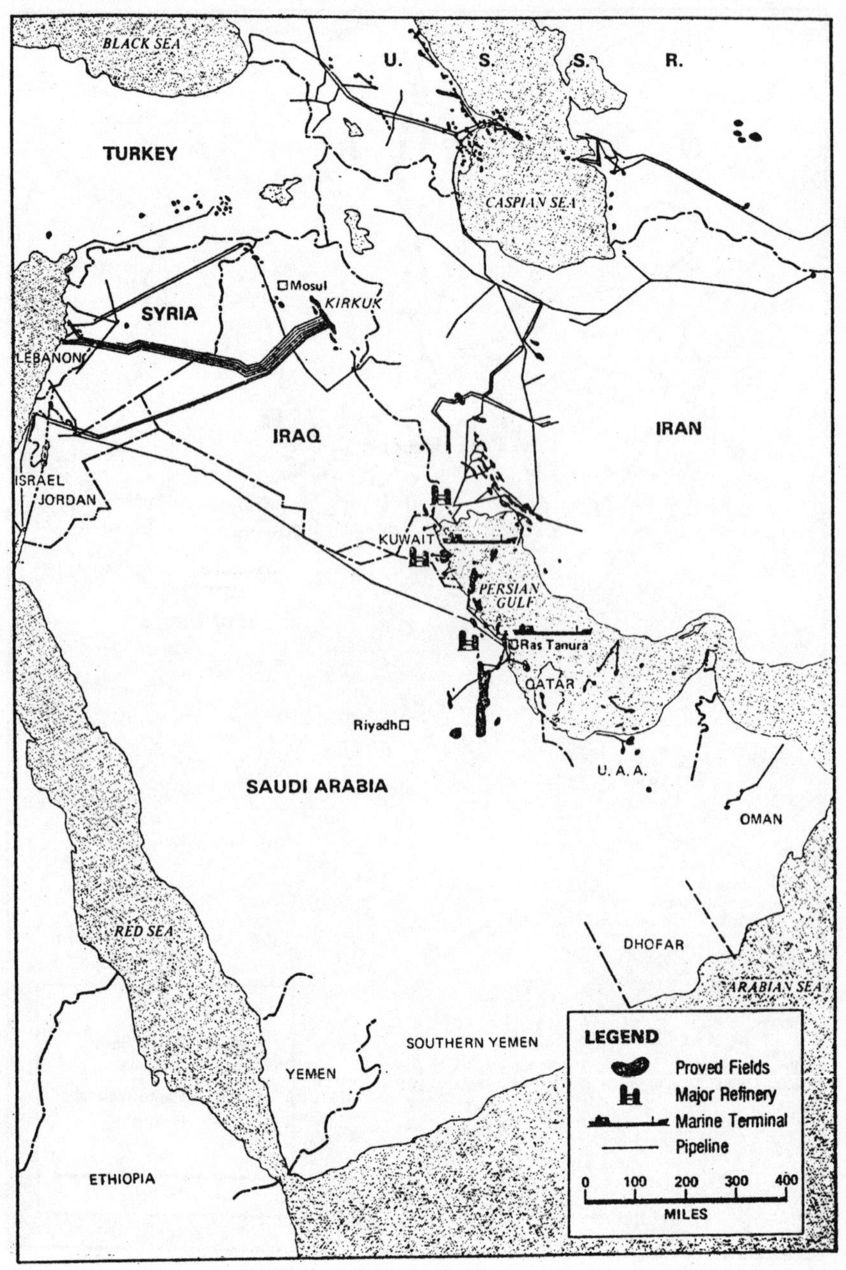

Map 6.

PERSIAN GULF OIL FIELDS

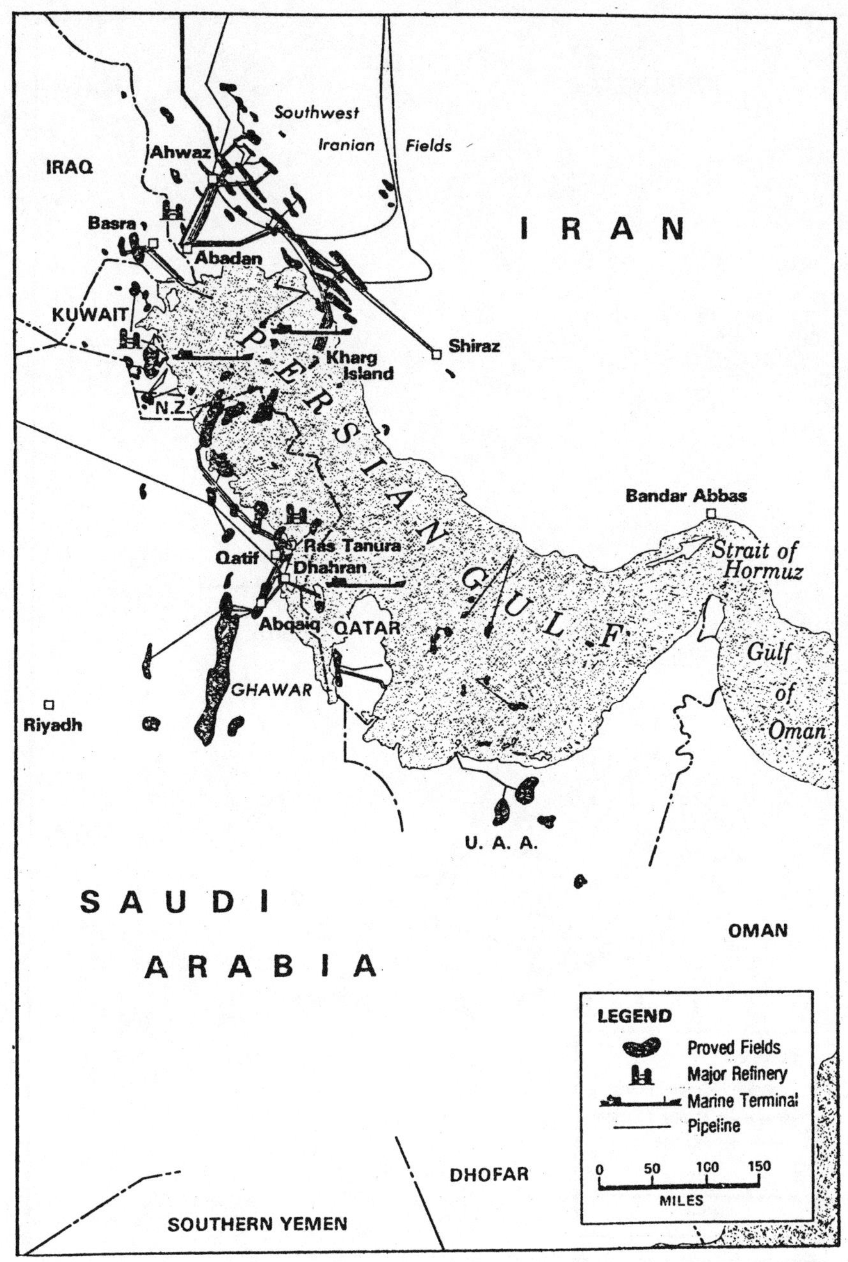

Map 7.

LIBYAN OIL FIELDS

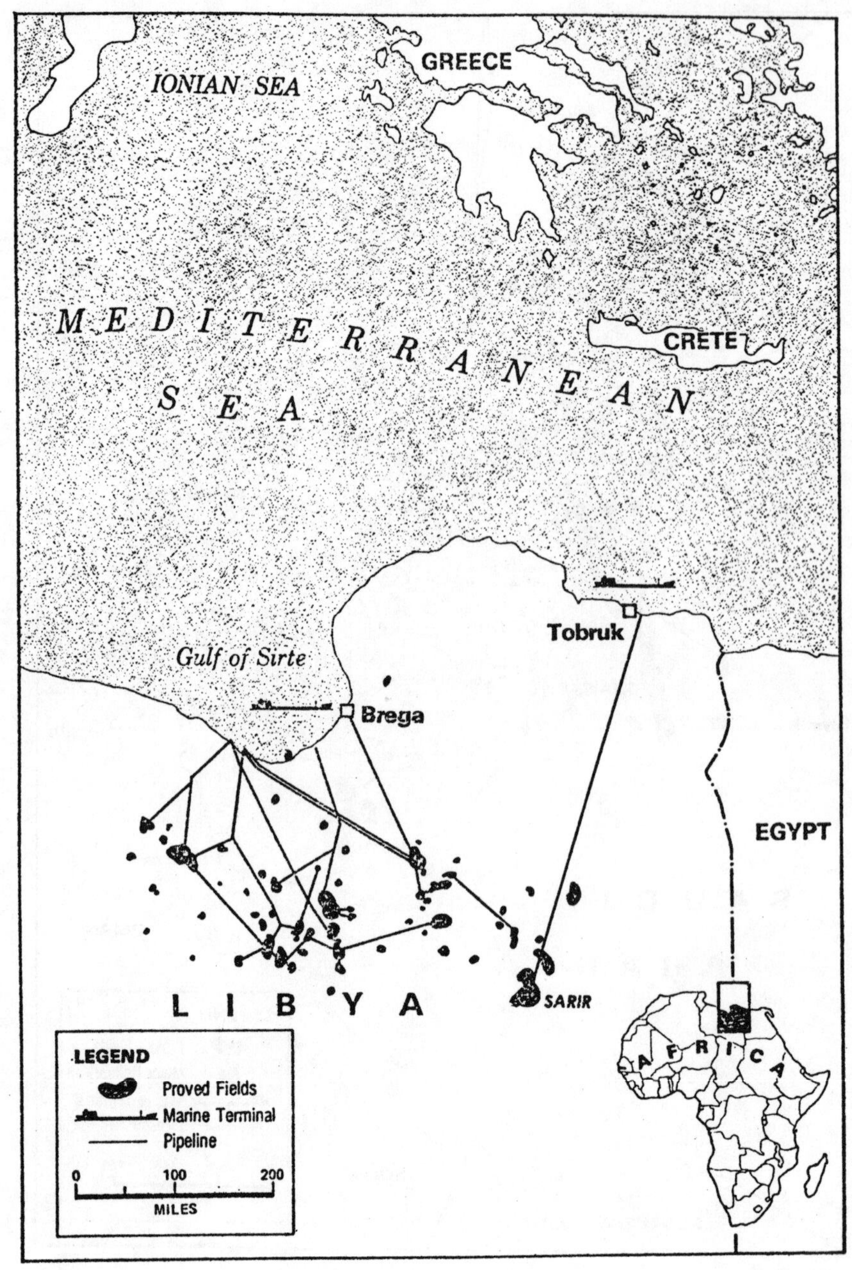

Map 8.

ALGERIAN OIL FIELDS

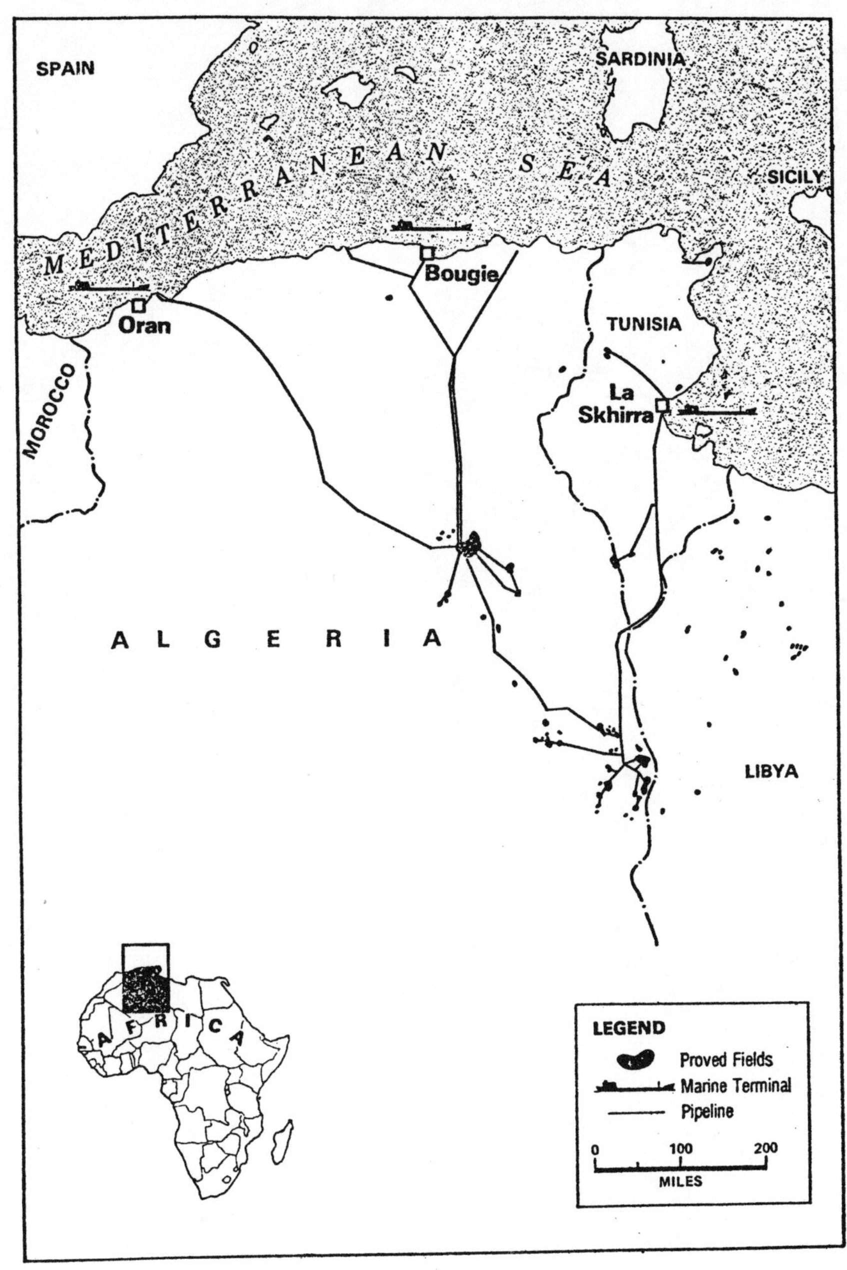

93d Congress } COMMITTEE PRINT
1st Session }

DATA AND ANALYSIS CONCERNING THE POSSIBILITY OF A U.S. FOOD EMBARGO AS A RESPONSE TO THE PRESENT ARAB OIL BOYCOTT

PREPARED FOR THE

COMMITTEE ON FOREIGN AFFAIRS

BY THE

FOREIGN AFFAIRS DIVISION, CONGRESSIONAL RESEARCH SERVICE, LIBRARY OF CONGRESS

NOVEMBER 21, 1973

U.S. GOVERNMENT PRINTING OFFICE
WASHINGTON : 1973

DATA AND ANALYSIS CONCERNING THE POSSIBILITY OF A U.S. FOOD EMBARGO AS A RESPONSE TO THE PRESENT ARAB OIL BOYCOTT

On the basis of the data available, the leverage available to the Arabs through their oil boycott far exceeds any leverage that might be available to the United States through a food embargo since the Arabs can meet their relatively small food import needs from other sources in the world market, while the United States cannot meet its relatively large petroleum import needs from other sources.

In order to understand the impact of a potential U.S. food embargo upon the Arab oil boycotters, certain basic facts about the nature of the Arab food market should be made clear. In the present situation there are two main categories of Arab countries. In one category are the oil exporters who are participating in the boycott: Libya, Algeria, Abu Dhabi, Kuwait, Bahrain, Qatar, Saudi Arabia, Iraq, and Syria. In the other category is Egypt. The countries in the first category obtain the majority of their foreign exchange through exports of petroleum, and, except for Algeria, whose greater population and development needs have limited the size of the growth, all have increased their foreign exchange reserves dramatically in the last 4 years. Finally, except for Algeria, they all have relatively small populations and total food requirements. Egypt, on the other hand, has a large and rapidly growing population, few natural resources, and has experienced continual chronic foreign exchange shortages since the closing of the Suez Canal—its main foreign exchange earner.

Probably the most significant economic characteristic of the food import market for the countries in both categories is the extremely decentralized, competitive nature of their cereals purchases. In the last year, major purchases of either wheat or rice have been made in the United States, France, Pakistan, Canada, Australia, Thailand, the Soviet Union, through Singapore and Hong Kong, and, according to Agriculture Department sources, perhaps from the People's Republic of China.

An examination of the figures for total wheat exports to the Arab countries since 1963 indicates that there have been large variations in amounts purchased and countries of origin (see table A). The main reason for this is, except for Egypt's reaction to the 1967 war in cutting off wheat imports from the United States for political reasons, that the Arab countries have been very attentive to price and non-price competitive factors in their grain buying. Thus, substantial grain sales by Australia in 1971 and 1972, and by Canada in 1970 and 1971 were made largely because they were on concessional terms, or because the seller offered to assist in the construction of milling facilities in the buyers' country. In the tight world grain market in 1973 the Arabs turned to the lowest cost seller, in this case it was the United States.

Probably the second most significant characteristic of the Arab food import market is the large amount of transshipping that takes place. Much of the wheat and rice for Saudi Arabia, for example, is purchased and recorded as an import in Kuwait, Iraq, the United Arab Emirates. The variations which appear from year to year in the food import statistics of many of the Arab countries may only indicate a larger or smaller amount of transshipment rather than changes in demand or domestic supply. With the major characteristics of the buyers kept in mind, an examination of the figures in table B for estimated wheat supply of all Arab countries indicates that, except for the provisional 1973 data, the United States has never supplied more than 10.2 percent of the total supply of wheat to the area (16 countries). However, two countries have been more dependent upon U.S. supplies in the last few years than other states in the Arab world. Specifically, Saudi Arabia and Algeria have purchased sizable quantites of U.S. cereals (see table D). From 1967 to 1972, Saudi Arabia imported about three-quarters of its wheat and wheat flour requirements. These imports have ranged from 280,000 to 370,000 metric tons annually. The U.S. portion of total Saudi wheat imports has ranged from 28 to 40 percent—with a provisional 1973 figure of 63 percent (see table C). Since 1967, Algeria has imported an average of 30 percent of its wheat consumption. During this period, total Algerian wheat imports have ranged from 337,000 to 800,000 metric tons a year. (A provisional 1973 figure indicates imports of 1.1 million metric tons.) The U.S. percentage of Algerian imports averaged 47 percent, with a high of 68 percent of imports in 1969 and a low of 17 percent in 1970. The amount of U.S. wheat exports to Algeria since 1967 has ranged from 121,000 metric tons in 1971 to a provisional 1973 figure of 575,000 metric tons (see table C).

While table C on supply of wheat and flour and the U.S. annual share of imports indicates that Algeria and Saudi Arabia are the most heavily dependent of all Arab countries upon the United States for wheat imports, it must be kept in mind that the total for these two countries has never exceeded 850,000 metric tons (1973 provisional data). This figure should be contrasted against the size of the world wheat export market of 73.5 million metric tons in 1972 and 55.5 million metric tons in 1971, or the size of U.S. wheat exports: 32.5 million metric tons in 1972, 16 million metric tons in 1971. Furthermore, the wheat import total for the entire Arab world (16 countries) has never exceeded 9.2 million tons from all sources. Of that 9.2 million tons, the United States provided 13.3 percent (see table B).

Two-thirds of U.S. rice exports to the Middle East have gone to Saudi Arabia. These exports have averaged about 65,000 metric tons a year since 1969. (See table F.) Since recent total Saudi Arabian imports of rice have been about 195,000 metric tons a year, the United States has been providing about one-third of Saudi Arabian rice requirements. And, according to U.N. statistics, since the Saudi Arabians produce only 2 to 3 percent of their rice consumption, it can safely be said that the United States has provided about one-third of Saudi Arabian rice consumption in the last few years. Because of the effect of recent floods in Pakistan, which annually had exported 100,000 metric tons of Basmati rice to Saudi Arabia, U.S. rice exports to the entire Arabian Peninsula are expected to exceed 170,000 metric tons in fiscal year 1974. Counting uses in other countries, this is over 80 percent of the consumption of rice in Saudi Arabia. To give some idea of the magnitude of this figure, about 938,000 metric tons are expected to be imported into the Middle East and Turkey in 1973 from all sources. In 1972, worldwide U.S. rice exports amounted to 2 million metric tons, while the world rice export market was 8.2 million metric tons. Thus, for 1972–73, U.S. rice exports comprise about one-quarter of the world rice export market and about the same percentage of the rice exports to the entire Middle East.

Having discussed the nature of the Arab cereals market and examined the import patterns of the two largest importers, it is now possible to discuss the impact upon these countries of a potential U.S. grain embargo. First of all, not counting 1973, which is an exceptional year, the Arab oil producers, except for Algeria and Suadi Arabia, are for all practical purposes completely independent of U.S. food exports. Kuwait, Libya, Iraq, Syria, the United Arab Emirates, and the Gulf States are dependent upon the United States, at most, for 5 percent of their food imports (see table D). Algeria and Saudi Arabia are more dependent upon U.S. cereals but, as greviously noted, the 850,000 metric tons of wheat they have purchased from the United States in 1973 is an extremely small amount of the world wheat export market. If an embargo of rice exports were specifically aimed at Saudi Arabia, the Saudis could do either of two things to deal with the embargo: they could attempt to locate the rice in the open market (a good possibility, especially in a barter deal for oil) or they could increase purchases of wheat, which is more widely available (as the Indians did in 1973 when their rice stocks were seriously depleted and additional rice supplies could not be obtained).

While the 1973 purchases of wheat in this country by Syria and Iraq are unusual, the important thing is not their existence or amount, but that they have already been concluded and the grain shipped. Thus, any U.S. embargo would not be felt, even assuming total inaction by the Arabs, until next year when the stocks are depleted.

Furthermore, because Arab grain purchases are so decentralized, and the size of the individual states purchases so small in world market terms, future purchases could be made from Canada, Australia, or even from this country by third country middle men without attracting suspicion. The very structure of the U.S. grain export market is another factor that would work against the effectiveness of any embargo to the Arab world alone. Because the U.S. market is highly decentralized, it would be impossible for the original seller to determine the ultimate destination of the grain.

Finally, except for Egypt, because of their very substantial foreign exchange reserves, and the promise of even greater revenue as oil prices and output increase, the Arab countries are in an excellent position to outbid other potential food buyers in the world food market. Five dollars-a-bushel wheat can easily be purchased with $5-a-barrel oil. And, while the world market for food grains is tight, it is nowhere near as tight as the world market for petroleum. Grain supplies are available in sufficient quantities even though the buyer might have to pay higher prices for them. The same cannot be said about oil.

Data compiled by the Department of State indicate that the equivalent of 1.6 million barrels a day of crude and petroleum products is entering the United States today from the Arab countries.[1] This is equivalent to about 9.2 percent of present U.S. daily consumption of 17.3 million barrels a day. This figure includes direct crude oil shipments and shipments of refined products which have been processed in refineries outside of the United States from Arab feedstocks.[2] Present U.S. consumption has increased about 1 million barrels a day over 1972 and about 2.1 million barrels a day over 1971 when total consumption was 16.3 and 15.2 million barrels a day equivalent respectively.

During the period from 1970 to mid-1973, U.S. domestic production has actually fallen from 11.2 million barrels a day to 10.9 million barrels a day. Thus, while U.S. requirements were rising 2 million barrels a day, U.S. domestic production was falling 0.3 million barrels a day, leaving a shortfall of 2.3 million barrels a day in the last 3 years alone. The total shortfall for 1973 is expected to exceed 6.4 million barrels a day. (see table G).

The shortfall has not been made up entirely by the Arabs. During the period (1969–73) Canada has increased its shipments to the United States from 610,000 barrels a day to 1.1 million barrels a day. Similarly, Venezuela has increased its exports to the United States from 880,000 barrels a day to 2 million, Iran from 46,000 to 400,000 and Nigeria from 49,000 to 550,000 barrels a day. (1969 data, Department of Interior Minerals Yearbook; 1973 data, Department of State.) In 1969, U.S. oil imports from the Arab countries were running about 150,000 barrels a day. Today, as noted in the opening of this section, that figure is 1.6 million barrels a day, or 9.2 percent of consumption. As the figures indicate, U.S. dependence upon Arab oil producers is a recent phenomenon caused by continuous, large increases in consumption combined with gradually declining domestic production.

In the short term, there is little that can be done to increase domestic production. While the figures for domestic U.S. production may change due to increased prices making formerly uneconomic wells profitable again, the most recent data on domestic and offshore U.S. oil production indicate that the addition of Alaskan North Shore Oil will simply serve to stabilize the gradual decline in domestic U.S. production. And, in any case, North Shore oil is some 4 years in the future at the earliest. Furthermore, on the basis of steps taken last summer, long before the Middle East war, further increases from Canada seem highly unlikely. And, presently, Venezuela is reexamining its export policy because of fears that the current high levels of exports will rapidly deplete reserves. Only Iran and Nigeria have not threatened cuts in production although the Nigerians did double the price of their crude last week partly as a reaction to the boycott.

---

[1] This figure is an estimate of the level of imports at this time based upon projections from the most up-to-date data on the actual deliveries of Arab crude and petroleum products.

[2] The latter is important because a very large percentage of the oil entering the United States originating from the Arab countries has been either transshipped through or refined in third countries before it reaches the United States. The most recent figures based upon direct shipments of crude to the United States would indicate that the United States is dependent upon the Arabs for only 4–5 percent of its total consumption rather than 9–10 percent as it actually is.

TABLE A.—WHEAT EXPORTS TO ARAB COUNTRIES FROM MAJOR EXPORTERS 1964–72 AND JANUARY–SEPTEMBER 1973

Country [1]	1946	1965	1966	1967	1968	1969	1970	1971	1972	January–September 1973
Metric tons (thousands):										
United States	1,498	1,393	1,498	945	981	671	1,015	1,104	986	1,766
U.S.S.R	202			1,200	298	301	234	200		
Australia	344	235	274	571	497	243	445	2,336	2,570	
Canada	20	40	12	16	150	42	1,058	1,233	560	
France	260	475	361,	604	1,140	1,147	256	40	593	
Total wheat imports from all sources	2,335	2,539	3,538	4,578	4,065	2,705	3,645	6,275	5,768	7,380
Approximate share of wheat imports from (percent):										
United States	64.2	54.9	42.3	20.6	24.1	24.8	27.8	17.6	17.1	23.9
U.S.S.R	8.7			26.2	7.3	11.1	6.4	3.2		
Australia	14.7	9.3	7.7	12.5	12.2	9.0	12.2	37.2	44.6	
Canada	.9	1.6	.3	.3	3.7	1.6	29.0	19.6	9.7	
France	11.1	18.7	10.2	13.2	28.0	42.0	7.0	.6	10.3	

[1] Individual country's data based on their exports to these countries.

Source: U.S. Department of Agriculture.

TABLE B.—ESTIMATED WHEAT SUPPLY OF ARAB COUNTRIES, 1966–73[1]

	1966	1967	1968	1969	1970	1971	1972	1973
	1,000 METRIC TONS							
Total supply	10,114	12,780	14,271	10,982	12,524	15,595	17,562	16,800
Wheat production	5,114	6,502	8,635	7,294	7,686	7,903	10,424	7,600
Imports: total	5,136	6,307	5,656	3,718	4,873	7,722	7,458	9,280
Imports from United States	2,207	1,259	1,209	816	1,275	1,330	1,369	2,250
Exports	170	37	120	30	35	30	320	80
	PERCENT							
Percent of total supply imported from all sources	50.8	49.3	39.6	33.8	38.9	49.5	42.5	55.2
Percent of total supply provided by United States	21.8	9.8	8.5	7.4	10.2	8.5	7.8	13.3

[1] Egypt, Sudan, Libya, Morocco, Algeria, Tunisia, Lebanon, Syria, Saudi Arabia, Iraq, Yemen, Oman, Qator, UAE, Kuwait.

Source: U.S. Department of Agriculture.

TABLE C.—SUPPLY OF WHEAT AND WHEAT FLOUR IN SELECTED COUNTRIES AND U.S. SHARE OF IMPORTS, ANNUAL 1967–73

[In thousands of metric tons]

	1967	1968	1969	1970	1971	1972	1973
Egypt:							
Total supply	3,908	3,810	2,774	2,768	4,076	4,972	5,197
Imports	2,687	2,284	1,517	1,252	2,506	3,356	3,340
Imports from United States	103						530
Percent of imports from United States	3.8						15
Saudi Arabia:							
Total supply	494	410	398	430	475	520	554
Imports	344	280	248	280	325	370	434
Imports from United States	123	91	79	98	91	150	225
Percent of imports from United States	35	32	31	35	28	40	63
Algeria:							
Total supply	1,984	2,236	1,747	1,837	1,913	2,400	1,110
Imports	718	702	421	337	713	800	1,110
Imports from United States	205	343	288	229	121	496	575
Percent of imports from United States	28	49	68	67	17	62	51

TABLE C.—SUPPLY OF WHEAT AND WHEAT FLOUR IN SELECTED COUNTRIES AND U.S. SHARE OF IMPORTS, ANNUAL 1967-73—Continued

[In thousands of metric tons]

	1967	1968	1969	1970	1971	1972	1973
Iraq:							
Total supply	1,042	1,576	1,191	1,159	1,767	1,955	1,700
Imports	176	205	2	100	953	195	700
Imports from United States	25				8	8	144
Percent of imports from United States	14					4	20
Syria:							
Total supply	1,149	854	1,048	1,392	1,625	1,960	1,140
Imports	100	254	44	542	750	360	340
Imports from United States	85				181	51	50
Percent of imports from United States	85				24	14	14

TABLE D.—U.S. AND WORLD FOOD EXPORTS TO SELECTED ARAB COUNTRIES

[In millions of dollars]

	A			B			C			D			E		
	U.S. exports of foodstuffs and live animals—category 0			U.S. exports of cereals (including wheat and rice—category 04)			Estimated world total agricultural imports by Arab countries			Estimated total foodstuff imports by Arab countries			U.S. percentage of estimated total foodstuff imports		
	1970	1971	1972	1970	1971	1972	1970	1971	1972	1970	1971	1972	1970	1971	1972
Saudi Arabia	26	22	32	20	18	26	218	225	263	207	213	250	12	10	12
Kuwait	3	4	4		1	1	80	81	139	76	77	132	3	5	3
Libya	1	1	2			1	122	155	173	116	147	164	1		1
Iraq		4	1		4		69	199	75	66	189	71		2	1
Syria		11	3		11	3	103	110	55	94	106	52		10	5
Algeria	14	9	33	14	9	30	153	189	208	145	180	198	9	5	16
Egypt	9	3	6	8	2	5	208	294	377	198	279	358	4	1	1
UAE	3	1		1		1									
Oman							102	104	117	96	100	111	6	2	
Qatar	3	1		1											

Sources: Columns A and B, U.S. Commerce Department, foreign trade series FT-455. Column C, U.S. Department of Agriculture data. Columns D and E calculated by author.

TABLE E.—RICE PRODUCTION AND ESTIMATED TOTAL SUPPLY IN THE NEAR EAST, ANNUAL 1966-73

[In thousands of metric tons]

Country	1966	1967	1968	1969	1970	1971	1972	1973 estimate
Total production	869	1,072	1,024	1,036	1,188	942	1,118	948
Total imports	496	372	393	418	561	713	655	968
Total supply	1,365	1,444	1,417	1,454	1,749	1,665	1,773	1,916

RICE IMPORTS BY ARAB COUNTRIES, ANNUAL 1966-72 AND ESTIMATE FOR 1973

	1966	1967	1968	1969	1970	1971	1972	1973 estimate
Iraq	1	10		1	2	97	45	135
Saudi Arabia	142	125	124	151	233	220	167	195
Kuwait	47	19	42	27	39	55	51	94
Bahrein	18	9	19	8	26	28	28	32
United Arab Emirates	25	27	45	34	44	48	64	88
South Yemen	28	29	28	60	46	40	30	33
Other Arabian Peninsula states	23	17	27	22	28	26	27	29
Syria	32	36	44	30	40	50	56	49

Source: U.S. Department of Agriculture.

TABLE F.—U.S. RICE EXPORTS TO MIDDLE EAST COUNTRIES, FISCAL YEARS

[Metric tons]

Country	1968	1969	1970	1971	1972	1973
Saudi Arabia	60,211	59,613	70,148	48,439	80,780	57,000
South Yemen	7,191	11,154	13,433	1,700	2	1
Kuwait	11,868	8,651	2,634	2,193	5	2
Arabian Peninsula States	4,387	2,346			1	1
Libya		486	1,036	946	3	2
Bahrain	1,404	2,095				
Israel	7,712	12,836	13,312	12,144	10,000	11,000

Source: U.S. Department of Agriculture.

TABLE G.—LEADING ARAB CRUDE OIL SUPPLIERS TO THE UNITED STATES 1971–72

[1,00C barrels a day of crude]

	Abu Dhabi	Algeria	Iraq	Kuwait	Libya	Qatar	Saudi Arabia	Total
1971	105.4		40.1	31.5	153.3	1.7	156.7	488.7
1972	113.3	81.7	18.3	38.9	173.6	3.5	197.3	626.6

Source: Middle East Economic Digest Oct 12 1973.

U.S. DOMESTIC PRODUCTION OF CRUDE AND GAS LIQUIDS

[Million barrels a day]

Year		Year	
1969	10.8	1972	11.1
1970	11.2	1973 (estimated)	10.9
1971	11.1		

U.S. DOMESTIC TOTAL CONSUMPTION

[Million barrels a day]

Year		Year	
1969	14.1	1972	16.3
1970	14.7	1973 (estimated)	17.3
1971	15.2		

Source: Department of Interior Bureau of Mines, 1973 data, Department of State.

TABLE H.—ESTIMATED TOTAL AGRICULTURAL IMPORTS BY MIDEAST AND NORTH AFRICAN COUNTRIES, ANNUAL 1966–73 AND ESTIMATE FOR 1973

[In thousands of dollars]

Country	1966	1967	1968	1969	1970	1971	1972	1973
Egypt	317,322	343,397	243,357	193,700	208,800	294,834	377,000	458,000
Libya	61,645	84,775	86,188	93,501	122,748	155,768	173,885	200,000
Algeria	169,174	184,796	168,863	92,900	153,555	189,359	208,000	300,000
Morocco	160,047	165,251	175,885	113,309	157,252	190,021	197,000	220,000
Tunisia	52,452	75,249	52,162	69,962	91,638	80,207	83,300	95,000
Syria	72,700	56,300	70,000	65,200	103,000	110,000	55,000	72,000
Iraq	92,800	73,400	82,700	65,700	69,200	199,880	75,000	170,000
Kuwait	50,000	60,000	65,000	70,000	80,000	81,800	139,800	153,600
Saudi Arabia	111,222	106,462	131,641	140,589	218,000	225,000	263,000	350,000
Gulf Area	77,000	81,000	93,000	97,000	102,000	104,000	117,000	130,000
Yemen	2,000	3,000	2,500	3,000	4,000	7,000	11,000	16,000
Yemen Democratic Republic	5,000	4,000	3,500	4,000	6,000	8,000	12,000	14,000

Source: U.S. Department of Agriculture.

COMMENTARY

Oil: The Issue of American Intervention

Robert W. Tucker

I

THE turning points in history, we are told, are commonly events whose real significance can only be understood at distant remove. To those who directly experience them, these events are the occasion for endless controversy and uncertainty. At the time, the only point of agreement may be that something unusual has occurred and, as a result, the accustomed order of things will never again be the same. Although the new landscape is not illuminated for all to see, the sensitive observer intuitively grasps that something extraordinary has happened.

Do the changes that have occurred in the world oil market during the past year, and the world's response to those changes, qualify as a "significant event" in the sense indicated above? To most observers, the answer would seem clear. The preponderant view is that these changes, when taken together with their effects, present and expected, represent one of the two or three signal developments of the postwar period. There are, of course, the usual differences in assessment. To many, the principal import of the crisis immediately brought on by the fourfold increase in oil prices is that it affords a spectacular demonstration, though only the first of many such demonstrations, of the growing power of the new and developing states. To be sure, oil is conceded to be an exceptional case, given the basic and pervasive role it plays in industrial economies. Even so, the expectation is that the example set by the Organization of Petroleum Exporting Countries (OPEC) will be followed by others, with at least varying degrees of success. Thus the oil crisis is seen to presage a radical shift in power as between the developed and capitalist states and those states that until only yesterday formed no more than the impotent objects of the international system.

To others, the essential meaning of the oil crisis is that the developed and capitalist states are at the end of a long period of rapid economic growth made possible in large measure by the cheap raw materials of the undeveloped world (cheap, of course, because of the imbalance of political and economic power). A corollary of the shift-in-power view, this end-of-an-epoch argument comes in several versions which range from the relatively optimistic to the quite pessimistic and even the near apocalyptic. For those of a more optimistic bent, the oil crisis—with all the immense difficulties it may immediately impose—may well prove to be a blessing in disguise if it serves to drive home the lesson that we must mend our wasteful and mindless ways. While forcing us to develop alternative sources of energy with a sense of purpose and degree of effort that otherwise would have appeared only at a later and much more critical period, it may also prompt us to consider seriously the dilemmas of societies that have made material growth their overriding social and political imperative. For the pessimists, however, the oil crisis is nothing so much as an early warning signal of the disaster that in all likelihood awaits future generations. Not only does it clearly point to the ultimate limits to growth but, more significantly in the shorter run, to the increasing pressures we will be subject to by those whose numbers grow daily at an ever greater rate and who are determined to share an ever larger piece of a cake that no longer can be considered as indefinitely expansible.

The point need not be labored. Save perhaps for the most resolute of optimists, there appears to be something for nearly everyone in the oil crisis. It has been regularly invoked as evidence of the inescapable need for increased interdependence among nations. Yet it may also be invoked as evidence of the need to make the nation as independent as possible of the international environment, or, at least, of the material constraints of this environment. Not infrequently, the two responses have been urged almost simultaneously by American officials. While professing to see in the oil crisis the imperative of interdependence, they have also exhorted the nation on the necessity of getting on with "Project Independence." It is easy enough to criticize statesmen for apparently inconsistent responses. What is worth emphasis is the varied and often inconsistent response of those who do not bear official responsibility. Yet the oil crisis may be used with some plausibility at least as evidence for a number of widely divergent interpretations about the world at this period in history.

II

GIVEN an "event" that has so many dimensions, it is unavoidable that the individual observer will be forced to pick and choose among what strike him as the more significant aspects. The resulting interpretation need not for that reason be arbitrary. Certainly, the interpretations noted above cannot be considered arbitrary because they focus primarily upon certain features of the oil crisis while relegating other features to a peripheral position. But if they are not arbitrary, they are at least curious in that with rare exception they fail to evince the slightest interest in the one feature of the oil crisis that clearly differentiates it so far from international crises in the past: the absence of the meaningful threat of force.

At first consideration, this apparent absence of force as an element in the crisis seems astonishing. At least it must seem astonishing to those who assume *some* continuity with the past. The very meaning of a crisis in the relations of states has traditionally been defined as a conflict over interests deemed vital by the contending parties and in which the use of force is considered an ever-present possibility. The crisis at hand surely meets the first criterion, though it just as surely has lacked the second. This is one reason, and most likely the major reason, that it has appeared so unstructured when judged in terms of our experience with past international crises. Suddenly, we find ourselves in a strange universe. Whether this universe is largely one of our deliberate choice and design is a question that may for the present be left in abeyance. But however the question is answered, it is clearly the absence of the credible threat of force which renders plausible the expectation that the interests placed in jeopardy by present oil prices will not be preserved in the near future. Moreover, it is the near future that must concern us most. The conflict of interest between the major OPEC countries and oil-importing nations will wither away if and when new energy sources are developed or very considerable oil reserves outside OPEC are discovered. Although expert opinion varies on both prospects, neither seems likely to materialize before the early to middle 1980's. Assuming the maintenance of something close to the present price structure for oil, how do we get from here to there without those disagreeable intervening consequences we are reminded of almost daily? And the problem is precisely one of getting from here to there. An emphasis on the long—or longer—run is all well and good, provided it is remembered that the short run is still our only way to the long run.

We know how the oil crisis would have been resolved until quite recently. Indeed, until quite recently it seems safe to say that it would never have arisen because of the prevailing expectation that it would have led to armed intervention. It is important to underline this point lest the utter novelty of the present situation be lost. We are not discussing here the growing indisposition of strong powers in this century to resort to military intervention against small and militarily weak states where the vital interests of the former are not in jeopardy. Nor, for that matter, are we concerned with the alleged tendency of strong powers to view more restrictively their vital interests justifying, if need be, military intervention against the small and weak. It may be conceded that there has been a change occurring over several decades in the propensity of the strong to resort to force against the weak, though the scope of the change, its causes, and its permanence remain less than clear. What is of relevance here, though, is that the case histories which are presumed to testify to this change provide no real precedent for the instance at hand if judged in terms of the magnitude of the interests at stake. On the contrary, until as recently as the middle 1960's, what the instances of armed intervention demonstrate is that great powers continued to manifest a willingness to use force against small states to vindicate interests which affected their well-being less than it is likely to be affected by a continuation of the policies pursued today by the major OPEC countries.

III

How, then, are we to explain that what has been a time-honored alternative in situations of comparable gravity has apparently been dismissed by governments, particularly the American government, and has only seldom been openly and seriously discussed in influential circles outside government? Is the appearance deceptive? Do we have here an instance of *pensons-y toujours, n'en parlons jamais?* It would hardly seem so. (And if this were the case, it would surely be inappropriate in the present circumstances.) There is no evidence that the alternative of military intervention, or the credible threat of intervention, has been given serious consideration by the American government. There may well be, and probably are, contingency plans for military intervention in the Persian Gulf drawn up within the past year by some Pentagon planning staff. But such plans exist for almost any conceivable contingency, and their existence indicates next to nothing about the seriousness with which governments consider the prospect of armed intervention. That prospect becomes credible to others when the upper reaches of bureaucracy manifest a receptiveness to employing armed force as one distinctly possible solution, when high officials make this receptiveness known through statements, however guarded, and when the actions otherwise taken by a government do not compromise the legitimacy and prejudice the success or the costs of military intervention, should it ultimately be chosen.

Once the record to date is set against these commonplace criteria, there is not much room left for doubt. Instead of leaving the option of armed intervention open, the American government has all but foreclosed it. It is true that governments have been known to reverse what has appeared to be a set policy, but in this case a reversal is made very difficult by the repeated acknowledgment that force is not a meaningful option and, even more, would be an entirely unjustified response to the actions taken by the OPEC countries. Nor is this particular legitimization of OPEC actions offset by the recent statements of President Ford and Secretary Kissinger to the effect that unreasonable action on the part of the major oil producers involves the risk of world depression, the consequent breakdown of world order and safety, and the rise to power of governments that might have fewer scruples about their international behavior. Quite apart from being a rather demeaning way for a great power to behave, these statements probably frighten Western publics more than they do the elites in the major oil-producing states for whom they are intended. At the same time, the American government has underscored its good faith in renouncing military intervention by its projected massive sale of arms—the newest and the best—to Saudi Arabia and Iran. Saudi officials have been quite candid in saying that a major purpose of their arms is to protect their vast underground treasure. Only the obtuse will ask against whom.

If the dismissal of military intervention or the credible threat of intervention must be taken at face value, is it redundant to ask why it has been dismissed? Obviously it is embarrassing to do so, else the question would have been pressed long ago. By a kind of unspoken convention, even to ask the question apparently indicates that one is simply out of touch with the realities of today's world, that one is a latter-day Colonel Blimp or, for the more sophisticated, an imperialist *manqué*. Yet it is doubtful that the same question, raised in roughly comparable circumstances, would have had the same reception fifteen or even ten years ago. It might have been turned aside after due consideration, but it would not have been quietly dismissed with pained expression. That it is so turned aside today, and by those who once were persuaded that the nation's well-being and international position might well warrant military intervention in the Congo, and did warrant military intervention in Vietnam and the Dominican Republic, must surely hold out some moral for us that is of more than passing interest.

There is, indeed, a good deal to be learned by considering the reasons that have been given, though only rarely and then with a rather patronizing air, in rejecting the possibility of using force or posing a credible threat of force. In summary form they are: that military intervention, though confined to a relatively restricted area, would prove technically very difficult, if not impossible, to carry through successfully, even if it is assumed that the Russians would not respond with force; that even if technically feasible, intervention would in all likelihood have to be undertaken unilaterally and would provoke the strong condemnation of our major allies, not to mention the complete estrangement of the developing world; that a militarily difficult and politically inexpedient action would also be unnecessary since there are means by which the financial and economic dislocations attending current oil prices can be contained and ultimately managed; and, finally, that military intervention against any of the major oil producers would be seen as an act of moral bankruptcy by the nation itself and, for this reason alone, would not be countenanced by public opinion.

These are the major reasons for dismissing the prospect of military intervention. There are others—for example, the conviction that intervention anywhere in the Middle East would give rise to widespread acts of terrorism in the Western nations—but the above seem quite enough. It is clear that if any one of them is well-taken, then the alternative raised in these pages must be put aside. One does not seriously consider a course of action, distasteful in any circumstances, that must in the instant case prove impossible, self-defeating, unnecessary, or utterly debilitating from a moral standpoint. Still, it is astonishing that few have found anything particularly instructive in what is presumably the almost utter irrelevance of military power to a conflict that involves vital interests. The prevailing view implies a revolutionary change in the very nature of international society. Yet those who take this view appear to find the change so indisputable as scarcely to deserve attention.

IV

Even if we grant for the time being the argument that armed intervention as a means for resolving the oil crisis is militarily unfeasible, politically inexpedient, and morally repugnant, it does not follow that there are plausible grounds for believing there is a satisfactory "way out" of the crisis. Military intervention, or the credible threat of intervention, may be rejected. Is this rejection compatible with avoiding the distinct possibility of an economic and political disaster bearing more than a superficial resemblance to the disaster of the 1930's? The words "distinct possibility" are chosen deliberately and with care. A possibility, even though distinct, is not a certainty. Nor is it a probability, though it comes rather close to one. Those who insist that armed intervention be ruled out so long as we are confronted only with a distinct possibility of disaster are perfectly at liberty to do so. But candor does at least require them to concede that this is what they mean when they say, that intervention is unnecessary. For there is a general consensus, which includes most of the "optimists," that if the present situation goes on unaltered, a disaster resembling the 1930's is indeed a distinct possibility and that it would have as its immediate and precipitating cause the present oil price. This being so, it is irrelevant, though true, to be reminded that the current economic malaise—above all, the global inflation—had its origins in conditions largely unrelated to the price of oil today and would persist even if this price were drastically lowered. A generally sick man who also happens to be hemorrhaging will not be saved from bleeding to death by being reminded of the other and more deeply-rooted causes of his ill health.

IS THERE a remedy for stopping the hemorrhage caused by the present price of oil which renders the threat or use of force unnecessary? If there is, it has yet to be advanced. After endless discussion we learn from the experts that the crisis can be *safely* resolved only if the price is drastically reduced. In the absence of this reduction, the principal "solutions" that are advanced inspire little confidence. The "recycling" solution is increasingly seen by many, and not without reason, as a sophisticated conjuring act, though a conjuring act nonetheless, if it does not lead to the kind of long-term investment in the importing states that permits the latter to provide goods and services to pay for their debts. In the form it is all too likely to take, recycling can lead only to an undermining of the credit-worthiness of many states and, ultimately, to widespread default or repudiation of debt. But even if the massive capital flows to the Arab states were recycled in the form of long-term investments, in all probability these flows would concentrate in only a very few states and precisely the states that have the least need of them. Who would buy the goods and services arising from this investment if the principal creditor states have insufficient need, and if the many poor and debt-ridden states have insufficient means? Moreover, there are limits to the investment capital any state will want to permit when it is directly controlled by foreign governments and can at any time be used for political leverage. This consideration applies not only to direct investment but, in lesser degree, to indirect investment as well after it reaches a certain magnitude.*

At issue here is not whether there are technical solutions to the vast financial drain resulting from present oil prices. No doubt there are, if only in the sense that any economic problem has a

* Determinedly optimistic economists are fond of quantifying the transfer of wealth successful recycling would entail. The exercise is designed to show us that "after all" this transfer would not amount to a great deal when set against the combined GNP of the developed capitalist states. While not particularly illuminating in economic terms, the exercise is quite revealing of the basic outlook that views the transfer with apparent equanimity. Equally revealing is the relative equanimity with which the prospect of a growing control over the most active and productive resources of Western economies is viewed, and this despite the fact that we have not the slightest assurance of the uses to which this control might be put.

strictly technical solution. At issue is whether there is a solution that, while accomplishing what must be the objectives of recycling, is also politically plausible. The essential objective of any recycling plan must be to insure that countries running large oil-related deficits will have available to them funds sufficient to meet their foreign-exchange needs. This might be accomplished through an arrangement whereby the principal recipients of the recycled funds make what will have to be for the most part soft loans to both developed and undeveloped states unable to pay for oil imports. Better still would be an arrangement whereby the principal recipients of recycled funds and some of the major producer states combine to accomplish the same end. The risks would be split between the OECD and OPEC states, and the indispensable lenders of last resort would be, among the former, the United States and West Germany, and, among the latter, Saudi Arabia and one or two other major producers. According to its proponents, the risks would then be manageable because spread out. When defaults occur, as inevitably they will occur, they are so shared that they can be made bearable.

As a technical solution, something along these lines would probably meet the problem of recycling. At least many economists have assured us that it can be thus resolved, and although their record of late is not exactly one to inspire blind faith, there seems no apparent reason to doubt them. The difficulty is that the proposed solution not only requires a degree of cooperation that has been quite rare among states in the past, but a willingness to take risks that is very nearly unprecedented save in war. Expectedly, the Arab states have to date shown no disposition at all to cooperate in the kind of plan considered here or to take the risks it necessarily implies. As to the major developed states, in response to an American initiative, they have only recently begun to explore a proposal for a $25-billion oil recycling fund. This "safety net" facility would operate within the OECD framework and would be designed to protect the members against financial collapse in the event their reserves and credit are exhausted. In turn, each participant would undertake the obligation to reduce dependence on imported oil and avoid resort to restrictive trade practices. In addition, a deficit country in applying to the managing board of the fund might be required, as a precondition of support, to make changes in its domestic economic policy. Establishment of the fund, then, would pose substantial political problems if it were to operate effectively. In the form it has been reported, the fund still represents a rather modest commitment for the U.S. ($8 billion). Finally, among American officials, it seems to be predicated on Treasury Secretary Simon's unwavering conviction that "the question is not whether oil prices will fall, but when they will fall." Even so, this plan would still leave unresolved a number of very serious issues which are unaffected by recycling—at least by the recycling that concentrates investment primarily in a very few developed states.

There is, of course, a simple alternative to the various forms of recycling, and it is to consume less oil. Minor reductions apart, this alternative assumes governments in the major importing states that have sufficient authority and will to take draconian measures. Such governments are not common today, and even if they were, there is no way by which oil imports might be financed out of current income without creating such shortages in energy as would result in a sharp decline of economic activity. The alternative of drastically reduced energy consumption would thus lead to a reduction in living standards. Even then, the problem of financing oil imports out of current income might remain, given the decline in trade that would attend a general decline in productivity.

These considerations are not materially affected by the kind of cooperative arrangement the major consumers—minus France—reached in the draft agreement worked out in Brussels this past September. That agreement, with its detailed commitment to oil-sharing in the event of a new Arab embargo, may prevent, if effectively implemented, a repetition of the disaster of the 1973 winter. It may also serve, as it is designed to serve, as an important means for eventually reducing present dependence on Middle East oil by facilitating a shift to alternative energy sources. All this *may* happen if the major importers demonstrate a degree of solidarity that, under pressure, they have yet to demonstrate. Even so, it remains extremely doubtful that the agreement creating an International Energy Agency can accomplish its immediate objective of forcing current prices down without taking measures that none of the participating governments is prepared to take.

Thus we are back to the starting point. The oil price must come down if the crisis, with all its latent dangers, is to be overcome, but no one knows how this is to be achieved within the short-to-medium term. Those who persist in believing that a modest cut in consumption will suffice to break the price structure set by the cartel conveniently ignore the history of OPEC, which affords little support for this belief. Moreover, they ignore what should by this time be apparent to all: that the major producer governments are not moved simply by economic calculation. The Shah of Iran now dreams the dreams of his ancestors, and the Western world, by its actions, encourages him to do so. The Arabs now dream of righting a humiliation that for centuries has lain deeply embedded in their consciousness. Why should men be "reasonable," according to Western lights, when they have come so far and so fast by being unreasonable?

V

IF THE view that business as usual, though with appropriate innovations, affords no persuasive, or even plausible, grounds for avoiding disaster, elementary prudence counsels that we at least raise the question of employing extraordinary means for resolving the crisis. Is military intervention technically feasible? Clearly the answer will depend, in the first place, on geography. Since it is impossible to intervene everywhere, the feasibility of intervention depends upon whether there is a relatively restricted area which, if effectively controlled, contains a sufficient portion of present world oil production and proven reserves to provide reasonable assurance that its control may be used to break the present price structure by breaking the core of the cartel politically and economically. The one area that would appear to satisfy these requirements extends from Kuwait down along the coastal region of Saudi Arabia to Qatar. It is this mostly shallow coastal strip less than 400 miles in length that provides 40 per cent of present OPEC production and that has by far the world's largest proven reserves (over 50 per cent of total OPEC reserves and 40 per cent of world reserves). Since it has no substantial centers of population and is without trees, its effective control does not bear even remote comparison with the experience of Vietnam.

The view that armed intervention is not technically feasible is persuasive, then, if it can be shown that the military difficulties of seizing and holding this area for an indefinite period are beyond our capabilities. If this view is correct, it says a great deal about the significance of American military power and its uses today, for it would be hard to find a group of states with a weaker collective military capability.* It is another matter entirely to argue the military unfeasibility of intervention by evoking the threat of Russian counter-intervention. But the specter of Russian counter-intervention lacks plausibility unless it is assumed that the Russians now enjoy a sense of military superiority sufficiently great on both the conventional and strategic levels as to permit them to deny what is to the United States, and surely to its major allies, a vital interest. For all the talk, however, about their global conventional capabilities, the Russians still lack the naval forces needed for effective interposition in the Persian Gulf. And for all the talk about our declining conventional capabilities, the United States still possesses at this point sufficient global forces to intervene. Moreover, even if the Russians possessed the forces necessary for effective naval interposition, the balance of perceived interest, as distinguished from the balance of military forces, is certainly against the Russians in this instance. The Russians simply do not have the interest here that we have. For this reason, they would be less prone to take the risks we would be prepared to take, and on any realistic assessment of Russian military capabilities today, those risks would be very considerable. Nor is it a sufficient response to these considerations to argue that the Russians might be tempted to rash action, if not to increase their political standing in the Middle East, then from fear that inaction would lead to a complete loss of standing. The political standing of the Russians would be increased in any event, since even strong verbal opposition —let alone the likely moving of troops into neighboring Iraq—would turn the Russians into the momentary heroes of the Arab world. (It is the distinct possibility that the Russians would move

* The transitory nature of this impotence should not be overlooked. In 1973-74 Western arms sales to the Persian Gulf have been reported in excess of $3 billion, and have included such sophisticated equipment as the F-14 fighter, Harpoon anti-ship missile, and a variety of SAM systems. Although it will be at least a year before these weapons enter Arab inventories in sizable numbers, their eventual availability will undercut the current U.S. dominance both in quality and in quantity.

forces into Iraq which would necessitate establishing a substantial American military presence in Kuwait as one of the first moves in intervening.)

Does the record of Russian behavior in recent years suggest that these considerations are too complacent? Surely the Russian response to the events in Czechoslovakia in 1968 does not do so, for Czechoslovakia was seen to raise a threat to imperial security and, beyond this, to threaten the structure of Soviet power and the very integrity of the Soviet state. Even then, what is impressive in retrospect is that, in view of the critical interests at stake, Soviet leadership proved so hesitant and vacillating about intervening. It is true that in the October 1973 war Russian behavior was marked by the *appearance* of a greater propensity for taking risks. Yet it remains an open question whether this appearance concealed a reality that is still characterized by a low risk-taking propensity. No one knows whether the Russians would in fact have airlifted several of their divisions to Egypt had the fighting not ceased. And even if they had done so, there is a world of difference between placing several divisions before Cairo (to face a foe who had no intention of advancing on Cairo) and taking an action that would put them in direct conflict with American forces. Moreover, in moving toward an open clash with American forces, the Russians would presumably be defending a regime with which they have no manner of commitment nor are likely to have, again in clear contrast to the October war.

To ESTABLISH that only a relatively restricted area need be seized and held, and to minimize the prospect of Russian counterintervention, only sets the broad conditions in which a military intervention might be successful. These conditions are admittedly very far from assuring its success. In all probability, a swift operation would be mandatory, not only to reduce whatever residual prospect there might be for counter-intervention, but, more importantly, to minimize destruction to the oil wells and supporting facilities—that is, to the pipe lines, pumping stations, loading jetties, etc. It is the anticipated destruction of the oil facilities that has been insistently raised by those who have dismissed the technical feasibility of employing military power in the Persian Gulf. Intervention would prove self-defeating, the argument runs, if only because we would inherit a shambles that might well take eight or nine months to repair. Is the assumption of systematic destruction from the wells to the terminal areas a realistic one? No one can answer the question with any real confidence. Much would depend upon the swiftness with which the initial phase of the operation were carried out. Yet even if it is conceded that, though swift, there would still be ample warning time—and this concession seems only reasonable—doubt must persist over the shambles we would presumably inherit. The kind and scope of the destruction commonly envisaged evokes the thoroughness of the destruction wrought by German forces during World War II as they withdrew from the East. Would the Arabs match this record? There is little in their past behavior to suppose that they would.

Let us, however, make the worst-case assumption. What then? The answer is almost certainly that we would be deprived of oil from the occupied area not for eight or nine months, but for three or four months and possibly less. Obviously, the operation would never be undertaken without making an inventory of the vital items of equipment that would be needed for early shipment. Of these items, the only ones clearly in short supply are the large-diameter pipelines peculiar to high-production areas. Even in this instance, though, there is little reason to assume that resupply within three months would prove beyond our capabilities.

It does not follow from these calculations that the importing nations must therefore have reserves which would permit self-sufficiency for at least a period of three months. Unless OPEC reacts by imposing a complete embargo, a 60- to 90-day reserve would prove quite sufficient even for the major importers (Western Europe and Japan), since most of present oil exports would remain unaffected. Of course, the possibility cannot be excluded that at least some OPEC countries would resort to an embargo, and particularly the remaining Arab states. As against this possibility, however, there is the consideration that almost all the remaining OPEC countries are revenue consumers and would be hard pressed to undertake an embargo for any appreciable period. Save for Libya, this is true even of the remaining Arab states. Then, too, the embargo would presumably be directed most critically against nations that, given their dependence on oil imports, would at the very least divorce themselves from, if not condemn, the American action. Instead of putting effective pressure on the United States to back down from its chosen course of action, an embargo might eventually provoke a hostile reaction from many of its hapless victims. Finally, it is not to be excluded that an embargo would be met by setting those entering it on notice that the newly fixed price of oil, once the Persian Gulf facilities were repaired (and production markedly expanded), would suffer still further as a result of any attempted embargo. With the core of the cartel broken, it is not only difficult to see such countries as Iran or Venezuela accepting this risk, it is even difficult to see Libya doing so.

These remarks on the military feasibility of intervention are very general. Many will insist they are much too general. To show the feasibility of intervention, it has been argued, it is the details which must be considered one by one with careful planning. Sweeping generalizations are of limited value. All this is quite true. But who has made for the most part sweeping generalizations about intervention in the Persian Gulf? Surely not the few who have ventured to suggest the feasibility of intervention. It is rather those who assure us that intervention is impossible. What is more, the assumption has been allowed to pass almost unchallenged that the burden of proof must rest upon those who dissent from the judgment that intervention in the Persian Gulf is not militarily feasible. Given the American force structure and the experience we possess, however, why is it unreasonable to insist that the burden of proof rests upon those who insist we lack the military capability to intervene successfully?

Nor is this all. Those who dismiss the feasibility of intervention on military grounds ought at least to acknowledge the simple logic of their position. If the argument is conceded that we cannot intervene now, it also follows that we cannot intervene even if the Arabs should impose an embargo in the future—only this time a truly harsh and crippling embargo. Let us suppose that within the next year there is another round of fighting in the Middle East and that this time the Arabs are very badly beaten. Let us also suppose that the Arabs react to their defeat by imposing an embargo. What then? Are we to conclude that in these circumstances there will be no disposition to use force because of the reasons given above? Many of the naysayers of today are prepared to admit that in these circumstances we might well be compelled to intervene. Yet if we are unable to do so now, how will we be able to do so then? For the Russians will still be with us and still threatening to put down their presumably "massive forces" in the Persian Gulf, and the Arabs will still be threatening to destroy everything. Our means to prevent all this will not be substantially different then from what they are today. If this is so, the conclusion must be drawn that the world is presently living quite at the mercy of the Arabs and the Russians.

VI

THE prevailing, if not universal, assumption that military intervention would have to be taken unilaterally and, initially at least, in the face of condemnation by most of the world, is probably well-founded. At least, it is well-founded if one assumes intervention under present circumstances. No one should underestimate the importance of this likelihood of widespread opposition, and particularly the opposition of at least some major allies. While the latter would feel themselves placed in a very vulnerable position as a result of American intervention, the shoe has not yet begun to pinch badly enough in Western Europe and Japan to cause men to shed illusions now deeply-ingrained. Once economic, social, and ultimately political conditions were to deteriorate to a point apparent to nearly all, the attitude toward intervention in Western Europe at least would almost certainly alter. But by this time the disease might have progressed sufficiently that the costliness of cure would in all probability be proportionate to a lack of sensitivity over the methods employed. It is naive to believe that nothing could be worse than the course of action under consideration in these pages.

It is the reaction of Western Europe and Japan that must for obvious reasons concern us most. This is not to imply that the reaction of the developing nations is of no concern, but only that it must rank lower in the scale of concerns any policy must weigh. The attitudes of the developing world—or, at least, much of it—would predictably be far harsher than those of the developed states, and for reasons too apparent to warrant discussion. On this, the record of the past year affords considerable evidence. The Indian government, to take perhaps the most notable example, has yet to say a critical word on current oil prices that have played havoc with the Indian economy and have brought many thousands of Indians closer to death by starvation. Even so, it defies belief that the developing nations, like the developed nations, would view with anything but relief, however disguised, a break in the petroleum price structure that followed a successful military intervention in the Persian Gulf. In the manner of Frederick the Great's description of Maria Theresa on the morrow of the division of Poland ("She wept, yet she took"), developed and undeveloped would deplore the action—though in considerably varying degree—while accepting with alacrity the benefits flowing from it.

This anticipation of at least a temporarily isolated America may be overly pessimistic, particularly with respect to Western Europe, and even under present circumstances. It is in keeping, however, with the attempt here not to gloss over or minimize the liabilities of armed intervention. At the same time, it is only reasonable to assume that the eventual reaction to intervention would depend very much on what the United States government did to elicit the consent, if not the cooperation, of its allies and, more generally and importantly, what it did after having seized and occupied the area in question. It is not only that the United States would have to act in as even-handed a manner as possible, which means refusing to punish those who had gone out of their way to condemn the intervention; it would also have to impose upon itself a policy of self-denial —at least until the temporary period of threatened or actual shortages passed. If any importer's share of oil is to decrease markedly during this period, it should be the state that is best prepared to shoulder the burden and that is least subject to reprisal. All this is evident fair play and indispensable to establish the *bona fides* of the American action. In addition, a system of allocation would probably be acceptable—and, indeed, workable—only if a fixed price were set for the allocated oil.

We pass over the issue of what this administered price should be in order to be judged reasonable to the interests of both producers and consumers. Clearly, the oil price would be designed to influence the structure of the world energy market. It would be absurd and self-defeating to propose a price close to present production costs in the Middle East. On the other hand, it would not be unreasonable to set a price below projected costs of alternative sources of energy, though not so much below as to discourage active development of these sources. It is entirely legitimate, in fixing the price, to respond to the demand that it should thereafter change in relation to the change in the price of goods oil producers must import from oil-consuming nations. It is equally legitimate to respond to the view that the major oil companies not be given a favored position and not be permitted to continue to enjoy their exorbitant profits. Any military intervention that failed to provide an equitable allocation of the oil on a cost-plus basis would be seen, and with no little justification, as a raw display of American imperialism. In any event, it would be widely seen in that light by those whose outlook permits no other interpretation. But there is no reason that this view should be permitted to enjoy some plausibility, and every reason that it should not. A rough basis for judging the relative disinterest with which intervention might be carried out would be if the major oil companies were just about as unhappy over the prospect as the Arabs.

But why consider intervention at all when we must bear its burdens although we enjoy the least vulnerable position among the major oil importers? Why accept the material, political, and moral costs of intervening when we can weather the storm with perhaps the least difficulty? These questions are voiced, remarkably enough, by many who have given consistent support to America's global enterprise over the past generation. For those of us who have been skeptical of this enterprise, the questions are at least understandable, if misplaced. But for those who have supported it, they can only appear gratuitous. Even the few among us who have argued for a radical contraction of America's interests and commitments have done so on the assumption that the consequences of an American withdrawal would not be a world in which America's political and economic frontiers were coterminous with her territorial frontiers, and in which societies that share our culture, institutions, and values might very possibly disappear. No doubt, some of us were mistaken in overestimating the extent to which other centers of power were prepared to provide for their own security. I for one am prepared to plead guilty to this, though I am still persuaded that if Western Europe and Japan remain political eunuchs today, the responsibility must be found as much in the character of American foreign policy as in the reaction of those who, while resenting their continued dependence, have been unwilling to make the efforts necessary to change the relationship.

The issue of responsibility apart, the fact is that Western Europe and Japan are still dependent upon the United States for their security. Oil is part of that security, considered in a broader sense than simply physical security, and a very vital part. There is no difficulty, then, in answering the question why we should undertake what would be at best a difficult and distasteful action on behalf of those who, while having a more immediate and compelling interest, are unwilling to act. We would presumably take the action because we have a vital interest in the fate of those unwilling—and unable—to act. Nor should there be any illusions about the inability of Western Europe to cope effectively with the oil crisis. The argument that today's Europe could deal with the Arabs if not for the interference of the Americans is even less persuasive than the argument that today's Europe could deal on its own with the Russians. Indeed, the two arguments are really one, since if the Europeans could in fact deal with the Russians independently of America, then they might well be able to deal with the Arabs. Unfortunately, they can do neither.

In part, an argument applied to the Arabs that would never be seriously applied directly to the Russians stems from a belief that the Arabs would become much more tractable over oil were it not for the support America insists on giving to Israel. In its extreme, though unspoken, version, this is the belief that if Israel could by some magic be exorcized, the position of the Arabs would change overnight. Though it is nonsense, the belief has its attractions and these attractions may yet find wide appeal. Israel does provide an apparent justification for Arab intransigence over oil, even if the justification is transparent. Certainly, the Shah of Iran has had no need of an Israel to justify his intransigence. Nor do the Arabs. The prospect of becoming economic superpowers, with all that this entails, is quite enough.

These considerations are not affected by the consequences that intervention would have on Israel's position. Clearly, intervention would in all likelihood markedly improve that position. It would be both useless and insincere to deny the benefits accruing to Israel from intervention, just as it is both useless and insincere to deny the present linkage between the oil crisis and the steady erosion of Israel's position. What is of relevance here, though, is that the interest in oil would be unchanged with or without Israel. That Israel will be affected, and critically so, whatever the outcome of the oil crisis, is foreordained by geography. To reject consideration of intervention on the grounds that it would be little more than a thinly disguised pro-Israel move is either to ignore this geographical reality or to imply that we must permit, under cover of an apparent "evenhandedness," the almost certain deterioration of Israel's position even at the expense of other interests that are clearly of vital concern to us. In this view is to be found a rare combination of obtuseness and perversity.

VII

THERE remains the argument that military intervention in the Persian Gulf would on moral grounds alone not be countenanced by domestic public opinion. Nor is it only the public that would presumably find in the act a manifestation of complete moral bankruptcy. One has the distinct impression that the foreign-policy elite shares this view and that in the certitude with which the public's supposed reaction is diagnosed there is something close to a wish-fulfilling prophecy. It is a curious reaction coming from those who once found no great difficulty, moral or otherwise, in supporting the intervention in Vietnam or who, in finally abandoning their support for intervention, did so not on moral grounds, but because they concluded Vietnam could not have a successful outcome or that, whatever the outcome, the costs had become disproportionate to the interests at stake. Perhaps their present reaction to the prospect of armed intervention in the Persian Gulf is not so curious, though, given this record. It is not surprising that, having lacked a sense of balance, moral and otherwise, in that most painful experience, they should lack a sense of balance today, and that we should find the law of compensation—or rather of overcompensation—at work.

At issue here is not whether there is some clear moral or legal basis for justifying armed intervention in the Persian Gulf, but whether public opinion would be morally outraged by the action. Though it is not uncommon to find them confused, these are two quite different questions. There is no need for positive moral approval, let alone moral fervor, by the public so long as it consents to the need for the action. There may even be considerable gain in the absence of that element which has so often attended policy in the past. The difficulty, of course, is that the public has been long habituated to support the use of force only in cases which have been made to appear as necessary for the containment of Communism, in turn equated with the nation's security. Could the public be induced, in the shadow of Vietnam, to support a military intervention that bore no apparent or tangible relation to the containment of Communism, itself a factor of diminishing importance in determining the public's disposition? No one can say. Put in the abstract, the question itself may be rather meaningless. It would take on meaning only after a concerted effort had been made to persuade the public that the alternatives to intervention were laden with dangers to the nation's well-being. Even then it remains an open question whether an administration could obtain public support, or tolerance, for intervention in the absence of events at home that, once plainly visible, would require little further effort in persuasion. In this instance, the choice might well be between a public that would oppose intervention so long as the interests at stake were not clear, and could not readily be made clear, and a public that would support intervention only when these interests had unfortunately become only too clear.

The point is worth emphasis that we simply do not know what might bring the public to support intervention in the Persian Gulf. If the public viewed such intervention as another Vietnam, they would most assuredly oppose it. But if intervention were to promise success at relatively modest cost, opinion might well move in the direction of support, and particularly if unemployment were to rise to 8 or 9 per cent. Moreover, in this instance, by contrast to Vietnam, the existence of an all-volunteer military force would preclude the painful issues once raised by the draft. Nor is it at all clear that the Left would take the same position toward intervention in the present case as it did toward Vietnam. For the effects of the current oil price on many poor countries do not endear the major oil producers to much of the Left. The relative ease with which Vietnam could be depicted as an attempt to preserve American domination over the developing states, a domination alleged to serve only American interests, would be difficult to repeat today, and this despite the inadequately perceived effects of the oil crisis.

VIII

It is instructive that on the few occasions military intervention has been discussed in the context of the oil crisis, such discussion has almost invariably proceeded by making what are very close to worst-case assumptions.

The outcome of the exercise is thus all but foreclosed, particularly once Russian counter-intervention is assumed. This insistance upon finding catastrophe in every corner if military intervention were undertaken affords a striking contrast to past behavior. It is surely not to be decried for that reason; a greater concern for the liabilities attending the use of force would have served us well in the last decade. Even so, a virtual obsession with worst-case assumptions has its own pathology of inaction. In this instance, it suggests that when men do not wish to undertake a certain course of action, they will find any number of reasons for not doing so.

A plausible case for rejecting intervention out of hand cannot be made to rest upon the argument no one would care to deny—that the successful use of force in the Persian Gulf depends upon our having the answers to many questions which we simply cannot answer with assurance. The evident implication of the argument is that in the absence of these answers we are far better advised to continue on the present and presumably the known course. But the present course also has its uncertainties, and by this time we have little excuse for not appreciating how numerous and potentially serious they may be. It is a sobering exercise to review the record of the very recent past and to find how badly off the mark almost all predictions of the nature and magnitude of the oil crisis have been. Even those who seemed at the time Cassandras, in retrospect appear as unguarded optimists. In dizzying succession one demand has led almost as soon as it was made to yet another. As a result, little confidence is left in the stability of a situation that has already brought us to an impasse which presently affords no politically discernible way out. In these circumstances it is excessive, to say the least, to insist that the many uncertainties admittedly attending intervention be answered with assurance before the use of force can be seriously considered. Equally, it is excessive to insist that before using force one must exhaust all other remedies, when the exhaustion of all other remedies is little more than the functional equivalent of accepting chaos. What may be reasonably demanded is a critical weighing—however rough and approximate it must necessarily be—of the uncertainties and dangers attending military intervention as opposed to the hazards of continuing along the present course. Those who dismiss intervention refuse even to make the effort.

Instead, we are almost daily subjected to speculation about the more profound dimensions of our predicament. Confronted with "impossible alternatives," many find an apparent solace in substituting philosophy for policy. Europeans are heard to argue that the West is now paying the price for the past century or more. In America, there is the now fashionable theme—naturally enough yesterday's heresy—that we have reached the outer edges of our power and that we must learn to accommodate ourselves to events and trends we may comprehend but cannot alter. A supposedly deeper historical understanding—the new maturity, as it were—thus leads to a kind of quietism. *Tout comprendre c'est tout pardonner.* The dilemmas of action are thereby overcome by denying their reality. This detached wisdom of passivity has no doubt its proper place. It may even express the truth about our present plight, though if it does, the more practical conclusions that should be drawn from it are scarcely the conclusions which are commonly drawn. It is equally plausible to surmise, however, that the obsession with the West's past sins, and the sudden attraction to events and trends beyond our control to alter, are often little more than rationalizations of political incompetence and the failure of will.

At the same time, an apparent pessimism and resignation before the inevitable may, and often does, conceal an optimism that takes for granted that we will somehow have our way in the end. If force is ruled out, it is in part because we assume, whether consciously or unconsciously, that the Arabs are, after all, still only Arabs, and that in the deadly game we are now playing with them, generations of political superiority and economic supremacy must count for something. To this assumption is added the belief that we still do hold the trumps when all is said and done. No longer able to comfort ourselves with yesterday's thought that the Arabs cannot drink their oil, we have been able to find a serviceable substitute in today's thought that the Arabs cannot bury their dollars. The hostages thereby turn out to be the hostage-holders, since foreign debt can always be wiped out through default and foreign investment can always be redeemed through expropriation. One can only hope that this latest argument designed to reassure us that all will end well enjoys a better fate than its predecessor.

THERE is much more than this in the explanation of the refusal seriously to consider force as an alternative in the oil crisis.

It has been said many times, though it bears repeating, that we are confronted here with a special case in that it involves actions which have long been regarded as within the sovereign prerogatives of states. The exclusive control a state may exercise over its natural resources implies the power, or license, to take such action as has resulted in the present crisis. To this must be added the legacy of Vietnam which evidently weighs heavily upon those who in the broadest sense managed the war, and probably much more so than it weighs upon the public at large. Finally, there is the pervasive and still growing conviction among the foreign-policy elites, a conviction clearly related to though not identifiable with the Vietnam experience, that military power has lost most of its former utility. The concomitant of this conviction is that force has also lost its legitimacy, save in the most restrictively defined circumstances.

These considerations round out, in all likelihood, the explanation for the current rejection of force as a real option in the Middle East. To treat them with the care they deserve would carry us far beyond the confines of this essay. Here it must suffice to point out that it is almost always the "special cases" which constitute the classic dilemmas of statecraft. It may be true that although the price set by the oil cartel constitutes very injurious action toward consumer states, there is little in international law that forbids such behavior. But in this sense, the Cuban missile crisis also was a special case, since there was little, if anything, in international law and practice that forbade the Soviet Union from sending nuclear missiles to Cuba or Cuba from accepting them. The critical issue at stake in the Cuban missile crisis was not whether the actions precipitating the crisis were within the sovereign prerogatives of states, but whether in the exercise of those prerogatives, the vital interests of other states were placed in jeopardy. It is the same issue that is in question in the oil crisis, however one cares to answer this question. Moreover, the same issue would remain if the Arab states were to impose an embargo, and this time a serious embargo. In imposing an embargo, no less than in imposing an unsupportable oil price, the Arab states would be exercising their sovereign rights over the disposal of their natural resources. There are those who nevertheless are now prepared to draw a line here and to insist that an embargo would be a just cause for force. But if the price for oil promises the same effects ultimately as an embargo, it is not easy to see the legal or moral basis for the distinction thereby drawn.

There is little to be served by making once again the already well-worn and unavoidably abrasive observations on the legacy of Vietnam. But it is important to address, however briefly, the broad conviction that armed force has lost most of its former utility and legitimacy. If this conviction is well-founded, then those who hold it should draw the appropriate conclusions for American foreign policy. The principal conclusion to be drawn—that the present structure of American interests in the world must change, and radically so—may be avoided only by assuming that in place of an obsolete policy of power and intervention we may substitute a policy of pacific interdependence rather than one that clearly points toward isolationism. The oil crisis is providing us with a supreme object lesson in the politics of interdependence, though, and to date the lesson is not very reassuring. If there is a moral to be drawn from the crisis that bears on the new interdependence, it is that interdependence is all too likely a prelude to a new autarchy—at least for those who can afford it. That, after all, is the meaning of "Project Independence."

In truth, however, the oil crisis is not a manifestation of interdependence in the sense that proponents of interdependence have in mind when using the term. Nor is it, clearly, a manifestation of the "old politics." Instead, it is the latest manifestation—though by far the most spectacular to date—of an egalitarianism which, if permitted to run its logical course, is likely to result first in chaos and then in an international system far harsher than today's, or even yesterday's, system.

War—The Ultimate Antitrust Action

By Andrew Tobias

With the world walking along the edge of financial collapse, depression, and massive human suffering (in the less-developed countries), a number of influential people—most notably the president of the United States and his secretary of state—have recently begun talking about how unthinkable, as a solution to our oil-related economic problems, military action would be. That in turn has started some people thinking about military action.

Even before the twin Ford/Kissinger speeches of September 23, which a Kissinger aide confirms were indeed coordinated, serious people were considering—and almost unanimously rejecting—war as a solution to our problems. They are still almost unanimously rejecting it. But that they would consider it at all is a measure of the gravity of the world situation.

And there are those few serious people who have considered it and, privately, advocate it. (Whether they would actually give the command if it were theirs to give is another story.) Early in September, before talk of confrontation was making headlines, the director of research of a prominent Wall Street firm told me that he thought the United States should, now, seize the Saudi Arabian oil fields, or get someone else to do it for us. A well-respected leader of the financial community, strictly off the record, agreed. And while neither anticipated immediate action, both thought that a violent outbreak over the Persian Gulf oil treasure, in one form or another, was almost inevitable.

Walter Levy, the best-known international oil expert, while he does not advocate the use of force, fears that nations may be driven to irrational acts—and in the not too distant future —if what he calls "unmanageable oil prices" are not reduced.

"My initial reaction to that whole military scenario," a Federal Energy Administration official told me, "is that it's a bunch of goddamned New York bankers trying to protect their investments overseas."

In fact, opinions among New York bankers vary. But it's true that they have been thinking about the problem. "Jesus, your timing is uncanny," one investment banker told me, again before the president's speech in Detroit. "We had a long debate about that last night." I interviewed both sides of the debate and offer them as being fairly typical of what's being said these days:

NAVY PINSTRIPE: "If things really get bad in this country, the potential social upheavals will force the government to look outside. And if the government wants to preserve itself, or if the system wants to preserve itself, it will naturally have to take into consideration what the hell are 6 million people in Saudi Arabia or 3 million people in Libya or 1 million people in the Trucial States—what the hell right do they have, as it would be put, to put us out of business, in effect? And when people get desperate, they can find plenty of rationalizations. 'We found that oil, we invested in it, we had contracts for it. . . .' You can make thousands of arguments.

"The American people are just not going to put up with not owning their own houses, with high unemployment . . . the American people will turn, aggressively, to look for the cause. ["My clients are really enraged," an institutional salesman told me, "that we could have lost so much in Vietnam, and then here, where our vital interests are at stake, we do nothing."]

"I don't see this happening in the immediate future because there are a lot of steps that can be taken in the interim to conserve energy in this country. And I think Ford is setting up these summits as a way of preparing the public for severe measures that have to be taken. As a result, there will be a period of a year, or whatever, while these measures are being taken, and while there is still hope of getting this thing under control. But I think it will be very hard to reorient a ship that's so far turned. (I'm not saying, by the way, that I think the Arabs are the only ones responsible for our problems; American economic policies—guns *and* butter, etc.—are responsible, too. Not to mention just the weather.)

"You know, six months ago this would have been looked on as totally unacceptable conversation, okay? Today it's acceptable, and almost reasonable, but people have an emotional revulsion to war and it's talked about in muted tones. Six months from now I think it's something that will be talked about among serious people as a serious alternative. And a year from now I think it might be fashionable."

CHARCOAL PINSTRIPE: "I think it's a totally crazy idea. There might conceivably be a scenario where it could be justified—if they refused to sell us any oil at all, for example—and the argument might have some more weight after we had gone through some very austere moments . . . but to consider it now?

"The argument for doing it, you know, can best be summed up: 'Are we going to let a bunch of desert *nomads* hold us ransom and hold the *whole world* ransom—these people who live in *tents*?' And in fact I heard that expressed with a certain amount of sincerity by the president of an international copper company.

"But besides its being offensive, it's ludicrous. Saudi Arabia happens to be one of our close allies. We would so shock and horrify our friends the Iranians they would wonder what good it is to be an ally of these guys. Not to mention the rest of the oil-producing countries.

"You know, invading Saudi Arabia is not what the cold war equation is all about. The Soviet Union would probably oppose us and oppose us very strongly were we to consider such a thing."

NAVY PINSTRIPE: "It's my personal point of view that the Russians will never fight a war with the Americans over something other than an invasion of Eastern Europe or the Soviet Union. The Russians, in my negotiations with them [Navy Pinstripe does a lot of East-West trade deals], are very prudent and cautious people. They drive a hard bargain and are full of bluster—until they see that you are really walking away. And I think they would do the same thing here. If they knew that it meant survival to the West, and that we meant business, the Russians would never fight a war over people that they themselves don't respect. Remember, the Arabs are not liked in Russia. You don't think the Russians are going to risk their whole country for Libya, do you? [A variant of this argument is that we would "simply make a deal with the Russians." Another wheat deal, perhaps.]

"There is no question in my mind that seizing and maintaining the Saudi oil fields would be a minor operation from our point of view."

CHARCOAL PINSTRIPE: "Bullshit. You can't get marines over there until you start flying them, and you can't produce a massive airlift without mobilizing a certain amount of our own forces; or else you would have to send the bloody Sixth Fleet [Charcoal Pinstripe is a lieutenant commander in the reserves] all the way around the horn of Africa and get it off the coast of Saudi Arabia—unless you wanted to march them across Egypt and across the canal and down the Sinai Peninsula, and eventually into Saudi Arabia. If you did manage to take it over, you would have a tremendous amount of patrolling to do to try to prevent sabotage of the pipelines, which extend all over the country, and you'd end up with a mini-Algeria.

"And I think from a cold war point of view this would have horrendous results. And it would have absolutely no justification in fact! This inflation problem has been largely self-created, and we cannot blame the Arabs for it. In Italy it's the militant trade unions, more than the Arabs, who have gotten things so messed up. The Arabs have done something that is perfectly rational from their standpoint—they've got a dwindling asset and they're trying to make it as valuable as they can.

"You know, one of the things that traditionally happen—it happened in Germany, it happened in Japan—is the foreign-devil theory, where people take internal domestic problems and say these are caused by the foreign devils who are raping the country, and all that sort of thing. I would be very concerned if we had some demagogue say that the way to get out of this is to beat the Arabs up and get cheap, abundant oil. It's a dangerous topic; people get easily carried away."

Around this point in the typical debate one party starts talking about the United States as a diabetic and the Arabs as withholding our insulin unless we pay outrageous prices; the other party talks of the United States as a heroin addict about to mug the Middle East; and the first party insists that it's the Middle East mugging the heroin addict—and that being hooked on energy is more constructive than being hooked on heroin.

But it is time to open the discussion to the rest of the wardrobe of opinion. *Could* we, technically, pull off an invasion of one of the nations belonging to the Organization of Petroleum Exporting Countries (O.P.E.C.) and keep the oil flowing? (Saudia Arabia is the country most often considered, because it has most of the world's oil, a small population, and an even smaller army. Though, in fact, it is the Venezuelans and the Iranians who seem to be putting the screws to us most tightly.) If so, *should* we do such a thing? And in any case, might we or some other country try it?

Herman Kahn, the futurist: "It would be fairly easy to knock over any one of those countries—but you got to go in and kill people to do it. It's very difficult to kill people on an enterprise that's immoral, illegal, and long-lasting. Day after day those pictures would show up on television: two Arabs killed, ten Arabs killed." Herman Kahn doesn't see it happening. We haven't the stomach to mount such an enterprise now, he says.

Tad Szulc, the journalist: "It would be a terribly foolish thing to do, open a can of worms—but having said that, there is always someone who is foolish enough to do something like this."

Someone like us, perhaps? "Look," Szulc says, "there's contingency planning for anything you want to mention, because there are an awful lot of colonels and generals who do nothing but plan contingencies, you know. And I think every government has got a contingency plan for invading the moon, with conventional forces. But I just don't see anybody at this stage making such a decision. Now, what happens six months from now. . . . Obviously there is no policy here."

A noted British financier: "Well, I would think it's unlikely in the course of a year. I would think the time for that kind of talk would have been back when the increases were put on. America doesn't suffer enough from this, and America is really the power that is most likely to get round to that line of thought. Japan is the other one.

Professor M. A. Adelman, of M.I.T., has never been considered "soft" on what he terms "Arab blackmail." In fact *Forbes* labeled him a "gunboat professor." But under most circumstances, he would not advocate an attempt to seize the oil.

"What I am told," he says, "is that such an operation would be feasible if you mounted a sufficiently large effort from the beginning. Which means you've got to have all your technicians on board, land them quickly, and get started. You can restore oil fields that have been blown up. Experience in World War II indicates that.

"But whether it should be done all depends on what the alternatives are. If you had a cutback of 25 per cent of the oil production in most of these countries, the way you had last fall, I would suppose that it would be an overreaction, and you wouldn't want to do it. If there had been a 100 per cent cutback, or even a good deal less than that, then it's not a question anymore of should it be done—it just would be done. Because the nations wouldn't let themselves starve and freeze in the dark. Period. And you can quote me on that, because it seems just obvious. I'm not even advocating anything. There's nothing to advocate. The consuming countries would just move in. It's just like predicting a change in the weather, only with a much greater chance of success."

And what if production were not cut back substantially, but prices were kept at the current level or even raised a bit? Send in the marines? "It's just not true," insists the gunboat professor, "that we can't live over the next five years with these prices. You can keep these figures in mind, and you can quote them: the O.P.E.C. loot amounts to about $100 billion a year, and world G.N.P. is about $5,000 billion. So it's a matter of 2 per cent. Well, the world can live with that. Now, for countries like the U.S.A., it just means that we pay a bit more. We transfer our wealth abroad in return for oil. In countries like India, it really is an acute crisis and undoubtedly it means starvation for many thousands of Indians. But rightly or wrongly, India and countries like it do not have the political power to do much about it, and indeed they've been almost as painfully obsequious and lickspittle to the producing countries as the United States has.

"So, like it or not, the world can take it perfectly well, and will take it, and I would say nobody can have much confidence in whether prices go much higher or much lower, but I give a slight edge to prices going higher."

As for the damage that massive "petrodollar" accumulations are causing the world financial system, Adelman agrees the damage is real, but maintains it is "essentially a temporary problem."

If you can't get a gunboat professor to salute when you run this invasion scenario up the flagpole, you won't get as much as a click-of-the-heels from within the State Department itself. "It makes no sense whatsoever," My Source told me with what *appeared* to be spontaneous sincerity. (After reading *Tinker, Tailor, Soldier, Spy*—or, come to think of it, the Watergate tape transcripts—I take nothing at face value.) "People talk about seizing the Saudi oil fields? There are so many reasons . . . it's the most absurd thing I've ever heard of. That's my problem, I guess [in being a little at a loss for words], because in the first place, I can't conceive of a situation so shortly after Vietnam where this would be generally accepted by the American people—unless it, you know, I could, I suppose, imagine a situation if our industry had ground to a halt because we didn't have oil that maybe if it got bad enough the frustration level might reach a point where it might be acceptable, but certainly it would take a great deal more than the currently foreseeable problems. Beyond that, the number of forces that would necessarily be involved would be great. Quite great. And beyond that, nobody in his right mind would expect the Soviets to stand by and watch it happen. So I just think there are any number of reasons why it's patently absurd."

In his speech to the U.N. last month Kissinger scared hell out of some people when he said, "What has gone up by political decision [O.P.E.C. oil prices] can be reduced by political decision [the question is, whose?]." But My Source, who "worked closely with Henry on this speech," says that "in the first place, it never entered our heads that the speech in *any way* implied any form of military intervention. In fact, I can read through the entire thing and not find a veiled threat anywhere, though I will admit that that's to a degree because I'm too close to it, and maybe fresh eyes can read it and say, 'Aha! There's a veiled threat.'

"I think it was a gloomy speech—I think it was a gloomy subject. But I don't accept that it was threatening in any way."

And, in fact, taken at face value and read in its entirety—not in snippets out of context—the speech seems more an urgent call to cooperation than a call to arms. Talking about nuclear proliferation, massive starvation, and the breakdown of world economic order, Kissinger was pointing out, urgently, that these are threats inherent in the present world situation—and that therefore cooperation is essential. You can read that "Cooperate or we'll beat your brains out." Or you can read it "We must all cooperate, or we shall sink together." The only thing is, admittedly—and, really, it goes without saying—if the O.P.E.C. countries gave us no alternative but to fight or sink, we would certainly fight.

"I just can't believe that they would be that uncompromising," a vice-president of Morgan Guaranty Trust with considerable expertise in the Middle East told me, "and that they would fail to recognize the threat they would be posing to the world economy. Because they would certainly be running themselves into the ground. I mean, I don't think they have a sort of suicidal urge to bring everybody down—quite the contrary. I think the chances are good that reason will prevail. I get the impression that the decision-makers on both sides are pretty responsible, in the final analysis, and realize that we are interdependent. I'm not alarmed, in other words, personally.

"Take the open letter to President Ford from the president of Venezuela. It's pretty verbose, if you like, but in the middle of all that it's pretty conciliatory. He's saying, 'We're willing to work things out.' He didn't promise anything, but he certainly didn't say, you know, 'Forget it.' And I think his letter is representative of most of the thinking in O.P.E.C."

There are, in all, thirteen members of O.P.E.C., but the two most important are Saudi Arabia and Iran:

Saudi Arabia has most of the world's oil and is a traditional ally, staunchly anti-Communist. We have 6,000 military advisers in Saudi Arabia, ranging from generals to master sergeants, and we are building an air defense system for them, which will be ready around 1978 or 1979. The Saudis have said they want to lower the cost of oil. One reason is to help us; the other reason is to hurt Iran, whom the Saudis fear. Iran, with 30 million people, a sophisticated army, and the beginning of a powerful economy, can use all the money its oil will bring, and so a cut in price means slowing down its military and economic expansion, whereas a cut in oil revenue for the Saudis means nothing. There are two reasons why the Saudis have not pushed down the price. First, they are afraid of their more populous and more militant neighbors. Second, King Faisal is a very religious man. "I think the religious thing is probably dominant," says an official of the Federal Energy Administration involved in international affairs. "It's not economics. You know, King Faisal is old, and praying in Jerusalem may be his life's goal at this stage. That's why some people think we are going to have a renewal of the embargo this winter. And that's not at all impossible if things don't progress politically.

"I think Yamani [the oil minister] would genuinely like to lower prices. He's more Western oriented [Harvard Law, 1955-56], and he has a better appreciation of the Iranian threat. But the power, of course, is with the king. And he sees things more in terms of Arab brotherhood."

Iran is not an Arab country. The shah has visions (literally) of Iran's becoming a major power, and to that end, I'm told, either has in hand or on order two destroyers from Litton Industries, a couple of aircraft carriers he is trying to lease, 850 Chieftain tanks from Britain, 600 helicopters, about 110 Phantoms, 80 F-14's, and so forth and so on. In the words of one war buff, "This guy's building up an incredible military force."

Which means if we ever wanted to invade Iran, we had best waste no time whatever. However, it is unlikely we would ever want to invade Iran. Inasmuch as she, also, is a close ally and staunchly anti-Communist. More likely, Iran will in a few years (if not sooner) invade her unfriendly, Communist neighbor to the west, Iraq (an oil producer of modest proportions), and then, while she's at it, perhaps knock off Kuwait, too—perhaps splitting these two prizes with Saudi Arabia, to keep that country quiet, or even going all the way and attempting to seize the Saudi oil fields (which are conveniently in the eastern part of the country, on the Gulf), plus Abu Dhabi, Oman, and Qatar. That would leave Iran, in the words of novelist Paul Erdman, who has been working on all this for his next book, "with (a) all the oil in the world, (b) all the money in the world, and (c) the most important real estate in the Middle East."

It is precisely the Saudi dependence on us to keep such a thing from happening that should be our point of leverage in this situation—but so far it hasn't done us much good.

There is no question that the consuming countries are in a bind. *The New York Times* has said, repeatedly, that we "must take effective economic action against the international oil cartel" to force down the price of oil. Unfortunately, there is no very effective economic action we can take. A food boycott would never work—the relatively little food O.P.E.C. needs would come from someone; perhaps even the Russians. *The Wall Street Journal* is not the only one to have called *The Times*'s proposal to limit the amount of funds O.P.E.C. could invest in any one consuming country "silly." And while it is certainly vital for us to cut back energy consumption and pull out all stops in increasing production—this may not be enough to force down oil prices. About the only way to "force" prices down is with what you might call the ultimate antitrust action. Force. But even that, if it were done half-heartedly, could prove unsuccessful or disastrous. Less dramatic, but more probable, perhaps, are the peaceful ways in which the world may muddle through:

In the first place, there is the possibility, simply, of compromise between producers and consumers. Even if that compromise is reached with the threat of war lurking in the background. As Walter Levy puts it: "Fundamentally, you know, I take the position: you do not produce oil sitting on bayonets. I don't know what you do when you take over a country by force. You have guerrilla movements, you have destruction of facilities and all these kinds of problems. But who knows what happens when people are desperate? I believe the important thing from our side as well as the producing side is to avoid it. And the mere fact that certain things may occur that make no sense whatever, but which would be extremely destructive to us as well as the producing countries—that may be the means through which agreement is achieved. You know, the deterrent effect of, what should I say, potentially irrational behavior. Which I would never advocate, but it's there, the danger."

Second, there is the possibility of the United States' guaranteeing Israel's pre-1967 borders, both to protect Israel from attack from without, and to protect her neighbors from attack from within. Along with, presumably, some compromise on Jerusalem. This might mollify much of the Arab intransigence on oil prices and production. It would be an expensive and unpleasant position to be put in, but less so than the position we're currently in.

Third, there is the possibility that the cartel will simply fall apart, as cartels have been known to do. So far this one has proved surprisingly strong. But if the world cuts back its oil demands sharply, through conservation measures, then the cartel would in turn have to cut back its production (and revenues) sharply in order to maintain the price. And it is in allocating cutbacks that cartels generally fail. Iran, for example, might be unwilling to cut back very much at all. Why then would Saudi Arabia and Kuwait agree to cut back? They have no interest in strengthening Iran; and to Saudi Arabia, with oil reserves of perhaps 100 years, a barrel not sold today is in effect put at the end of the line and not sold for 100 years—which in current dollars makes it virtually worthless. "This idea that a barrel of oil in the ground is as valuable as a barrel in the bank is a lot of crap," says Herman Kahn, of the Hudson Institute, who expects the price of oil to *decline* steadily over the next few years—even if, for face-saving reasons, the price remains constant while world inflation gradually eats away at the real price.

(Even if a program of stringent energy conservation did not actually force a price reduction from the cartel, it would go a long way to solving the problem, at least in this country. According to the Federal Energy Administration, for example, in 1972, the latest year for which figures are available, there were 34 million "small" passenger cars on the road, and 62 million "standards," which includes everything else. The small cars averaged just under 22 miles per gallon; the standards, just over eleven. Simply by switching from standards to small cars—from Impalas to Vegas—we would save 1.8 million barrels of oil a day, give or take—or about *30 per cent* of our total imports. And 30 per cent of the outflow of our wealth into O.P.E.C. hands. Obviously this switch cannot be made overnight. But while it's happening, the same oil could be saved by driving slower, driving smoother, and, as a last resort, actually—dare I say it?—driving less. Adding similar energy savings from heating, air conditioning, lighting, and industry, one can imagine that the "unconscionable ransom" we are being forced to pay for oil might be reduced to next to nothing. This is why measures like a really large excise tax on gasoline, the proceeds of which could be returned in the form of a tax credit to low- and middle-income taxpayers, might be a good idea.)

Fourth, there is some reason to think that even if the price does not come down, we can live with it. Rimmer de Vries, vice-president of the Morgan bank, outlined this case persuasively on September 23 at a conference in Beirut. De Vries does not believe that actual dollar accumulations will be anything like the World Bank forecast, by which O.P.E.C. member countries would build up $650 billion in excess reserves by 1980 and $1.2 trillion by 1985. He assumes that demand for O.P.E.C. oil will grow more slowly than was projected when prices were one-fifth their current level, whereas imports by the O.P.E.C. countries from consuming countries will rise very rapidly. He also expects foreign aid from O.P.E.C. countries to the less-developed countries to rise substantially. Under his assumptions, the O.P.E.C. reserve funds would peak four or five years from now at around $300 billion, by which time O.P.E.C. expenditures would equal revenues. Huge as this figure is, de Vries thinks it is not beyond the ability of the world financial system to handle.

If, in fact, the world can manage for the next four or five years, then prospects may improve substantially. By then oil from the North Slope of Alaska and from the North Sea should be flowing (Britain hopes to be an *exporter* of oil by 1980), and much of the exploration that is going on now will undoubtedly be bearing fruit. Five years from now we might also have made some progress running our nuclear plants, or even in exploiting in greater amounts our 3.2 trillion tons of coal.

Such a mess. It's enough to make the stock market go down and down, while stock in Northrop, a defense contractor with a lot of Middle Eastern contracts, hits new highs.

It is frustrating that our friends the Arabs and the Venezuelans and the Canadians, et al., seem so unsympathetic to what we perceive as urgent global problems; and frustrating that we consuming countries, with all our economic power, can do relatively little about it. And in frustration lie the seeds of irrationality.

Nor do the Arabs make it easier for us to keep our heads when they say they have raised oil prices to compensate for the inflation of *our* exports, and that if we lower our prices, they will consider lowering theirs. Number one, oil prices have vastly outstripped world prices as a whole. Number two, the O.P.E.C. countries broke long-term contracts and allowed consumers no time whatever to adjust—which, when the commodity is as indispensable as oil and the screws are turned as tight as they have been, would seem to qualify as a highly hostile act. Number three, the O.P.E.C. countries export so much more than they import that Western inflation does not even begin to justify the 400 per cent hike in the price of oil. We could give the Saudis *free* food if they cut oil prices 5 per cent!

One hopes that out of the jawboning and posturing and outrageous demands will come a good old-fashioned compromise. But it is almost as though we were being baited. If and when America will lose its collective temper, however unjustified we might be, and however imperialistic or callous that might make us look, is not an idle question. And that it is not—that war could be considered by serious people as a last resort to our economic problems—is almost enough to make you join a car pool.

How to Blow Up an Oil Well

Conversations with officials at three oil and pipeline companies suggest that, if we seized the Saudi oil fields, we could probably keep a good deal of oil flowing, despite the inevitable harassment. It could take a while, though, to get production going again if the Saudis used any imagination in blowing up the fields when they saw our choppers landing.

Pipelines are the most vulnerable, but least effective, point of sabotage. Not only are they easily patrolled in the desert—you can see for ten miles from a helicopter, I'm told—they are also no cinch to blow up. "The pipe they've got there is 30 and 36 inches, most of it, of solid welded steel half an inch or more thick. A roving band of eight or ten guerrillas with a couple of hand grenades—they would have a hell of a time blowing it up. It takes someone who knows what he's doing," one engineer told me. Moreover, if the right men and equipment are on hand, a pipeline break can be mended in a matter of a day or two.

"If you really wanted to shut a country down," I was told, "you would go after the wells and the pump stations. But to really wreck a pump station you'd have to have some technical expertise and an awful lot of dynamite, because the equipment is heavy and it doesn't blow apart too easily." Still, to a saboteur it would be worth the effort, because one well-blown pump station can shut a pipeline down for six months or more. Ninety days, minimum. "Of course there are numbers of countries and numbers of pipelines," mused another of my engineers, rising to the intellectual challenge, "but I must say that with the right men and the right equipment I might be able to keep 80 per cent of it knocked out of operation."

Yet the kind of "Yankee know-how" this would take would be on the side of keeping the oil flowing, and this man goes on to say, "I believe if a military effort were exerted you could get the oil out reasonably well and manage under conditions of harassment. (Unless, of course, the Russians wanted to come in and zap you.) But it wouldn't be easy." The others agreed.

As for the wells themselves, the usual procedure—to do it right—is, "you maybe drop a charge down the well and then maybe pour cement, pour junk, scrap iron, rails—anything you can get down through the bore of the well. That kind of just wrecks the whole situation."

But even so, he says, "with competent drilling contractors and a lot of money behind you you could still bring the field back in six months or a year. Actually, oil and gas installations are really pretty hard to take out of service for any length of time unless you control the real estate around them. They're pretty hard to take out from the air, because oil stuff is spread out, you know." Of course, we've been selling our friends there some pretty sensational weapons.

—A. T.

THE NEED FOR NEGOTIATED REFORMS

JOHN H. JACKSON

Let me begin by first dealing with a few of the remarks made by Stanley Metzger. I have had some conversations with him over the past year or two on the subject that he has raised. One of the things that interests me is how Professor Metzger recognizes himself to be a "minority of one" in his appraisal of the Trade Act of 1974,[1] in the sense that so many other groups, including economists, do not seem to share his pessimism about the statute.

I must say that this statute *is* something of a disappointment. I do not mean to defend it in all its particularities, even though I had a hand in drafting it. In fact, I can say that I have the best of two worlds: I think I can claim some credit for a few of the good things in the Act, but I left the government before some of the disappointing things happened. In any event, I do think there is some cause for optimism, and I want to review a few of those in the context of the topic today.

First, I would like to look at the statute and at the international trade negotiation. After that I shall turn to the question of so-called short supply, which in a sense is hard to discuss in the broader context of international trade reform. It is so new that it is difficult to grasp the contours of what we need or what we mean in terms of international trade reform in the context of the short supply problem, if indeed there is one.

As to the statute, one must ask whether we are better with it or without it at any given point in time. It was my judgment throughout most of the last two years, and I am glad this judgment was shared by many people, that we *are* better with it. There was a point when I was a bit nervous about it. However, I would reiterate one

1. Trade Act of 1974, Pub. L. No. 93-618, 88 Stat. 1978.

of the points Stanley Metzger mentioned—the escape clause[2] of the 1962 statute has posed some very real problems over the decade for the management of the United States trade policy. I do not say that in an "ideal world" we would not have been able to live with it, but we did not have an ideal world and there were protectionist pressures rising. One of the functions of an escape clause is to let a little steam out of those pressures so that we might avoid the kinds of encouragement, the kinds of pressures, the kinds of developments toward protectionism, that resulted in a number of measures in the 1960s, including for instance, a textile agreement, the steel voluntary agreement, and others. Thus, one of the reforms examined in depth by the Williams Commission involved the escape clause, and I would say that the Williams Commission provided the basic intellectual framework for a good deal of the trade bill.

I would also say that the basic overall results conformed not too discouragingly with the recommendations of the Williams Commission Report.[3] With respect to the escape clause itself, one of the ideas was to break the so-called "link" with trade concessions. As you are aware, in order to get an affirmative finding from the Tariff Commission, it was necessary to show that injury in domestic industries was due to increased imports, and in turn those increased imports were due to some trade concessions.[4] It was thought that the latter causal connection put such a restriction on the opportunity to get an escape clause that it was bottling up these various pres-

---

2. *See* 19 U.S.C. § 1901(b) (1970) providing in part:

> Upon the request of the President upon resolution of either the Committee on Finance of the Senate or the Committee on Ways and Means of the House of Representatives, upon its own motion, or upon the filing of a petition, the Tariff Commission shall promptly make an investigation to determine whether, as a result in major part of concessions granted under trade agreements, an article is being imported into the United States in such increased quantities *as to cause, or threaten to cause, serious injury to the domestic industry* producing an article which is like or directly competitive with the imported article.
>
> . . . .
>
> . . . [I]ncreased imports shall be considered to cause, or threaten to cause, serious injury to the domestic industry concerned when the Tariff Commission finds that such increased imports *have been the major factor in causing, or threatening to cause, such injury.*

Id. (emphasis added).

3. Commission on International Trade and Investment Policy, United States International Economic Policy in an Interdependent World (1971) [hereinafter cited as Williams Comm'n Report].

4. *See* note 2 *supra*.

sures. The Williams Commission faced the general policy issue of whether there ought to be means for adjustment, including the possibility of import relief, in the case where imports were causing injury to industry, regardless of whether there was a trade or tariff concession on the items.[5] I must say that by this time, however, there were so many trade and tariff concessions that one could almost find the trade and tariff concession "link" in any situation if one were willing to rely on a loose causal-type connection. In any event, the Williams Commission's judgment was to break the link to concessions. It was recognized that it has some risks. I still think it has some risks, the effects of which can only be determined over time.

As to the respective powers of the International Trade Commission (formerly the Tariff Commission) and the President, however, I was much encouraged with the way matters unrolled this past fall. The House and Senate Trade Act conference was able to restore a great deal of discretion in the President allowing him to refrain from using import restraint in the case of an affirmative finding by the Trade Commission. Not only is it stated that the President may find in the national interest that the imposition of import restraints would be harmful, but he is also authorized to, and indeed must, take into account a large number of other factors. Those factors include some interesting ideas, for example, the effects on consumers, the possibility of adjustment assistance (now modestly revised in levels of help, but greatly opened up in terms of access under the new Act), and matters that might effect economic relationships with our allies or trading partners. All these considerations can be factored in.[6] So, in one sense, despite the terrors of Watergate and other such problems, we may have increased the possibility of a President holding the line against protectionist forces. It remains to be seen how this will work, and, as I mentioned earlier, there are some risks.

But what is to be gained through the Trade Act? I think that the principal gain, and one that has been overlooked by some of the developing countries in their chagrin about the preference title, is the opportunity now for the United States to participate fully in and move forward with the trade negotiation. I have been asked if the trade negotiation is designed to provide any progress, or intended simply to hold the line. I cannot answer that question. I think that the original design was to provide for *some* progress, but even if it

5. Williams Comm'n Report, *supra* note 3, at 45—69.

6. Trade Act of 1974, Pub. L. No. 93-618, §§ 201—84, 88 Stat. 2011—41.

merely preserves the status quo, I think that would be a real contribution.

Perhaps my optimism is of the same intensity as Stanley Metzger's pessimism. He sees the glass half empty and I see it half full. In that sense, if we do hold the line, I think that would be a significant contribution. During all the turmoil, with the great stress on the balance of payments, during the past year, we have not had a competing deterioration of trade by import restrictions throughout the world. That is partly due to the point that Professor Metzger mentioned, namely the so-called "standstill" agreement.[7] It has operated in the context of the monetary arrangements, not using import trade account measures in an attempt to correct the problem of the oil balance of payments which Mr. Southard was mentioning. We have facing us at least a device for holding the line, namely the ongoing international negotiation.

Let me turn to that a moment—what can the negotiation do? There is a whole spectrum of possibilities. I think that it will probably take some time for the negotiation to get rolling. In fact, some say that there may not be anything very significant accomplished until after the 1976 presidential election, for obvious political reasons. As you come to recognize the very real problems of executive branch credibility in negotiations abroad, it may well be that nothing significant will occur until 1976 except to hold the line against protectionist pressures that may develop in this country and abroad. But there are some things that can be done.

First, in my view, this series of trade negotiations should be the last so-called "round" of trade negotiations. That view is not yet widely shared. I am putting it forward, partly to share with you today and to explain what I mean. We have, since 1947, developed a pattern of having spurts or surges of trade and tariff negotiations. The idea goes something like this: you have a major round of negotiations and every thing works in an interrelated fashion. On the last day of the authority, you somehow miraculously come to some sort of agreement, with everything in its place, and you have some sort of reciprocity.

That technique is becoming outmoded. I am very fearful that if we think in terms of continuing that technique for decades to come, we will be doing a great disservice. On the contrary, I think we must begin thinking in terms of permanent, ongoing negotiation, that is, an institutional structure that will allow the kinds of agreements

7. *See* Metzger, pp. 1150—52 *supra*.

and the kind of development of rules and norms (as well as resolution of disputes on these measures) that will help prevent, foresee, or at least ameliorate some of the problems that we seem to be facing with increased severity.

In terms of the current negotiation, both the Trade Act of 1974 and negotiation contain the seeds to move in that direction. Let me explain one such matter in the Trade Act of 1974. Stanley Metzger mentioned the fact that non-tariff barriers must be returned to Congress for approval, and that is true. The technical language of the bill reads, "non-tariff barriers negotiated under this section must be returned to the Congress."[8] This leaves open the possibility that some agreements made in other contexts need not be returned to Congress, if the President otherwise had authority. But I believe that this will be a controversial point, and we will have to await developments. It is part and parcel of the ongoing constitutional crisis in executive-congressional relations.

However, there are some interesting features in the procedure of the Act by which these agreements and possible legislative changes will be taken back to Congress. Those of you who have followed the passage of the Trade Act of 1974 know that we started with the idea of a veto procedure, that is, these agreements and implementing orders would be laid before Congress for a certain period of time and, if neither house rejected them, they would become law.[9] That was the proposed "one-house veto" procedure. The rationale for not using a "two-house veto" procedure was that with the one-house version we would preserve the relative bargaining status of each of the three major participants in legislation: the President, the House of Representatives, and the Senate. If any one of those three participants refused to go along, then we would have neither any change nor any legislation. The House of Representatives bought that idea, and the bill that came out of the Ways and Means Committee[10] appropriately added some measures to safeguard the whole procedure and to ensure that the provision would not be bottled up in committee.

The Senate did not agree to that procedure,[11] and worried—appropriately, I think—about the problem of presidential

---

8. Trade Act of 1974, Pub. L. No. 93-618, § 102, 88 Stat. 1982.

9. H.R. 10710, § 102, 93d Cong., 1st Sess. (1973) (as reported without amendment). *See* H.R. Rep. No. 571, 93d Cong., 1st Sess. (1973).

10. H.R. 10710, 93d Cong., 1st Sess. (as amended and passed by House Dec. 12, 1973).

11. *See* S. Rep. No. 1298, 93d Cong., 2d Sess. (1974).

power in a Watergate year; it was concerned about that kind of procedure which they thought might amount to a basic constitutional change. They opted for the idea of positive legislation being required to approve any non-tariff barrier agreement (NTB) and implementing legislation.[12] They preserved three essential features of the veto procedure, however: 1) the automatic committee discharge—the legislation and the agreement must, after 45 days in committee, be reported out and go to the floor of either house; 2) the limited debate—no filibustering and a limit of 20 hours of debate in either house; and 3) no amendments—the "closed rule" on the provisions in either house.[13] We now have, therefore, the means to get a total vote from each house of Congress on a measure, and presumably to get something near to a majority consensus from both houses on these proposed measures rather quickly.

There is a draft agreement on standards new on the table, and it might be possible for governments to complete it and for us to bring it back and put it through this procedure very quickly. I say that for several reasons. First, as I said, we ought to move away from the idea of having massive negotiations, all wrapped up in one instant before midnight on the last day of the authority of negotiations. We ought to become accustomed to the idea of devoting continuous attention to some of these problems which are simply too complex to handle in one big package. Second, I think it would be very salutary—indeed, it may be essential in the light of the concern of some of our trading partners over executive branch authority—to move in this direction in order to demonstrate that there is some authority in the United States, with the combined cooperation of the President and the Congress under this new procedure. If it fails, then I must say that my optimism will diminish or my pessimism will increase, and I may even be joining Stanley Metzger's ranks. But I have confidence—a fair amount of confidence—that it will not fail, and that the quick approval of such an agreement will have an overall beneficial effect on the negotiation.

That particular procedure has in it the basis of a procedure that could continue after the five year period authorized for the negotiations. As you know, the tariff negotiating authority,[14] as well as the special non-tariff barrier fast-track authority,[15] expires in five years. It could well be that at the end of five years Congress would be

12. *Id.*
13. *Id.*
14. Trade Act of 1974, Pub. L. No. 93-618, § 101, 88 Stat. 1982.
15. *Id.* § 102(b).

amenable to extending that particular procedure for the NTB agreement. By that time, hopefully, the problem of tariffs will not be severe if we can utilize the full measure of tariff reduction authority which we have now. There may be no further need for tariff negotiations, or further tariff negotiations could be minor, in the form of adjustments, with the one exception being the problem of United States tariff disparities which we will still have to face in some way.

There are other items which should be mentioned here. One of the great problems we have in international economic affairs today is a lack of an institutional framework or system able to cope with the difficulties we currently face. No one denies that these problems could be the cause of severe international conflagrations. I do not know how to guess at the scenario. I can see the possibilities of the developing countries getting themselves in terrible balance of payments binds, not having the credits to buy or import the essential needs of food and nutrition, and this in turn causing wars. I can see problems between the major powers, jockeying for position in certain areas of the world and having protected states act as surrogates in the conflicts. These situations can all be visualized and economics will have a major role in some of these dangers.

There was a great deal said earlier in this Meeting about whether in fact we had a short supply problem, and there were many who said there is no short supply problem. The view articulated was that there may be a high price problem or there may be a producer government cartel problem, but there is no short supply problem. I am not enough of an economist to be able to predict, but it is certainly true that there is *some* problem of great magnitude. I would also say that in all probability the difficulty today may not be the most serious problem two or five years from now. Indeed, I think Stanley Metzger has contributed to our sense of perspective by saying that despite the so-called short supply problem we may really have a problem of *market access* in the traditional sense in the next few years, given the current state of the world economy.

The question is, do we have the international mechanisms to cope with those kinds of problems. I fear that we do not. We may be able to deal with these problems in an ad hoc manner as we have in the past, but the central organization that was meant to deal with them, namely the General Agreements on Tariffs and Trade (GATT),[16] has grounds for despair within it, in the sense that it involves a number

16. General Agreement on Tariffs and Trade, Oct. 30, 1947, 61 Stat., Vols. 5, 6, T.I.A.S. No. 1700 (entered into force for the United States Jan. 1, 1948).

of rules and principles, some of which are outdated and others of which do not adequately cover our new problems. It also has, in my opinion, a very deficient system for either the formulation of new rules or for the settlement of disputes. It is my hope that this new negotiation will give some attention to these institutional problems as well as the substantive problems of either holding the line against protectionism or advancing the line and developing further trade liberalization.

Indeed, it seems that there are more or less three approaches or methodologies that governments can use to attack problems of international economics today. One is the bargaining or swap technique. This is the technique that has gone on "par excellence" since the 1934 Reciprocal Trade Agreements Act,[17] and it has been enormously successful. I do not in any way wish to denigrate what has been accomplished by that process, and I think we need to act in a way such that those gains are preserved.

A second technique is what might be called the "norm or rule formulation" technique. It is less like swapping a dollar for a watch or swapping so many tariff concessions on one side for so much trade coverage on the other. It is more like saying, "If certain rules were in place and governments followed those rules, we would all be benefited further." Those rules might involve such things as an injury determination in the countervailing duty area, or might involve certain government procurement-type standards that national administrations would have to follow. There are areas of endeavor that are becoming more important than tariffs and which do not easily lend themselves to what I call the bargaining or swap technique. The reason is that the idea of reciprocity was always difficult to implement, even in the case of tariffs. But try to determine the reciprocity, if you will, that results from some of these rules that might be implemented regarding non-tariff barriers. I think it is impossible. I believe that people simply cannot predict exactly what will happen to trade flows because of the development of such rules. Further, if you have a more flexible exchange rate system, there is no need to predict what will happen to the trade flows as a result of those rules. I would hope that we would begin to turn considerably more attention to this second kind of technique of international economic endeavor, and more away from the bargaining or swap technique.

The third technique is one that I have already mentioned, namely

17. Act of June 12, 1934, ch. 474, §§ 1—4, 48 Stat. 943.

the institutional technique. What we need is as much attention to *how* the rules are made as to what should be *in* those rules. In other words, we must give some attention to how nations should get together and formulate rules. I do not mean to include those spurious rules, the rules which are held up and waved as propaganda by certain groups that may have control of one assembly or another. I refer to rules that would indicate meaningful commitment by the forces of power in the world as well as the forces that feel they are "owed" something as a matter of justice, or in philosophical terms. This may be hinting at some kind of a differential voting system, but I decline to go into that at this point.

This brings me, finally, to the question of short supply itself. All I have said so far also applies to the short supply problem, if one exists. There can be short supply negotiations going on in the new Multinational Trade Negotiations (MTN). Whether they will go on there or in some other forum is going to depend more on internal bureaucratic squabbles in this country than on any sort of inherent forum jurisdiction in the international sense. However, it is possible for some such negotiations to go on in the MTN locus.

Some interesting swaps are possible, if one applies the bargaining or swap technique. There are market access for supply access swaps: "We assure you food if you assure us oil" and various swaps of that type. But suppose you turn to a norm formulation system. What kind of norms would be necessary or advisable in order to approach some of the recent problems we have experienced? That is puzzling, because it is not at all clear just exactly what the problems are. Let me suggest a few, however.

I see the underlying problem to be that which we have roughly characterized as the short supply problem of recent years. First, a change in the terms of trade, that is, one group of countries or one group of suppliers or producers trying to gain for themselves an advantage with respect to the price of one good over another good in the world economy. How can we solve that problem on any sort of objective philosophical basis? I am not certain we can, unless we adopt some sort of medieval notion of "fair" price. In other words, the problem really challenges the whole notion of free market allocation and free market forces. Perhaps it will mean that by returning to some concept of fair price, the oil producing countries will make a claim along the lines that "this is our national heritage being sucked out of the ground, and in x years it's going to be gone, leaving us to be poor desert nomads again; therefore, during that period of time we have the right to gain for ourselves a new type of living, new industries, and new capital inputs." I must say there is some appeal in that sort of claim. But I do not know how one can determine what the rule ought to be in such a case.

Second, it seems to me that one of the problems is suddenness. If you let the markets act, things will adjust themselves in the long run. Indeed, I think Mr. Southard might even give us a prognostication that over a period of six or eight years it is conceivable that we will not have the kind of problem we are now facing, or at least think we are facing . By that time, perhaps there will be enough imports by those countries to offset the reduced revenues they will have if price and production fall. In any event, the real problem is the suddenness of action and we need some kind of norm in this respect. Perhaps we could somehow devise a system that would call for certain consultations, or a delay, or a particular time for other countries to take actions that would adjust and ameliorate the harm inflicted on their economies. I am reminded of some of the mechanisms which have evolved to give relief from a sudden increase in imports, for example, the escape clause and adjustment assistance,[18] where we admit there are industries that would be hurt by imports, and those industries perhaps should change into producing items other than the ones they are now producing. This is simply a matter of time and tiding them over.

The third norm that I would suggest raises the question of whether we can approach, in an international forum, some kind of restraint from linking economic decisions to political short run advantages. This is a highly volatile area, and I think again the United States probably has been as culpable as other nations in this regard. Nevertheless, it is worth a try.

The final point that I would make is that we might be able to come to some norm or realization of a rule against the use of force, in any context, in trying to wring from other countries the supplies which are part of what you might call their national patronage. Again, I would decline to go into that in detail, but to me it seems a sensible proposition.

Thus you have my current analysis on a somewhat more upbeat and somewhat more optimistic tone than our other two participants on this panel. Again, as I say, it may simply be an attempt to characterize the half empty glass as being half full.

---

18. The adjustment assistance program began under the Trade Expansion Act of 1962, 19 U.S.C. § 1901(c)(1), (2). The program has been continued and modified by the Trade Act of 1974, Pub. L. No. 93-618, §§ 201—84, 88 Stat. 2011—41.

PART III

LEGAL FRAMEWORK

(REFERENCES)

UNITED NATIONS DOCUMENTS

CHARTER OF THE UNITED NATIONS

We the Peoples of the United Nations Determined

to save succeeding generations from the scourge of war, which twice in our lifetime has brought untold sorrow to mankind, and

to reaffirm faith in fundamental human rights, in the dignity and worth of the human person, in the equal rights of men and women and of nations large and small, and

to establish conditions under which justice and respect for the obligations arising from treaties and other sources of international law can be maintained, and

to promote social progress and better standards of life in larger freedom,

And for these ends

to practice tolerance and live together in peace with one another as good neighbours, and

to unite our strength to maintain international peace and security, and

to ensure, by the acceptance of principles and the institution of methods, that armed force shall not be used, save in the common interest, and

to employ international machinery for the promotion of the economic and social advancement of all peoples,

Have Resolved to Combine our Efforts to Accomplish these Aims

Accordingly, our respective Governments, through representatives assembled in the city of San Francisco, who have exhibited their full powers found to be in good and due form, have agreed to the present Charter of the United Nations and do hereby establish an international organization to be known as the United Nations.

CHAPTER I

PURPOSES AND PRINCIPLES

Article 1

The Purposes of the United Nations are:

1. To maintain international peace and security, and to that end: to take effective collective measures for the prevention and removal of threats to the peace, and for the suppression of acts of aggression or other breaches of the peace, and to bring about by peaceful means, and in conformity with the principles of justice and international law, adjustment or settlement of international disputes or situations which might lead to a breach of the peace;

2. To develop friendly relations among nations based on respect for the principle of equal rights and self-determination of peoples, and to take other appropriate measures to strengthen universal peace;

3. To achieve international cooperation in solving international problems of an economic, social, cultural, or humanitarian character, and in promoting and encouraging respect for human rights and for fundamental freedoms for all without distinction as to race, sex, language, or religion; and

4. To be a center for harmonizing the actions of nations in the attainment of these common ends.

Article 2

The Organization and its Members, in pursuit of the Purposes stated in Article 1, shall act in accordance with the following Principles.

1. The Organization is based on the principle of the sovereign equality of all its Members.

2. All Members, in order to ensure to all of them the rights and benefits resulting from membership, shall fulfill in good faith the obligations assumed by them in accordance with the present Charter.

3. All Members shall settle their international disputes by peaceful means in such a manner that international peace and security, and justice, are not endangered.

4. All Members shall refrain in their international relations from the threat or use of force against the territorial integrity or political independence of any state, or in any other manner inconsistent with the Purposes of the United Nations.

5. All Members shall give the United Nations every assistance in any action it takes in accordance with the present Charter, and shall refrain from giving assistance to any state against which the United Nations is taking preventive or enforcement action.

6. The Organization shall ensure that states which are not Members of the United Nations act in accordance with these Principles so far as may be necessary for the maintenance of international peace and security.

7. Nothing contained in the present Charter shall authorize the United Nations to intervene in matters which are essentially within the domestic jurisdiction of any state or shall require the Members to submit such matters to settlement under the present Charter; but this principle shall not prejudice the application of enforcement measures under Chapter VII.

Article 51

Nothing in the present Charter shall impair the inherent right of individual or collective self-defense if an armed attack occurs against a Member of the United Nations, until the Security Council has taken measures necessary to maintain international peace and security. Measures taken by Members in the exercise of this right of self-defense shall be immediately reported to the Security Council and shall not in any way affect the authority and responsibility of the Security Council under the present Charter to take at any time such action as it deems necessary in order to maintain or restore international peace and security.

CHAPTER VIII

REGIONAL ARRANGEMENTS

Article 53

1. The Security Council shall, where appropriate, utilize such regional arrangements or agencies for enforcement action under its authority. But no enforcement action shall be taken under regional arrangements or by regional agencies without the authorization of the Security Council, with the exception of measures against any enemy state, as defined in paragraph 2 of this Article, provided for pursuant to Article 107 or in regional arrangements directed against renewal of aggressive policy on the part of any such state, until such time as the Organization may, on request of the Governments concerned, be charged with the responsibility for preventing further aggression by such a state.

2. The term enemy state as used in paragraph 1 of this Article applies to any state which during the Second World War has been an enemy of any signatory of the present Charter.

CHAPTER IX

INTERNATIONAL ECONOMIC AND SOCIAL COOPERATION

Article 55

With a view to the creation of conditions of stability and well-being which are necessary for peaceful and friendly relations among nations based on respect for the principle of equal rights and self-determination of peoples, the United Nations shall promote:

a. higher standards of living, full employment, and conditions of economic and social progress and development;

b. solutions of international economic, social, health, and related problems; and international cultural and educational cooperation; and

c. universal respect for, and observance of, human rights and fundamental freedoms for all without distinction as to race, sex, language, or religion.

Article 56

All Members pledge themselves to take joint and separate action in cooperation with the Organization for the achievement of the purposes set forth in Article 55.

DRAFT DECLARATION ON RIGHTS AND DUTIES OF STATES

Report of the International Law Commission, 9 June 1949.
GAOR, IV, Supp. 10 (A/925), pp. 7–10.

Whereas the States of the world form a community governed by international law,

Whereas the progressive development of international law requires effective organization of the community of States,

Whereas a great majority of the States of the world have accordingly established a new international order under the Charter of the United Nations, and most of the other States of the world have declared their desire to live within this order,

Whereas a primary purpose of the United Nations is to maintain international peace and security, and the reign of law and justice is essential to the realization of this purpose, and

Whereas it is therefore desirable to formulate certain basic rights and duties of States in the light of new developments of international law and in harmony with the Charter of the United Nations,

The General Assembly of the United Nations adopts and proclaims this

DECLARATION ON RIGHTS AND DUTIES OF STATES

ARTICLE 1. Every State has the right to independence and hence to exercise freely, without dictation by any other State, all its legal powers, including the choice of its own form of government.

ARTICLE 2. Every State has the right to exercise jurisdiction over its territory and over all persons and things therein, subject to the immunities recognized by international law.

ARTICLE 3. Every State has the duty to refrain from intervention in the internal or external affairs of any other State.

ARTICLE 4. Every State has the duty to refrain from fomenting civil strife in the territory of another State, and to prevent the organization within its territory of activities calculated to foment such civil strife.

ARTICLE 5. Every State has the right to equality in law with every other State.

ARTICLE 6. Every State has the duty to treat all persons under its jurisdiction with respect for human rights and fundamental freedoms, without distinction as to race, sex, language, or religion.

ARTICLE 7. Every State has the duty to ensure that conditions prevailing in its territory do not menace international peace and order.

ARTICLE 8. Every State has the duty to settle its disputes with other States by peaceful means in such a manner that international peace and security, and justice, are not endangered.

ARTICLE 9. Every State has the duty to refrain from resorting to war as an instrument of national policy, and to refrain from the threat or use of force against the territorial integrity or political independence of another State, or in any other manner inconsistent with international law and order.

ARTICLE 10. Every State has the duty to refrain from giving assistance to any State which is acting in violation of article 9, or against which the United Nations is taking preventive or enforcement action.

ARTICLE 11. Every State has the duty to refrain from recognizing any territorial acquisition by another State acting in violation of article 9.

ARTICLE 12. Every State has the right of individual or collective self-defence against armed attack.

ARTICLE 13. Every State has the duty to carry out in good faith its obligations arising from treaties and other sources of international law, and it may not invoke provisions in its constitution or its laws as an excuse for failure to perform this duty.

ARTICLE 14. Every State has the duty to conduct its relations with other States in accordance with international law and with the principle that the sovereignty of each State is subject to the supremacy of international law.

ESSENTIALS OF PEACE

Resolution 290 (IV) of the General Assembly, 1 December 1949.
GAOR, IV, Resolutions (A/1251), p. 13.

The General Assembly

1. Declares that the Charter of the United Nations, the most solemn pact of peace in history, lays down basic principles necessary for an enduring peace; that disregard of these principles is primarily responsible for the continuance of international tension; and that it is urgently necessary for all Members to act in accordance with these principles in the spirit of co-operation on which the United Nations was founded;

Calls upon every nation

2. To refrain from threatening or using force contrary to the Charter;

3. To refrain from any threats or acts, direct or indirect, aimed at impairing the freedom, independence or integrity of any State, or at fomenting civil strife and subverting the will of the people in any State;

4. To carry out in good faith its international agreements;

5. To afford all United Nations bodies full co-operation and free access in the performance of the tasks assigned to them under the Charter;

6. To promote, in recognition of the paramount importance of preserving the dignity and worth of the human person, full freedom for the peaceful expression of political opposition, full opportunity for the exercise of religious freedom and full respect for all the other fundamental rights expressed in the Universal Declaration of Human Rights;

7. To promote nationally and through international co-operation, efforts to achieve and sustain higher standards of living for all peoples;

8. To remove the barriers which deny to peoples the free exchange of information and ideas essential to international understanding and peace;

Calls upon every Member

9. To participate fully in all the work of the United Nations;

Calls upon the five permanent members of the Security Council

10. To broaden progressively their co-operation and to exercise restraint in the use of the veto in order to make the Security Council a more effective instrument for maintaining peace;

Calls upon every nation

11. To settle international disputes by peaceful means and to co-operate in supporting United Nations efforts to resolve outstanding problems;

12. To co-operate to attain the effective international regulation of conventional armaments; and

13. To agree to the exercise of national sovereignty jointly with other nations to the extent necessary to attain international control of atomic energy which would make effective the prohibition of atomic weapons and assure the use of atomic energy for peaceful purposes only.

PEACE THROUGH DEEDS

Resolution 380 (V) of the General Assembly, 17 November 1950.
GAOR, V, Supp. 20 (A/1775), pp. 13–14.

The General Assembly,

Recognizing the profound desire of all mankind to live in enduring peace and security, and in freedom from fear and want,

Confident that, if all governments faithfully reflect this desire and observe their obligations under the Charter, lasting peace and security can be established,

Condemning the intervention of a State in the internal affairs of another State for the purpose of changing its legally established government by the threat or use of force,

1. Solemnly reaffirms that, whatever the weapons used, any aggression, whether committed openly, or by fomenting civil strife in the interest of a foreign Power, or otherwise, is the gravest of all crimes against peace and security throughout the world;

2. Determines that for the realization of lasting peace and security it is indispensable:

(1) That prompt united action be taken to meet aggression wherever it arises;

(2) That every nation agree:

(a) To accept effective international control of atomic energy, under the United Nations, on the basis already approved by the General Assembly in order to make effective the prohibition of atomic weapons;

(b) To strive for the control and elimination, under the United Nations, of all other weapons of mass destruction;

(c) To regulate all armaments and armed forces under a United Nations system of control and inspection, with a view to their gradual reduction;

(d) To reduce to a minimum the diversion for armaments of its human and economic resources and to strive towards the development of such resources for the general welfare, with due regard to the needs of the underdeveloped areas of the world;

3. Declares that these goals can be attained if all the Members of the United Nations demonstrate by their deeds their will to achieve peace.

SECRETARY-GENERAL OF THE UNITED NATIONS, REPORT ON THE QUESTION OF DEFINING AGGRESSION

U.N. Doc. A/2211 (October 3, 1952) (footnotes omitted)

273. From the point of view of form, three categories of definitions may be distinguished: enumerative, general and combined.

274. The *enumerative definitions* give a list of the acts regarded as acts of aggression. In most cases, the authors of these definitions have regarded it as essential that the enumeration should be exhaustive, which means that only the acts enumerated constitute acts of aggression. Some authors, however, have proposed that the international organs should be empowered to treat as acts of aggression acts other than those enumerated in the definition.

275. The *general definitions,* instead of listing the acts of aggression, are couched in general terms which cover the entire class of cases to be included. It is left to the international organs to determine the scope of the terms when specific cases are brought before them.

276. The *combined definitions* are a combination of the two preceding types. They contain, first, general terms and, second, a list, but a list which is not exhaustive. Their object is merely to describe the principal forms of aggression.

. . .

(ii) *What constitutes indirect aggression?*

414. The characteristic of indirect aggression appears to be that the aggressor State, without itself committing hostile acts as a State, operates through third parties who are either foreigners or nationals seemingly acting on their own initiative. Representatives who have referred to indirect aggression have sometimes mentioned it in general terms, and at other times have pointed to certain facts which, in their view, constitute indirect aggression.

415. Indirect aggression is a general expression of recent use (although the practice itself is ancient), and has not been defined. The concept of indirect aggression has been construed to include certain hostile acts or certain forms of complicity in hostilities in progress. . . .

416. What will be considered here are cases of indirect aggression which do not constitute acts of participation in hostilities in progress, but which are designed to prepare such acts, to undermine a country's power of resistance, or to bring about a change in its political or social system.

. . .

(b) *Intervention or interference in the affairs of another State*

420. This may assume the most varied forms: e.g., encouraging a party, paying it funds, sending weapons, etc.

. . .

(c) *Violation of the political integrity of a country by subversive action* . . .

2. Economic Aggression

(a) *Emergence of the concept of economic aggression*

441. The concept of economic aggression is new. Economic aggression was covered in the draft definition submitted to the Sixth Committee by Bolivia on 11 January 1952, which states:

> "Also to be considered as an act of aggression shall be . . . unilateral action to deprive a State of the economic resources derived from the fair practice of international trade, or to endanger its basic economy, thus jeopardizing the security of that State or rendering it incapable of acting in its own defence and co-operating in the collective defence of peace."

. . .

445. It will be noted that article 16 of the Charter of the Organization of American States signed at Bogotá on 30 April 1948 states that:

> "No State may use or encourage the use of coercive measures of an economic or political character in order to force the sovereign will of another State and obtain from it advantages of any kind."

(b) *Criticism of the concept of economic aggression*

446. The concept of economic aggression appears particularly liable to extend the concept of aggression almost indefinitely. The acts in question not only do not involve the use of force, but are usually carried out by a State by virtue of its sovereignty or discretionary power. Where there are no commitments a State is free to fix its customs tariffs and to limit or prohibit exports and imports. If it concludes a commercial treaty with another State, superior political, economic and financial strength may of course give it an advantage over the weaker party; but that applies to every treaty, and it is difficult to see how such inequalities, which arise from differences in situation, can be evened out short of changing the entire structure of international society and transferring powers inherent in States to international organs.

DRAFT CODE OF OFFENSES AGAINST THE PEACE AND SECURITY OF MANKIND

Adopted by the International Law Commission, 28 July 1954.
GAOR, IX, Supp. 9 (A/2693), pp. 11–12.

ARTICLE 1. Offences against the peace and security of mankind, as defined in this code, are crimes under international law, for which the responsible individuals shall be punished.

ARTICLE 2. The following acts are offences against the peace and security of mankind:

(1) Any act of aggression, including the employment by the authorities of a State of armed force against another State for any purpose other than national or collective self-defence or in pursuance of a decision or recommendation of a competent organ of the United Nations.

(2) Any threat by the authorities of a State to resort to an act of aggression against another State.

(3) The preparation by the authorities of a State of the employment of armed force against another State for any purpose other than national or collective self-defence or in pursuance of a decision or recommendation of a competent organ of the United Nations.

(4) The organization, or the encouragement of the organization, by the authorities of a State, of armed bands within its territory or any other territory for incursions into the territory of another State, or the toleration of the organization of such bands in its own territory, or the toleration of the use by such armed bands of its territory as a base of operations or as a point of departure for incursions into the territory of another State, as well as direct participation in or support of such incursions.

(5) The undertaking or encouragement by the authorities of a State of activities calculated to foment civil strife in another State, or the toleration by the authorities of a State of organized activities calculated to foment civil strife in another State.

(6) The undertaking or encouragement by the authorities of a State of terrorist activities in another State, or the toleration by the authorities of a State of organized activities calculated to carry out terrorist acts in another State.

(7) Acts by the authorities of a State in violation of its obligations under a treaty which is designed to ensure international peace and security by means of restrictions or limitations on armaments, or on military training, or on fortifications, or of other restrictions of the same character.

(8) The annexation by the authorities of a State of territory belonging to another State, by means of acts contrary to international law.

(9) The intervention by the authorities of a State in the internal or external affairs of another State, by means of coercive measures of an economic or political character in order to force its will and thereby obtain advantages of any kind.

(10) Acts by the authorities of a State or by private individuals committed with intent to destroy, in whole or in part, a national, ethnic, racial or religious group as such, including:

(i) Killing members of the group;

(ii) Causing serious bodily or mental harm to members of the group;

(iii) Deliberately inflicting on the group conditions of life calculated to bring about its physical destruction in whole or in part;

(iv) Imposing measures intended to prevent births within the group;

(v) Forcibly transferring children of the group to another group.

(11) Inhuman acts such as murder, extermination, enslavement, deportation or persecutions, committed against any civilian population on social political, racial, religious or cultural grounds by the authorities of a State or by private individuals acting at the instigation or with the toleration of such authorities.

(12) Acts in violation of the laws or customs of war.

(13) Acts which constitute:

(i) Conspiracy to commit any of the offences defined in the preceding paragraphs of this article; or

(ii) Direct incitement to commit any of the offences defined in the preceding paragraphs of this article; or

(iii) Complicity in the commission of any of the offences defined in the preceding paragraphs of this article; or

(iv) Attempts to commit any of the offences defined in the preceding paragraphs of this article.

ARTICLE 3. The fact that a person acted as Head of State or as responsible government official does not relieve him of responsibility for committing any of the offences defined in this code.

ARTICLE 4. The fact that a person charged with an offence defined in this code acted pursuant to an order of his Government or of a superior does not relieve him of responsibility in international law if, in the circumstances at the time, it was possible for him not to comply with that order.

Resolution of Non-Intervention[1]

"*The General Assembly,*

"*Deeply concerned* at the gravity of the international situation and the increasing threat to universal peace due to armed intervention and other direct or indirect forms of interference threatening the sovereign personality and the political independence of States,

"*Considering* that the United Nations, in accordance with their aim to eliminate war, threats to the peace and acts of aggression, created an Organization, based on the sovereign equality of States, whose friendly relations would be based on respect for the principle of equal rights and self-determination of peoples and on the obligation of its Members to refrain from the threat or use of force against the territorial integrity or political independence of any State,

"*Recognizing* that, in fulfilment of the principle of self-determination, the General Assembly, in the Declaration on the Granting of Independence to Colonial Countries and Peoples contained in resolution 1514 (XV) of 14 December 1960, stated its conviction that all peoples have an inalienable right to complete freedom, the exercise of their sovereignty and the integrity of their national territory, and that, by virtue of that right, they freely determine their political status and freely pursue their economic, social and cultural development,

"*Recalling* that in the Universal Declaration of Human Rights the General Assembly proclaimed that recognition of the inherent dignity and of the equal and inalienable rights of all members of the human family is the foundation of freedom, justice and peace in the world, without distinction of any kind,

"*Reaffirming* the principle of non-intervention, proclaimed in the charters of the Organization of American States, the League of Arab States and the Organization of African Unity and affirmed at the conferences held at Montevideo, Buenos Aires, Chapultepec and Bogotá, as well as in the decisions of the Asian-African Conference at Bandung, the First Conference of Heads of State or Government of Non-Aligned Countries at Belgrade, in the Programme for Peace and International Co-operation adopted at the end of the Second Conference of Heads of State or Government of Non-Aligned Countries at Cairo, and in the declaration on subversion adopted at Accra by the Heads of State and Government of the African States,

"*Recognizing* that full observance of the principle of the non-intervention of States in the internal and external affairs of other States is essential to the fulfillment of the purposes and principles of the United Nations,

"*Considering* that armed intervention is synonymous with aggression and, as such, is contrary to the basic principles on which peaceful international co-operation between States should be built,

"*Considering further* that direct intervention, subversion and all forms of indirect intervention are contrary to these principles and, consequently, constitute a violation of the Charter of the United Nations,

"*Mindful* that violation of the principle of nonintervention poses a threat to the independence, freedom and normal political, economic, social and cultural development of countries, particularly those which have freed themselves from colonialism, and can pose a serious threat to the maintenance of peace,

"*Fully aware* of the imperative need to create appropriate conditions which would enable all States, and in particular the developing countries, to choose without duress or coercion their own political, economic and social institutions,

"*In the light of the foregoing considerations, solemnly declares:*

"1. No State has the right to intervene, directly or indirectly, for any reason whatever, in the internal or external affairs of any other State. Consequently, armed intervention and all other forms of interference or attempted threats against the personality of the State or against its political, economic and cultural elements, are condemned.

"2. No State may use or encourage the use of economic, political or any other type of measures to coerce another State in order to obtain from it the subordination of the exercise of its sovereign rights or to secure from it advantages of any kind. Also, no State shall organize, assist, foment, finance, incite or tolerate subversive, terrorist or armed activities directed towards the violent overthrow of the regime of another State, or interfere in civil strife in another State.

"3. The use of force to deprive peoples of their national identity constitutes a violation of their inalienable rights and of the principle of non-intervention.

"4. The strict observance of these obligations is an essential condition to ensure that nations live together in peace with one another, since the practice of any form of intervention not only violates the spirit and letter of the Charter of the United Nations but also leads to the creation of situations which threaten international peace and security.

"5. Every State has an inalienable right to choose its political, economic, social and cultural systems, without interference in any form by another State.

---

[1] Resolution 2131 (xx) adopted by the General Assembly on December 21, 1965.

"6. All States shall respect the right of self-determination and independence of peoples and nations, to be freely exercised without any foreign pressure, and with absolute respect for human rights and fundamental freedoms. Consequently, all States shall contribute to the complete elimination of racial discrimination and colonialism in all its forms and manifestations.

"7. For the purpose of the present Declaration, the term 'State' covers both individual States and groups of States.

"8. Nothing in this Declaration shall be construed as affecting in any manner the relevant provisions of the Charter of the United Nations relating to the maintenance of international peace and security, in particular those contained in Chapters VI, VII and VIII."

UNITED NATIONS CONFERENCE ON THE LAW OF TREATIES

Convention on the Law of Treaties. Done at Vienna on 23 May 1969

The States Parties to the present Convention,

Considering the fundamental role of treaties in the history of international relations,

Recognizing the ever-increasing importance of treaties as a source of international law and as a means of developing peaceful co-operation among nations, whatever their constitutional and social systems,

Noting that the principles of free consent and of good faith and the *pacta sunt servanda* rule are universally recognized,

Affirming that disputes concerning treaties, like other international disputes, should be settled by peaceful means and in conformity with the principles of justice and international law,

Recalling the determination of the peoples of the United Nations to establish conditions under which justice and respect for the obligations arising from treaties can be maintained,

Having in mind the principles of international law embodied in the Charter of the United Nations, such as the principles of the equal rights and self-determination of peoples, of the sovereign equality and independence of all States, of non-interference in the domestic affairs of States, of the prohibition of the threat or use of force and of universal respect for, and observance of, human rights and fundamental freedoms for all,

Believing that the codification and progressive development of the law of treaties achieved in the present Convention will promote the purposes of the United Nations set forth in the Charter, namely, the maintenance of international peace and security, the development of friendly relations and the achievement of co-operation among nations,

Affirming that the rules of customary international law will continue to govern questions not regulated by the provisions of the present Convention,

Have agreed as follows:

PART III

OBSERVANCE, APPLICATION AND INTERPRETATION OF TREATIES

SECTION 1: OBSERVANCE OF TREATIES

Article 26

Pacta sunt servanda

Every treaty in force is binding upon the parties to it and must be performed by them in good faith.

Article 27

Internal law and observance of treaties

A party may not invoke the provisions of its internal law as justification for its failure to perform a treaty. This rule is without prejudice to article 46.

PART V

Invalidity, termination and suspension of the operation of treaties

SECTION 2: INVALIDITY OF TREATIES

Article 46

Provisions of internal law regarding competence to conclude treaties

1. A State may not invoke the fact that its consent to be bound by a treaty has been expressed in violation of a provision of its internal law regarding competence to conclude treaties as invalidating its consent unless that violation was manifest and concerned a rule of its internal law of fundamental importance.

2. A violation is manifest if it would be objectively evident to any State conducting itself in the matter in accordance with normal practice and in good faith.

Article 51

Coercion of a representative of a State

The expression of a State's consent to be bound by a treaty which has been procured by the coercion of its representative through acts or threats directed against him shall be without any legal effect.

Article 52

Coercion of a State by the threat or use of force

A treaty is void if its conclusion has been procured by the threat or use of force in violation of the principles of international law embodied in the Charter of the United Nations.

Article 53

Treaties conflicting with a peremptory norm of general international law
(jus cogens)

A treaty is void if, at the time of its conclusion, it conflicts with a peremptory norm of general international law. For the purposes of the present Convention, a peremptory norm of general international law is a norm accepted and recognized by the international community of States as a whole as a norm from which no derogation is permitted and which can be modified only by a subsequent norm of general international law having the same character.

UNITED NATIONS CONFERENCE ON THE LAW OF TREATIES

Declarations and resolutions adopted by the Conference
Done at Vienna on 23 May 1969

Declaration on the prohibition of military, political or economic coercion in the conclusion of treaties

The United Nations Conference on the Law of Treaties,

Upholding the principle that every treaty in force is binding upon the parties to it and must be performed by them in good faith,

Reaffirming the principle of the sovereign equality of States,

Convinced that States must have complete freedom in performing any act relating to the conclusion of a treaty,

Deploring the fact that in the past States have sometimes been forced to conclude treaties under pressure exerted in various forms by other States,

Desiring to ensure that in the future no such pressure will be exerted in any form by any State in connexion with the conclusion of a treaty,

1. *Solemnly condemns* the threat or use of pressure in any form, whether military, political, or economic, by any State in order to coerce another State to perform any act relating to the conclusion of a treaty in violation of the principles of the sovereign equality of States and freedom of consent;

2. *Decides* that the present Declaration shall form part of the Final Act of the Conference on the Law of Treaties.

DECLARATION ON PRINCIPLES OF INTERNATIONAL LAW CONCERNING FRIENDLY RELATIONS AND CO-OPERATION AMONG STATES IN ACCORDANCE WITH THE CHARTER OF THE UNITED NATIONS

Approved by General Assembly Resolution 2625 (XXV) of Oct. 24, 1970. U.N.Gen.Ass.Off.Rec. 25th Sess., Supp. No. 28 (A/8028), p. 121.

PREAMBLE

The General Assembly,

Reaffirming in the terms of the Charter of the United Nations that the maintenance of international peace and security and the development of friendly relations and co-operation between nations are among the fundamental purposes of the United Nations,

Recalling that the peoples of the United Nations are determined to practise tolerance and live together in peace with one another as good neighbours,

Bearing in mind the importance of maintaining and strengthening international peace founded upon freedom, equality, justice and respect for fundamental human rights and of developing friendly relations among nations irrespective of their political, economic and social systems or the levels of their development,

Bearing in mind also the paramount importance of the Charter of the United Nations in the promotion of the rule of law among nations,

Considering that the faithful observance of the principles of international law concerning friendly relations and co-operation among States and the fulfilment in good faith of the obligations assumed by States, in accordance with the Charter, is of the greatest importance for the maintenance of international peace and security and for the implementation of the other purposes of the United Nations,

Noting that the great political, economic and social changes and scientific progress which have taken place in the world since the adoption of the Charter give increased importance to these principles and to the need for their more effective application in the conduct of States wherever carried on,

Recalling the established principle that outer space, including the Moon and other celestial bodies, is not subject to national appropriation by claim of sovereignty, by means of use or occupation, or by any other means, and mindful of the fact that consideration is being given in the United Nations to the question of establishing other appropriate provisions similarly inspired,

Convinced that the strict observance by States of the obligation not to intervene in the affairs of any other State is an essential condition to ensure that nations live together in peace with one another, since the practice of any form of intervention not only violates the spirit and letter of the Charter, but also leads to the creation of situations which threaten international peace and security,

Recalling the duty of States to refrain in their international relations from military, political, economic or any other form of coercion aimed against the political independence or territorial integrity of any State,

Considering it essential that all States shall refrain in their international relations from the threat or use of force against the territorial integrity or political independence of any State, or in any other manner inconsistent with the purposes of the United Nations,

Considering it equally essential that all States shall settle their international disputes by peaceful means in accordance with the Charter,

Reaffirming, in accordance with the Charter, the basic importance of sovereign equality and stressing that the purposes of the United Nations can be implemented only if States enjoy sovereign equality and comply fully with the requirements of this principle in their international relations,

Convinced that the subjection of peoples to alien subjugation, domination and exploitation constitutes a major obstacle to the promotion of international peace and security,

Convinced that the principle of equal rights and self-determination of peoples constitutes a significant contribution to contemporary international law, and that its effective application is of paramount importance for the promotion of friendly relations among States, based on respect for the principle of sovereign equality,

Convinced in consequence that any attempt aimed at the partial or total disruption of the national unity and territorial integrity of a State or country or at its political independence is incompatible with the purposes and principles of the Charter,

Considering the provisions of the Charter as a whole and taking into account the role of relevant resolutions adopted by the competent organs of the United Nations relating to the content of the principles,

Considering that the progressive development and codification of the following principles:

(*a*) The principle that States shall refrain in their international relations from the threat or use of force against the territorial integrity or political independence of any State, or in any other manner inconsistent with the purposes of the United Nations,

(*b*) The principle that States shall settle their international disputes by peaceful means in such a manner that international peace and security and justice are not endangered,

(*c*) The duty not to intervene in matters within the domestic jurisdiction of any State, in accordance with the Charter,

(*d*) The duty of States to co-operate with one another in accordance with the Charter,

(*e*) The principle of equal rights and self-determination of peoples,

(*f*) The principle of sovereign equality of States,

(*g*) The principle that States shall fulfil in good faith the obligations assumed by them in accordance with the Charter, so as to secure their more effective application within the international community, would promote the realization of the purposes of the United Nations,

Having considered the principles of international law relating to friendly relations and co-operation among States,

1. *Solemnly proclaims* the following principles:

The principle that States shall refrain in their international relations from the threat or use of force against the territorial integrity or political independence of any State, or in any other manner inconsistent with the purposes of the United Nations

Every State has the duty to refrain in its international relations from the threat or use of force against the territorial integrity or political independence of any State, or in any other manner inconsistent with the purposes of the United Nations. Such a threat or use of force constitutes a violation of international law and the Charter of the United Nations and shall never be employed as a means of settling international issues.

A war of aggression constitutes a crime against the peace, for which there is responsibility under international law.

In accordance with the purposes and principles of the United Nations, States have the duty to refrain from propaganda for wars of aggression.

Every State has the duty to refrain from the threat or use of force to violate the existing international boundaries of another State or as a means of solving international disputes, including territorial disputes and problems concerning frontiers of States.

Every State likewise has the duty to refrain from the threat or use of force to violate international lines of demarcation, such as armistice lines, established by or pursuant to an international agreement to which it is a party or which it is otherwise bound to respect. Nothing in the foregoing shall be construed as prejudicing the positions of the parties concerned with regard to the status and effects of such lines under their special régimes or as affecting their temporary character.

States have a duty to refrain from acts of reprisal involving the use of force.

Every State has the duty to refrain from any forcible action which deprives peoples referred to in the elaboration of the principle of equal rights and self-determination of their right to self-determination and freedom and independence.

Every State has the duty to refrain from organizing or encouraging the organization of irregular forces or armed bands, including mercenaries, for incursion into the territory of another State.

Every State has the duty to refrain from organizing, instigating, assisting or participating in acts of civil strife or terrorist acts in another State or acquiescing in organized activities within its territory directed towards the commission of such acts, when the acts referred to in the present paragraph involve a threat or use of force.

The territory of a State shall not be the object of military occupation resulting from the use of force in contravention of the provisions of the

Charter. The territory of a State shall not be the object of acquisition by another State resulting from the threat or use of force. No territorial acquisition resulting from the threat or use of force shall be recognized as legal. Nothing in the foregoing shall be construed as affecting:

(*a*) Provisions of the Charter or any international agreement prior to the Charter régime and valid under international law; or

(*b*) The powers of the Security Council under the Charter.

All States shall pursue in good faith negotiations for the early conclusion of a universal treaty on general and complete disarmament under effective international control and strive to adopt appropriate measures to reduce international tensions and strengthen confidence among States.

All States shall comply in good faith with their obligations under the generally recognized principles and rules of international law with respect to the maintenance of international peace and security, and shall endeavour to make the United Nations security system based on the Charter more effective.

Nothing in the foregoing paragraphs shall be construed as enlarging or diminishing in any way the scope of the provisions of the Charter concerning cases in which the use of force is lawful.

The principle that States shall settle their international disputes by peaceful means in such a manner that international peace and security and justice are not endangered

Every State shall settle its international disputes with other States by peaceful means in such a manner that international peace and security and justice are not endangered.

States shall accordingly seek early and just settlement of their international disputes by negotiation, inquiry, mediation, conciliation, arbitration, judicial settlement, resort to regional agencies or arrangements or other peaceful means of their choice. In seeking such a settlement the parties shall agree upon such peaceful means as may be appropriate to the circumstances and nature of the dispute.

The parties to a dispute have the duty, in the event of failure to reach a solution by any one of the above peaceful means, to continue to seek a settlement of the dispute by other peaceful means agreed upon by them.

States parties to an international dispute, as well as other States, shall refrain from any action which may aggravate the situation so as to endanger the maintenance of international peace and security, and shall act in accordance with the purposes and principles of the United Nations.

International disputes shall be settled on the basis of the sovereign equality of States and in accordance with the principle of free choice of means. Recourse to, or acceptance of, a settlement procedure freely agreed to by States with regard to existing or future disputes to which they are parties shall not be regarded as incompatible with sovereign equality.

Nothing in the foregoing paragraphs prejudices or derogates from the applicable provisions of the Charter, in particular those relating to the pacific settlement of international disputes.

The principle concerning the duty not to intervene in matters within the domestic jurisdiction of any State, in accordance with the Charter

No State or group of States has the right to intervene, directly or indirectly, for any reason whatever, in the internal or external affairs of any other State. Consequently, armed intervention and all other forms of interference or attempted threats against the personality of the State or against its political, economic and cultural elements, are in violation of international law.

No State may use or encourage the use of economic, political or any other type of measures to coerce another State in order to obtain from it the subordination of the exercise of its sovereign rights and to secure from it advantages of any kind. Also, no State shall organize, assist, foment, finance, incite or tolerate subversive, terrorist or armed activities directed towards the violent overthrow of the régime of another State, or interfere in civil strife in another State.

The use of force to deprive peoples of their national identity constitutes a violation of their inalienable rights and of the principle of non-intervention.

Every State has an inalienable right to choose its political, economic, social and cultural systems, without interference in any form by another State.

Nothing in the foregoing paragraphs shall be construed as affecting the relevant provisions of the Charter relating to the maintenance of international peace and security.

The duty of States to co-operate with one another in accordance with the Charter

States have the duty to co-operate with one another, irrespective of the differences in their political, economic and social systems, in the various spheres of international relations, in order to maintain international peace and security and to promote international economic stability and progress, the general welfare of nations and international co-operation free from discrimination based on such differences.

To this end:

(*a*) States shall co-operate with other States in the maintenance of international peace and security;

(*b*) States shall co-operate in the promotion of universal respect for, and observance of, human rights and fundamental freedoms for all, and in the elimination of all forms of racial discrimination and all forms of religious intolerance;

(*c*) States shall conduct their international relations in the economic, social, cultural, technical and trade fields in accordance with the principles of sovereign equality and non-intervention;

(*d*) States Members of the United Nations have the duty to take joint and separate action in co-operation with the United Nations in accordance with the relevant provisions of the Charter.

States should co-operate in the economic, social and cultural fields as well as in the field of science and technology and for the promotion of international cultural and educational progress. States should co-operate in the promotion of economic growth throughout the world, especially that of the developing countries.

The principle of equal rights and self-determination of peoples

By virtue of the principle of equal rights and self-determination of peoples enshrined in the Charter of the United Nations, all peoples have the right freely to determine, without external interference, their political status and to pursue their economic, social and cultural development, and every State has the duty to respect this right in accordance with the provisions of the Charter.

Every State has the duty to promote, through joint and separate action, realization of the principle of equal rights and self-determination of peoples, in accordance with the provisions of the Charter, and to render assistance to the United Nations in carrying out the responsibilities entrusted to it by the Charter regarding the implementation of the principle, in order:

(*a*) To promote friendly relations and co-operation among States; and

(*b*) To bring a speedy end to colonialism, having due regard to the freely expressed will of the peoples concerned;

and bearing in mind that subjection of peoples to alien subjugation, domination and exploitation constitutes a violation of the principle, as well as a denial of fundamental human rights, and is contrary to the Charter.

Every State has the duty to promote through joint and separate action universal respect for and observance of human rights and fundamental freedoms in accordance with the Charter.

The establishment of a sovereign and independent State, the free association or integration with an independent State or the emergence into any other political status freely determined by a people constitute modes of implementing the right of self-determination by that people.

Every State has the duty to refrain from any forcible action which deprives peoples referred to above in the elaboration of the present principle of their right to self-determination and freedom and independence. In their actions against, and resistance to, such forcible action in pursuit of the exercise of their right to self-determination, such peoples are entitled to seek and to receive support in accordance with the purposes and principles of the Charter.

The territory of a colony or other Non-Self-Governing Territory has, under the Charter, a status separate and distinct from the territory of the State administering it; and such separate and distinct status under the Charter shall exist until the people of the colony or Non-Self-Governing Territory have exercised their right of self-determination in accordance with the Charter, and particularly its purposes and principles.

Nothing in the foregoing paragraphs shall be construed as authorizing or encouraging any action which would dismember or impair, totally or in part, the territorial integrity or political unity of sovereign and independent States conducting themselves in compliance with the principle of equal rights and self-determination of peoples as described above and thus possessed of a government representing the whole people belonging to the territory without distinction as to race, creed or colour.

Every State shall refrain from any action aimed at the partial or total disruption of the national unity and territorial integrity of any other State or country.

The principle of sovereign equality of States

All States enjoy sovereign equality. They have equal rights and duties and are equal members of the international community, notwithstanding differences of an economic, social, political or other nature.

In particular, sovereign equality includes the following elements:

(*a*) States are juridically equal;

(*b*) Each State enjoys the rights inherent in full sovereignty;

(*c*) Each State has the duty to respect the personality of other States;

(*d*) The territorial integrity and political independence of the State are inviolable;

(*e*) Each State has the right freely to choose and develop its political, social, economic and cultural systems;

(*f*) Each State has the duty to comply fully and in good faith with its international obligations and to live in peace with other States.

The principle that States shall fulfil in good faith the obligations assumed by them in accordance with the Charter

Every State has the duty to fulfil in good faith the obligations assumed by it in accordance with the Charter of the United Nations.

Every State has the duty to fulfil in good faith its obligations under the generally recognized principles and rules of international law.

Every State has the duty to fulfil in good faith its obligations under international agreements valid under the generally recognized principles and rules of international law.

Where obligations arising under international agreements are in conflict with the obligations of Members of the United Nations under the Charter of the United Nations, the obligations under the Charter shall prevail.

GENERAL PART

2. *Declares* that:

In their interpretation and application the above principles are interrelated and each principle should be construed in the context of the other principles.

Nothing in this Declaration shall be construed as prejudicing in any manner the provisions of the Charter or the rights and duties of Member States under the Charter or the rights of peoples under the Charter, taking into account the elaboration of these rights in this Declaration.

3. *Declares further* that:

The principles of the Charter which are embodied in this Declaration constitute basic principles of international law, and consequently appeals to all States to be guided by these principles in their international conduct and to develop their mutual relations on the basis of the strict observance of these principles.

Charter of Economic Rights and Duties of States

On 12 December 1974, the General Assembly adopted the Charter of Economic Rights and Duties of States, contained in resolution 3281 (XXIX). It was adopted by a roll-call vote of 120 in favour to 6 against, with 10 abstentions. In the preamble of the resolution, the Assembly stressed the fact that "the Charter shall constitute an effective instrument towards the establishment of a new system of international economic relations based on equity, sovereign equality, and interdependence of the interests of developed and developing countries".

PREAMBLE

THE GENERAL ASSEMBLY,

Reaffirming the fundamental purposes of the United Nations, in particular, the maintenance of international peace and security, the development of friendly relations among nations and the achievement of international co-operation in solving international problems in the economic and social fields,

Affirming the need for strengthening international co-operation in these fields,

Reaffirming further the need for strengthening international co-operation for development,

Declaring that it is a fundamental purpose of this Charter to promote the establishment of the new international economic order, based on equity, sovereign equality, interdependence, common interest and co-operation among all States, irrespective of their economic and social systems,

Desirous of contributing to the creation of conditions for:

(a) The attainment of wider prosperity among all countries and of higher standards of living for all peoples,

(b) The promotion by the entire international community of economic and social progress of all countries, especially developing countries,

(c) The encouragement of co-operation, on the basis of mutual advantage and equitable benefits for all peace-loving States which are willing to carry out the provisions of this Charter, in the economic, trade, scientific and technical fields, regardless of political, economic or social systems,

(d) The overcoming of main obstacles in the way of the economic development of the developing countries,

(e) The acceleration of the economic growth of developing countries with a view to bridging the economic gap between developing and developed countries,

(f) The protection, preservation and enhancement of the environment,

Mindful of the need to establish and maintain a just and equitable economic and social order through:

(a) The achievement of more rational and equitable international economic relations and the encouragement of structural changes in the world economy,

(b) The creation of conditions which permit the further expansion of trade and intensification of economic co-operation among all nations,

(c) The strengthening of the economic independence of developing countries,

(d) The establishment and promotion of international economic relations, taking into account the agreed differences in development of the developing countries and their specific needs,

Determined to promote collective economic security for development, in particular of the developing countries, with strict respect for the sovereign equality of each State and through the co-operation of the entire international community,

Considering that genuine co-operation among States, based on joint consideration of and concerted action regarding international economic problems, is essential for fulfilling the international community's common desire to achieve a just and rational development of all parts of the world,

Stressing the importance of ensuring appropriate conditions for the conduct of normal economic relations among all States, irrespective of differences in social and economic systems, and for the full respect for the rights of all peoples, as well as the strengthening of instruments of international economic co-operation as means for the consolidation of peace for the benefit of all,

Convinced of the need to develop a system of international economic relations on the basis of sovereign equality, mutual and equitable benefit and the close interrelationship of the interests of all States,

Reiterating that the responsibility for the development of every country rests primarily upon itself but that concomitant and effective international co-operation is an essential factor for the full achievement of its own development goals,

Firmly convinced of the urgent need to evolve a substantially improved system of international economic relations,

Solemnly adopts the present Charter of Economic Rights and Duties of States.

CHAPTER I

Fundamentals of international economic relations

Economic as well as political and other relations among States shall be governed, *inter alia*, by the following principles:

(a) Sovereignty, territorial integrity and political independence of States;

(b) Sovereign equality of all States;

(c) Non-aggression;

(d) Non-intervention;

(e) Mutual and equitable benefit;

(f) Peaceful coexistence;

(g) Equal rights and self-determination of peoples;

(h) Peaceful settlement of disputes;

(i) Remedying of injustices which have been brought about by force and which deprive a nation of the natural means necessary for its normal development;

(j) Fulfilment in good faith of international obligations;

(k) Respect for human rights and fundamental freedoms;

(l) No attempt to seek hegemony and spheres of influence;

(m) Promotion of international social justice;

(n) International co-operation for development;

(o) Free access to and from the sea by land-locked countries within the framework of the above principles.

CHAPTER II

Economic rights and duties of States

Article 1

Every State has the sovereign and inalienable right to choose its economic system as well as its political, social and cultural systems in accordance with the will of its people, without outside interference, coercion or threat in any form whatsoever.

Article 2

1. Every State has and shall freely exercise full permanent sovereignty, including possession, use and disposal, over all its wealth, natural resources and economic activities.

2. Each State has the right:

(a) To regulate and exercise authority over foreign investment within its national jurisdiction in accordance with its laws and regulations and in conformity with its national objectives and priorities. No State shall be compelled to grant preferential treatment to foreign investment;

(b) To regulate and supervise the activities of transnational corporations within its national jurisdiction and take measures to ensure that such activities comply with its laws, rules and regulations and conform with its economic and social policies. Transnational corporations shall not intervene in the internal affairs of a host State. Every State should, with full regard for its sovereign rights, co-operate with other States in the exercise of the right set forth in this subparagraph;

(c) To nationalize, expropriate or transfer ownership of foreign property, in which case appropriate compensation should be paid by the State adopting such measures, taking into account its relevant laws and regulations and all circumstances that the State considers pertinent. In any case where the question of compensation gives rise to a controversy, it shall be settled under the domestic law of the nationalizing State and by its tribunals, unless it is freely and mutually agreed by all States concerned that other peaceful means be sought on the basis of the sovereign equality of States and in accordance with the principle of free choice of means.

Article 3

In the exploitation of natural resources shared by two or more countries, each State must co-operate on the basis of a system of information and prior consultations in order to achieve optimum use of such resources without causing damage to the legitimate interest of others.

Article 4

Every State has the right to engage in international trade and other forms of economic co-operation irrespective of any differences in political, economic and social systems. No State shall be subjected to discrimination of any kind based solely on such differences. In the pursuit of international trade and other forms of economic co-operation, every State is free to choose the forms of organization of its foreign economic relations and to enter into bilateral and multilateral arrangements consistent with its international obligations and with the needs of international economic co-operation.

Article 5

All States have the right to associate in organizations of primary commodity producers in order to develop their national economies to achieve stable financing for their development, and in pursuance of their aims, to assist in the promotion of sustained growth of the world economy, in particular accelerating the development of developing countries. Correspondingly all States have the duty to respect that right by refraining from applying economic and political measures that would limit it.

Article 6

It is the duty of States to contribute to the development of international trade of goods, particularly by means of arrangements and by the conclusion of long-term multilateral commodity agreements, where appropriate, and taking into account the interests of producers and consumers. All States share the responsibility to promote the regular flow and access of all commercial goods traded at stable, remunerative and equitable prices, thus contributing to the equitable development of the world economy, taking into account, in particular, the interests of developing countries.

Article 7

Every State has the primary responsibility to promote the economic, social and cultural development of its people. To this end, each State has the right and the responsibility to choose its means and goals of development, fully to mobilize and use its resources, to implement progressive economic and social reforms and to ensure the full participation of its people in the process and benefits of development. All States have the duty, individually and collectively, to co-operate in order to eliminate obstacles that hinder such mobilization and use.

Article 8

States should co-operate in facilitating more rational and equitable international economic relations and in encouraging structural changes in the context of a balanced world economy in harmony with the needs and interests of all countries, especially developing countries, and should take appropriate measures to this end.

Article 9

All States have the responsibility to co-operate in the economic, social, cultural, scientific and technological fields for the promotion of economic and social progress throughout the world, especially that of the developing countries.

Article 10

All States are juridically equal and, as equal members of the international community, have the right to participate fully and effectively in the international decision-making process in the solution of world economic, financial and monetary problems, *inter alia,* through the appropriate international organizations in accordance with their existing and evolving rules, and to share equitably in the benefits resulting therefrom.

Article 11

All States should co-operate to strengthen and continuously improve the efficiency of international organizations in implementing measures to stimulate the general economic progress of all countries, particularly of developing countries, and therefore should co-operate to adapt them, when appropriate, to the changing needs of international economic co-operation.

Article 12

1. States have the right, in agreement with the parties concerned, to participate in subregional, regional and interregional co-operation in the pursuit of their economic and social development. All States engaged in such co-operation have the duty to ensure that the policies of those groupings to which they belong correspond to the provisions of the Charter and are outward-looking, consistent with their international obligations and with the needs of international economic co-operation and have full regard for the legitimate interests of third countries, especially developing countries.

2. In the case of groupings to which the States concerned have transferred or may transfer certain competences as regards matters that come within the scope of the present Charter, its provisions shall also apply to those groupings, in regard to such matters, consistent with the responsibilities of such States as members of such groupings. Those States shall co-operate in the observance by the groupings of the provisions of this Charter.

Article 13

1. Every State has the right to benefit from the advances and developments in science and technology for the acceleration of its economic and social development.

2. All States should promote international scientific and technological co-operation and the transfer of technology, with proper regard for all legitimate interests including, *inter alia,* the rights and duties of holders, suppliers and recipients of technology. In particular, all States should facilitate the access of developing countries to the achievements of modern science and technology, the transfer of technology and the creation of indigenous technology for the benefit of the developing countries in forms and in accordance with procedures which are suited to their economies and their needs.

3. Accordingly, developed countries should co-operate with the developing countries in the establishment, strengthening and development of their scientific and technological infrastructures and their scientific research and technological activities so as to help to expand and transform the economies of developing countries.

4. All States should co-operate in exploring with a view to evolving further internationally accepted guidelines or regulations for the transfer of technology, taking fully into account the interests of developing countries.

Article 14

Every State has the duty to co-operate in promoting a steady and increasing expansion and liberalization of world trade and an improvement in the welfare and living standards of all peoples, in particular those of developing countries. Accordingly, all States should co-operate, *inter alia,* towards the progressive dismantling of obstacles to trade and the improvement of the international framework for the conduct of world trade and, to these ends, co-ordinated efforts shall be made to solve in an equitable way the trade problems of all countries, taking into account the specific trade problems of the developing countries. In this connexion, States shall take measures aimed at securing additional benefits for the international trade of developing countries so as to achieve a substantial increase in their foreign exchange earnings, the diversification of their exports, the acceleration of the rate of growth of their trade, taking into account their development needs, an improvement in the possibilities for these countries to participate in the expansion of world trade and a balance more favourable to developing countries in the sharing of the advantages resulting from this expansion, through, in the largest possible measure, a substantial improvement in the conditions of access for the products of interest to the developing countries and, wherever appropriate, measures designed to attain stable, equitable and remunerative prices for primary products.

Article 15

All States have the duty to promote the achievement of general and complete disarmament under effective international control and to utilize the resources freed by effective disarmanent measures for the economic and social development of countries, allocating a substantial portion of such resources as additional means for the development needs of developing countries.

Article 16

1. It is the right and duty of all States, individually and collectively, to eliminate colonialism, *apartheid,* racial discrimination, neo-colonialism and all forms of foreign aggression, occupation and domination, and the economic and social consequences thereof, as a prerequisite for development. States which practise such coercive policies are economically responsible to the countries, territories and peoples affected for the restitution and full compensation for the exploitation and depletion of, and damages to, the natural and all other resources of those countries, territories and peoples. It is the duty of all States to extend assistance to them.

2. No State has the right to promote or encourage investments that may constitute an obstacle to the liberation of a territory occupied by force.

Article 17

International co-operation for development is the shared goal and common duty of all States. Every State should co-operate with the efforts of developing countries to accelerate their economic and social development by providing favourable external conditions and by extending active assistance to them, consistent with their development needs and objectives, with strict respect for the sovereign equality of States and free of any conditions derogating from their sovereignty.

Article 18

Developed countries should extend, improve and enlarge the system of generalized non-reciprocal and non-discriminatory tariff preferences to the developing countries consistent with the relevant agreed conclusions and relevant decisions as adopted on this subject, in the framework of the competent international organizations. Developed countries should also give serious consideration to the adoption of other differential measures, in areas where this is feasible and appropriate and in ways which will provide special and more favourable treatment, in order to meet the trade and development needs of the developing countries. In the conduct of international economic relations the developed countries should endeavour to avoid measures having a negative effect on the development of the national economies of the developing countries, as promoted by generalized tariff preferences and other generally agreed differential measures in their favour.

Article 19

With a view to accelerating the economic growth of developing countries and bridging the economic gap between developed and developing countries, developed countries should grant generalized preferential, non-reciprocal and non-discriminatory treatment to developing countries in those fields of international economic co-operation where it may be feasible.

Article 20

Developing countries should, in their efforts to increase their over-all trade, give due attention to the possibility of expanding their trade with socialist countries, by granting to these countries conditions for trade not inferior to those granted normally to the developed market economy countries.

Article 21

Developing countries should endeavour to promote the expansion of their mutual trade and to this end may, in accordance with the existing and evolving provisions and procedures of international agreements where applicable, grant trade preferences to other developing countries without being obliged to extend such preferences to developed countries, provided these arrangements do not constitute an impediment to general trade liberalization and expansion.

Article 22

1. All States should respond to the generally recognized or mutually agreed development needs and objectives of developing countries by promoting increased net flows of real resources to the developing countries from all sources, taking into account any obligations and commitments undertaken by the States concerned, in order to reinforce the efforts of developing countries to accelerate their economic and social development.

2. In this context, consistent with the aims and objectives mentioned above and taking into account any obligations and commitments undertaken in this regard, it should be their endeavour to increase the net amount of financial flows from official sources to developing countries and to improve the terms and conditions thereof.

3. The flow of development assistance resources should include economic and technical assistance.

Article 23

To enhance the effective mobilization of their own resources, the developing countries should strengthen their economic co-operation and expand their mutual trade so as to accelerate their economic and social development. All countries, especially developed countries, individually as well as through the competent international organizations of which they are members, should provide appropriate and effective support and co-operation.

Article 24

All States have the duty to conduct their mutual economic relations in a manner which takes into account the interests of other countries. In particular, all States should avoid prejudicing the interests of developing countries.

Article 25

In furtherance of world economic development, the international community, especially its developed members, shall pay special attention to the particular needs and problems of the least developed among the developing countries, of land-locked developing countries and also island developing countries, with a view to helping them to overcome their particular difficulties and thus contribute to their economic and social development.

Article 26

All States have the duty to coexist in tolerance and live together in peace, irrespective of differences in political, economic, social and cultural systems, and to facilitate trade between States having different economic and social systems. International trade should be conducted without prejudice to generalized non-discriminatory and non-reciprocal preferences in favour of developing countries, on the basis of mutual advantage, equitable benefits and the exchange of most-favoured-nation treatment.

Article 27

1. Every State has the right to enjoy fully the benefits of world invisible trade and to engage in the expansion of such trade.

2. World invisible trade, based on efficiency and mutual and equitable benefit, furthering the expansion of the world economy, is the common goal of all States. The role of developing countries in world invisible trade should be enhanced and strengthened consistent with the above objectives, particular attention being paid to the special needs of developing countries.

3. All States should co-operate with developing countries in their endeavours to increase their capacity to earn foreign exchange from invisible transactions, in accordance with the potential and needs of each developing country and consistent with the objectives mentioned above.

Article 28

All States have the duty to co-operate in achieving adjustments in the prices of exports of developing countries in relation to prices of their imports so as to promote just and equitable terms of trade for them, in a manner which is remunerative for producers and equitable for producers and consumers.

CHAPTER III

Common responsibilities towards the international community

Article 29

The sea-bed and ocean floor and the subsoil thereof, beyond the limits of national jurisdiction, as well as the resources of the area, are the common heritage of mankind. On the basis of the principles adopted by the General Assembly in resolution 2749 (XXV) of 17 December 1970, all States shall ensure that the exploration of the area and exploitation of its resources are carried out exclusively for peaceful purposes and that the benefits derived therefrom are shared equitably by all States, taking into account the particular interests and needs of developing countries; an international régime applying to the area and its resources and including appropriate international machinery to give effect to its provisions shall be established by an international treaty of a universal character, generally agreed upon.

Article 30

The protection, preservation and the enhancement of the environment for the present and future generations is the responsibility of all States. All States shall endeavour to establish their own environmental and developmental policies in conformity with such responsibility. The environmental policies of all States should enhance and not adversely affect the present and future development potential of developing countries. All States have the responsibility to ensure that activities within their jurisdiction or control do not cause damage to the environment of other States or of areas beyond the limits of national jurisdiction. All States should co-operate in evolving international norms and regulations in the field of the environment.

CHAPTER IV

Final provisions

Article 31

All States have the duty to contribute to the balanced expansion of the world economy, taking duly into account the close interrelationship between the well-being of the developed countries and the growth and development of the developing countries, and the fact that the prosperity of the international community as a whole depends upon the prosperity of its constituent parts.

Article 32

No State may use or encourage the use of economic, political or any other type of measures to coerce another State in order to obtain from it the subordination of the exercise of its sovereign rights.

Article 33

1. Nothing in the present Charter shall be construed as impairing or derogating from the provisions of the Charter of the United Nations or actions taken in pursuance thereof.

2. In their interpretation and application, the provisions of the present Charter are interrelated and each provision should be construed in the context of the other provisions.

Article 34

An item on the Charter of Economic Rights and Duties of States shall be inscribed in the agenda of the General Assembly at its thirtieth session, and thereafter on the agenda of every fifth session. In this way a systematic and comprehensive consideration of the implementation of the Charter, covering both progress achieved and any improvements and additions which might become necessary, would be carried out and appropriate measures recommended. Such consideration should take into account the evolution of all the economic, social, legal and other factors related to the principles upon which the present Charter is based and on its purpose.

TREATIES

GENERAL AGREEMENT ON TARIFFS AND TRADE SIGNED AT GENEVA, ON 30 OCTOBER 1947

Article I

General Most-Favoured-Nation Treatment

1. With respect to customs duties and charges of any kind imposed on or in connection with importation or exportation or imposed on the international transfer of payments for imports or exports, and with respect to the method of levying such duties and charges, and with respect to all rules and formalities in connection with importation and exportation, and with respect to all matters referred to in paragraphs 1 and 2 of Article III, any advantage, favour, privilege or immunity granted by any contracting party to any product originating in or destined for any other country shall be accorded immediately and unconditionally to the like product originating in or destined for the territories of all other contracting parties.

2. The provisions of paragraph 1 of this Article shall not require the elimination of any preferences in respect of import duties or charges which do not exceed the levels provided for in paragraph 3 of this Article and which fall within the following descriptions :

(a) preferences in force exclusively between two or more of the territories listed in Annex A, subject to the conditions set forth therein;

(b) preferences in force exclusively between two or more territories which on July 1, 1939, were connected by common sovereignty or relations of protection or suzerainty and which are listed in Annexes B, C and D, subject to the conditions set forth therein;

(c) preferences in force exclusively between the United States of America and the Republic of Cuba;

(d) preferences in force exclusively between neighbouring countries listed in Annexes E and F.

3. The margin of preference on any product in respect of which a preference is permitted under paragraph 2 of this Article but is not specifically set forth as a maximum margin of preference in the appropriate Schedule annexed to this Agreement shall not exceed :

(a) in respect of duties or charges on any product described in such Schedule, the difference between the most-favoured-nation and preferential rates provided for therein; if no preferential rate is

provided for, the preferential rate shall for the purposes of this paragraph be taken to be that in force on April 10, 1947, and, if no most-favoured-nation rate is provided for, the margin shall not exceed the difference between the most-favoured-nation and preferential rates existing on April 10, 1947;

(b) in respect of duties or charges on any product not described in the appropriate Schedule, the difference between the most-favoured-nation and preferential rates existing on April 10, 1947.

In the case of the contracting parties named in Annex G, the date of April 10, 1947, referred to in subparagraphs *(a)* and *(b)* of this paragraph shall be replaced by the respective dates set forth in that Annex.

Article II

Schedules of Concessions

1. *(a)* Each contracting party shall accord to the commerce of the other contracting parties treatment no less favourable than that provided for in the appropriate Part of the appropriate Schedule annexed to this Agreement.

(b) The products described in Part I of the Schedule relating to any contracting party, which are the products of territories of other contracting parties, shall, on their importation into the territory to which the Schedule relates, and subject to the terms, conditions or qualifications set forth in that Schedule, be exempt from ordinary customs duties in excess of those set forth and provided for therein. Such products shall also be exempt from all other duties or charges of any kind imposed on or in connection with importation in excess of those imposed on the date of this Agreement or those directly and mandatorily required to be imposed thereafter by legislation in force in the importing territory on that date.

(c) The products described in Part II of the Schedule relating to any contracting party, which are the products of territories entitled under Article I to receive preferential treatment upon importation into the territory to which the Schedule relates, shall, on their importation into such territory, and subject to the terms, conditions or qualifications set forth in that Schedule, be exempt from ordinary customs duties in excess of those set forth and provided for in Part II of that Schedule. Such products shall also be exempt from all other duties or charges of any kind imposed on or in

connection with importation in excess of those imposed on the date of this Agreement or those directly and mandatorily required to be imposed thereafter by legislation in force in the importing territory on that date. Nothing in this Article shall prevent any contracting party from maintaining its requirements existing on the date of this Agreement as to the eligibility of goods for entry at preferential rates of duty.

2. Nothing in this Article shall prevent any contracting party from imposing at any time on the importation of any product

(a) a charge equivalent to an internal tax imposed consistently with the provisions of paragraph 1 of Article III in respect of the like domestic product or in respect of an article from which the imported product has been manufactured or produced in whole or in part;

(b) any anti-dumping or countervailing duty applied consistently with the provisions of Article VI;

(c) fees or other charges commensurate with the cost of services rendered.

3. No contracting party shall alter its method of determining dutiable value or of converting currencies so as to impair the value of any of the concessions provided for in the appropriate Schedule annexed to this Agreement.

4. If any contracting party establishes, maintains or authorizes, formally or in effect, a monopoly of the importation of any product described in the appropriate Schedule annexed to this Agreement, such monopoly shall not, except as provided for in that Schedule or as otherwise agreed between the parties which initially negotiated the concession, operate so as to afford protection on the average in excess of the amount of protection provided for in that Schedule. The provisions of this paragraph shall not limit the use by contracting parties of any form of assistance to domestic producers permitted by other provisions of this Agreement.

5. If any contracting party considers that a product is not receiving from another contracting party the treatment which the first contracting party believes to have been contemplated by a concession provided for in the appropriate Schedule annexed to this Agreement, it shall bring the matter directly to the attention of the other contracting party. If the latter agrees that the treatment contemplated was that claimed by the first contracting party, but declares that such treatment cannot be accorded because a court or other proper authority has ruled to the effect that the product involved cannot be classified under the tariff laws of such contracting party so as to permit the treatment contemplated in this Agreement, the two contracting parties, together with any other contracting parties substantially interested, shall enter promptly into further negotiations with a view to a compensatory adjustment of the matter.

6. *(a)* The specific duties and charges included in the Schedules relating to contracting parties members of the International Monetary Fund, and margins of preference in specific duties and charges maintained by such contracting parties, are expressed in the appropriate currency at the par value accepted or provisionally recognized by the Fund at the date of this Agreement. Accordingly, in case this par value is reduced consistently with the Articles of Agreement of the International Monetary Fund by more than twenty per centum, such specific duties and charges and margins of preference may be adjusted to take account of such reduction; *Provided* that the CONTRACTING PARTIES (i.e. the contracting parties acting jointly as provided for in Article XXV) concur that such adjustments will not impair the value of the concessions provided for in the appropriate Schedule or elsewhere in this Agreement, due account being taken of all factors which may influence the need for, or urgency of, such adjustments.

(b) Similar provisions shall apply to any contracting party not a member of the Fund, as from the date on which such contracting party becomes a member of the Fund or enters into a special exchange agreement in pursuance of Article XV.

7. The Schedules annexed to this Agreement are hereby made an integral part of Part I of this Agreement.

Article XI

GENERAL ELIMINATION OF QUANTITATIVE RESTRICTIONS

1. No prohibitions or restrictions other than duties, taxes or other charges, whether made effective through quotas, import or export licenses or other measures, shall be instituted or maintained by any contracting party on the importation of any product of the territory of any other contracting party or on the exportation or sale for export of any product destined for the territory of any other contracting party.

2. The provisions of paragraph 1 of this Article shall not extend to the following :

(a) export prohibitions or restrictions temporarily applied to prevent or relieve critical shortages of foodstuffs or other products essential to the exporting contracting party;

(b) import and export prohibitions or restrictions necessary to the application of standards or regulations for the classification, grading or marketing of commodities in international trade;

(c) import restrictions on any agricultural or fisheries product, imported in any form, necessary to the enforcement of governmental measures which operate :

(i) to restrict the quantities of the like domestic product permitted to be marketed or produced, or, if there is no substantial domestic production of the like product, of a domestic product for which the imported product can be directly substituted; or

(ii) to remove a temporary surplus of the like domestic product, or, if there is no substantial domestic production of the like product, of a domestic product for which the imported product can be directly substituted, by making the surplus available to certain groups of domestic consumers free of charge or at prices below the current market level; or

(iii) to restrict the quantities permitted to be produced of any animal product the production of which is directly dependent, wholly or mainly, on the imported commodity, if the domestic production of that commodity is relatively negligible.

Any contracting party applying restrictions on the importation of any product pursuant to sub-paragraph *(c)* of this paragraph shall give public notice of the total quantity or value of the product permitted to be imported during a specified future period and of any change in such quantity or value. Moreover, any restrictions applied under (i) above shall not be such as will reduce the total of imports relative to the total of domestic production, as compared with the proportion which might reasonably be expected to rule between the two in the absence of restrictions. In determining this proportion, the contracting party shall pay due regard to the proportion prevailing during a previous representative period and to any special factors which may have affected or may be affecting the trade in the product concerned.

3. Throughout Articles XI, XII, XIII and XIV the terms " import restrictions " or " export restrictions " include restrictions made effective through state-trading operations.

Article XIII

Non-discriminatory Administration of Quantitative Restrictions

1. No prohibition or restriction shall be applied by any contracting party on the importation of any product of the territory of any other contracting party or on the exportation of any product destined for the territory of any other contracting party, unless the importation of the like product of all third countries or the exportation of the like product to all third countries is similarly prohibited or restricted.

2. In applying import restrictions to any product, contracting parties shall aim at a distribution of trade in such product approaching as closely as possible to the shares which the various contracting parties might be expected to obtain in the absence of such restrictions, and to this end shall observe the following provisions :

(a) wherever practicable, quotas representing the total amount of permitted imports (whether allocated among supplying countries or not) shall be fixed, and notice given of their amount in accordance with paragraph 3 *(b)* of this Article;

(b) in cases in which quotas are not practicable, the restrictions may be applied by means of import licences or permits without a quota;

(c) contracting parties shall not, except for purposes of operating quotas allocated in accordance with sub-paragraph *(d)* of this paragraph, require that import licences or permits be utilized for the importation of the product concerned from a particular country or source;

(d) in cases in which a quota is allocated among supplying countries, the contracting party applying the restrictions may seek agreement with respect to the allocation of shares in the quota with all other contracting parties having a substantial interest in supplying the product concerned. In cases in which this method is not reasonably practicable, the contracting party concerned shall allot to contracting parties having a substantial interest in supplying the product shares based upon the proportions, supplied by such contracting parties during a previous representative period, of the total quantity or value of imports of the product, due account being taken of any special factors which may have affected or may be affecting the trade in the product. No conditions or formalities shall be imposed which would prevent any contracting party from utilizing fully the share of any such total quantity or value which has been allotted to it, subject to importation being made within any prescribed period to which the quota may relate.

3. *(a)* In cases in which import licences are issued in connection with import restrictions, the contracting party applying the restrictions shall provide, upon the request of any contracting party having an interest in the trade in the product concerned, all relevant information concerning the administration of the restrictions, the import licences granted over a recent period and the distribution of such licences among supplying countries; *Provided* that there shall be no obligation to supply information as to the names of importing or supplying enterprises.

(b) In the case of import restrictions involving the fixing of quotas, the contracting party applying the restrictions shall give public notice of the total quantity or value of the product or products which will be permitted to be imported during a specified future period and of any change in such

quantity or value. Any supplies of the product in question which were en route at the time at which public notice was given shall not be excluded from entry; *Provided* that they may be counted so far as practicable, against the quantity permitted to be imported in the period in question, and also, where necessary, against the quantities permitted to be imported in the next following period or periods; and *Provided* further that if any contracting party customarily exempts from such restrictions products entered for consumption or withdrawn from warehouse for consumption during a period of thirty days after the day of such public notice, such practice shall be considered full compliance with this sub-paragraph.

(c) In the case of quotas allocated among supplying countries, the contracting party applying the restrictions shall promptly inform all other contracting parties having an interest in supplying the product concerned of the shares in the quota currently allocated, by quantity or value, to the various supplying countries and shall give public notice thereof.

4. With regard to restrictions applied in accordance with paragraph 2 *(d)* of this Article or under paragraph 2 *(c)* of Article XI, the selection of a representative period for any product and the appraisal of any special factors affecting the trade in the product shall be made initially by the contracting party applying the restriction; *Provided* that such contracting party shall upon the request of any other contracting party having a substantial interest in supplying that product or upon the request of the CONTRACTING PARTIES, consult promptly with the other contracting party or the CONTRACTING PARTIES regarding the need for an adjustment of the proportion determined or of the base period selected, or for the reappraisal of the special factors involved, or for the elimination of conditions, formalities or any other provisions established unilaterally relating to the allocation of an adequate quota or its unrestricted utilization.

5. The provisions of this Article shall apply to any tariff quota instituted or maintained by any contracting party, and, insofar as applicable, the principles of this Article shall also extend to export restrictions and to any internal regulation or requirement under paragraphs 3 and 4 of Article III.

Article XX

GENERAL EXCEPTIONS

Subject to the requirement that such measures are not applied in a manner which would constitute a means of arbitrary or unjustifiable discrimination between countries where the same conditions prevail, or a disguised restriction on international trade, nothing in this Agreement shall be construed to prevent the adoption or enforcement by any contracting party of measures :

I. *(a)* necessary to protect public morals;

(b) necessary to protect human, animal or plant life or health;

(*c*) relating to the importation or exportation of gold or silver;

(*d*) necessary to secure compliance with laws or regulations which are not inconsistent with the provisions of this Agreement, including those relating to customs enforcement, the enforcement of monopolies operated under paragraph 4 of Article II and Article XVII, the protection of patents, trade marks and copyrights, and the prevention of deceptive practices;

(*e*) relating to the products of prison labour;

(*f*) imposed for the protection of national treasures of artistic, historic or archaeological value;

(*g*) relating to the conservation of exhaustible natural resources if such measures are made effective in conjunction with restrictions on domestic production or consumption;

(*h*) undertaken in pursuance of obligations under intergovernmental commodity agreements, conforming to the principles approved by the Economic and Social Council of the United Nations in its Resolution of March 28, 1947, establishing an Interim Co-ordinating Committee for International Commodity Arrangements; or

(*i*) involving restrictions on exports of domestic materials necessary to assure essential quantities of such materials to a domestic processing industry during periods when the domestic price of such materials is held below the world price as part of a governmental stabilization plan; *Provided* that such restrictions shall not operate to increase the exports of or the protection afforded to such domestic industry, and shall not depart from the provisions of this Agreement relating to non-discrimination;

II. (*a*) essential to the acquisition or distribution of products in general or local short supply; *Provided* that any such measures shall be consistent with any multilateral arrangements directed to an equitable international distribution of such products or, in the absence of such arrangements, with the principle that all contracting parties are entitled to an equitable share of the international supply of such products;

(*b*) essential to the control of prices by a contracting party undergoing shortages subsequent to the war; or

(*c*) essential to the orderly liquidation of temporary surpluses of stocks owned or controlled by the government of any contracting party or of industries developed in the territory of any contracting party owing to the exigencies of the war which it would be uneconomic to maintain in normal conditions; *Provided* that such measures shall not be instituted by any contracting party except after consultation with other interested contracting parties with a view to appropriate international action.

Measures instituted or maintained under part II of this Article which are inconsistent with the other provisions of this Agreement shall be removed as soon as the conditions giving rise to them have ceased, and in any event not later than January 1, 1951; *Provided* that this period may, with the concurrence of the CONTRACTING PARTIES, be extended in respect of the application of any particular measure to any particular product by any particular contracting party for such further periods as the CONTRACTING PARTIES may specify.

Article XXI

SECURITY EXCEPTIONS

Nothing in this Agreement shall be construed

(a) to require any contracting party to furnish any information the disclosure of which it considers contrary to its essential security interests; or

(b) to prevent any contracting party from taking any action which it considers necessary for the protection of its essential security interests

(i) relating to fissionable materials or the materials from which they are derived;

(ii) relating to the traffic in arms, ammunition and implements of war and to such traffic in other goods and materials as is carried on directly of indirectly for the purpose of supplying a military establishment;

(iii) taken in time of war or other emergency in international relations; or

(c) to prevent any contracting party from taking any action in pursuance of its obligations under the United Nations Charter for the maintenance of international peace and security.

Article XXII

CONSULTATION

Each contracting party shall accord sympathetic consideration to, and shall afford adequate opportunity for consultation regarding, such representations as may be made by any other contracting party with respect to the operation of customs regulations and formalities, anti-dumping and countervailing duties, quantitative and exchange regulations, subsidies, state-trading operations, sanitary laws and regulations for the protection of human, animal or plant life or health, and generally all matters affecting the operation of this Agreement.

Article XXIII

Nullification or Impairment

If any contracting party should consider that any benefit accruing to it directly of indirectly under this Agreement is being nullified or impaired or that the attainment of any objective of the Agreement is being impeded as the result of *(a)* the failure of another contracting party to carry out its obligations under this Agreement, or *(b)* the application by another contracting party of any measure, whether or not it conflicts with the provisions of this Agreement, or *(c)* the existence of any other situation, the contracting party may, with a view to the satisfactory adjustment of the matter, make written representations or proposals to the other contracting party or parties which it considers to be concerned. Any contracting party thus approached shall give sympathetic consideration to the representations or proposals made to it.

2. If no satisfactory adjustment is effected between the contracting parties concerned within a reasonable time, or if the difficulty is of the type described in paragraph 1 *(c)* of this Article, the matter may be referred to the Contracting Parties. The Contracting Parties shall promptly investigate any matter so referred to them and shall make appropriate recommendations to the contracting parties which they consider to be concerned, or give a ruling on the matter, as appropriate. The Contracting Parties may consult with contracting parties, with the Economic and Social Council of the United Nations and with any appropriate inter-governmental organization in cases where they consider such consultation necessary. If the Contracting Parties consider that the circumstances are serious enough to justify such action, they may authorize a contracting party or parties to suspend the application to any other contracting party or parties of such obligations or concessions under this Agreement as they determine to be appropriate in the circumstances. If the application to any contracting party of any obligation or concession is in fact suspended, that contracting party shall then be free, not later than sixty days after such action is taken, to advise the Secretary-General of the United Nations in writing of its intention to withdraw from this Agreement and such withdrawal shall take effect upon the expiration of sixty days from the day on which written notice of such withdrawal is received by him.

Provisional agreement between the United States of America and the Kingdom of Saudi Arabia in regard to diplomatic and consular representation, juridical protection, commerce and navigation.[1] *Signed November 7, 1933.*

The Undersigned,

Mr. Robert Worth Bingham, Ambassador Extraordinary and Plenipotentiary of the United States of America at London, and Sheikh Hafiz Wahba, Minister of the Kingdom of Saudi Arabia at London, desiring to confirm and make a record of the understanding which they have reached in the course of recent conversations in the names of their respective Governments in regard to diplomatic and consular representation, juridical protection, commerce and navigation, have signed this Provisional Agreement:

Article I.

The diplomatic representatives of each country shall enjoy in the territories of the other the privileges and immunities derived from generally recognized international law. The consular representatives of each country, duly provided with exequatur, will be permitted to reside in the territories of the other in the places wherein consular representatives are by local laws permitted to reside; they shall enjoy the honorary privileges and the immunities accorded to such officers by general international usage; and they shall not be treated in a manner less favorable than similar officers of any other foreign country.

Article II.

Subjects of His Majesty the King of the Kingdom of Saudi Arabia in the United States of America, its territories and possessions, and nationals of the United States of America, its territories and possessions, in the Kingdom of Saudi Arabia shall be received and treated in accordance with the requirements and practices of generally recognized international law. In respect of their persons, possessions and rights, they shall enjoy the fullest protection of the laws and authorities of the country, and they shall not be treated in regard to their persons, property, rights and interests, in any manner less favorable than the nationals of any other foreign country.

Article III.

In respect of import, export and other duties and charges affecting commerce and navigation, as well as in respect of transit, warehousing and other facilities, the United States of America, its territories and possessions, will accord to the Kingdom of Saudi Arabia, and the Kingdom of Saudi Arabia will accord to the United States of America, its territories and possessions, unconditional most-favored nation treatment. Every concession with respect to any

[1] Arabic text not printed.

duty, charge or regulation affecting commerce or navigation now accorded or that may hereafter be accorded by the United States of America, its territories and possessions, or by the Kingdom of Saudi Arabia to any foreign country will become immediately applicable without request and without compensation to the commerce and navigation of the Kingdom of Saudi Arabia and of the United States of America, its territories and possessions, respectively.

Article IV.

The stipulations of this Agreement shall not extend to the treatment which is accorded by the United States of America to the commerce of Cuba under the provisions of the Commercial Convention concluded between the United States and Cuba on December 11, 1902, or the provisions of any other commercial convention which hereafter may be concluded between the United States of America and Cuba. Such stipulations, moreover, shall not extend to the treatment which is accorded to the commerce between the United States of America and the Panama Canal Zone or any of the dependencies of the United States of America or to the commerce of the dependencies of the United States of America with one another under existing or future laws.

Nothing in this Agreement shall be construed as a limitation of the right of either Government to impose, on such terms as it may see fit, prohibitions or restrictions of a sanitary character designed to protect human, animal, or plant life, or regulations for the enforcement of police or revenue laws.

Nothing in this Agreement shall be construed to affect existing statutes of either country in relation to the immigration of aliens or the right of either Government to enact such statutes.

Article V.

The present stipulations shall become operative on the day of signature hereof and shall remain respectively in effect until the entry in force of a definitive treaty of commerce and navigation, or until thirty days after notice of their termination shall have been given by the Government of either country, but should the Government of the United States of America be prevented by future action of its legislature from carrying out the terms of these stipulations, the obligations thereof shall thereupon lapse.

Article VI.

The English and Arabic texts of the present agreement shall be of equal validity.

Signed at London this seventh day of November, one thousand nine hundred and thirty-three.

Robert Worth Bingham [seal]
[Signature and seal of Sheikh Hafiz Wahba]

Treaty between the United States of America and Iraq respecting commerce and navigation. Signed at Baghdad December 3, 1938; ratification advised by the Senate of the United States August 1, 1939; ratified by the President of the United States August 30, 1939; ratified by Iraq May 1, 1940; ratifications exchanged at Baghdad May 20, 1940; proclaimed by the President of the United States May 29, 1940.

BY THE PRESIDENT OF THE UNITED STATES OF AMERICA.

A PROCLAMATION.

WHEREAS a Treaty of Commerce and Navigation between the United States of America and the Kingdom of Iraq was concluded and signed by their respective Plenipotentiaries at Baghdad on the third day of December, one thousand nine hundred and thirty-eight, the original of which Treaty, being in the English and Arabic languages, is word for word as follows:

TREATY OF COMMERCE AND NAVIGATION BETWEEN THE UNITED STATES OF AMERICA AND THE KINGDOM OF IRAQ.

The United States of America and His Majesty the King of Iraq, taking cognizance of the provisions of Article 7 of the Convention, signed at London January 9, 1930, to which the United States of America, Great Britain, and Iraq are Parties, whereby on the termination of the special relations existing between His Britannic Majesty and His Majesty the King of Iraq, negotiations shall be entered into between the United States and Iraq for the conclusion of a treaty in regard to their future relations, have resolved to conclude a treaty of Commerce and Navigation and for that purpose have appointed as their Plenipotentiaries:

THE PRESIDENT OF THE UNITED STATES OF AMERICA:
PAUL KNABENSHUE,
Minister Resident of the United States of America at Baghdad.
HIS MAJESTY THE KING OF IRAQ:
His Excellency Sayid TOWFIK AL SWAIDI,
Minister for Foreign Affairs.

Who, having communicated to each other their full powers found to be in due form, have agreed upon the following articles:

Article 1.

In respect of import and export duties, all other charges imposed on or in connection with importation or exportation, and the method of levying such duties and charges, as well as in respect of transit, warehousing and customs formalities, and the treatment of commercial traveler's samples, the United States of America will accord to Iraq and Iraq will accord to the United States of America, its territories and possessions, unconditional most-favored-nation treatment.

Therefore, no higher or other duties shall be imposed on the importation into or the disposition in the United States of America, its territories or possessions, of any articles the growth, produce or manufacture of Iraq than are or shall be payable on like articles the growth, produce or manufacture of any other foreign country.

Similarly, no higher or other duties shall be imposed on the importation into or the disposition in Iraq of any articles the growth, produce or manufacture of the United States of America, its territories or possessions, than are or shall be payable on like articles the growth, produce or manufacture of any other foreign country.

Similarly, no higher or other duties shall be imposed in the United States of America, its territories or possessions, or in Iraq, on the exportation of any articles to the other or to any territory or possession of the other, than are payable on the exportation of like articles to any other foreign country.

Any advantage, of whatsoever kind, which either High Contracting Party may extend to any article, the growth, produce or manufacture of any other foreign country shall simultaneously and unconditionally, without request and without compensation, be extended to the like article the growth, produce or manufacture of the other High Contracting Party.

The stipulations of this Treaty regarding the treatment to be accorded by each High Contracting Party to the commerce of the other do not extend:

(a) to the advantages now accorded or which may hereafter be accorded by the United States of America, its territories or possessions or the Panama Canal Zone to one another or to the Republic of Cuba. The provisions of this paragraph shall continue to apply in respect of any advantages now or hereafter accorded by the United States of America, its territories or possessions or the Panama Canal Zone to one another, irrespective of any change in the political status of any of the territories or possessions of the United States of America;

(b) to any advantages in customs matters which Iraq may grant to goods the produce or manufacture of Turkey, or of any country whose territory was in 1914 wholly included in the Ottoman Empire in Asia;

(c) to any advantages which are, or may in the future be accorded by either Party to purely border traffic within a zone not exceeding ten miles (15 kilometres) wide on either side of the customs frontier;

(d) to any advantages in customs matters which are, or may in the future be accorded to States in customs union with either High Contracting Party so long as such advantages are not accorded to any other State.

Article II

Having regard to the volume and nature of the trade between the two countries it is agreed that in all that concerns matters of prohibitions or restrictions on importations and exportations each of the two countries will accord, whenever they may have recourse to the said prohibitions or restrictions, to the commerce of the other country treatment equally favorable to that which is accorded to any other country and that in the event either country establishes or maintains import or customs quotas, or other quantitative restrictions, or any system of foreign exchange control, the share of the total permissible importation of any product or of the total exchange made available for importation of any product of the other country shall be equal to the share in the trade in such product which such other country enjoyed in a previous representative period.

Article III

Vessels of the United States of America will enjoy in Iraq and Iraqi vessels will enjoy in the United States of America treatment not less favorable than that accorded to national vessels or the vessels of the most favored nation.

The coasting trade of the High Contracting Parties is exempt from the provisions of this Article and from the other provisions of this Treaty, and is to be regulated according to the laws of each High Contracting Party in relation thereto. It is agreed, however, that vessels of either High Contracting Party shall enjoy within the territory of the other with respect to the coasting trade the most-favored-nation treatment.

Article IV

Nothing in this Treaty shall be construed to prevent the adoption of measures prohibiting or restricting the exportation or importation of gold or silver, or to prevent the adoption of such measures as either Government may see fit with respect to the control of the export or sale for export of arms, ammunition or implements of war, and in exceptional circumstances, all other military supplies. It is agreed, further, that nothing in this Treaty shall be construed to prevent the adoption or enforcement of measures relating to neutrality or to rights and obligations arising under the Covenant of the League of Nations.

Subject to the requirement that, under like circumstances and conditions, there shall be no arbitrary discrimination by either High Contracting Party against the other High Contracting Party in favor of any third country, nothing in this Treaty shall be construed to restrict the right of either High Contracting Party to impose (1) prohibitions or restrictions designed to protect human, animal, or plant health or life or national treasures of artistic, historical or archaeological value; (2) prohibitions or restrictions applied to products which as regards production or trade are or may in the future be subject within the country to state monopoly or monopolies exercised under state control; or (3) regulations for the enforcement of revenue or police laws.

Each of the High Contracting Parties agrees that, in respect of the foreign purchases of any state monopoly for the importation, production, or sale of any commodity or of any agency having such monopoly privileges, the commerce of the other High Contracting Party shall receive fair and equitable treatment, and that, in making its foreign purchases, such monopoly or agency will be influenced solely by those considerations which would normally be taken into account by a private commercial entreprise interested solely in purchasing goods on the most favorable terms.

Article V

Should measures be taken by either High Contracting Party seriously affecting the chief exports of the other Party, the Party taking such measures will give sympathetic consideration to any representations which the other Party may make in respect to such measures. If agreement with respect to the question or questions involved in such representations shall not have been reached within ninety days from the date of the receipt of the said representations the Government making the representations may, notwithstanding the provisions of Article VII, terminate this Treaty, such termination to be effective at the expiration of thirty days from the date of the receipt of a notification given subsequent to the expiration of the ninety-day period provided herein.

Article VI

The present Treaty shall, from the day on which it comes into force supplant Article 7 of the convention between the United States of America and Great Britain and Iraq signed at London January 9, 1930, in so far as commerce and navigation are concerned.

Article VII

The present Treaty shall take effect in all its provisions on the thirtieth day after the exchange of ratifications, and shall continue in force for the term of three years from that day. If neither High Contracting Party notifies to the other at least one year in advance an intention of terminating the Treaty upon the expiration of the aforesaid period of three years, the Treaty shall remain in full force and effect after the aforesaid period and until one year from such a time as either of the High Contracting Parties shall have notified to the other an intention of terminating the Treaty.

Article VIII

The present Treaty shall be ratified and the ratifications thereof shall be exchanged at Baghdad as soon as possible.

In witness whereof the respective Plenipotentiaries have signed the present Treaty and have affixed their seals thereto.

Done in duplicate in the English and Arabic languages, which have the same value and shall have equal force, at Baghdad this 3rd day of December, 1938, of the Christian Era, corresponding with the 10th. day of Shawaal, 1357, of the Hijra.

[SEAL] PAUL KNABENSHUE
[SEAL] T. SWAIDI

AND WHEREAS the said Treaty has been duly ratified on both parts, and the ratifications of the two Governments were exchanged in the city of Baghdad on the twentieth day of May, one thousand nine hundred and forty;

AND WHEREAS the said Treaty, in accordance with Article VII thereof, shall take effect on the thirtieth day after the exchange of ratifications, that is to say, on June nineteenth, one thousand nine hundred and forty;

NOW, THEREFORE, be it known that I, Franklin D. Roosevelt, President of the United States of America, have caused the said Treaty to be made public to the end that the same and every article and clause thereof may be observed and fulfilled with good faith by the United States of America and the citizens thereof, on and after the nineteenth day of June, one thousand nine hundred and forty.

IN TESTIMONY WHEREOF, I have hereunto set my hand and caused the Seal of the United States of America to be affixed.

DONE at the city of Washington this twenty-ninth day of May, in the year of our Lord one thousand nine hundred and forty, [SEAL] and of the Independence of the United States of America the one hundred and sixty-fourth.

FRANKLIN D ROOSEVELT

By the President:

CORDELL HULL

Secretary of State.

MUSCAT AND OMAN AND DEPENDENCIES

Amity, Economic Relations and Consular Rights

Treaty and protocol signed at Salalah December 20, 1958;
Ratification advised by the Senate of the United States of America April 28, 1959;
Ratified by the President of the United States of America May 8, 1959;
Ratifications exchanged at Salalah May 11, 1960;
Proclaimed by the President of the United States of America July 8, 1960;
Entered into force June 11, 1960.

BY THE PRESIDENT OF THE UNITED STATES OF AMERICA

A PROCLAMATION

WHEREAS a treaty of amity, economic relations and consular rights between the President of the United States of America and the Sultan of Muscat and Oman and Dependencies, together with a protocol relating thereto, was signed at Salalah on December 20, 1958, the originals of which treaty and protocol, being in the English and Arabic languages, are word for word as follows:

TREATY OF AMITY, ECONOMIC RELATIONS AND CONSULAR RIGHTS BETWEEN THE PRESIDENT OF THE UNITED STATES OF AMERICA AND THE SULTAN OF MUSCAT AND OMAN AND DEPENDENCIES

The President of the United States of America and Sultan Said bin Taimur bin Faisal, Sultan of Muscat and Oman and Dependencies, desirous of promoting friendly relations between the two countries and of encouraging mutually beneficial trade and closer economic intercourse generally have resolved to conclude a Treaty of Amity, Economic Relations and Consular Rights, and have appointed as their Plenipotentiaries:

The President of the United States of America:

Walter K. Schwinn, Consul General of the United States of America;

The Sultan of Muscat and Oman and Dependencies, Sultan Said bin Taimur bin Faisal, in person,

Who have agreed as follows:

Article I

There shall be firm and enduring peace and sincere friendship between the United States of America and the Sultanate of Muscat and Oman and Dependencies.

Article II

1. Nationals of either Party shall, subject to the laws relating to the entry and sojourn of aliens, be permitted to enter the territories of the other Party, to travel therein freely, and to reside at places of their choice. Nationals of either Party shall in particular be permitted to enter the territories of the other Party and to remain therein for the purpose of: (a) carrying on trade between the territories of the two Parties and engaging in related commercial activities; or (b) developing and directing the operations of an enterprise in which they, or companies of their nationality by which they are employed and which they represent in a responsible capacity, have invested or are actively in process of investing a substantial amount of capital. Each Party reserves the right to exclude or expel aliens on grounds relating to public order, morals, health and safety.

2. Nationals of either Party shall receive all possible protection and security within the territories of the other Party. When any such national is in custody, he shall receive reasonable and humane treatment, and, on his request, the nearest consular representative of his country shall be notified as soon as possible. He shall be promptly informed of the accusations against him, allowed ample facilities to defend himself and given a prompt and impartial disposition of his case.

3. Nationals of either Party within the territories of the other Party shall, either individually or through associations, enjoy freedom of conscience and religious toleration and enjoy the right to engage in religious worship. They shall be accorded most-favored-nation treatment with respect to engaging in philanthropic, educational and scientific activities. They shall be enabled to communi-

cate by legal means with other persons inside or outside such territories. The provisions of this paragraph shall be subject to the right of either Party to apply measures that are necessary to maintain public order and to protect public morals and safety.

Article III

1. Companies constituted under the applicable laws and regulations of either Party shall be deemed companies thereof and shall have their juridical status recognized within the territories of the other Party. As used in the present Treaty, "companies" means corporations, partnerships, companies and other associations, whether or not with limited liability and whether or not for pecuniary profit.

2. Nationals and companies of either Party shall have free access to the courts of justice and administrative agencies within the territories of the other Party, in all degrees of jurisdiction, both in defense and in pursuit of their rights. Such access shall be allowed upon terms no less favorable than those applicable to nationals and companies of such other Party or of any third country, including the terms applicable to requirements for deposit of security. It is understood that companies not engaged in activities within the country shall enjoy the right of such access without any requirement of registration or domestication.

Article IV

1. Each Party shall at all times accord fair and equitable treatment to nationals and companies of the other Party, and to their property and enterprises, and shall refrain from applying unreasonable or discriminatory measures that would impair their legally acquired rights and interests.

2. Property of nationals and companies of either Party, including direct and indirect interests in property, shall receive all possible protection and security within the territories of the other Party. Such property shall not be taken except for a public purpose, nor shall it be taken without the prompt payment of just compensation. Such compensation shall be in an effectively realizable form and shall represent the full equivalent of the property taken; and adequate provision shall have been made at or prior to the time of taking for the determination and payment thereof.

3. The dwellings, offices, warehouses, factories and other premises of nationals and companies of either Party located within the territories of the other Party shall not be subject to entry or molestation without just cause. Official searches and examinations of such premises and their contents shall be made only according to law and with all possible regard for the convenience of the occupants and the conduct of business.

Article V

1. Nationals and companies of either Party shall be accorded national treatment with respect to establishing, as well as with respect to acquiring interests in, enterprises for engaging in commercial activities within the territories of the other Party. Moreover, nationals and companies of such Party shall in no case be accorded

treatment less favorable than that accorded to nationals and companies of any third country with respect to establishing or acquiring interests in enterprises for engaging in industrial and other business activities within the territories of such other Party. The provisions of this paragraph do not include the practice of professions.

2. Neither Party shall discriminate against enterprises established within its territories that are owned or controlled by nationals and companies of the other Party, as compared with any other enterprises engaged in like activities, in the application of any laws, rules, or regulations affecting the conduct of such enterprises.

3. Nationals and companies of either Party shall enjoy the right to continued control and management of their enterprises within the territories of the other Party; shall be permitted to engage accountants and other technical experts, executive personnel, attorneys, agents and other specialized employees of their choice, regardless of nationality but subject to the provisions of Article II regarding the entry and sojourn of aliens; and shall be permitted without discrimination to do all other things necessary or incidental to the effective conduct of their affairs.

Article VI

1. Nationals and companies of either Party shall be accorded most-favored-nation treatment within the territories of the other Party with respect to leasing real property needed for their residence or for the conduct of activities pursuant to the present Treaty, and national treatment with respect to: (a) purchasing or otherwise acquiring personal property of all kinds, subject to any limitations on acquisition of shares in enterprises that may be imposed consistently with Article V, and (b) disposing of property of all kinds by sale, testament, or any other legal manner.

2. Nationals and companies of either Party shall be accorded within the territories of the other Party effective protection in the exclusive use of inventions, trade marks and trade names, upon compliance with the applicable laws and regulations, if any, respecting registration and other formalities.

Article VII

1. Nationals and companies of either Party shall not be subject to the payment of taxes, fees or charges within the territories of the other Party, or to requirements with respect to the levy and collection thereof, more burdensome than those borne by nationals, residents and companies of any third country. In the case of nationals of either Party residing within the territories of the other Party, and of nationals and companies of either Party engaged in trade or other gainful pursuit or in non-profit activities therein, such taxes, fees, charges and requirements shall not be more burdensome than those borne by nationals and companies of such other Party.

2. Each Party, however, reserves the right to: (a) extend specific tax advantages only on the basis of reciprocity, or pursuant to agreements for the avoidance of double taxation or the mutual protection of revenue; and (b) apply special requirements as to the exemptions of a personal nature allowed to nonresidents in connection with income and inheritance taxes.

3. Companies of either Party shall not be subject, within the territories of the other Party, to taxes upon any income, transactions or capital not reasonably allocable or apportionable to such territories.

Article VIII

1. Each Party shall accord to products of the other Party, from whatever place and by whatever legally authorized carrier arriving, and to products destined for exportation to the territories of such other Party, by whatever route and by whatever legally authorized carrier, treatment no less favorable than that accorded like products of, or destined for export to, any third country, in all matters relating to: (a) customs duties, as well as any other charges, regulations and formalities levied upon or in connection with importation and exportation; and (b) internal taxation, sale, distribution, storage and use.

2. Neither Party shall impose restrictions or prohibitions on the importation of any product of the other Party, or on the exportation of any product to the territories of the other Party, unless the importation of the like product of, or the exportation of the like product to, all third countries is similarly restricted or prohibited.

3. Either Party may impose prohibitions or restrictions on sanitary or other customary grounds of a noncommercial nature, or in the interest of preventing deceptive or unfair practices, provided such prohibitions or restrictions do not arbitrarily discriminate against the commerce of the other Party.

4. Each Party reserves the right to accord special advantages: (a) to adjacent countries in order to facilitate frontier traffic, or (b) by virtue of a customs union or free trade area of which either Party may become a member, so long as it informs the other Party of its plans and affords such other Party adequate opportunity for consultation. Each Party, moreover, reserves rights and obligations it may have under the General Agreement on Tariffs and Trade,[1] and special advantages it may accord pursuant thereto.

Article IX

1. The Parties recognize that the development of their economic relations will benefit from conditions of maximum freedom with respect to carrying out financial payments and transfers between their respective territories and between nationals and companies of the two Parties. Accordingly, each Party undertakes to refrain from applying restrictions on such payments except to the extent that shortages of foreign exchange may require. In that event, the Party applying restrictions undertakes to administer them in a manner not to influence disadvantageously the competitive position of the commerce, transport or investment of capital of the other Party in comparison with the commerce, transport or investments of any third country.

2. Nationals and companies of either Party shall be accorded treatment no less favorable than that accorded nationals and companies of the other Party, or of any third country, with respect to all matters relating to importation and exportation.

3. Neither Party shall impose any measure of a discriminatory

nature that hinders or prevents the importer or exporter of products of either country from obtaining marine insurance on such products in companies of either Party.

Article X

1. Between the territories of the two Parties there shall be freedom of commerce and navigation.

2. Vessels under the flag of either Party, and carrying the papers required by its law in proof of nationality, shall be deemed to be vessels of that Party both on the high seas and within the ports, places and waters of the other Party.

3. Vessels of either Party shall have liberty, on equal terms with vessels of the other Party and on equal terms with vessels of any third country, to come with their cargoes to all ports, places and waters of the other Party open to foreign commerce and navigation. Such vessels and cargoes shall in all respects be accorded national treatment and most-favored-nation treatment within the ports, places and waters of such other Party; but each Party may reserve exclusive rights and privileges to its own vessels with respect to the coasting trade and inland navigation.

4. Vessels of either Party shall be accorded national treatment and most-favored-nation treatment by the other Party with respect to the right to carry all products that may be carried by vessel to and from the territory of such other Party; and such products shall be accorded treatment no less favorable than that accorded like products carried in vessels of such other Party, with respect to: (a) duties and charges of all kinds, (b) the administration of the customs, and (c) bounties, drawbacks and other privileges of this nature.

5. Vessels of either Party that are in distress shall be permitted to take refuge in the nearest port or haven of the other Party, and shall receive all possible friendly treatment and assistance.

6. The term "vessels," as used herein, means all types of vessels, whether privately owned or operated, or publicly owned or operated; but this term does not, except with reference to paragraphs 2 and 5 of the present Article, include fishing vessels or vessels of war.

Article XI

1. The present Treaty shall not preclude the application of measures:

(a) regulating the importation or exportation of gold or silver;

(b) relating to fissionable materials, the radioactive byproducts thereof, or the sources thereof;

(c) regulating the production of or traffic in arms, ammunition and implements of war, or traffic in other materials carried on directly or indirectly for the purpose of supplying a military establishment;

(d) necessary to fulfill the obligations of a Party for the maintenance or restoration of international peace and security, or necessary to protect its essential security interests;

(e) denying to any company in the ownership or direction of which nationals of any third country or countries have directly or indirectly the controlling interest, the advantages of the present Treaty, except with respect to recognition of juridical status and with respect to access to courts of justice and to administrative tribunals and agencies; and

(f) regarding its national fisheries and the landing of the products thereof.

2. The present Treaty does not accord any rights to engage in political activities.

3. The most-favored-nation provisions of the present Treaty relating to the treatment of goods shall not extend to advantages accorded by the United States of America or its Territories and possessions, irrespective of any future change in their political status, to one another, to the Republic of Cuba, to the Republic of the Philippines, to the Trust Territory of the Pacific Islands or to the Panama Canal Zone.

Article XII

Each Party shall have the right to send consular representatives to the other Party, subject to the approval of such other Party as to the persons appointed and the places at which they reside. Such consular representatives shall be permitted to perform such consular functions and shall enjoy such privileges and immunities as are in accordance with international law and practice and as provided in the protocol to this Treaty.

Article XIII

Each Party shall accord sympathetic consideration to, and shall afford adequate opportunity for consultation regarding, such representations as the other Party may make with respect to any matter affecting the operation of the present Treaty.

Article XIV

The territories to which the present Treaty extends shall comprise all areas of land and water under the sovereignty or authority of the United States of America, other than the Panama Canal Zone and the Trust Territory of the Pacific Islands, and of the Sultan of Muscat and Oman and Dependencies.

Article XV

The present Treaty shall replace and terminate as between the United States of America and the Sultan of Muscat and Oman and Dependencies the treaty of amity and commerce signed at Muscat September 21, 1833.[1]

Article XVI

1. The present Treaty shall be ratified, and the ratifications thereof shall be exchanged at Muscat as soon as possible.

2. The present Treaty shall enter into force one month after the day of exchange of ratifications. It shall remain in force for seven years and shall continue in force thereafter until terminated as provided herein.

3. Either Party may, by giving one year's written notice to the other Party, terminate the present Treaty at the end of the initial seven-year period or at any time thereafter.

In witness whereof Walter K. Schwinn, Consul General of the United States of America, on behalf of the President of the United States of America, Dwight D. Eisenhower, and Sultan Said bin Taimur bin Faisal, Sultan of Muscat and Oman and Dependencies, on his own behalf, have signed the present Treaty and have affixed thereto their respective seals.

Done in duplicate in the English and Arabic languages, both equally authentic, at Salalah in the Kingdom of Oman, this twentieth day of December one thousand nine hundred fifty-eight, which corresponds to the ninth day of Jumada II one thousand three hundred seventy-eight.

[SEAL] Walter K. Schwinn

[SEAL]